CONTINENTAL DRIFT

CONTINENTAL

EMILY APTER

DRIFT

FROM NATIONAL CHARACTERS

TO VIRTUAL SUBJECTS

THE UNIVERSITY OF CHICAGO PRESS

CHICAGO AND LONDON

Emily Apter is professor of comparative literature and French at the University of California, Los Angeles. She is author of *Feminizing the Fetish: Psychoanalysis and Narrative Obsession in Turn-of-the-Century France* and coeditor of *Fetishism as Cultural Discoursi.*

The University of Chicago Press, Chicago 60637
The University of Chicago Press, Ltd., London
© 1999 by The University of Chicago
All rights reserved. Published 1999

08 07 06 05 04 03 02 01 00 99   5 4 3 2 1
ISBN (cloth): 0-226-02349-4
ISBN (paper): 0-226-02350-8

Library of Congress Cataloging-in-Publication Data

Apter, Emily S.
    Continental drift : from national characters to virtual
subjects / Emily Apter.
        p.   cm.
    Includes bibliographical references and index.
    ISBN 0-226-02349-4. — ISBN 0-226-02350-8 (pbk.)
    1. France—Civilization—20th century—Influence.   2. National
characteristics, French.   3. Virtual reality—Social aspects.   4.
Postcolonialism—France.   5. Nationalism—History—20th century.
6. Intellectual life—History—20th century.   I. Title.
DC33.7 .A695   1999
944.083—ddc21   98-46153
                                                                        CIP

CONTENTS

A gallery of illustrations follows page 20

Preface   vii

Acknowledgments   xiii

Introduction   1
Continental Theory on Different Continents

NATIONAL CHARACTERS

1 Uprooted Subjects   25
Barrès and the Politics of *Patrimoine*

2 Saints at Stake   39
Joan of Arc as National Pathography

3 Out of Character   61
Camus's French Algerian Subjects

4 Character Assassination   77
Racial Pathologies, Colonial Crimes—Fanon,
Mannoni, Lacan, Paulhan

METROPOLITAN MASQUERADES

5 Harem   99
Scopic Regimes of Power/Phallic Law

6 Ethnographic Travesties   113
Alibis of Gender and Nation in the Case of Elissa Rhaïs

7 Acting Out Orientalism   131
Stereotype, Performativity, the Isabelle Eberhardt Effect

8 Cleopatra's Nose   149
Characterology and the Modern Subject
in Belle Epoque Paris

VIRTUAL COLONIES

9 The Dance of Colonial Seduction   167
Flaubert and the Line of Desire

10 The Landscape of Photogeny   179
"Morocco" in Black and White

11 Impotent Epic   195
The Crisis of Literary Tourism in the Age
of Mechanical Reproduction

12 Postcolonial Cyberpunk   213
Dirty Nationalism in the Era of Terminal Identities

13 Nomadologies of Tomorrow   225
The Deleuzean Worldscape

   Notes   239

   Index   277

In the immediate aftermath of the French elections of spring 1997, in which President Chirac woefully miscalculated his mandate and inadvertently returned the Socialists to power, it appears that France's Gaullist national calling became defunct. Perhaps this failure of old-style nationalism is only temporary; perhaps it has merely migrated to a more virulent, if still minoritarian, party of right-wing, nationalist xenophobia under the direction of Jean-Marie Le Pen. Whatever the political turns in store, the elections were interpreted as symptomatic of the death of old-style nationalism. The erosion of a belief in national destiny inherited from the Maurrasians, coupled with the attraction to technologically mediated citizenship in a global, laissez-faire economy, is the context in which I situate the far-ranging themes addressed in this book. In broadest terms, what I have attempted to trace is the dissolution of a national subject, honored by traditional fields of literary and area studies, into postnational and virtual reshapings of subjectivity in modern or futuristic genres.

The book is divided into interrelated sections, each exemplifying continental theory conceived and practiced in a global frame. The sections—national characters, metropolitan masquerades, virtual colonies—engage consistently with structuring themes: the erosion of national character as an anchor of subjectivity in the advance of a mobile, geomorphic vision of continentalism; the relationship between cultural stereotypes and the ethics of character; the connections among imperialism, modernity and futurity in the formation of the modern subject; and the virtualization of identity in the era of cybernetics and electronic diaspora. Unifying the book is an emphasis on the play between intellectual and disciplinary faultlines within modern subject-formation, and the shearing away of landmass (literal and figurative) from continental or national perimeters. From earthquakes to race wars to "astrocentric" perspectives on cultural universalism, the topographies of millennial identity are shown simultaneously to appropriate and transform age-old narratives of national consciousness, imperial time and place, and "character building."

Though a rough chronological progression is implied in the title—
from national characters *to* virtual subjects—I avoid narratives of causa-
tion, following instead a jagged time-line. In the place of a master-thesis
demonstrating how a monumental subject disintegrates into an amorphous condition of postnational screen-being, I have preferred to treat national character as an idea that haunts the past, present, and future in
unpredictable ways. Thus, I assume that national character was never a firm
or fixed topology in some primordial first place of turn-of-the-century
nation-building, just as I assume that the modern subject—that phantasmatic construct of postimperial selfhood—never had its unitary ontology
eviscerated at precise temporal junctures. Similarly, the colonial unconscious was never a "thing" that suddenly made its apparition as a result of
colonial anthropology's encounter with psychoanalysis; nor did virtuality
suddenly become a constitutive problem of identity with the advent of new
media technologies.

This said, the book's investigation of subjectivity in the colonial period
tries to respect established parameters of colonial and postcolonial history
while observing conceptual linearity in the organization of chapters. I begin in the introduction by considering how French culture and critical theory have migrated through the humanities, generating novel disciplinary
admixtures that really have no equivalent in Europe. The aim is to assess, in
a modest way, where French theory has gone and is going as it defines itself
beyond the hexagon. Though pedagogical concerns associated with teaching a European "foreign" language and culture within a global humanities
curriculum inform the attempt to define a postcolonial francophone studies, the major emphasis is on tracking the "drift" of European theory (ontology) in postcolonial and postnational critiques of identity.

In the section entitled "National Characters," I deal with the theme of
national character by investigating how the historic rhetoric of roots and
soil (popularized by Maurice Barrès in the 1890s) fares under the contemporary onslaught of those twin challenges to a national heritage culture:
immigration and multiculturalism. This heritage culture, crystallized in
France as a deliverance narrative of national destiny in the legend of Joan
of Arc (appropriated by Le Pen), is approached as a manifestation of the
modern monstrous. Another chapter, on Albert Camus's elusive Euro-
African subject, explores the difficulties, both now and in Camus's time, of
trying to establish a hybrid subject under conditions of binational splitting
in Algeria. Here I confront the problem of recalcitrant, recrudescent nationalisms. Though on the face of it, Algeria's current political crisis involves internally focused civil strife (on the order of competing ethnic and regional
claims, or the deadlock between conservative Islam and corrupt secular

rule), nationalism, I would argue, still matters to Algerian politics. Whether it is the vestigial form of French national culture that complicates the politics of Arabization and westernization, or the nationalism forged by the FLN in the wake of independence (given powerful state ceremonial forms under Boumedienne in the seventies), a condition of volatile binationalism prevails. It affects both Maghrebian immigrants living within French borders as insider/outsiders, and Algerians of multiple political stripes in North Africa who hold on to French culture as a vital link to Western media, information technology, and secular ways of life.

The mutations of nationalism in the era of imperialism have received expert assessment by political theorists and historians too numerous to list. For my own particular purposes, the work of Ernst Renan, Charles-Robert Agéron, Charles-André Julien, Frantz Fanon, Aimé Césaire, Albert Memmi, Pierre Nora, Samir Amin, Emmanuel Wallerstein, Ferdinand Braudel, Etienne Balibar, Pierre Bourdieu, Abdelmalek Sayad, Achille Mmembe, Liah Greenfeld, Jean-François Lyotard, Abdelkebir Khatibi, Jean-Luc Nancy, Edward Said, Homi K. Bhabha, and Arjun Appadurai has been particularly valuable in trying to interpret the French colonial legacy.[1] Rather than summarize their writings, I rely on them to inform the project's historical and theoretical purview. My interest is not in providing an exhaustive account of national character in philosophies of world history (Herder, Kant, Hegel, Hume, Gobineau, Taine, Maurras et al.), but in giving full rhetorical play to the notion as I focus on the way in which nationalism in the colonies, much like anti-Semitism at the time of the Dreyfus affair, functioned compensatorily to acquit France of its fin-de-siècle inferiority complex toward Germany (*la défaite* of 1870) and Great Britain (envied as the first industrial power, the greater empire in India and Africa). The conqueror-colon who returned an image of aggrandized Frenchness to a demoralized nation emerges as a character prototype of outsized proportions. It was with an eye to placing this monstrous character "under analysis" that I exhumed the feud between Frantz Fanon and Octave Mannoni over colonial psychopathology. Their disagreements are edifying for today's readers not only because of the content (the characterology of the colonizer), but also because of the way they confronted heuristic complexities that continue to impinge on psychoanalytic approaches to race and identity.

As the book proceeds to the section "Metropolitan Masquerades," it argues that national character—whether it is the "civilized" character of the colonial civil servant inventing empire in a distant outpost, or the Orientalist diva acting out colonial fantasies in a metropolitan sphere—was in many respects scripted for the colonies out of literary and theatrical cultural productions. Placing renewed emphasis on the stereotype as a stamp or mold of national consciousness that curtails free-fall interpretations of performative identity, I assign signal importance to the realist tradition within colonial narrative. As a repository of racial, ethnic, and gender caricatures and exoticist cartoons of landscape and local color, colonial realism often functioned as the handmaiden to colonial ideology, offering literary stereotypes as the *stoff* of national character.

I also advance the hypothesis that early feminism, Western and non-Western, had a complex stake in these enactments of colonial power. Social reformers, wives, and missionaries, inspired to participate in the colonizing mission as founders of schools and hospitals, had their anticolonial *and* feminist sensibilities awakened by the visible brutalities of settler regimes. Alternatively, many women would hypocritically assert the colonizer's right abroad while delegitimating patriarchal claims at home. Significant tensions between First and Third World feminism exemplified in colonial fiction have held fast in debates over the strategic aims of global feminism: the works stand not only as historical curiosities with a singular relevance to contemporary feminist discourses, but also give narrative form to what Judith Butler has called "the psychic life of power."

Sexual addiction and material hardship were often thematically twinned in women's *littérature coloniale*. At the turn of the century, Isabelle Eberhardt would inspire subsequent generations of French feminists to imitate her refusal of patriarchal European convention in favor of a body-punishing, nihilist nomadology in the North African desert. A decade later, a best-selling Algerian woman author named Elissa Rhaïs achieved celebrity as an "authentic" purveyor of scenes from the lives of destitute dancers, abused wives, and abandoned prostitutes. This unique form of colonial feminism, invented in and reexported from the colonies to the metropole, helped (ironically enough) to breathe new life into decadent Orientalist stereotypes. Thaïs, Sémiramis, Cleopatra, and Salome were revivified by a generation of New Woman performers, from Sarah Bernhardt to Ida Rubenstein, emerging as icons of feminine empowerment. In this context, it is perhaps no accident that psychoanalysis, with its gender-neutral categories of the modern subject, seems in retrospect to have worked to quell the threat of feminist hypercharacterology.

In dealing with what I occasionally refer to as colonial phantasms (most evident with respect to the harem topos), I have been concerned that the very articulation of such a notion could foster the misleading impression that colonialism was merely a fantasy of the colonizer rather than a dialectically fraught material and psychic history, as much defined by the colonized as the colonizer. The question inevitably arises of whether a critical appraisal of what Jacqueline Rose has called "states of fantasy" ultimately domesticates or unseats the impact of Europeanization. Though I would argue that it is virtually impossible to evoke and critique the eroticization of power inherent in colonial fictions without to some extent retainting the subject under review, or reenacting a problematic drama of subjection, I would hope that the consistently critical framings of each chapter will be seen to alleviate some of these concerns.

In the "Virtual Colonies" section, the book evaluates the impact of visual technologies (early cinema and tourist photography) and new media on the subject of colonial history. Problems of colonial vision (as in the figuration of colonial desire in the staging of dance numbers), are analyzed through an archive of major and minor texts of imperial and metropolitan literary historiography. I also examine the crisis of travel writing in the face of early cinema and cheap photographic reproduction ("impotent epic") and the problem of "black and light" in filmic representations of colonial cities ("the landscape of photogeny"). Questions of colonialism and visuality are addressed together because I am persuaded that part of what made the so-called modern subject modern was its mediation by new visual technologies. Conquest and national hegemony were strengthened by aerial vision or a mass diffusion of images that allowed a European nation to project a picture of the world (an obvious controlling fantasy). At the same time, new anxieties around the loss of an ethnically or racially pure identity were aggravated by technologies that enhanced cross-cultural nearness or produced potentially miscegenated spaces.

If colonialism depended for its efficacy on its ability to represent itself visually, thus engendering a kind of first order of virtuality in and through ethnographic travesties, a second order of virtual colonies can be identified in the age of cyber. The final chapters of the book trace what happens to postcolonial subjectivity when it is electronically mediated or screened. In an attempt to wrench the intellectual topography of colonialism from its twilight temporality in postcolonial theory, I look at experiments in Third World or multicultural cyberpunk, digital diaspora, and the invention of "race aliens" or "Afrofuturists" in the era of the postnation.

ACKNOWLEDGMENTS

The main title of this book, *Continental Drift,* must inevitably be related to my own temporal and geographical dislocations during the period in which it was written. I began the research in 1989 under the auspices of a University of Pennsylvania postdoctoral fellowship. Between northern California and New York, I spent two years negotiating bicoastal schizophrenia before alighting for four years in Los Angeles. The traumatic L.A. earthquake of 1994 marked the moment when cavernous cracks in the freeways and spidery splits in the plaster made the idea of "continental rift" an appropriate theme for what I was working on. As I finished writing the book, during a leave from Cornell University in the spring of 1997, the landing gear froze on my prop plane as I took off from La Guardia. The book I happened to be reading, and which I used to steady my nerves until we managed, somehow, to land, was Russell Banks's novel *Continental Drift* (a book that shared its title with geological, seismic studies of plate tectonics). The story of a New Hampshire repairman on the skids who finds himself caught in the hallucinatory horror of shipwreck as a runner of Haitian boat people off the Florida coast, Banks's fictional work got me back to terra firma; it thus seemed only fitting that the same title should serve an assessment of the intellectual swerves and dips in continental theory.

Generous research funding from the University of California, Davis, and exchanges with valued colleagues there—Georges Van Den Abbeele, Marc Blanchard, and Catherine Kudlick in particular—fostered methodological reflection on the relationship between French studies and postcolonial theory. T. J. Clark and Ann Wagner provided a special opportunity to share work in progress with faculty and students at Berkeley. At the University of Chicago Humanities Center, the Shelby Cullom Davis Center of Historical Studies at Princeton, the Getty Center in Los Angeles, the Whitney Museum Education Program in New York, the Institute of Contemporary Art and the Architectural Association in London, the University of Rochester, the French Cultural Studies Institute at Northwestern University, the Society for the Humanities at Cornell University, and the Cultural

Studies Center at UC Santa Cruz, I tested drafts of chapters and enjoyed the benefit of trenchant critique. I am particularly grateful to Arjun Appadurai, Natalie Zemon Davis, Tom Reese, Michael Anne Holly, Jonathan Culler, Dominick La Capra, Mary Kelly, Mark Cousins, Carla Freccero, Françoise Lionnet, and Lawrence Kritzman for making these invaluable intellectual opportunities possible.

For their permission to reprint previously published portions of the book, my thanks to the editors of *Substance* 76–77 (1995), *Modern Language Notes* (summer 1997), *Architecture New York* 16 (spring 1996), *Differences: A Journal of Feminist Cultural Studies* (spring 1992), *Suitcase: A Journal of Transcultural Traffic* (1995), *After Colonialism: Imperial Histories and Postcolonial Displacements* (Princeton University Press, 1995), *Spectacles of Realism: Body, Gender, Genre* (University of Minnesota Press, 1995), and *Performance and Cultural Politics* (Routledge, 1996).

Many of the concerns addressed in this book were sparked by colleagues, friends, and students at UCLA. Collaborations and discussions with Ali Behdad, Jenny Sharpe, Peter Wollen, Janet Bergstrom, Ken Reinhardt, Debora Silverman, Sam Weber, Babak Nahid, Victoria Sams, and Tamara Ho inform the interdisciplinary range of the book. Grants from UCLA's Academic Senate and Center for the Study of Women made successive summers of research and sabbatical leave in Paris possible. I am also indebted to the debates over French national identity that anchored our faculty seminar on French Culture and Theory at the University of California Humanities Research Institute at Irvine.

A special note of gratitude must be conveyed to Alan Thomas, esteemed editor at the University of Chicago Press; to Judith Butler, whose work has provided consistent theoretical points of departure; to Homi K. Bhabha, whose writings on the stereotype, and on Fanon, proved crucial; to Margaret Cohen, whose ideas about what constitutes the realist archive helped focus my thoughts on gender and the literary field; to Lawrence Kritzman, whose commitment to a critical French studies and intellectual collaborations I cannot imagine doing without; to Tom Conley, whose eloquent critique of the manuscript was immensely helpful; and to Ernest Pascucci, former student and beloved friend, who coaxed me to revise a recalcitrant chapter, and who tragically took his life in the spring of 1997.

For her unique friendship, literary wit, and camaraderie I give warmest thanks to Leslie Dick.

My father, David Apter, a political scientist whose first book was on decolonization in Ghana, has been an important goad and critic as I have thought through theoretical paradigms of the colonial legacy. He served as a "native informant" on historical points, particularly on the genesis of dependency theory in the period of neoimperialism.

Eleanor Apter provided intellectual and personal support throughout the book's production.

This book is dedicated to Anthony Vidler and to our son Nicolas, vital mainstays in a life of continual continental displacement.

Colonies: S'attrister quand on en parle.

                    FLAUBERT, *Dictionnaire des idées reçues*

INTRODUCTION

CONTINENTAL THEORY ON

DIFFERENT CONTINENTS

As the French, along with other national subjects within the so-called New Europe, find themselves interrogating the boundaries and limits of national identity in the light of rising anti-Semitism, ethnic cleansing, racial or ethnic claims to citizenry, and the socioeconomic pressures of immigration, those concerned with the global politics of French culture have found themselves drawn to postcolonial theory as a source of useful, if often problematic, critical paradigms. The colonial legacies of France, Britain, Spain, Portugal, and to a lesser degree Germany and Holland, have been restudied and redebated in conferences, lectures, and research centers throughout North America. Often amalgamated with African-American, Afro-Caribbean, French-Asian, transnational, and diaspora studies, postcolonialism has generated a lengthy and fast-growing bibliography, and, increasingly, humanities departments advertise positions calling for expertise in the field of postcolonial studies.

Although there are obviously complex reasons postcolonialism has become a code-language elected to speak to the issues of multiculturalism, canon realignment, global decentering, revisionist historiography, identity politics, and cultural hermeneutics in the North American academy, one thing is clear: there is really no commensurate intellectual movement on the European continent. Many French intellectuals seem to have difficulty in grasping the pertinence of postcolonial theory to the contemporary politics of culture, despite their recognition that Maghrebian, Caribbean, West African, and Indo-Chinese exclusion from mainstream *francité* continues to inflect internal political and cultural affairs as well as the export of French culture abroad. Though it has existed for a long time in France, francophone research still tends to be confined to policy analysis, institutes of international relations, and area studies. Even the most recent volumes of Pierre Nora's richly textured *Les Lieux de mémoire*, with their New Historical attention to the mystificatory components of national identity, clumsily justify their choice not to include Algiers or Montreal as *hauts lieux*, or psychotopographies worthy of revisionist nostalgia. Nora suggests that consideration of these places would lead to indulging in "personal, arbitrary vagabondage," implying that the sites deemed worthy of inclusion—Lascaux, Alésia, Vézelay, Notre-Dame de Paris, the Loire chateaus, Sacré-Coeur, the Eiffel Tower—had somehow eluded these personalistic criteria:

> The series on privileged sites poses an entirely different kind of problem. Where outside its heart could one admit that the heart of France beats most intensely? The temptation was strong here to allow for the choice of entirely personal places and moments, in order to endow them with a historical problematic, as Michelet endowed Ouessant and the circus of Gavarnie with a geopolitical problematic. Or again, to profit from the occasion to introduce places outside the hexagon such as Algiers, London, Fort-de-France, or even Montreal, which precisely this year celebrates the 350th anniversary of its foundation. But against this individual and arbitrary vagabondage we have preferred three less controversial criteria: the aura of large temporal strata, the homogeneity of examples—resonant sites, important places and monuments of demonstrative power—and finally, the authorization of the collective or foreign gaze. The intersection of these criteria has dictated the list.[1]

Though one could certainly locate comparable memory lapses and territorial omissions in the way in which the United States has taken stock of its imperialist past (only relatively recently has Vietnam been declassified in the American psyche, and most of U.S. intervention in Latin America has yet to be worked through in the psychoanalytic sense), it is still surprising for those working in French studies to encounter so many taboos intact when it comes to investigating former French interests in Africa, the Middle East, and Indochina, not to speak of the Algerian Revolution and the complex postcolonial culture left in its wake in both France and North Africa.

Part of France's reluctance to confront its colonial past, beyond the obvious negative history of national political decline and the more immediate obsession with preserving French cultural integrity, may be attributable to the fear and confusion provoked by the most recently anointed forms of conservative Islam. The epidemic of assassinations of Algerian in-tellectuals (morbidly dubbed "intellocide") in 1993—Djilali Lyabès, Laadi Flici, Hafid Senhadri, Mahfoud Bouceb, the writer Tahar Djaout—by hard-line *islamistes* has been roundly denounced in the French press, but at the same time the condemnation of *intégrisme* mingles uncomfortably with Western ignorance of Islam and a reflexive sympathy toward members of North Africa's westernized elite. So-called Fundamentalism tests Western democratic tolerance for moral relativism (witness the First/Third World schisms at the June 1993 Vienna conference over the universality of *les droits de l'homme)* and squeezes the intellectual Left's cherished "politics of difference." For Western feminism, the ethical conflicts provoked by non-laico-assimilationist interpretations of Islam have been particularly irk-some, as can be seen in Hélène Cixous's text *Vivre l'orange* (1975). Written at the time of Khomeini's rise to power, a French *pied noir,* Jewish feminist such as Cixous found herself at pains, despite her self-identification as an exilic, semi–Third World subject, to be open-minded about religious dif-ference when it entailed an orthodoxy drastically restrictive of women's rights (as defined by occidental norms). This kind of breach between West-ern and non-Western criteria of subjective self-determination, mirrored to some extent in Britain in the divergent reactions to the Rushdie affair, re-mains a source of continual unease within the politics of Western post-colonialism.

But putting aside for the moment the enormously complicated and volatile issue of Islam's intersection with nationalism and its collisions with ethnicity, feminism, and secular definitions of human rights, it still seems worth opening up the question of what postcolonial studies *à la française* would look like if it were framed constructively to examine the residual politics of France's notorious *mission civilisatrice.* Though it would risk becoming a caricature of what the French intelligentsia already likes to caricature—namely, a field of study deemed "politically correct"—French postcolonialism, in its more nuanced incarnations, could pose a healthy challenge to ideological universalism, metropolitan narcissism, cultural "pasteurization," and the critically underexamined institutional tenets of national language and literature. It could give rise to a consideration of na-tional identity focusing on the points of contact between a "New Europe" of the future and the "old Europe" of the colonial aftermath; as in, for ex-ample, a phenomenon that might be called the *harki-ization* of Europe, whereby the specific situation of the *harkis* (pro-French Algerians who found themselves stranded in civil and territorial no-man's-land after the Algerian War) would be generalized to apply to myriad ethnic minorities throughout Europe whose cause is of little vital interest to any of the larger nation-states. French postcolonial criticism could reinvigorate the links between political philosophy and literary/cultural analysis. It could broaden the parameters of translation to encompass a polyglot identity in the arts, a fait accompli, according to a *Libération* editorial in which the playwrights Jean-Christophe Bailly and Michel Deutsch announced that to speak of "foreign authors" is an atavism in an era that is fundamentally already "translated."[2] Finally, postcolonial criticism could foster the inclusion of francophone studies within a framework other than that of "enlightened" assimilationism, thus leading to a broader interest in French studies abroad.[3]

After several decades of investment in French theory "for its own sake," French critiques of the modern subject have themselves come under heavy criticism for their putative devaluation of history and identity, yet the fascination with applying theory to the history of representation and to archival, materialist history remains fast. Consistently deployed to rethink subjective agency, French theory makes itself felt within new subfields: feminism and the "new" art history, the history of *mentalités* and its redefinition within New Historicism, the study of decolonization and modernity in the postwar period, colonialism and the history of spatial identity, psychoanalysis, filmic representation and the marketing of "Frenchness," the politics of immigration and national consciousness, the deconstruction of cultural and national stereotypes. In the more limited field of literary criticism, the extrahexagonal impulse in French studies has prompted attention to the *mise-en-rapport* of "classic" political reflection on nation-formation, conquest, and linguistic usurpation (Montesquieu, Herder, Benjamin Constant, de Maistre, Tocqueville, Renan); French critical writing on exoticism and exile (from Victor Segalen to Tveztan Todorov); francophone theories of language and racial identity (Frantz Fanon, Edouard Glissant, V. Y. Mudimbe, Abdelkedir Khatibi, Réda Bensmaia, Achille Mbembe); cultural transpositions of Anglo-Indian critical theory and historiography (Homi K. Bhahba, Gayatri Chakravorty Spivak, Sara Suleri, Satya Mohanty, Ashis Nandy, Arjun Appadurai), and North American or American-based deconstructions of Orientalism and Africanism (Edward Said, Henry Louis Gates, Christopher Miller, Timothy Mitchell, Lisa Lowe, Masao Miyoshi, Ella Shohat).

Like many working to enlarge the intellectual and territorial compass of French studies, I have drawn on these sources with an eye to making the traditional generic, narrative, and stylistic categories of literary criticism operative in nuancing questions of cultural ontology. The objective has been to avoid some of the particularist mantras and truisms calcifying inside the rhetoric of "difference" while at the same time taking seriously *different* categories of thinking colonial subjectivity.

In theorizing and researching national identity-fracture, I have been conscious of the difficulties and rewards of dispatching culturally specific theories to distant or contiguous geopolitical contexts. Quite some time ago, James Clifford characterized the locomotive, portmanteau quality of postcolonial criticism as itself a transnational fact of interdisciplinary everyday life:

> Old geopolitical oppositions are transformed into sectors within western and non-western societies. Hot/cold, historical/mythic, modern/traditional, literate/oral, country/city, center/periphery, first/third ... are subject to local mix and match, contextual-tactical shifting, syncretic recombination, import-export. Culture is migration as well as rooting—within and between groups, within and between individual persons.[4]

Clifford's evocation of syncretism, salvage, and situational tactics captures one of the fundamental questions running through postcolonial studies; namely, when is "mix and match" a camouflaged expression of alienated colonial mimesis and when is it a syncretically reinvigorated form of global cultural identity? In Homi K. Bhabha's ascription, the latter is necessarily haunted by the former; "hybridity" is shadowed by mimicry:

> It is one of the ironic signs of our times that the Introduction to *The Real Me? Postmodernism and the Question of Identity* should be written by an anglicised postcolonial migrant who happens to be a slightly Frenchified literary critic. For in that hybridity of histories and cultures you have the spectacle of the simulacral: the corrosive craft of colonial mimicry exposing the limits and borders of the sustaining subject of Western mimesis.[5]

In employing an oxymoron such as "corrosive craft" (or, as he does elsewhere, "sly civility"), Bhabha implies a kind of aesthetic fabrication of the cultural subject that simultaneously self-destructs, a partitive or morselated subject affirming itself in the world through the projection and erosion of its "native" base.[6]

Bhabha's observation alerts us to the risks, now as before, of the critic's reproduction, if not fabrication, of historic variations of colonial mimesis, variations, which we might characterize as brutal catachreses of identity, typified by what I am dubbing, after their linguistic invention in colonial education, *l'effet Yadtou* and *l'effet Thénonité. L'effet Yadtou* was unwittingly produced by André Malraux in his commentary on Picasso's masks:

> As early as the collection shown at the old Trocadéro, the plurality of African forms endowed that art with a virulent force, because those forms seemed not at all bound up with any common significance in the sense that historical forms are. . . . . painters were dumbfounded by their discovery of an inexhaustible inventiveness which they called the language of freedom. When one painter said, "Negro art is good because *il y a de tout,*" the freedom implied was expressed by painters in a play on words: they called it *"Yadtou"* art—the art of a tribe they had invented in order to name Negro art.[7]

Malraux recounts the anecdote surrounding "Yadtou art" by way of illustrating that African art, despite the disability of having "no history," could be ratified by virtue of its formalist offerings to European primitivism. The make-believe African tribal name Yadtou, itself a camouflage of a hidden European expression, *il y a de tout,* constitutes an emblem of colonial conquest; a European identity masquerading as African that, though it may refract European cultural grotesquerie back through the colonial gaze (thereby fissuring Europe's self-recognition), nonetheless remystifies European cultural appropriationism.

My second example, *l'effet Thénonité,* was coined by Sartre in his introduction to Fanon's *Les Damnés de la terre.* In the course of a rousing attack on France's "golden age" of assimilation Sartre wrote:

> It was not so long ago, the earth counted two billion inhabitants, five hundred million men and a billion natives. The first disposed of the Verb, the others borrowed it. . . . The European elite undertook to create an indigenous elite, they selected some adolescents, branded the principles of western culture on their foreheads with a red iron, they lined their mouths with sonorous gags, big pasty words that stuck to the teeth; after a brief sojourn in the metropole they were sent home, altered for life ("truqués"). These living lies had nothing left to say to their brothers; they echoed Europe. From Paris, from London, from Amsterdam we uttered the words "Parthénon! Fraternité!" and somewhere in Africa, in Asia, lips opened: "Thénon . . . nité" It was the golden age.[8]

"Thenonity" becomes here much more than a parapraxis that comically unsettles, through elision, icons of Western art such as the Parthenon or the Republican virtue of Fraternity. Thenonity is its own phenomenon, a term that names the inner violence of cultural self-unlearning, the estrangement of semantic value through parrot-speech, and the political terror of enforced pedagogical error.

This subjective violence, though it may be subdued in the context of late-twentieth-century academic canon wars and disciplinary turf-battles, flashes forth in the multicultural university, where, for the last decade, minority constituencies have equated the hegemony of European humanities curricula with the warping of consciousness and the suppression of inter-ested (in the sense of "in one's own interest") knowledge. Even if it is ad-mitted that American secessionist ideologies of identity fit uncomfortably around the contours of Third World cultural cosmopolitanism (where in general the intelligentsia has remained in active dialogue with the metro-pole), Eurocentrism seems inevitably compromised by its colonial or impe-rialist association with ideological force-feeding.

Continentalism Adrift

The drift away from the European continent in the definition of national language disciplines outside of Europe seems inevitable in the light of new imperatives to globalize the canon. Circa the mid-1980s, what North Amer-ican humanities departments called continental theory, continental phi-losophy, or, to use the common parlance shorthand, "deconstruction," was put on the defensive. The curtailment of funding sources for foreign-lan-guage study coincided with the arrival of a new generation of graduate stu-dents whose threshold of endurance for theory's notorious difficulty was substantially lower than that of their predecessors. Even those critics of the (long-dead) "Yale School" who once championed the theoretical vanguard began to trumpet a "new literariness" to ward off the excesses of an increas-ingly demonized cultural studies. The word *deconstruction*, already some-thing of an archaism, was by the mid-1990s most commonly found as a pejorative term misdeployed by ideologues to decry what was wrong with the humanities.

On the cutting edge of criticism, deconstruction was largely sup-planted by cultural theory. As Jim Berkley wrote of Paul de Man's work in a paper subtitled "An Elegy for the Era of High Theory," "Despite his often ir-reproachable philosophical positions, his audacious negativity is more likely to strike us today as posturing, his bleak aesthetic of allegory as un-necessarily restrictive and annoyingly 'more-demystified-than-thou.'"[9] Weary of hermeneutic gongorism, morally singed by the "de Man Affair," cut loose from the prise of a European theory that seemed to have lost its younger progenitors, galvanized by the political urgency of minority dis-courses, and nostalgic for the bygone status of the public intellectual, a whole generation of deconstruction-trained critics looked to cathect else-where. The destabilizing reading practices that were part of a literary for-mation in the 1970s and 1980s were now applied to the "texts" of popular culture, historical narrative, gender identity, virtual reality, American and postcolonial politics, and so on. This residual propensity to textualize objects of analysis when textualization itself was understood to be a culturally freighted philosophical occidentalism created problems for many whose foundations were historically and politically grounded. Conversely, deconstructionists, with their profoundly discomfited relationship to "role models" or "positive images," often had severe difficulty with an identity politics that seemed to shore itself up through heroic histories of cultural subjects.

As a hermeneutic praxis, deconstruction's particular "construction" of continental philosophy, particularly in the United States, tended to purge the contextual specificity of the European continent. Though "good students" put their time in studying the French Hegelians (Kojève to Levinas) and phenomenologists (Husserl to Bachelard), continental theory began to lose its multiple voices, coalescing, bloblike, into a conceptual magma. Increasingly abstracted from its generative situation in postwar European history, it came to be associated with unfocused American political agendas within identity politics.

And yet, to ask what happened to the identity of deconstruction (Where did it go? What was it all about? Is it still here in another guise?) is, inevitably, to pose another kind of question: could there be a contemporary identity politics *without* the legacy of deconstruction?[10] Or, more pointedly still, was the long shadow of deconstruction largely responsible for rendering the category of identity in identity politics incoherent, fraught with irksome contradictions, mired in an essentialism debate that seemed to have no issue?

In the early days of cultural studies, deconstruction was seen as the bridge to a promising politics of identity; its ability to dislodge the dead fixity of eternal verities was treasured as a mode of semantic activism. The complexity of deconstruction's rhetorical conceits pressured the mind to project itself to a "different" place. Through diacritical invention, language was defamiliarized. Neologisms and syntactic intercessions broke up patterns of impacted, predictable meaning. The separation of prefixes and suffixes from verbal *racines* released lost or forgotten significations into the imagination. And then there was the visual mobilization of the page through narrative spacing and whimsical deformations of orthography and diction. Perhaps the most historic case in which deconstruction's graphological "deviance" was "identified" as potentially worthwhile for a nascent identity politics, was Henry Louis Gates's famous move toward an "écriture black." Read today, Gates's essay on the Signifyin(g) Monkey (as trope for the historic black vernacular parodics of the master's discourse) appears surprisingly indebted to Derridean "différance." I say surprisingly because today he would surely feel in no way compelled to address race matters via a deconstructive turn. "Perhaps," he wrote back in the mid-1980s, "replacing with a visual sign the *g* erased in the black vernacular shall, like Derrida's neologism, serve both to avoid confusion and the reduction of these two distinct sets of homonyms to a false identity and to stand as the sign of a (black) Signifyin(g) difference itself. The absent *g* is a figure of the Signifyin(g) black difference."[11]

In the period that has elapsed since Gates's appropriation of *différance* or Gayatri Spivak's insistence on "deconstructing" historiography within subaltern studies, a well-acknowledged divide has opened up between minority discourses and continental philosophy. The breach became glaringly visible in 1986 in the controversy that erupted between Derrida and Anne McClintock and Rob Nixon over the questionable political value of interrogating the word *apartheid* as a metonym for world racism, abstracted from the specific history of South Africa.[12] This early initiative to "identify deconstruction" (in the sense of consciously allying it with a global human-rights movement) came from Derrida himself, but one could say, in retrospect, that it backfired politically and has continued to do so as the McClintock/Nixon position has fanned out into a larger critique of deconstruction's obsession with Eurocentric philosophical problems: being, subjectivity, representation, and the real.

Derrida himself has arguably been the most effective in eschewing doctrinaire applications of deconstruction. In *Jacques Derrida par Geoffrey Bennington et Jacques Derrida* he interrogates his own "Algériance" in relation to the philosophical stakes of deconstruction. In his more recent *Le Monolinguisme de l'autre*, he engages with questions of native language, translational metaphysics, and national belonging.[13] And in "Géopsychanalyse 'and the Rest of the World'" he dissects the colonial foundations of psychoanalysis. Derrida's title refers to a meeting held in London in 1976, where the International Psychoanalytic Association presented itself as a supranational institution invested with powers to disburse credentials, supervise training programs, and institute self-legitimating procedures of analysis. In its responsibility for regional supervision, it referred to the geographical areas not immediately under its jurisdiction as "game preserves" (the analogy to African safari and wildlife grounds is embarrassingly transparent). The official brief stated: "The association's main geographical areas are defined at this time as America north of the United States-Mexican border; all America south of that border, *and the rest of the world."*[14] For Derrida,

> It is too good an expression not to start with this last bit. It essentially names Europe, the country of origin and former capital of psychoanalysis, a body

covered with apparatuses and institutional tattoos, and, in this same "rest of the world," any territory that might still be considered virgin, all the places in the world where psychoanalysis, let's say it, hasn't yet planted its feet.[15]

[C'est un trop bon mot pour qu'on ne commence pas par ce reste. Il nomme au fond l'Europe, terre d'origine et vieille métropole de la psychanalyse, un corps couvert d'appareils et de tatouages institutionels et, dans le même "reste du monde," tout territoire encore vierge, tous les lieux du monde où la psychanalyse, disons-le, n'a pas encore mis les pieds.]

Derrida's analysis of "psychoanalysis à la carte" signals the obfuscated collusions between the institution's thirst for internationalist status and its underacknowledged implication in the history of colonial mentalities.[16]

Though, like psychoanalysis, deconstruction has been stigmatized for its elitist internationalism, it entered the age of cultural studies with strong interrogations of nation-ness, femme-ness, and race matters. In "being there" with a language of nonconformist discursive invention, deconstruction provided a vocabulary for ontological homelessness and denationalized consciousness that remains important for the nonreductive exfoliation of identity and cultural discourses. When nationalism "came back" in the late 1980s and 1990s conjoined to postcolonial theory, deconstruction remained initially coiled up inside; stored in orthography (as in Homi Bhabha's "dissemi[nation])," in critical demystifications of nationalism as a raced and gendered construct (Anne McClintock's "'No Longer in a Future Heaven': Nationalism, Gender, and Race"), or in hologrammatic projections of alienated nationalisms of the future (as in Benedict Anderson's "long-distance" or "E-mail nationalism" in which "the participant rarely pays taxes in the country in which he does his politics" and who is paradoxically "enabled by the very metropole that marginalizes him, to play national hero in a flash, on the other side of the planet").[17] In the late 1990s studies of nationalism continue to proliferate wildly, perhaps because, as Anderson's vision of E-mail nationalism presages, national identity disburses a nostalgic charge the more it erodes under the pressures of diaspora. The whimsical imperatives of roving corporate investment and labor outsourcing have meant that diaspora competes with national rootedness; poor people disperse to where the work is, and elites form, in Jenny Sharpe's words, a "transnational capitalist class whose members act in the interest of the global system. Like transnational corporations their allegiance is not to the nation-state but to a global consumerism that thrives on cultural hybridities."[18]

Sharpe's intimation of the multinationalization of culture industries, along with her surmise that Third World intellectuals help consolidate a hybridized or multicultural elite that is eminently deployable by transnational corporations, accords with what Philip McMichael has called "the colonization of nation-states" by "multilateral agencies, global firms, and global and regional free trade agreements."[19] There are stark implications here for the fate of national language departments or "foreign" literature programs: like the archaic myths of national character on which they are based, they will become increasingly meaningless as they cede sovereignty to interstate or common market cultural regulatory entities. Accordingly, French theory, which has already been misleadingly subsumed by the geographically and nationally amorphous nomenclatures of "continental philosophy," "critical theory," or the even more crudely simplified "Theory," will be progressively reduced to a critical affect radiating off global cultural transfers. Even the "nation" in transnationalism is destined to wither away within regimes of diasporic allegiance, unless a fiction of national autonomy is preserved as a marketing ploy, deemed useful for the identification of publishers' target audiences or the distribution of literary prizes and awards.

If French continental theory in the United States has been upstaged or rendered obsolete by transnational studies, it has been supplanted in France by a "born again" infatuation with American neoliberalism (Luc Ferry on the right, Alain Touraine on the left), and British-style analytic philosophy (the Wittgensteinianism of Jacques Bouveresse). The New Europe thus offers a fuzzy continentalization of culture in exchange for a Europeanized Americanism. Euros for dollars. Not surprisingly, this fast and loose deal-making in the culture industry has precipitated counteroffensives. Nationalist recidivism is evident in the endeavor to impose fines on companies that bastardize the French language with corrupting linguistic imports, as well as in the protectionist effort to contain the home market for American media product. In the press, American multiculturalism is routinely excoriated by pundits as a form of "wound culture" that stifles intellectual dialogue and cultural *rayonnement*. Alain Finkelkraut's response to a *New York Times* poll on how America is viewed from outside is symptomatic in this regard:

> A real paradigm shift has occurred with the decision to designate intellectual disciplines not by their method but by their subject. Henceforth what we have is not learning to understand but to heal: heal white heterosexual males of their superiority complex and give other people back their pride. Bring down the offenders, raise up the offended: such is the mission of the humanities in the era of multiculturalism.
> . . . The obsessional respect for feelings turns the game of seduction

into sexual harassment; the entire tradition of European art and literature stands convicted of ethnocentrism. Whereas "culture" in the singular was a kind of conversation, multiculturalism is an inquisition: the D.W.E.M.'s (dead white European males) and their current accomplices have been summoned before a tribunal thoroughly determined to liberate us from their hateful grip.

In France, too, you have to watch your step these days. The Gay Pride movement is powerful, and the expression of any skepticism about its mandate renders you a homophobe. And if you should have the temerity to criticize contemporary art, you're immediately denounced as a reactionary.

The "healing disease" is particularly virulent on American campuses, but conformism can establish its reign anywhere by brandishing the flag of subversion.[20]

Finkelkraut's aversion to identity politics deflects attention from the more difficult task of defining what he means by "`culture' as a kind of conversation." Such "conversation" seems to presume a common language, shared intentions, and good-faith terms of communication, which in turn risk masking a monolingualism offering no guarantees of dialogue with Islamic or non-Western immigrant populations.[21]

While Finkelkraut is more interested in criticizing the sectarianism of American intellectual interest groups than in defending a clearly defined vision of national culture, Marc Fumaroli (a distinguished scholar of classical rhetoric) has zealously pursued a mission to indict the Socialist state's cultural politics. In *L'Etat culturel: Essai sur une religion moderne* (1991), Fumaroli traced the origins of the cultural state to the colonial era, during which French civilization was codified within a bureaucratic apparatus and exported as part of the imperial mandate. Positing that it was no accident that the rise of the Ministry of Cultural Affairs coincided with the decline of the Ministry of the Colonies, Fumaroli implied that what was left over from the colonial period was transferred back home and turned on French subjects: "we are dealing with a neocolonization for internal use" [on a affaire à une néo-colonisation à usage interne].[22] Fulminating against the "technocratic philistinism" of the Mitterand government, Fumaroli ended his book wondering whether France will become "a cultural or multicultural space of the masses" or "the center of the only Europe worthy of love: the Europe of the spirit" (p. 305).

Though Fumaroli's polemic was widely dismissed for its reactionary hostility to non-French or popular cultures, his use of a Barrèsian rhetoric of national destiny anticipated what would become a more widespread nationalist revivalism in belletristic circles. As if aware, himself, of his swerve toward Barrèsianism, Fumaroli alludes to Barrès explicitly, but his allusion—"we are far from the polemic of *The Uprooted*"—reveals itself to be a mocking rhetorical flourish used not, as one might expect, to distance himself from Barrès, but rather, to underscore how much worse the cultural crisis has become since Barrès's time. Where Barrès had only to worry about the corrosive effect of Kantian abstraction, we postmoderns, Fumaroli contests, must confront a minister of culture (Jack Lang) who "subsidizes rap culture, imported from the savage neighborhoods *(quartiers ensauvagés)* of the New World."[23]

If here Fumaroli pursued his mission to stem the tide of invasive American popular culture, more recently he extended his polemical range to the arts. In the spring of 1997 he became tangentially embroiled in a mini-"affaire" that erupted when leading intellectuals associated with the Left—Jean-Pierre Vernant, Régis Debray, Claude Lévi-Strauss, Michel Serres, Jean Baudrillard, and Jean Clair (director of the Picasso Museum)—published articles in the right-wing journal *Krisis* denouncing the nullity of contemporary art in France. Known for its fascist leanings, specifically its revival of the stigmatization of modern works as "degenerate art," *Krisis* was considered to be a Le Pen–backed journal. It is edited by Alain de Benoist, author of a sympathetic volume on Hitler's favorite sculptor Arno Breker, and founding member of the New Right group Grèce (Groupe de recherche et d'études pour la civilisation européenne/Organization for the Research and Study of European Civilization).[24] While the motives for the left intellectual collaboration with *Krisis* remain inscrutable from this side of the Atlantic (were Baudrillard et al. seeking an *épater la gauche* effect? Did they genuinely believe such a move would spark meaningful dialogue?), and while it remains difficult to disentangle the critique of cultural mediocrity from the *Krisis* scandal, Fumaroli took advantage of the charged atmosphere when he published an interview with Jean Clair entitled "Contemporary Art Is at an Impasse" in *Le Figaro* (January 22, 1997). Here he furthered his earlier case against the "cultural state" by implying that high artistic standards are held hostage to state-subsidized institutions determining what is "médiatiquement correct" [mediatically correct].[25] In what appears to be a contradictory position (familiar enough if one looks at conservative cultural agendas in the United States), Fumaroli linked his crusade to reform French artistic standards with reduced state participation in cultural policy.

In its promotion of aesthetic codes that go back to the royal retinue (a culture of *galanterie, geste, raffinement,* and privileged intellection for its own sake), Fumaroli's study of the "genius of the French language," published in *Les Lieux de mémoire,* plays to the resurgent popularity of national-heritage culture.[26] This study of French eloquence as the crux of a nationalist universalism stands at the antipodes of much American-style

French studies, typified perhaps by Kristin Ross's examination of the demise of colonial nationalism during and after France's "dirty war" in Algeria.[27] Where Fumaroli mobilizes the machinery of classical rhetoric on behalf of relaunching *bienséance* as a national calling, Ross uses historical and visual juxtapositions to deflate national hubris. Hygiene, domesticity, and the machinery of Americanization are set against the gleamingly macabre "appliances" of Algerian torture. These bipolar conceptions of the stakes and methods of French studies, represented (synechdochally) by Fumaroli and Ross, exemplify the widening continental divide—specifically the drifting apart of France and the United States—within criticism and theory.

What Is the National Character of the Multinational Nation?

In the new studies of nationalism focusing on identity, national consciousness, national becoming, the posthistory of what the decolonization era termed "new nations," or the postnational "beyond," the category of national character fails to figure prominently, if at all.[28] Undoubtedly, we should conclude that it is a defunct or anachronistic term; a throwback to the era of Hyppolyte Taine or Gustave Lanson, for whom it mattered in consolidating Third Republic institutions and canons of national literature, or earlier, to the manners and customs definition of David Hume: (*Political Essays* of 1748, "Of National Characters"), itself informed by Caesar's description of the Gauls in *The Gallic Wars:*

> The vulgar are apt to carry all *national characters* to extremes; and having once established it as a principle, that any people are knavish, or cowardly, or ignorant, they will admit of no exception, but comprehend every individual under the same censure. Men of sense condemn those undistinguishing judgements: Though at the same time, they allow, that each nation has a peculiar set of manners, and that some particular qualities are more frequently to be met with among one people than among neighbors.
>
> . . . Different reasons are assigned for these *national characters;* while some account for them from *moral,* others from *physical* causes. By *moral* causes, I mean all circumstances which are fitted to work on the mind as motives or reasons, and which render a peculiar set of manners habitual to us. Of this kind are, the nature of the government, the revolutions of public affairs, the plenty or penury in which the people live, the situation of the nation with regard to its neighbours, and such like circumstances. By *physical* causes, I mean those qualities of the air and climate, which are supposed to work insensibly on the temper, by altering the tone and habit of the body,

and giving a particular complexion, which, though reflexion and reason may sometimes overcome it, will yet prevail among the generality of mankind, and have an influence on their manners.[29]

Hume's emphasis on the long arm of the public sphere shaping the moral ontology of the individual through economic hierarchies, government affairs, and foreign policy, anticipates Etienne Balibar's focus on the role of national-state intervention in the "whole space of private life."[30] But putting aside the intrinsic historical interest of Hume's arguments, it is not self-evident why one would want to exhume national character as the stamp of the public persona on the private individual, unless there were pointed reasons for doing so. For my concerns here, early theorizations of national character provide a vantage point from which to view present-day accounts of the subject that privilege mediatic publicity and cybernetic civic evacuation. Looking backward at the confident essentialism of Hume's idea of national character (epitomized by his endorsement of the truism that "people in the northern regions have a greater inclination to strong liquors, and those in the southern to love and women"), one can better measure the distance between the a priori status of national character during the Enlightenment and its relative tenuousness in late-twentieth-century projections of virtual, postnational citizenship.[31]

The great events in between, both of which clearly had a monumental impact on the status of national character as a discourse in France, were the French Revolution and the colonizing mission. Under the reign of the Jacobins, *instituteurs de langue française* were deployed as agents of "linguistic terror" to supervise the standardization of national language. The postrevolutionary emergence of what Renée Balibar and Dominique Laporte have characterized as "le français national" (with emphasis on this expression's conflation of "French national language" with "nationalized Frenchman" or French citizen-subject) was given eloquent substance by Abbé Grégoire's pamphlets. In his *Report on the necessity and means of abolishing patois and universalizing the usage of the French language,* written during the Terror, Grégoire fused an Enlightenment ideal of semantic transparency with a patriotic conception of national language. French, already elevated to superior status as the language truly expressive of reason, clarity, and truth, is accorded an even more singular role as that which mystically binds the spirit of *le peuple* to national greatness.[32]

As for the period of colonization, focused on in this book, new theories of racial superiority were yoked to a revitalized sense of national manifest destiny. The imperial venture provided endless trials through which the mettle of national will and national right could be tested. Citing Linda Colley's *Britons: Forging a Nation,* Jacqueline Rose underscores that "Britishness as it attempted to absorb all the nations of the Union under its sway . . . was inseparable from more brutal forms of self-fashioning. 'Regular *and violent* contact with peoples' defined the nation-state.'"[33] Michael Gorra makes a similar point via George Orwell's definition of the "Englishness of the English." British identity emerges as insular, island-formed, self-referential, circular, suspicious of outsiders, and historically consolidated through cultural tics ("devotion to hobbies, a love of flowers, solid breakfasts, gloomy Sundays"), and periodic revivals of "native" literary traditions (Philip Larkin's return to Thomas Hardy and the Georgian nature poets).[34]

National character and native literary tradition were, of course, comparably affirmed in France by suborning conquered peoples to French national culture. As Derrida noted in a lecture entitled "My Independence of Algeria: The Little Negative Theology of the Mother Tongue," delivered at Cornell University in 1996, the "colonial drive" was at its most effective in subjugating the Algerian people to a spectral power called France by instituting French as the national language of Algeria.[35] Derrida underscores the estranged sovereignty or "auto-heteronomy" of the language, by which he implies that French functioned as "the one" (the master-language to which every other form of speech and print culture defaults and defers), and the "other" (a distant, "fantastic" mother tongue, a natal inscription of familial foreignness on Algerian nationals). Though French was the official language of the colonies, it also remained forbidden (subject to "inderdict"), in the sense of unpossessable, remote, beyond the ken of Algerians, be they *pieds noirs* or *indigènes*. This bedrock of interdiction complemented the colonial suppression of Arabic and Berber as legitimate languages of study in the school system. In a curious twist, Derrida uses himself as a case history of linguistic self-hatred and dispossession when he confesses to his profound intolerance of heavily accented French. In describing his efforts to expunge traces of impurity from his own *pied noir* inflections, he reveals that deconstruction perhaps owes much of its impetus to its inventor's complex relation to his own linguistic assimilation. The urge to sully the purity of high French usage through deconstructive ungrammaticality may thus be seen as a psychic preservation of foreignness, a resistance to assimilation; a refusal of slavish fealty to the linguistic *doxa* that his educational upbringing taught him to desire.

If national language codes remain crucial to defining the legacy of national character in the postcolonial era, the same must be said of historic discourses of nationalism. When Ernest Gellner published his *Nations and Nationalism* in 1983, it looked to him as if nationalism were a neglected topic on the part of academic political philosophers.[36] A strong detractor of Elie Kedourie, whose lodestone volume *Nationalism,* published in 1960, is accused of rendering its subject a "contingent, avoidable aberration, accidentally spawned by European thinkers," Gellner insisted on dissociating doctrines from phenomena.[37] Seeking perhaps to contradict Tom Nairn's assertion that "the theory of nationalism has been inordinately influenced by nationalism itself,"[38] he decoupled nationalist thinkers from nationalism, defining the latter as "a distinctive species of patriotism . . . pervasive and dominant only under certain social conditions, which prevail in the modern world, and nowhere else."[39] For Gellner, these conditions include aspirations to cultural homogeneity, centralized education, and bureaucracy, and "a literate sophisticated high culture" that spawns "cultural chauvinism."[40] By indenturing modern nationalism to print culture, Gellner implicitly placed extreme weight on the role of national literature. Literary national culture emerges as the secular equivalent of Hegel's Protestant ethic; with a "priestless unitarianism" substituting for coreligionism as social glue.[41]

In the wake of several decades of canon questioning and high/low controversy it is difficult to interpret Gellner's conception of consensual high-culturalism as much more than a fantasy of civic uniformity, even if he is right to emphasize the critical role of literacy in the formation of modern nation-states. Responding to problematic aspects of Gellner's position, one is perhaps well advised to return to Ernst Renan's founding text *What Is a Nation?* (1882). For Renan, significantly enough, national language, like race, is not considered crucial as an epoxy of social cohesion:

> Languages are historical formations, which tell us very little about the blood of those who speak them and which, in any case, could not shackle human liberty when it is a matter of deciding the family with which one unites oneself for life or for death.[42]

Race and language are both deemed "dangerous" categories: "Such exaggerations enclose one within a specific culture, considered as national; one limits oneself, one hems oneself in. One leaves the heady air that one breathes in the vast field of humanity in order to enclose oneself in a conventicle with one's compatriots" (p. 50). Renan's staunch cultural cosmopolitanism leads him to identify collective memory as the "soul or spiritual principle" of the nation. Though he envisages a time when a "European confederation" will render nations obsolete as guarantors of liberty, he treats nationalism as a fact of his historical present; modeling his vision of national solidarity on concubinage ("the desire to live together") and on military sacrifice for the sake of civilization (p. 52).

Though he may have been wary of instantiating language as the essential social bond, by elevating civilization's role in sustaining national adhesion Renan conferred responsibility on the makers of national culture and official memory: historians, writers, artists, intellectuals. Here, we may surmise, he opened a space for rethinking nationalism's indebtedness to literary fabrications of national character. The invention of Marianne by Republican artists and writers; romanticism's consecration of Napoleon; realism's breviary of French types, including *ambitieux* angling for publicity and state power in the urban capital; naturalism's xenophobic patriotism and cult of Joan of Arc; colonial literature's lionization of settler frontiersmen; postwar epics of sacrifice and resistance on behalf of French soil; all furnished characterological prototypes that were actively recruited in assembling the construct of the French nation-state.[43]

Associated with an enduring tradition of *Bildung,* with Fichtean postulations of the spiritual unity between native language and national identity;[44] or with Judeo-Christian determinations of right and wrong, strong and weak, "character" has been replaced by articulations of ethical relations mediated by utilitarianism (felicific calculus); psychoanalysis (psychic investments and expenditures); political theories of cultural default to ethnic primordialism; literary theories of politics and genre (as in Fredric Jameson's controversial thesis that national allegory characterizes "Third-World Literature in the Era of Multinational Capitalism"), and New Age inspirationalism (as in "you can be who you want to be").[45] But it is perhaps time to put the problem of national character back into discussions of nationalism, in part because it functions like the stereotype in relation to performativity theory (a reality check to unbounded fabulations of diasporic openness), in part because it refocuses attention on the contemporary individual's atrophied relationship to the state, and in part because, in surviving as an unspoken *grundrisse* within national language and literature fields, it seeds a particular predicament for future disciplines: What will the national character of the multinational nation be (i.e., the nation whose borders are ridden roughshod over by transnational corporations)?[46]

The Imperium of Affect

In the absence of a reliable sense of what multinational character might turn out to be, I will submit that what we are left with is a confusing play of affects. Affects are gestures that are both affecting (moving, alluring, identificatory) and affected (hyperbolized, camped, "fake," mimetic of an absent reality). The world of affect seems to take up where the critique of performativity leaves off: that is, at the point where antiessentialism has become a given and the market in identity-production is oversaturated. The imperium of affect marks a return to "easy"; to feelings washing about in a depoliticized space of the transnational commodity. While Freudian affect is defined by small electrophysiological shocks, opposed drives, libidinal charges, and the "speaking body," Kleinian affect concerns "memories in feelings" (gratitude, envy, aggression, as translated into words), and the "feeling of selfhood" or subjectivity.[47]

Affect is about visual pleasure after aura has been drained off. Affect is about ethnic and racial particularisms that have lost their hard edges and become substitutable formulas or caricatures of nation, race, and gender. Orientalism, in much recent cultural production, emerges as a means of costuming the affect, garbing it in a fantastic culturalism, that scrambles ethnic profiles and depletes historical references to national character. Here, affect is about the indiscriminate, loving embrace of "others," of alterity as a domesticated exoticism replenishing Western reserves of the *intérieur,* and extending the repertory of poses and postures necessary to acting out bourgeois masquerades of identity.

Affect can also be about unfocused "resistance," small revolutions, desecrations of "positive images," outbreaks of *ressentiment,* agitprop tactics. Affect stages political events with realist expectations; that is, with perfect foreknowledge of the basic immunity of "the system" to its viral attacks. Cynical and deflationary, affect alludes to what happens to oppositional discourse when it turns into "happy" multiculturalism, a kind of "we-are-the-worldism," or hybridized *kulturfest.*[48] It is precisely this kind of pallid "diversity," typified by the morphed racializations of Benetton advertisements, that Donna Haraway associates with the marketing of "panhumanity": "Benetton produces a stunningly beautiful, young, stylish panhumanity composed by mix-and-match techniques. Diversity, like DNA, is the code of codes. Race, in Sarah Franklin's words, becomes a fashion accessory."[49]

For the cultural-studies critic Lawrence Grossberg, affect applies to the sensibility of mass culture and the understanding of "the popular": "Affect," he writes,

> points to the (relatively autonomous) production of what is normally experienced as moods and emotions by an asignifying effectivity. It refers to a dimension or plane of our lives that involves the enabling distribution of energies. While it is easy to conceptualize it as the originary (causal) libidinal economy postulated by psychoanalysis, . . . affect is not the Freudian

notion of disruptive (or repressed) pulsions of pleasure breaking through the organized surfaces of power; rather, it is an articulated plane whose organization defines its own relations of power and sites of struggle. . . . the recognition of an articulated plane of affect points to the existence of another politics, a politics of feeling . . . (good, bad or indifferent), a politics that Benjamin had acknowledged.[50]

If Grossberg defines affect as a mass-cultural materiality that embraces a Benjaminian "politics of feeling," he neglects to explore the full implications of its "asignifying effectivity." What kind of politics is affective without being effective? A politics of hyperreality and hypermimetism?

Affect is what comes (quite logically) after the performative subject. It is about miming the human when the human has come increasingly to be embodied in posthuman constructions. To be affected, in Roger Caillois's sense, is to see human-ness prefigured in the primitive repository of gestures and triggered responses archived in the behavior of the animal world; the camouflage of the praying mantis thus becomes an anticipation of humanoid enactments of defense and ego-building scaffolding.

Affects are the residue of the real; ghostly afterimages of attitudes, performances of human-ness, and attempts to simulate being a subject. Affects are crucial to robotics and cybernetics: if a cyborg can successfully simulate affect, it can become all too human. Affect bespeaks a politics of the virtual subject. But questions arise: Are these virtual subjects regressive? Mirror images of unconscious images (imagos) that are themselves delusional, phobic, and paranoid?

The answer is yes, provided that we remember that Lacan, following his teacher Clérambault and the aesthetic example of his surrealist contemporaries (Breton, Dalí, Crevel), destigmatized delusional automatism in his account of the psychic formation of the subject. As Sam Weber has noted, Lacan's famous mirror stage rests on the child's delusional mimicry, a self (mis)-recognition. Here we might be tempted to line up Lacanian delusionism with what Caillois characterized as "the psychological virtualities of man."[51] As the leftovers of instincts, as the residues of "mythic" behaviors that haunt the staging of the subject, affects become crucial to sustaining the illusion of identity, however dismantled.

While the aesthetics of affect clearly participate in the identity politics of performative mimicry, it remains to be seen whether they will acquire anything more than a circumstantial politics. In the meantime I will conjecture that affect has emerged as the "theory lite" version of virtual subjects who have little real stake in national, ethnic, or gender affiliations, as well as the anticipation of a critique of posthuman subjectivity at the end of the millennium.

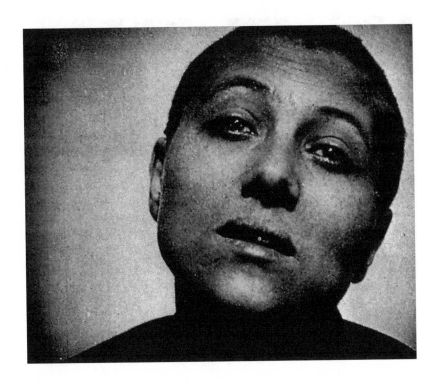

Still of Renée Falconetti in Carl Dreyer's *Joan of Arc* (1928). Falconetti was one of many playing Joan who afterward seemed to suffer an accursed life. (Photograph from Theresa Hak Kyung Cha, *Dictée* [Berkeley: Third Woman Press, 1995].)

Maurice Barrès at the Joan of Arc celebration at Compiègne in 1913. "The cult of Joan of Arc," Barrès wrote, "will involve the collaboration of religion, patriotism, poetry, and the spirit of war." He helped mount a successful campaign to create a national holiday in her honor. (Photograph from Harlinge-Viollet, reproduced in Michel Winock, *Le Siècle des intellectuels* [Paris: Seuil, 1997], p. 144.)

Plantu's cartoon of the National Front being burned at the stake (1995). By the early 1990s Jean-Marie Le Pen had firmly appropriated Joan of Arc as a symbol of national chauvinism and anti-immigration politics for his right-wing party Le Front National. (From Plantu, *Le Pire est à nous!* [Paris: Editions Le Monde, 1994].)

Still from flier for Isaac Julien's film *Frantz Fanon: Black Skin, White Mask* (1995). Isaac Julien's charismatic documentary confirms Fanon's resurgent image as a mythic black hero even as it establishes terms for a critical demystification of Fanon's emancipatory humanism and sexual politics. (From the archive of Isaac Julien.)

Harem Interior: The Handkerchief Favor, an example of Orientalist pornography from the 1830s. The haremization effect can be traced to the age-old European topos of visual curiosity and sexual fantasy. In the harem, new forms of love, exotic eroticisms, incubate and multiply. (Lithograph in the Bibliotheque Nationale, Paris.)

Sarah Bernhardt as Cleopatra. Bernhardt typifies turn-of-the-century feminine hypercharacterology, with its conflation of "acting" and "being." Not only was she celebrated for her role in Victor Sardou's *Cléopâtre*—which she played into her seventies—she had herself photographed in character, stretched out on a divan with jeweled girdle and arm-bracelet, an adoring female attendant at her knee. (Victoria and Albert Museum.)

Colette in *Egyptian Dream* (1907). Orientalist stereotypes were used as a means of outing sapphic love. Colette's revelation of her partnership with the marquise de Belboeuf in *Egyptian Dream* caused a furor in the theater. (Collection of Mme. Dreyfus-Valette, *Album Colette: Iconographie choisie* [Paris: Gallimard, 1984], plate 156, p. 90.)

Isabelle Eberhardt as a Bedouin man, 1895. Eberhardt's larger-than-life
biography, characterized by nomadism, addiction, and bicultural, bisexual
cross-dressing, inspired successive generations of feminists with an
"Eberhardt complex" that continues to this day, exemplified in the films of
Leslie Thornton. (From Annette Kobak, *Isabelle: The Life of Isabelle
Eberhardt* [New York: Vintage, 1990].)

THE

ANALYSIS

OF

BEAUTY.

Written with a view of fixing the fluctuating IDEAS of TASTE.

BY *WILLIAM HOGARTH.*

So vary'd he, and of his tortuous train
Curl'd many a wanton wreath, in fight of Eve,
To lure her eye.-------- Milton.

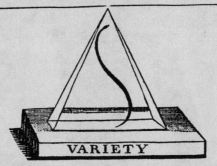

LONDON:

Printed by *J. REEVES* for the *AUTHOR,*
And Sold by him at his House in LEICESTER-FIELDS.

MDCCLIII.

5332

B

William Hogarth's "Line of Beauty," frontispiece to his *Analysis of Beauty.* Hogarth's serpentine line anticipates Lacan's "line of desire" (figured as an interior eight). This sinuous line has been reprised in renderings of Oriental dancers and modern-day pinups. Hogarth depicted the S-curve with a snake's head at the top, evoking the biblical serpent with a citation from Milton's *Paradise Lost.*

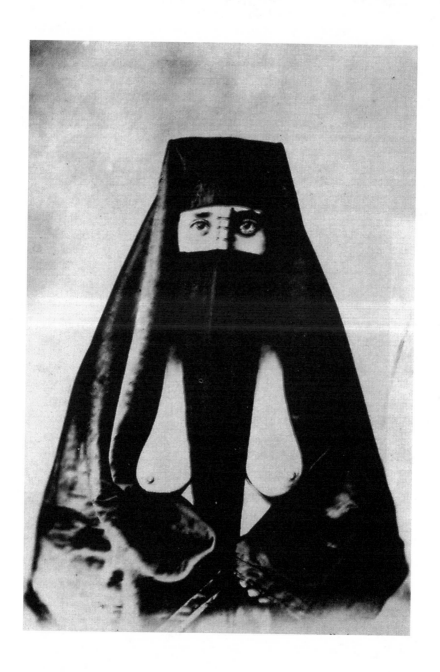

Postcard of North African woman, the last reproduced in Malek Alloula's *The Colonial Harem* (trans. Myrna Godzich and Wlad Godzich [Minneapolis: University of Minnesota Press, 1986]). The woman's eyes stare back at the camera with an apparent mixture of fear and obstinacy, as if to say, "Terminus. The figura serpentinata stops here."

Fez city wall, from André Chevrillon, *Visions du Maroc* (1933). Shadows, arrayed in complex bands and wedges of intense light or sprayed in Technicolor blue around a minaret at nightfall, emerge as a visual specialty of "Morocco" photographs and films, endowing them with a distinct aesthetic allure that might be called "colonial photogeny."

Tourist publicity, "Visitez la Tunisie," 1956. As the notion of photogeny is transferred from face to place, the problem of what gives a site its sex becomes entangled with the more difficult problem of identifying what is noir in the aesthetics of noir. (From Pascal Blanchard and Armelle Chatelier, eds., *Images et colonies* [Paris: BDIC-ACHAC, 1993].)

Film still of Gina Manès in Jean Epstein's *Coeur fidèle* (1923). This face superimposed on the landscape illustrates Epstein's theory of cinematic photogeny. The close-up turned the screen into a relief map: faces were transformed into kinetic flesh-lands; stark seascapes and barren landmasses became expressive faces. (From Jean Epstein, *Ecrits sur le cinéma,* vol. 1 [Paris: Editions Seghers, 1974].)

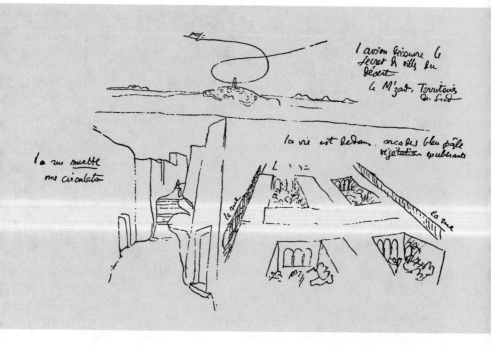

Detail from a drawing for Le Corbusier, *La Ville radieuse* (The radiant city) (1935). Le Corbusier described aerial vision as a "miracle of sagacity and order" that allowed what was viewed below to be "pried open like living shellfish." For André Malraux, the airplane was the Icarian hero of modernity, a miracle of whiteness, an apparatus synonymous with the triumph of Western civilization.

Still from *Geography,* choreographed and performed by the Ralph Lemon Company (1997). *Geography* may be seen as an example of Afrofuturism blending traditional African dance steps with techno-*bidonville* stage sets by Nari Ward and rhizomatic soundscore by Paul D. Miller, aka D. J. Spooky That Subliminal Kid. (Program catalog for *Geography,* Brooklyn Academy of Music's Next Wave Festival, 1997. Photo by T. Charles Erickson.)

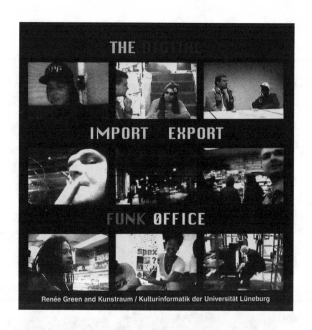

Renée Green, *Import-Export Funk Office*. Green's projects are in the forefront of experiments in Afrofuturism and digital diaspora. (Photograph from the artist's collection.)

CHARACTERS

1
UPROOTED SUBJECTS

BARRÈS AND

THE POLITICS

OF *PATRIMOINE*

Maurice Barrès's *Les Déracinés* (The uprooted), published in 1897 as the first in a trilogy of "novels of national energy," reverberates unexpectedly in contemporary debates over cultural identity. An ideologue of right-wing persuasion and "writer's writer," Barrès used the botanical metaphor of deracination to bolster the politics of anticosmopolitanism (often a code for anti-Semitism).[1] Arguing that trees, when uprooted from their native soil, sicken and die (a point hotly contested by André Gide, who pointed out that, quite to the contrary, cross-bred or hybrid arboricultures often proved to be the hardiest species), Barrès sought to reground French national identity in its provincial traditions and beliefs. Though Barrès's novel was about the reassertion of regional rather than national chauvinism, I would suggest that in contemporary France, universalist nationalism has become a new kind of regional chauvinism, particularly as played out in the realigned political map of the New Europe. Many of the particularist arguments that Barrès applied to the Lorraine, Brittainy, or Languedoc—what he called "la petite patrie" [the little homeland]—now seem appropriate to examine in relation to France's national cultural politics.

Barrès's title—*Les Déracinés*—seems to resonate with Zola's eugenic, organicist titles (*Germinal, Fécondité, La Terre*), despite the two writers's oppositional positioning during the Dreyfus affair. Published in the same year as Emile Durkheim's *Le Suicide* and André Gide's *Les Nourritures terrestres*, the novel places the moral responsibility for murder, committed by a student transplanted from Lorraine to Paris, on the shoulders of his *lycée* professor,

M. Bouteiller. A Kantian trained at the Ecole Normale, the instructor per-sonifies in the eyes of his detractors what Diane Rubenstein has character-ized (in relation to a later generation of *normaliens,* including Foucault and Althusser), as "the metonymic contagion between perverse subjectivities and French philosophy."[2] Thoroughly alienated from the soil, Bouteiller is portrayed as a metaphysical automaton: "a pedagogical product, a son of reason, a stranger to traditional, local or familial custom, a totally abstract being, virtually suspended in the void."[3] The restoration of nativist iden-tity and its by-product, the renewal of national energy, were linked by Bar-rès to an antidecadentist position, defined through a polemical assault on the pro-Dreyfus urban intellectuals who typified the Third Republic of Let-ters. Seeking to reverse "the village that died for France"[4] phenomenon, whereby the nation-state condemns the province to extinction, Barrès transformed provincialism into a form of national egoism: "Had I thought of the world the way I thought of Lorraine I would be in truth a citizen of humanity." This conditional formula indicates how ethnic particularism could be appropriated to modern French nationalism, in its turn convert-ible, according to Pierre Mille, into internationally exportable forms of national idealism.[5] Writing during the interwar years with uncanny pre-science, Mille envisaged Barrèsianism as a major political force that would sweep through the Balkans and the Third World, through "nations and races," that is, who "continue to feel the need of having [nationalistic] ideals stated, stressed, and featured for them in terms overheated with emo-tion."[6]

Barrès's political concoction of *boulangisme,* antiparliamentarianism, and socialism served him poorly in many of his electoral campaigns but earned him an immense popular following as a writer.[7] Ideologically he was indebted to the extremist racial ethnologies of Jules Soury, his profes-sor at the Ecole des Hautes. A precursor of Spengler, most renowned for his work on the central nervous system, Soury was obsessed with the twilight of French civilization, ascribable in his view to the Jewish spoliation of the French race. One of Barrès's early publications, entitled *Trois stations de psy-chothérapie* (1891) joins a Soury-based ideology of nervousness in the social body with the concept of deracination. Part 3 of this work focuses on the life of Marie Bashkirtseff, a Russian-born demimondaine artist who died at twenty-six. "La Légende d'une cosmopolite" (dedicated to "Néo-Catholics"), compares "ideological, thermal, and devotional stations" in the progress of a soul toward the exalted states of sensibility necessary to the production of art. Born of a Tainean conjunction between tempera-ment and milieux, these stations of sensibility are exemplified by Barrès in Goethe's connection to German landscape (the poet is featured outstretched beneath a strong tree in a bounteous Germanic countryside) or Balzac's identification with his nocturnal Parisian cell. Marie Bashkirtseff, by contrast, is presented as a precursor of the transient female cosmopolite that Barrès would build on fictively for Bérénice (the lesbian protagonist of *Le Jardin de Bérénice,* nicknamed "Petite-Secousse," or "Little Seizure," who is described as "a being of pure instinct in no way served by her milieu"), and Astiné Aravian, the exotic temptress of *Les Déracinés.*[8] "With what image, which customs, and which country" could Bashkirtseff be identified, Barrès queried. "This cosmopolite who has no heaven, no earth, no society, is an uprooted one. In the breviary of ideologues, to express moral bohemianism, so strangely entangled with refinement, mustn't one inscribe her in a vulgar but meaningful way, with the epithet *Notre-Dame du sleeping-car.*"[9] The sobriquet "Our Lady of the Sleeping-Car," with its morally suspect connotations of disaffiliation, homelessness, and promiscuity, yields a complex characterology of modern life built around the deracinated subject. Cleverly, Barrès deployed literary portraits of such cosmopolites to impugn the reputations of strangers to the nation. Marie's "vie errante" is metaphysically soldered to insatisfaction, exhaustion, a desirous, fevered attitude to the future, a body prey to fits of shaking and hypertrophy. Like the city of Rome in which Bashkirtseff temporarily resided, her personality dangerously micegenates baroque splendor ("une haute allure") with spiritual fatality, a life-world of nihilism.[10]

Against this barren ontology of dysfunctional national identity and extradited consciousness Barrès forged his *culte du moi*—a protofascist idolatry of the collective individual or mega-Self that was profoundly incoherent in the way much fascist thinking is: that is, unable to decide between statism and decentralization, collectivism and individualism, ontological emptying out and plenitudinous group identification, the *nonmoi* and the *sur-moi.*[11] In taking up the problem of individual identity in culture, Barrès bolstered his conservative vision of the self by restoring an agricultural denotation to culture's political usage (more in line with English convention), a kind of semantic "back to the land" movement, in relation to the *doxic* French sense of *la culture* as classical formation, aesthetic refinement, or intellectual cultivation.

In this context, the *racine* emerges as the bulbous master-trope of Barrès's *roman à thèse:* germinating in an epigraph drawn from Darwin describing the "stunted growth" of plants situated on steep hillsides (analogous, Barrès implies, to provincial youths ill-equipped to handle the peaks of the Kantian sublime), and sprouting anew in a chapter entitled "L'Arbre de M. Taine," in which the eminent literary historian and author of *Les Origines de la France contemporaine* makes a cameo appearance, passing the torch of his wisdom to one of the Lorrainean disciples. After paying a personal visit to Roemerspacher's modest student rooms, Taine counsels him to advance a new principle of "sociability" by remaining faithful to his compatriot "clan" and mindful of his regional origins: Nancy, Taine argues, could become the next Heidelberg, if its native sons work to establish an "exemplary social laboratory" conducive to group identity.[12] Roemerspacher accompanies Taine on his constitutional to the esplanade of the Invalides, where, stopping before his favorite tree, the philosophe delivers an extended peroration on the virtues of enracination:

> This tree will be my friend and adviser until the end of my days. Can you feel its biography? . . . This tree is the expressive image of a beautiful existence. It knows not that it does not move. Its young creative force, from the beginning, fixes its destiny and moves within it. Dare I say that it is its proper force? Not even, it is the eternal unity, the eternal enigma that manifests itself in each form. First under the soil, in the sweet moisture, in the underground night, the seed becomes worthy of light. And the light enables the fragile stem to develop, fortifying itself from one stage to the next. No need for an external master to intervene. The plane tree spreads its limbs, extends its branches, and disposes of its leaves from year to year until reaching perfection.[13]

Taine gleans an ethic of "the living soul and its engenderings" from the tree's exemplary rootedness. His lesson prompts the disciple to take stock of Taine's bodily presence: his tough physique and developed calf muscles bespeak his appurtenance to "the solid race of the Ardennes." This racial/rural marking of Taine's person signals the youth's conversion to the doctrine of mystic regional chauvinism.

As Barrès's student-heroes substitute Taine with the arch-anti-Semite patriot Paul Déroulède, the novel's doctrine evolves more pointedly in the direction of racist xenophobia. Defending "la vieille vie provinciale, celle qui avait ses racines profondes," the narrator describes the tragic loss of "saveur terrienne" in France's eastern territories, attributable to the arrival of "immigrants of the German race," who have modified and "spoiled" the native French type. On a national political scale, the narrator deplores the triumph of a soulless *fonctionnarisme*.[14] The drive to purge French culture of its foreign implants receives its narrative culmination in the brutal murder of Astiné Aravian, an Armenian seductress who has been the mistress of Sturel, the most high-minded of the band from Lorraine. Vilified as a "poison in the blood" (p. 423), a virus from the East, the feminine form of a drugged *patrimoine,* her character becomes, somewhat contradictorily, a place to park a mini–travel narrative through Ottoman landscape. Though all the charms of *dépaysement* are arrayed for the reader's delectation, there is a need to exorcise the foreign presence; Astiné's *lustmord* at the hands of the clan's "serfs" (Racodot and Mouchefrin) is recounted as a ritual sacrifice ostensibly committed in the name of *La Vraie République* (the students' underfunded journal), but more profoundly "justified" by the xenophobic logic of the *récit*. Decapitated and denuded beneath the impassive foliage of a tree in the outskirts of Billancourt, Astiné's bloodied corpse is offered like a victual to replenish the aridity of the French soul. Using the language of nationalist *élan vital*, Barrès describes the crime in morally ambiguous terms as an act of extraordinary energy. As Astiné expires with the final thought—"Comme ça m'ennuie de mourir!"—the narrator adds a final racist insult: "Mais eût-elle aimé viellir? Les Orientales s'alourdissent si fort!" [But would she have liked to grow old? Oriental women get so fat] (p. 427).

As many critics have noted, Barrès's imbrication of race and root came to a disgraceful pass in the Dreyfus affair and its aftermath.[15] This said, the language of Barrèsian roots is perhaps as ubiquitous in the present *fin de siècle* as it was at the turn of the century. Writers and critics from the left and the right, from the metropole and the postcolonies, currently lay claim to and disavow the term's charged symbolic capital. In a single issue of *Le Monde des Livres* of December 1995, the notion of roots surfaced in virtually every piece.[16] A review of Michel Serres's *Éloge de la philosophie en langue française* cited the author's neo-Barrèsian denunciation of Socialism's intellectual elite: "The *notables* and Parisian barons of the Socialist Party . . . contemptuous of the province, . . . disdainful of the country, cultivated, magnificently educated, *petits maîtres*, rich residents of the *beaux quartiers*, ignorant of poverty while blindly producing it, devoted to finance and business, intellectually dominant, quickly corrupted, swindlers in words and morals."[17] By contrast, an article on Paul Celan stresses the German Jewish poet's traumatic relationship to his native language, experienced as the installation of the culture of Auschwitz at the center of his being. "Was Celan first and foremost a poet of deracination?" the critic Nicolas Weill asks, answering his own question with a quote from the Turkish poet Zafer Senocak: "I followed the tracks of Celan and I stopped there where my roots got lost."[18] On the following page, a piece on the Zairean writer Sony Labou Tansi describes a passage from his posthumously published novel *Le Commencement des douleurs* evoking a postcolonial utopia—"une île vierge de colonisation, une terre sans histoire" [a colonially virgin island, a land without history].[19] In the dream of Tansi's protagonist, roots, in the sense of collective history, are forfeited for the sake of a psychic and territorial domain prior to colonization, an impossible space of "colony-lessness." And where Tansi evokes roots as the negation of violent colonial settlement,

Tahar Ben Jelloun, in another review, equivocates over the theme in relation to postcolonial identity politics. Paying homage to the late Moroccan
author of *"Ce Maroc!"* Mohammed Khair-Eddine, he praises the use of
Berber etymologies ("racines") but insists that "he was not the sort of writer
who felt torn between his mother tongue, Tamazight, and French. He was
beyond problems of identity and belonging. For him, everything was resolved through poetry."[20] Ben Jelloun's recourse to the pancultural virtue
of poetry dodges, to some extent, the vexed question of identity claims
and their relation to native speech. His position typifies that of many Third
World writers in exile, unable to reconcile ethnic antiessentialism with
nostalgia for linguistic origins; the "generative grammar" of a *muttersprache*
and the cultural *habitus* of a nonnative land.

    In rereading *Les Déracinés* in the 1990s, my interest has been to investi-
gate its relevance to *la politique identitaire* currently rivening France itself,
and, to a significant degree, the institutions in charge of transmitting
French culture abroad (French *services culturels* or academic departments of
French studies in the United States). In the field of international French
studies, the status of Frenchness as cultural *doxa* is far from clear. As Sandy
Petrey has pointed out, the wave of Francophilia that bolstered enroll-
ments in French departments in the postwar period has more or less
subsided. While the precarious material conditions of existence will undoubtedly affect the future of French studies far more than any other factor,
there is another level of difficulty besetting scholars working in the field
outside of France; one that has much more to do with the erosion of a common theoretical language of culture. The current *décalage* between France
and the United States in terms of how to approach the problem of the subject in relation to national identity and national language can be traced, at
least in part, to the tractability of the *racine* as psychic ideal of literary identification.

    If we follow the cyclical periodization of cosmopolitanism and provin-
cialism sketched in Gustave Lanson's essay of 1917, *La Fonction des influences étrangères dans le développement de la littérature française,* we might say
that at present, France is self-avowedly in an era of "at home with itself-
ness." Lanson wrote: "For centuries, one remarks in the literary life of
France—and it is one of its most curious characteristics—a kind of rhythm,
a seesaw motion making us alternatively open or closed to the importation
of foreign ideas or forms of art."[21] In surveying these pendulum swings,
Lanson's apparently benign intent was to encourage French writers to appropriate intelligently rather than imitate slavishly; his premises, however,
were stalwartly chauvinist: "it is a national misfortune," he affirmed,
"when the foreign genre pushes out the native genre, or when French ideas

are exterminated by ideas coming from outside."[22] Today, many French intellectuals seem to have fallen back on an old form of Lansonist national conviction; faith in *les valeurs sûres,* a heritage culture based on the sentiment that the legacy of the Enlightenment would be betrayed by "caving in" to particularist ethnic claims. While there may be persuasive arguments for guarding against aggravated sectarianism or Balkanization in the humanities, there is still the risk that this kind of reasoning remasks an old assimilationism, implicitly elevating French culture to the status of global universal and leading, de facto, to a reinvented provincialism in an international context.

If an inward-turning preoccupation with Frenchness or European-ness (comparable to the resurgent isolationism and parochialism currently sweeping much of Britain and North America), has arisen from the increasingly manifest prospect of a New Europe, it would be unfair to suggest that there has been an absence of French criticism of the new provincialism. Gilles Deleuze worked consistently throughout his career to develop a critical place for what he called *la littérature mineure,* or *minoritaire.* His concept of the rhizome, coinvented with Félix Guattari, emerges as a kind of "antiracine" (double entendre intended), or counterdiscourse of the Barrèsian doctrine of enracination that has been useful to Afro-Caribbean writers such as Edouard Glissant, Raphaël Confiant, Patrick Chamoiseau, and Jean Bernabé as a model for diasporic nomadologies and linguistic subjectivities of *créolité.*

Deflating the hierarchical tradition of *le fondement-racine,* on which sylvan Barrèsianism (and Western culture in general) rests, Deleuze and Guattari advocate a more brutal deformation of root culture than their Afro-Caribbean successors, claiming, "The tree and the root inspire a sad image of thought, ceaselessly imitating a multiple, based on a superior unity, from the center or the segment."[23] "In its difference from the roots of a tree," they argue, "the rhizome connects one random point *(un point quelconque)* to another; its traits do not necessarily refer to traits of the same nature, it puts into play very different regimes of signs, or even states of the nonsign."[24] A bastard root, "crabgrass" sign, or "cut-up *radicelle,"* designating multiplicities, strata, becomings, lines, folds, patchwork, chaos, imperceptibility, deterritorialization, the rhizome functions as a social pathogen, an antistatist virus or Agent Orange of nonassimilation. In its appeal for a revolutionary semantics that would profoundly disturb linguistic convention at its root, the rhizome responds to Jean Paulhan's *Les Fleurs de Tarbes ou la terreur dans les lettres* (1941), in which the bloodiest phase of the French Revolution—the Terror—is strategically evoked as a means of shaking language loose from the fetters of dead rhetorical formulas and *idées reçues.*[25]

Paulhan dreamed of wresting the sexual passion of brute sense from the conjugal staleness of conventional usage.

One could argue that despite his revolutionary intentions, Paulhan's fidelity to floral metaphors sustained and reproduced certain aspects of the Barrèsian botanical cliché. While the rhizome is undoubtedly more radical than the "flower of Tarbes," the question still remains: does it adequately expunge the conservative legacy of roots currently haunting contemporary identity politics? For Albert Memmi *(Le Racisme)*, one of the problems with identity politics is that, in bringing back some form of the discourse of roots, it risks reverting to nostalgic Barrèsianism. In a related point, the anthropologist Marc Augé notes that even though we commonly still use expressions such as "so-and-so is a 'real' Breton, Briton, Auvergnat or German, . . . in the meantime we have learned to distrust absolute, simple and substantive identities, on the collective as well as the individual level."[26] Augé's and Memmi's caveats attend to the potential for claustration and censure within identity claims, but they sidestep the issue, raised by Jacques Hassoun in his *Les Contrebandiers de la mémoire*, of what happens to cultural identification once the ethic of transmission has been relinquished in a diaspora situation. "Freedom from" the bounds of national, ethnic, and religious subjectivity is a freedom of loss and confusion. Distinguishing transmission (dialectical and inventive in narrative form) from tradition (a "narrative without fiction," imbued with *une géographie pathétique)*, Hassoun wants to make the art of transmitting culture comparable to the underground traffic in contraband; an exciting, clandestine operation through which something truly desired is offered and acquired.[27]

Like Hassoun, many Afro-Caribbean postcolonial thinkers have seemed loath to dispense entirely with the moral ecology of roots, using some form of it to temper the geographically abstracted metaphysics of location (symptomatic, say, of Homi Bhabha's articulations of ambivalence, or hybridity), while at the same time refusing categorization as regionalist, "doudouist" writers. In their *Eloge de la créolité* (1989), for example, Bernabé, Chamoiseau, and Confiant launch an appeal for a cultural "diversality" that "will obey all the demands of modern writing while taking *roots* in the traditional configurations of our orality."[28] For Glissant, in *Poétique de la relation*, Deleuze and Guattari's rhizome is explicitly appropriated as part of an effort to redefine the postcolonial *racine*. Facilitating transit from periphery to periphery; traversing or bypassing the metropole, it partitions the *tout-monde* into unpredictable "bits" of relationality.[29] Similarly, in Patrick Chamoiseau's novel *Texaco*, a new town built through bricolage on a petroleum site is defined not as a *bidonville* but as an "urban mangrove" that spawns a new kind of rhizomatic citizen; mutant, insurrectional, and postcolonial: "It may be hard to admit that in its anguished roots *(angoisse des racines)*, mousse-covered shadows, and murky waters, the mangrove can become a cradle for marine ecosystems. . . . But it does, like the sea, re-populating itself with new forms of life that bind chemicals to mangroves."[30] Alternatively, in Paul Gilroy's work, the rhizome may be identified with the "stereophonic, bilingual and bifocal cultural forms originated by, but no longer the exclusive property of, blacks dispersed within the structures of feeling, producing, communicating and remembering that I have heuristically called the black Atlantic world."[31] Where Deleuze and Guattari had paved the way for the rhizome's association with popular culture, in their formula rhizomatique = pop'analyse,"[32] Gilroy extends it aesthetically and historically to "the damaged signs" of music in which "politics exists on a lower frequency." This counterculture exists in the "fissures of modernity," helping to construct "an imaginary antimodern past and a postmodern yet-to-come."[33]

If the rhizome has served postcolonial theorists as a means of commemorating violent histories of ruptured filiation and purloined memory, it also describes the condition of the *jamais enraciné*, claimed at the beginning of the twentieth century as a subject position by André Gide in his challenge to Barrès's ideology of emplacement: "Born in Paris, of a father from Uzès and a mother from Normandy, where would you like me, M. Barrès, to enracinate myself?" he queried in 1902.[34]

The famous Gide-Barrès altercation, dubbed "La Querelle du Peuplier," or "quarrel of the poplar tree," may be read as an early version of the rhizome's contest with the *racine*. For Gide, arguing the case of the "abnormal" or eccentric individual was inextricable from his historic defense of homosexual exceptionality and difference (*Corydon,* 1911). To Barrès he insisted that the rule, without the exception, would lead to narrative inertia and a culturally enervated normalization: "If your hero Racodot had never left Lorraine, he would never have been assassinated; but nor would he have ever interested me in the least. . . . your book proves, despite your intentions, that dramatic interest lies in strange circumstances; one could say that *deracination constrains Racodot to originality.*"[35] Gide implied that regional severance was necessary for national genius; that uprooting a person from his native milieu was essential to his education in the etymological sense of *élever*—to be raised, or taken out of. Charles Maurras, a Barrès supporter, entered the fray at this juncture, asserting that Gide was confusing transplantation with deracination: "One only deracinates dead trees or those whom one wishes to sacrifice" [On ne déracine que les arbres morts ou ceux qu'on sacrifie] (p. 68). Gide seized on the Barrèsian rhetoric of *la terre et les morts:* "you're cutting off your nose to spite your face," he insisted, in pointing out that Maurras had pruned the very trees whose roots were nourished by the soil of the *patrimoine*, steeped in the blood of heros sacrificed for the future of France (p. 69).

The Gide-Barrès dispute emphasizes the extent to which determinations of modern identity stubbornly revert to literal figurations of the botanics of roots and the physicality of land. Gide, for example, may have been wary of the *racine*, but even he seemed unable to resist the appeal of hard rock. In an essay entitled "La Terre occidentale," also published in 1902, he wrote: "From the edge of the Norman forests, I evoke a smoldering rock—perfumed air wafts around it, confounding the smells of thyme and lavender, and the strident song of the crickets."[36] The crusty terrain around Arles is evoked as an "almost Latin land, of grave laughter, lucid poetry, and severe beauty. No softness here. The city is born of rock and guards its warm tones. In the hardness of rock the spirit of antiquity is fixed, inscribed in the living, hardened flesh of the race" (p. 73).

In substituting rock for root, and in reintroducing race, what did Gide accomplish ideologically? It appears that rock, in its layering and sedimentation, allowed for a certain strength of national character at the expense of *retardataire* regional gardening. Rock, at least for Gide, was associated with an exalted hybridity that inoculated culture against racial and national decline:

> To form and harden a country's sense of unity, the diverse elements that compose it must mingle, cross, and fuse. The doctrine of enracination, if too rigorously applied, risks, while protecting and accentuating French heterogeneity, creating a situation in which the diverse elements can never get on together: making Bretons, Normans, Lorrains, Basques more Breton, Norman, Lorrain, or Basque than French.[37]

Though he supported a classical idea of national genius, Gide avoided becoming a narrow partisan of literary nationalism. He noted with repugnance that some zealots were calling for an end to translation of foreign authors on the grounds that non-French or exoticist literature could be used to intoxicate the people of France. Gide adopted the stance of antiprotectionism: "nothing can impede the flight of words and ideas from crossing borders; it would be comparable to trying to prevent birds from flying over walls."[38] That said, it still seems apparent that, in falling back on the commonplace of "rock-hard" national unity, Gide embraced a familiar brand of enduring cultural chauvinism. Choosing between a rock and a hard place, he chose the rock; a decision that may have cost him a certain rhizomatic freedom. Something of this freedom may be found, for example, in Georges Perec's radically deterritorialized *espèces d'espaces* (1974). Here, Gide's classical rock is replaced by Perec's "Brighton rock" or "Rock's rock," a hard sticky candy commonly found in English seaside resort towns, and associated by Perec with ultrasituational spaces—dimly remembered pubs, hotel rooms, rented beds. In Perec's world, the rock of nations is as evanescent as the root of identity.[39]

According to Simone Weil, writing during the Occupation, the family, the village, the town, the country, the province, the region, in short, any geographical entity smaller than the nation, had, by 1940, ceased to have enracinating power. In a famous political essay imbued with Christian humanism, *L'Enracinement: Prélude à une déclaration des devoirs envers l'être humain*, she noted that when the nation becomes the sole carrier of roots, its "instant, vertiginous decomposition" is no surprise. The French had yielded to the Germans with open palms, she argued, because they had suppressed their *besoins terrestres* (a spiritual communalism as basic to existence as food), and rescinded a sense of social obligation.[40] Under these circumstances patriotism could only be redeemed through the dirty business of imperial conquest. The French, Weil warned, camouflaged their history of uprooting subject peoples with layers of republican rhetoric.

Filtered through Simone Weil's vision of antinationalist, ethical "enrooting," Barrès's idea of deracination seems little more than a subterfuge for colonial *ralliement*. Barrèsianism was, of course, a historic ingredient in the ideological confection of "L'Algérie Française," despite the fact that the very expression *French Algeria* is a contradiction in terms according to Barrèsian principles of ecocentric nativism. For how can a culture be true to its roots if it has deserted the ancestral domain to set up house in a land of strangers? And how, once house has been set up on expropriated soil, can a ruling class of *déracinés* govern an autochthonous population of *déracinés*? These are the questions that implicitly structure Pierre Bourdieu's remarkable study of agricultural enclosure and territorial disenfranchisement entitled *Le Déracinement: La crise de l'agriculture en Algérie*, coauthored with Abdelmalek Sayad, and published in 1964 in the wake of the Evian Accords.

The particular form of deadly colonial alienation that comes from the doubling of deracination from above and below is hauntingly registered in Claude Ollier's *La Mise en scène*, a *nouveau roman* set in Algeria that appeared in 1958 at the height of the Algerian War. This colonial thriller about a French engineer-profiteer charged with tracing a new route through the Atlas Mountains, returns us to the Barrèsian literalism of rock, soil, and earth, but writ large. The brute gigantism of mountain rock, described in every vein and crater ad nauseam, emerges as a virtual parody of "the epic land" that challenges colonial hubris, characteristic of the genre known as *littérature coloniale*. The engineer's "tunnel vision," as he works to construct a transport network that will eventually blast its way through stone and displace local boundaries, prevents him from seeing that he is gradually being trapped in an elaborate *comédie,* in which indigenous landowners replay, on him, the scene of a murder that he is trying to solve while carrying out his cartographic calculations. The lines on the half-erased map, made by the other engineer, zigzag and snake imperfectly around a *zone non cartographiée,* described as a "center of invisibility," a "stain in the form of an ellipse" tucked away in the fold of the map.[41] This place of doubled secrecy—the missing key to a successful mountain bypass and the place of his own future death—emerges as the effaced *racine;* the spot where the colon's *déracinement* converges with that of the *colonisé.* As if in conscious travesty of Barrèsian metaphors, Claude Ollier's novel provides a geological mapping of the way in which self-colonization and auto-uprooting arise from colonial eminent domain.

The politics of roots and the psychic phenomenon of identification continue, perhaps more than ever, to condition cultural exchange and disciplinary formation. As economic protectionism has bolstered ideologies of cultural insularity, tariff wars, translation barriers, copyright disputes, and prohibitive insurance policies have become their own kind of market force in the politics of reenracination. At the opposite pole, the philosophical tradition of phenomenology has carried over a discourse of roots in a nostalgic poetics of *heimat,* of ontological domesticity. Heideggerian black forests come caricaturally to mind, but within the French tradition I am thinking most pointedly of Gaston Bachelard's chapter on *la racine* in *La Terre et les rêveries du repos,* published shortly after the war (1948).[42] For Bachelard, the root qualifies as one of those "big images" of a culture's unconscious, of primal psychic reality. Metaphorized as a "strange opaque mirror," the root emerges as the obverse of aerial vision, an oxymoronic figure of "alive death" shooting backward below ground. For Bachelard, unburying the unconscious through psychoanalytic *labourage* involves a painful, sexually offensive digging. Once unearthed, the root, in its rage, is capable of leading the subject who tore it up to his or her death. Haunted by images of trees that have been mutilated or turned over as if in invitation to anal fornication, by the monstrous anfractuosity of Michelet's mountain roots, by Valéry's evocation of "thousands of roots" torquing into knots of being, by the "nauseating vegetalism" diagnosed by Sartre, and by the *Todtenbaum* or death-tree dominating his own earlier writings on *L'Eau et les rêves,* Bachelard envisages the root as a wild force of counterdomesticity, urging the subject to forsake the hearth and to heed the call of "being-in-earth" through acts of sex and ingestion. It is literature in Bachelard that mediates and tames this archaic drive, sublimating ecodesire into a phenomenology of nostalgia for *la maison natale.*

To conclude, I would argue that ever since European romanticism put nationalism in the place of the object within literary study, cultures have identified with national literatures, treating them as proxies for the nation. In the context of postrevolutionary France, the newly independent nations of Greece and Italy, or in the struggle for independence following the demise of colonialism in the postwar era, nationalist identification often took on a critical role. But in the present context, in which the nation is linguistically splintered across a postcolonial, postnational map, a nationalist cultural politics is either tethered to a nostalgic vision of an already dead past, or more problematically confronted by the difficult negotiation between reactionary essentialism and relativistic interpretation. Such a condition is, and has been since the turn of the century, bound to test the depth of national roots within a discipline, especially when that discipline is based on a national literature taught outside the nation, and poses the unsettling but ultimately fruitful question: What does *francité* signify when it is *déracinée,* that is, transplanted to another cultural context?

2 SAINTS AT STAKE

JOAN OF ARC AS

NATIONAL PATHOGRAPHY

Vocational Training

Since her death at the stake in 1431, Joan of Arc, the maid of Domremy, has survived as one of world history's unique national characters. The documents and legends recording descriptions of her androgynous persona, interlocution with God, military campaigns, trials, and extinction in flames, have been scrutinized by historians, mobilized by ideologues, and set in motion by artists, writers, and filmmakers.[1] My own interest centers on the way in which aspects of her legend exemplify a "pathologically" modern, monstrous subjectivity. A drama of the ego, or more specifically, of the nationalized, feminized ego revealed in all its psychic armature, is, I would argue, embedded in Joan's story, helping to explain its historical resiliency. A recent spate of avant-garde cultural productions created between 1980 and 1996 attests to the curious perdurability of the Joan legend, which uniquely combines mythic constructions of national character and feminist agency.

First Case: Richard Einhorn's 1995 opera/oratorio *Voices of Light,* performed against the backdrop of a vintage print of Carl Dreyer's 1928 cinematic masterpiece *The Passion of Joan of Arc,* itself recovered in 1981 from a Norwegian sanatorium. Committed to the musical construction of "a female hero," the libretto crafts a "file" built up from excerpts of Joan's letters and trial statements, as well as fragments of medieval misogynist poetry and passages from late medieval texts by female mystics: Christine de

Pizan, Marguerite Porete, St. Hildegard of Bingen, Beatrice of Nazareth. Performed primarily by women (including the conductor) the score relies on layered female voices and dialogic instrumental minimalism, resulting in a choral modernity cloaked in the New Medievalism. On the screen above the orchestra the Dreyer movie is visually contrapuntal, the camera fixating on the face of the vaudeville actress Renée Falconetti.[2] Dreyer's famous close-ups hinge on excruciating nodes of pain: Falconetti's knotted hands register torsions of inner suffering, her eyes lock onto the studs of the torture rack, her shaved head provides a bald target of public ire and abuse and is shown bursting into flames in the protracted scene at the stake. Einhorn's excavation of a mythic Joan, via Dreyer and the female mystics, capitalizes on the "interpellative" moment where divine calling and feminist vocation converge in a pageant of abjection.

Second Case: In a 1995 fiction-cum-compilation film entitled *From the Journals of Jean Seberg*, a Jean-Joan connection is contrived.[3] Directed by Mark Rappaport and starring Mary Beth Hurt, the movie implies that Jean Seberg's suicide may have been helped along by her Joan-like effacement at the hands of male directors, not least of them the New Wave director Jean-Luc Godard, who cut his auteur signature on Seberg's blank, frontal stare in *Breathless*. Rappaport's film investigates the strange curse that seems to have befallen actresses who played Joan of Arc on screen. Renée Falconetti endured abusive tirades from the director Carl Dreyer; the scene in which she was tonsured apparently brought her to the brink of mental breakdown; her son would die of AIDS-related complications. Jean Seberg was accidentally burned during the filming of the pyre scene, and Otto Preminger, seeming to savor the authenticity of her pain, conserved the incendiary take in the film's final cut and publicity trailer. Cast for their astonishing photogeneity, complexions that seemed to cry out for cinematic agons of shadow and light, the actresses selected to play Joan of Arc—Hedy Lamarr, Falconetti, Ingrid Bergman, Seberg—all, according to Rappaport's view, seemed to acquiesce in cinema's vampiric need to feed on youthful feminine faces. If, as George Bernard Shaw suggested, it is true that the role of Joan of Arc was for women actors what Hamlet was for men—an acme in performance credits—then it was an acme exacting egoic demission. Jean/Joan emerges in *From the Journals of Jean Seberg* as none other than God's prostitute, adhering to a credo of "aller jusqu'au boutisme" [he wants me to die]. To make this point crudely and emphatically, Rappaport introduces clips from obscure films directed by Seberg's husband, the brilliant French-Rumanian writer Romain Gary. Gary favored scenarios in which his wife played a nymphomaniac hankering for humiliation; it seems that for Gary, it was necessary to have her filmed fucked by everyone.

Third Case: Theresa Hak Kyung Cha's *Dictée,* a cult novel of Asian-American avant-gardism published in 1982, the year of the artist's tragic murder in New York City at age thirty-one. *Dictée* evokes Joan of Arc as one of many exemplary feminine characters (including Sappho, Thérèse de Lisieux, and the Korean nationalist heroine Yu Guan Soon), whose response to a higher calling enabled them to become forces of history. Folded into the formally fragmented biography of a Korean-American female narrator, this postcolonial Joan mobilizes audition against dictation and dictatorships. The book opens with a French *dictée* that literally forces the hand of the writing subject. The pupil makes mistakes, writing out the diacritical instructions ("aller à la ligne," "virgule," "fermez les guillemets").[4] This faulty transcription demonstrates not only the futility of colonial mimicry (where phonemes are revealed to be meaningless), but also the subliminal sadism of the imperial pedagogical imperative. Cha's Korea bears the scars of didactic ravaging; Catholic catechism, French grammar-rules, Chinese calligraphy; education under Japanese occupation, nationalist dogma, American cultural imperialism—each has left its trace of ideological force-feeding. In *Dictée* Joan of Arc has a double-edged status; she is part of the missionary fodder exported by the French to Korea, but she is also a node of feminist identification for the Korean schoolgirl; an initiatory face (the book contains a still of Falconetti in Dreyer's film) igniting the artist's thirst for a vocation.[5]

Interpellation, abjection, vocational training: these thematic strands emerge clearly from the avant-garde reprise of Joan's legend, contributing, perhaps, to another level of symbolic elephantiasis in Joan of Arc's semiotic history. Standing back, it would seem that each of these works, in different media, emphasizes the drama of subjectivation, or the subject's coming to subjecthood, as defined within the gendered terms of a feminist sense of calling. The relationship between feminism and interpellation, with the latter defined in an Althusserian sense as the subject's response to ideology's "call" or "hailing," informs Joan's iconic status as a gender anomaly (masculated femininity) whose supranatural agency is swelled by divine invocation.

In defining the subject of ideology, Althusser gave interpellation a preeminent role in political theory. Deriving from the Latin *interpellatus* yoking *inter* (between) with *pellere* (to drive, to urge), interpellation denotes first and foremost the concepts of interruption, interference, and interception. In a legal context, the term refers to a formal calling to account of a minister by a legislative assembly. Enfolding the notion of call *(appel)* qua "act of making a voice come to yourself," it also denotes calling, vocation, recruitment to a cause. All these connotations have been crucial to Lacan's insistence on the delusionary character of the mirror stage as well as to his earlier thesis on paranoia; a thesis that included, significantly enough, the case history of a certain Marcelle C., diagnosed by Lacan and other doctors as having a Joan of Arc complex.

Althusser's subject, confounding ideologically mediated values and beliefs with reality, lives similarly in delusion, blind to perceiving itself as a symptom or social formation produced by the dominant mode of production. As Etienne Balibar, Althusser's former student and coauthor, has emphasized, there is a close relation between *subject* and *subjectum* or *submission*. Indentured to the more or less legitimate authority of a superior power, for example a "supra-human sovereign" or "inner master," or "transcendent impersonal *law,*" this modern subject is "subjectivated," that is, held accountable to the "call." The inner subject, Balibar claimed:

> is basically a *responsible,* or an *accountable* subject, which means that he has to respond, to give an account *(rationem reddere)* of himself, i.e. of his actions and intentions, before another person, who righteously interpellates him. Not a Big Brother, but a Big Other—as Lacan would say—always already shifting in an ambivalent manner between the visible and the invisible, between individuality and universality.

The "crucial point" for Balibar is that "the 'subject,' for the first time bearing that name in the *political* field where it (he) is subjected *to* the sovereign, the lord, ultimately the Lord God, in the *metaphysical* field necessarily *subjects himself to himself* or, if you like, performs his own subjection."[6]

Is it so implausible to set up Joan of Arc as the prototypical recruit of metaphysical self-subjection? The aim here will be to enter Joan into the "graveyard of the subject" debate, a phrase coined by Joan Copjec in her critique of contemporary theories that would seemingly infer a death of agency in the story of late modern subject formation.[7] Much of this debate appears to devolve around how internalization of the law is defined: whether the law, or in Althusser's terms, the state apparatus, is performing us, or whether "the call" to subjecthood forms part of an ethics or working through of psychic trauma.

A synonym for state fetishism, the name of Joan of Arc has been historically identified on the right and the left with national destiny and theocratically self-authorizing political strategy. But it has also signified complicity between feminism and saintliness, or, in a darker vein, between the psychic masochism of abjected femininity and the self-extinguishing ethics of female martyrdom. "Martyrdom was the dream of my youth and this dream has grown with me within Carmel's cloisters," Cha's narrator confides. "With St. Agnes and St. Cecilia, I would present my neck to the sword, and like Joan of Arc, my dear sister, I would whisper at the stake Your Name, O JESUS."[8] Identification with Christ comes at the expense of the female body; the calling, paradoxically enough, is a call to subjective depletion.

Or is it? Writing in 1911, Charles Péguy recognized the unique militancy of this emptying out. "Une vocation trop profonde l'avait marquée" [a calling that went too far marked her], he noted.[9] But for Péguy, Joan of Arc's excessive interiorization of divine ordinance *wounded* the egoic character of chivalric laws (personified in Péguy): "Les lois savent toujours quand on leur manque" [these laws always know when you are not there for them], for they know you better than you thought you knew yourself; they read your heart and your secrets, they act as an x-ray performed by the social order.[10]

For Péguy, Joan of Arc incurred the wrath of the Law by having too large a say in determining by whom she would be interpellated. Such a position is anathema to the Law and its functionary, the ideological state apparatus, accustomed as it is to directing the performance. As Judith Butler reminds us in her reading of Althusserian ethics entitled "Conscience Doth Make Subjects of Us All," the Law does not suffer affronts to its hubris lightly. Prey to a "theological fantasy" that it "monopolizes the terms of existence" through its call to the subject, the Law exhibits a paranoid intolerance of the subject's attempt to cheat it of subjection.[11] Prompted by the "animating reprimand" of the Law, the subject, in Butler's ontological scheme, comes into being through a ritual of self-acquittal that reproduces the work of social relations.[12] Like Joan, then, the subject must go on trial as part of the "labor" of its right to self-subjection.

Here is where Joan of Arc's suicidal refusal to accept the official allegation of apostasy intersects with the drama of subjugated subjectivity. For what is Joan of Arc a name for if not a wounding of the ego of theocratic ideology? The Maid's interpellation by a higher voice emerges as a heroic attempt to rob the Church of its subjectivating claim. Like Judge Shreber in Freud's case history of *dementia paranoides*, Joan of Arc is in the grip of a conviction that she has been elected to "be" the Law.[13] Miming the law's delusion of grandeur, she arrogates to herself the power to subjectivate and be subjected to; she is both performative and predicate, not unlike the foundational God of Althusser's state apparatus:

> God thus defines himself as the Subject *par excellence*, he who is through himself and for himself ("I am that I am"), and he who interpellates his subject, the individual subject to him by his very interpellation, i.e. the individual named Moses. And Moses, interpellated-called by his Name, having recognized that it "really" was he who was called by God, recognizes that he

is a subject, a subject *of* God, a subject subjected to God, *a subject through the Subject and subjected to the Subject.*[14]

Joan's occupation of *both* the place of the subject and the place of the Law not only reveals the nonsingular, polyvocal identity of the Law (split, in the case of Joan of Arc, between God's "true" voice and its earthly transmitter, the Church), it also highlights the delusional character of the subject's call to psychic arms, a delusion that, as we know, was crucial to Lacan's theory of subject formation.

In 1928–29 Lacan wrote an article "Structures des psychoses para- noiaques" in *La Semaine des Hôpitaux de Paris* in which he replaced Cléram- bault's "syndrome of mental automatism" with "structure," and absorbed Clérambault's theory of erotomania or delusions of love (as in "The queen of England loves me") within the larger framework of paranoia. Cléram- bault apparently greeted this text with apoplexy; convinced that his ideas were being stolen, he accused Lacan of plagiarism.[15] Delusion and para- noia seem thus to have had a contagious effect on their own theorizations.

In 1931 Lacan coauthored (and in a sense cocurated) a case history with Pierre Migault and J. Lévy-Valensi, entitled "Ecrits 'inspirés': Schizo- graphie" ("Inspired" writings: Schizography), concerning a thirty-four- year-old schoolteacher, Marcelle C. Though she gives an initial impression of being in possession of her faculties, she exhibits a stubborn resistance to *subjection:* "Je ne veux être soumise à personne. Je n'ai jamais voulu admet- tre la domination d'un homme" [I want to submit to no-one. I never wanted to admit male domination].[16] In hindsight, Marcelle C. seems to be suffering from a case of acute feminism, set in full tilt against the patriar- chal myopia of the psychiatric establishment.

Prey to what Lacan qualifies as "hyperidealism," Marcelle believes that she has a unique historical mission, that "she is a new Joan of Arc," but "bet- ter educated, at a higher level of civilization."[17] Convinced that she is put on earth for the purpose of guiding governments and regenerating social values, her agenda includes state sponsorship of "a center dedicated to top international and military affairs" (p. 367). Where Clérambault diagnoses her as having a paranoid character and has her interned after she demands 20 million francs in compensation for intellectual and sexual deprivation, Lacan is more concerned with understanding the grounds on which rest her "polymorphous delirium." According to Lacan, it took months to gauge the nature of her dictations, not, properly speaking, voices, but ex- periences of "psychic affinities," "intuitions," "spiritual revelations," "a sense of direction" (p. 368). Her "inspirations" have diverse paternalist ori- gins ranging from General Foch, to President Georges Clemenceau, to her academic supervisor, to her grandfather. Inexplicably, so it seems, signs encountered in the street become pregnant with significance. Everything is a mise-en-scène; details become heavily weighted expressions of destiny: "I thought that my case was becoming an affair of parliament," she grandiosely maintained.

As the prolific author of texts at once lubricious, hermetic, and politically millenarian, Marcelle intrigued Lacan; who may have discovered his hermeneutical talents in analyzing the graphological deformities ("schizographies") of her texts. Nothing, Lacan concluded, was less inspired in a spiritual sense, than these so-called texts of inspiration. It is when thought is limited and impoverished that automatism kicks in to make up the deficit. The sense of exteriority (the instructions come from without) forms part of the delusional apparatus of pathological egomania.

That Marcelle C. may have been clinically certifiable is difficult to contest; there remains, however, the problem of the content of her interpellations, written, as her doctors would have it, in code. "J'ai subi le joug de la défense" [I endured the yoke of defense]. Lacan deciphers the statement, arguing that she mistakenly substituted "defense" for "oppression" (he reads "I endured the yoke of oppression"); but what if we were to interpret Marcelle's writings more to the letter, situating them in the broader context of voices and feminine subjectivities?[18] Here we might let the French notion of *subir* resonate with that cluster: subject, submission; subjection; subjugation; subjectivation. In light of these associations, Marcelle might be seen indeed to "submit to defense," rather than oppression. She mobilizes a psychic rampart (delusional egomania) to construct a monstrous feminist agency. Another enunciation reveals a variation on this theme of persecutory recuperation: "Vous êtes atterrés parce que je vous hais au point que je vous voudrais tous sauvés" [You are dismayed/floored because I hate you to the point of wanting you all saved] (p. 378). As Lacan points out, Marcelle characteristically inverts the terms of accusation, heroically retrieving her importance to the other (as the other's savior) from the ashes of incrimination. In another letter, addressed to the president of the Republic, a comparably self-serving verbal convolution reveals its link to a nationalistic sense of purpose: Marcelle evokes the "peril of a perverse nation" that puts itself on the back of a scrawny harlequin; raining blows on the "one who wants nothing for herself" (p. 370). Lacan also takes stock of Marcelle's predilection for portentous neologisms. Words such as *oraie* (formed, he argues from *roseraie* or rosary and used by Marcelle to designate a good economic prospect [as in conducive to producing gold, *or*]) underscore the bipolar valency of her speech, both oracular and fiduciary. In the case of the word *vendredettes* there is not only, as Lacan ventures, a reference to Friday classes, but also (why doesn't Lacan remark on this?) a homonymic allusion to "debts for sale." Through this secret language of political redemption and injured moral economy, Marcelle C. emerges as an enigmatic Joan of Arc of the clinic, as baffling and politically strident as her fifteenth-century fore-bear. Like Joan of Arc, clinging to the conviction that she alone can save France's honor or receive God's collect call, like Judge Shreber, convinced that he alone has been chosen for union with God "in the fore-courts of Heaven," that he alone will act as the Redeemer on earth, Marcelle C. demonstrates the subject's desire to usurp the power of the Law through a self-accrediting linguistic order of interpellation.

Of course, as Lacan describes it, the ego is always submitting to the crushing recognition that it fails to measure up to its ego ideal, assuaging its disappointment with compensatory fantasy. But what makes this tru-ism of subject-formation play differently in the Joan of Arc legend is the way in which defense and delusion are mobilized to pierce the ego of the Law. As in the case of Senatspräsident Shreber, ordered by God to change into a woman, so Joan of Arc effects a sex-change as a barrier against the subject-shattering force of the Law. Where Shreber's feminized body soft-ened into the state of voluptuousness associated with *jouissance* and celes-tial blessedness *(seligkeit)*, Joan's body hardens into masculinity through war wounds and coats of armor. This militancy of the ego, delusional, megalomaniac, paranoid, and projective though it may be, becomes ob-jectively "real" on the sex-crossed body of the subject, endowing the sub-ject with a performative agency of suprahuman proportions. In gendering the "call" or interpellative moment in the destiny of the subject (national-izing it in the process), Joan of Arc "fools" the law into calling its subject by its own name.

Gilles and Jeanne: Pathographic Hagiography

Having concentrated thus far on the psychic implications of the militancy of the ego, I now want to introduce the more historically resonant issue of national character; specifically the way in which the nationalizing of the ego plays out against the backdrop of the "pathology" of the modern sub-ject. In focusing on the relationship between pathography and hagiogra-phy in the construction of exceptional subjects of history, I will review the bizarrely intercalated lives of Joan of Arc and Gilles de Rais, actors and con-temporaries at the siege of Orléans in 1428, each the other's counterpart in matters of sexual ambivalence, each, at different moments, embodiments of radical evil in the national imaginary. I will also analyze the political di-mension of their profiles as perverts of patriotism, or contestants of ecclesiastic and civic normalization. Placing themselves above the Sovereign, conferring on themselves the privilege of interlocution with the Big Other (Satan, God the Father), confusing the boundaries between saintliness and sacrilege, their stories exemplify a monstrous posthumanism recuperated by apologists of nihilistic modernity from the Marquis de Sade to Nietzsche, Bataille, and Heidegger. Sartre's redemptive celebration of Jean Genet's criminality in his philosophical biography *Saint Genet* and David Halperin's "gay hagiography" *Saint Foucault,* which pays tribute to Foucault as a historian of sex whose reprise of the antique "'culture of the self' took the form of new and more intense modes of ethical subjectivation— and of new and more elaborate technologies of self-transformation,"[19] may be situated on a continuum stretching back to Saint Joan, the paramount forebear perhaps, of the performatively exorbitant modern subject. In many respects, I will argue further, the call received by Joan of Arc from God, urging her to rescue the city of Orléans from its English marauders, corresponds in latter-day terms to what has been deemed most monstrous in the Althusserian theory of ideological interpellation, itself (as we have seen) interpretable as an interiorized call ensuring obeisance to dominant values, the subjection of the subject to the Big Other of the modern state. Though at one level Joan's response to the call may have exposed (and in exposing challenged) the apparatus of state power, at another level her martyrdom and legendary status were proof that the state could nationally produce her in the form of patriotic myth and official narrative, successfully remasking itself in the process.

Gilles de Rais (1404–40) was a wealthy nobleman who emerged in the popular imagination as a negative Joan of Arc. Chosen, because of his superior military reputation, to be Joan's special protector, he apparently fought by her side at the liberation of Orléans. After coronating Charles II, he supervised an account of the Maid's life and record of battle entitled *Mystery of Orléans.* Like Joan he was accused of heresy and sacrilege, and like her, he expired in a notorious public execution. His case history inspired vivid reconstruction, ranging from J.-K. Huysmans's *Là-bas* (1891) to Georges Bataille's *Le Procès de Gilles de Rais* (1965) (containing translations of Latin sources by Pierre Klossowski) to, most recently, Michel Tournier's fabulistic *Gilles & Jeanne* (1983), in which the life of the female saint in male dress is insidiously intertwined with that of a diabolical and effeminate Gilles. The sodomizer and murderer of scores of young boys, Gilles was characterized by Bataille as an "ogre" whose existence fascinated and repelled: "a force that seduces and dominates, . . . a nobility of violence that sees nothing, and to which there is no resistance."[20] For Bataille, Gilles was a variant of Lacan's "Kant with Sade" or Nietzsche's Socrates; a *monstrum in animo* scorning moral fictions, clinging to instinct, championing negative dialectics, seducing and subjugating his disciples.

It is in this role of demonic superman that Gilles de Rais emerges as an intertext for twentieth-century allegories of *ancien régime* depravity and revolutionary terror alike. Emphasizing the sinister underbelly of the Enlightenment, Bataille confected a revisionist pathography of Gilles de Rais in the same way that he had already, along with Maurice Heine, Pierre Klossowski, and Jean Paulhan, reconfigured and in the process radically repoliticized the *vita sexualis* of the marquis de Sade.[21]

Bataille's fascination in the early sixties with Gilles as an archetypal hero *noir* whose lust murders of eight hundred boys foreshadowed macabre scenes from the writings of Sade, may be seen as an extension of the rereading of Sade that he and fellow members of the Collège had systematically undertaken in the late thirties. But, though novel in their recuperation and rehabilitation of Sade's work, these essays of the thirties should themselves be placed in a broader historical context, informed as they were by an earlier period's medicalization of celebrated authors and historic personages. Jules Michelet's *Jeanne d'Arc* (1853), Charles Monselet's *Restif de la Bretonne* (1854), Victor Hugo's *Quatrevingt-treize* (1874), the Goncourt brothers' *La du Barry* (1878), or Hyppolyte Taine's *Psychologie des chefs jacobins* (1884) constitute only a fraction of the literary works that spawned, influenced, or derived from a comparable array of medical analogues. A veritable counterpoint between fictive text and actual case history marked the second half of the nineteenth century. The annals of early psychiatry from the 1850s to the 1920s featured Marie Antoinette (stigmatized as prostitute and nymphomaniac) and Louis XVI (allegedly sexually impotent), Jean-Jacques Rousseau (analyzed ad nauseam as masochist, exhibitionist, fetishist, and repressed homosexual), Rétif de la Bretonne (whose foot fetishism gradually took on the name brand *rétifomanie)*, and the marquis de Sade (branded a *satyrographomane*, or "erotomaniac of the pen") as the favored subjects of nosological récits.[22] From P. L. Jacob's *Curiosités de l'histoire de France* (1858) to Richard von Krafft-Ebing's *Psychopathia Sexualis* (1882), from Oskar Panizza's (author of the *Council of Love) Pyschopathia Criminalis* (1898) to Dr. Augustin Cabanès's *Le Cabinet secret de l'histoire* (1900), and from Havelock Ellis's *Studies in the Psychology of Sex* (1936) to Magnus Hirschfeld's *Geschlechts Anomalien und Perversionen* (1957), legendary biographies were pathologized; that is, built up as medical dossiers and collected like so many rare specimens.[23] Each case study was placed on display, demonstrating individually the determinative traits of a given perversion, obsession, or paranormal *idée fixe*, and exemplifying as a totality the taxonomy of criminal anomaly.

Gilles de Rais emerges within this psychohistorical museum as, on the one hand, a metonymy for a "perversion all his own" (that is, a sadism beyond sadism, or "crime of all crimes"), and, on the other, as a typological prefiguration of Sade. Sade himself had accorded the Maréchal de Rays a place of honor as a distinguished ancestor in the art of agalomania when he invoked his example in *Justine* and *La Philosophie dans le boudoir*. Gilles's crimes, sadistic *avant la lettre,* gave expression to the enigma of pleasure in cruelty well before Krafft-Ebing christened the phenomenon in Sade's name. During the nineteenth century, Sade, like Gilles, was associated with an elite corps of master-criminals: Jack the Ripper, Andreas Bichel, Sergeant Bertrand (the famous necrophiliac), and the Hungarian Countess Bathory, "whose lust," according to Havelock Ellis, "could only be satisfied through the death of innumerable victims."[24]

A number of specific structural parallels also linked Sade's life and work to Gilles's pathography. Like that of Sade, the story of Gilles de Rais occupies generic space between Charles Perrault's ethnographically grounded folktale—Bluebeard—and the tabloid or *fait divers* (we think here of Sade's trial for administering Spanish fly to the Marseille prostitutes read in tandem with the sex murder trial of Gilles).[25] Bluebeard and his castle also coincide with Gilles de Rais and his *châteaux-fort* at Tiffauges and Champtocé, which in turn are readily aligned with Sade and the uncanny present-day ruins of La Coste. Moreover, the name of Gilles's initial accomplice in debauchery, his cousin Gilles de Sillé, bears a homophonic (and perhaps not accidental) resemblance to the name of Sade's fictive Chateau de Silling, which, like Tiffauges, contained a rationalized plan for interring torture victims in their respective chambers.

Gilles de Rais may also be said to have anticipated Sade in the area of his "greatest" cultural achievement, namely, his ability to devise a language, syntax, and logic for the most nuanced modalities of sexuality and torture. Though Sade's place as foremost fabulist of outlaw eroticism will always be secure (Gilles, it must be remembered, was no writer, and Sade in his actual deeds was far from being the worst of criminals), one can argue that, using his own body and that of his pubescent victims as the instruments of his craft, Gilles "wrote" the legend of the most sadistic of crimes.[26] And, to anchor this textual simile still further, there are also the actual documents of the trial, which appear in retrospect to be palimpsests of *120 Days of Sodom*. This opus of cruelty, if one can call it that, consists of formal accusations levied against Gilles, as in "Item: . . . that he was and is a relapsed heretic, a sorcerer, a sodomite, an invoker of evil spirits, a diviner, a strangler of the innocent, an apostate, an idolater, having deviated from the faith, hostile to it, a diviner and sorcerer."[27] The transcription of Gilles's confession in-

cluded grisly details of the murders. Not content to kill, Gilles and his accomplices devised elaborate mise-en-scènes: ejaculating on the children
before slashing their bellies, carefully separating heads from bodies with
daggers, suspending them on meat hooks, strangling them with rope while
sodomizing them, making love to infantile corpses, gleaning voyeuristic
pleasure from the contemplatation of their eviscerated organs.[28]

Taken up and faithfully retransposed virtually point for point in their
respective epochs by Huysmans, Bataille, and Tournier, this composite of
spiraling abominations—scopophilia, pedophilia, flagellation, rape, de-
filement, protracted murder, coprophilia, decapitation, evisceration, an-
thropophagy, necrophilia, and a kind of consummate sadism projected by
the assassin's infernal laugh—forms a litany of horror that for Bataille at
least, must be endlessly repeated while at the same time allowed to speak
for itself. As the official deposition chillingly reveals, the congestion of so
many acts of profanation, together with the ingenious details of this experiment in demonic pederasty, make of Gilles's confession a rival document
to the most hyperbolic passages penned in the hand of *le divin Marquis*.
What Paulhan would characterize as "that sublimely forceful quality of a
language beyond language," which would in turn provide Bataille and
Klossowski with their inspiration for a pornography "beyond pornography" (from *L'Histoire de l'oeil* to *Roberte, ce soir*), was common to both Gilles
and Sade.[29] As Stuart Schneiderman has observed, the criminological perversion represented by Gilles de Rais is so beyond words that it literally
bears no name. To signify the infernal recipe of sadoerotic tortures concocted by this fifteenth-century nobleman, one has recourse only to the
name of the perpetrator himself.

Finally, and perhaps most interesting for a pychopolitical interpretation of the revolutionary Terror, Gilles and de Sade may be seen to form an
uneasy triumvirate with Citizen Marat, whose own legacy and reputation
were persistently medicalized throughout the nineteenth century. As Eric
Walter has shown, Marat's excessive zeal for justice was thought to have
embarked the Revolution on the murderous course of eating its own. Along
with Saint-Juste and Robespierre, Marat, according to Dr. Cabanès, was a
victim of "revolutionary neurosis." Incarnating satanic Jacobinism, a condition characterized by "human bloodletting," "homicidal furors," and
"method in madness," Marat's demonic silhouette fit neatly over that of
Gilles de Rais's, particularly insofar as both were distinguished in the popular imagination by their putative propensity for necrophilic cannibal-
ism.[30] In defining the tropes of what Michelet called the pathology of the
Terror, we might now be tempted to revise Peter Weiss's play *Marat/Sade* as
Marat/Sade/Gilles.

In his essay of 1939 for the Collège de Philosophie, "Le Marquis de Sade et la Révolution," Pierre Klossowski gave further substance to Michelet's "pathology of the Terror," arguing that Sade, aware that he himself was an "abscess" on the afflicted body politic, promulgated a political nihilism that was the essence of the perversion of justice.[31] In becoming the mouthpiece of pure crime Sade could be seen as the architect of that confounding of bloodletting with justice that characterized the revolutionary Terror. But the serious problem that the Terror posed for Sade, Klossowski claims, was how to preserve the transgressive aura of criminality in a republican *utopie du mal* founded on the inversion of virtue and vice. Once regicide was history, how could you continue to obtain the sadoerotic frisson produced by the fantasy of royal sacrifice? Where could you go from there? According to Klossowski, Sade understood the risk of forfeiting crime in a republic in which virtue was founded on atheism, regicide, and murder. In the reversed hierarchy of values represented by the Terror, murder was so bureaucratized that it no longer retained its power of horror.

Exploring how to procure and suspend this power of horror, Bataille, seeming to pick up where Klossowski had left off, made his fortuitous discovery of the Gilles de Rais file. As Genet was for Sartre, so Gilles was for Bataille: the model of a politically irrecuperable criminal consciousness. The smoky atmosphere of necromancy and Faustian sacrilege surrounding Gilles's experiments in alchemy, once combined with the afterglow of his heroic past as a codefender, with Joan of Arc, of France's national destiny, served to elevate his sex crimes to the heights of "the marvelous." It was this just this feeling of marvelous terror that accompanied Bataille's presentation of the trial as one of the consummate events of history: Of the maréchal de Rais's trial, Abbé Bossard wrote that it "was in every aspect, the counterpart of Joan of Arc." But he adds: "Both comprise the two most famous affairs of the Middle Ages, and also perhaps of Modern Times."[32]

Presaging the "society of the spectacle," to use Guy Debord's terms, Gilles's final calvary, like his trial, produced a mass hysteria almost "marvelous" in its excess. Descriptions of the scene were greatly enhanced so as to give them the aura of pageantry and miracle. In a thesis on Gilles de Rais containing passages that greatly influenced Huysmans's *Là-bas,* the abbé Bossard scenographically depicted Gilles's contraction of the Christian fervor emanating from the crowd:

> Through a natural effect of misfortune, not without precedent in the history of crime, in the midst of growing anguish, faith revives itself in the breath of a double sentiment, shame and repentance. These deep emotions, never before experienced, even in the torment of remorse, shake him violently and throw him from this moral torpor engulfing him: like a flower

weighed down by mud, he raised himself up little by little under the rain of heaven, this soul heavily bent down towards the earth, washed by his tears, rises slowly towards God.[33]

As shown here, Gilles de Rais's conversion and apotheosis imparted a kind of black grandeur to his demise at the stake. It also gave his legend over to Christic comparison. There was even an episode during the trial which seemed to reiterate the Savior's cry: "Why hast thou forsaken me?" Queried by the president of the court as to his motives for violating, strangling, and incinerating his victims, Gilles, momentarily losing control of courtroom decorum, replied in French instead of Latin: "Alas! Monseigneur, you are tormenting yourself and me with." Through the magical principle of inversion Gilles de Rais, Michelet's premier "beast of extermination," passed into history as a candidate for hagiography.

Inversion is, of course, the rather obvious principle governing the play of recursive substitutions in the pathography and exploited thematically in virtually every rendition of Gilles de Rais's legend. Used as a synonym for homosexuality in the nineteenth century, the term invert (as distinct from pervert, meaning "twisted sexual nature") implied "that the individual's sexual feelings were turned inward on himself or toward his own sex."[34] In Michel Tournier's *Gilles & Jeanne* the concept of "benign inversion" is used not only to denote the religious convertibility of a satanic Gilles de Rais into a saintly Joan of Arc, but also to describe the bi-gendered or doubly inverted figure created by their composite psycholiterary profiles. Jeanne is portrayed as a *garçonne* or superior ephebe whose martyrdom is mystically bound up with Gilles's subsequent need to perform acts of violent pollution. In Tournier's psychoanalytically constructed fable the double martyrdom of Gilles and Jeanne implicates a society that refuses to tolerate ambiguous forms of sexuality from androgyny to pederasty to sadomasochism.[35]

Perhaps what distinguishes the pairing of Gilles and Jeanne is the way in which both afforded examples of transgender linked to perversely modern political personalities. If Gilles prefigured the mass executioner associated with the Terror, Joan, at least for the historian Jules Michelet, personified the Enlightened modern subject, a force of light against mob unreason.

> Joan's eminent originality was her common sense. This sets her apart from the multitude of enthusiasts who, in ages of ignorance, have swayed the masses. In most cases, they derived their power from some dark contagious force of unreason. Her influence, on the contrary, was due to the clear light she was able to throw upon an obscure situation.[36]

As had Gilles's, Joan's trial set a standard of spectacularity. Accused of heresy and political sedition, vilified as a supernatural virgin whose inviolable body cast a kind of hex, obstinate in her refusal to abandon masculine attire, Joan of Arc's judges, in Michelet's words, "resolved to stage a great and terrible public scene."[37] She was carted to the marketplace of Rouen and placed atop a huge pyre:

> The pyre had been made so high, so the executioner could only reach its base; he would not be able to shorten the torture, and mercifully to dispatch the victim, as he usually did, and so to spare her the flames. In this case, they wanted to make sure that justice would not be cheated, that the fire would not simply devour a corpse; they wanted her literally burnt alive; they wanted her, hoisted atop this mountain of fuel, above the encircling spears and swords, to be in plain sight for everyone in the market place.[38]

As did Gilles, Joan made the scene of her death a privileged site of dialogue with God. Her last word—"Jesus"—was said to have been miraculously written in the flames that licked her charred body. As in the case of Gilles de Rais, Joan's legend was polemically relaunched in the aftermath of the Dreyfus affair. Anatole France published his *Vie de Jeanne d'Arc* in two volumes in 1908, and Charles Péguy's *Le Mystère de la charité de Jeanne d'Arc* appeared in 1910. In addition to drawing implicit parallels between Joan's martyrdom and Dreyfus's wrongful punishment, both works were read as Dreyfusard apologies for individual liberty in the face of morally illegitimate governments.[39] In a similar vein, though in a different genre (cultural history), Gilles de Rais also profited from Dreyfusard revisionism. A chapter of Salomon Reinach's monumental study of world-historical sacred practices (*Cultes, mythes et religions,* 1912) attempted to rehabilitate Gilles, marshaling evidence that he had been politically scapegoated much like Joan of Arc.[40] A prominent Jewish intellectual himself, Reinach was renowned in France for remaining a steadfast supporter of Dreyfus throughout the affair.

As onetime favorites of the king they both served; as historic constructs of a radical evil so extreme that it touched an obverse holiness; as subjects whose positioning outside the Law endowed them with extraterrestrial status, Gilles and Joan were diabolically twinned. But the history of Joan of Arc begins to diverge radically from that of Gilles when it comes to matters of national fetishism. Gilles went down in history as the worst of criminals and as an impenitent spendthrift whose addiction to pomp and extravagant purchase so infuriated the king that he suspected him of rivalry in standards of noble splendor. Joan, by contrast, was resurrected as the pre–World War I icon of French national chauvinism. In his *Autour de*

Jeanne d'Arc Maurice Barrès recounted his successful campaign, as a member of the Ligue des Patriotes, to create a national fete day in her honor. "The cult of Joan of Arc," Barrès wrote polemically, "will involve the collaboration of religion, patriotism, poetry, and the spirit of war."[41] This bellicose reinvention of Joan on the eve of her canonization in 1920 was echoed in a royalist vein in a popular ditty by Charles Maurras, founder of the Action Française: "The [national] Heritage maintained / And the Fatherland saved / By the monarchy restored."[42] And another archconservative, Léon Daudet, described in his souvenirs the process whereby Juliette Adam built her Joan of Arc cult around the Maid's reputation as one who never despaired in time of war. The victory of the Marne was characterized by Adam as "our Poitiers of 1914, where not only was the German turned back for good, but also Germanism."[43]

Gabriel Jacobs has noted that Marshall Pétain would reprise Joan's status as a paragon of Frenchness during the Occupation: "Martyr of National Unity, Jeanne d'Arc is the symbol of France."

> Some writers presented her less as the precursor of Vichy than as the embodiment of heroic grandeur and saw her story as the Triumph of the Will. Jean Jacoby, the author of works whose titles did not hide his political colors—*Le Front Populaire en France et les égarements du socialisme moderne, Le Déclin des grandes démocraties et le retour à l'autorité, La Race*—was drawn to a Jeanne in whom he saw a manifestation of iron resolution and fascist vitality. In his *Scènes de la vie de Jeanne d'Arc* of 1941 he rejected Anatole France's *magnum opus* on the life of Joan on account of its author's "sordide sectarisme." For him, Anatole France had hidden the true Joan, whose heart had indeed been full of charity, but who in no way had sought reform or so-called social justice: "Elle ne se plonge pas dans les masses," Jacoby insisted, "ne spécule pas sur leurs sentiments."[44]

Claimed by Resistance writers, as well as by those on the right, Joan of Arc's name increasingly acquired the density of an ideologeme—something on the order of *God, country, Communism*—a semantic accretion of symbolic and historical capital. Though her trial carried the ugly connotations of a perverse contagion in the body politic, her unwavering loyalty to the French king (despite his delivery of her over to the English), allowed royalist, nationalist, Catholic partisans to disimplicate themselves from the historical record of civil and theological injustice. A holy relic of the French right, the Maid and her cult became synonymous with xenophobic nationalism, Catholic revivalism, and jingoistic militarism in the decade leading up to Vichy. Her monstrous attributes—cross-dressing, androgyny, soldierly masculinity—were conveniently suborned to a myth of French triumphalism.

Unlike Joan of Arc, Gilles de Rais could never funnel the perverse metonymy of his name into a purified national allegory. However, he could be seen as competing with her as a perversely modern subject; perverse in the sense of paranormal, inhuman, subjectively destitute, a being interpellated by the beyond of representation. It is here that we might return to Joan's voices and the problem of interpellation. I would argue that one way in which Joan's story is rife with possibilities for modernity is that it yields a subject defined not by humanist individualism, but rather, by an automaton-like obeisance to dictation from outside and above—the big Telephone in the sky (what Avital Ronnell has dubbed "Dasein's collect call to itself").[45]

In Michelet's account of Joan's communion with long-distance voices, one of the twentieth century's great ontological dramas seems to have been historically prestaged by the auditions of a fifteenth-century virgin shepherdess. Michelet's work begins with a depiction of Joan as a young girl standing in her father's garden on a summer day of fasting. Looking in the direction of the church, she perceives a dazzling light and hears a voice: "Joan, be a good and dutiful child, go often to church." Voices that she identifies with St. Michael urge her: "Joan, go thou to the assistance of the king of France, and thou shalt restore his kingdom to him." When asked in what language the celestial voices communicate, she says only that it is a tongue that she understands. During her trial, she insists with unbending conviction that her saints exhort her "to willingly submit to everything and that God would come to her aid."[46] The voices address her as "Joan the Maid, daughter of God," and exact prostration of her will: "Accept everything with a willing heart; be not dismayed at the thought of martyrdom; for it will lead you at last to the kingdom of Heaven" (p. 82). According to Michelet, on dying she uttered the words, "Yes, my voices came from God, my voices did not deceive me!" (p. 121). Joan's vocation defined itself around the absolute injunctions of a God-language, a kind of glorified Telephone that, to quote Avital Ronnell again, "offers itself as instrument of the destinal alarm."

To conclude on a more contemporary note: it is perhaps none other than Althusser himself, theorist of modern interpellation, who emerges, at least in biographical terms, as something of a twentieth-century theoretical counterpart of the composite portrait of Gilles and Joan. After a fervent engagement with Catholicism in his youth he turned to Communism. Throughout his life he suffered from bouts of manic-depression, madness, inner voices, and personal demons. In 1980 his life changed forever when—by accident?—he strangled his wife Hélène in their apartment at the Ecole Normale Supérieure. He never went to trial (successfully pleading insanity) but spent the rest of his life intermittently imprisoned in mental hospitals, a ward of the very state apparatus that he, like Foucault, had made the object of social critique. Indeed, Althusser's autobiography, published in 1985 some five years after the tragedy, and titled *The Future Lasts Forever,* reads like a pathography of the perverse modern subject.[47] His account of the murder is bloodchillingly tender. He describes his own hands as they lovingly massage his wife's neck and then move, as if impelled by an exterior power, toward lethal gestures.[48]

While collecting newspaper clippings about the murder, Althusser noted that one journalist had compared him to a Japanese killer who, having murdered and cannibalized a Dutch woman, went on to write a bestseller about the crime. Althusser, one could say, emerges as a kind of Gilles de Rais caught in the vise of the Maid's calling, only this time the "call" is not from God, but from ideology as a force of production and alienation. As Slavoj Žižek has argued, with

> Althusser . . . the "individual" which is interpellated into subject is not conceptually defined, it is simply a hypothetical X which must be presupposed *into subjects.* The "point de capiton" is the point through which the subject is "sewn" to the signifier, and at the same time the point which interpellates individual into subject by addressing it with the call of a certain master-signifier ("Communism," "God," "Freedom," "America")—in a word, it is the point of the subjectivation of the signifier's chain.[49]

It is in this context, perhaps, that reflection on Joan's extraordinary history might provide an interesting way of reflecting not only on the modern conditions of saintly calling, but also on their darker side: the modern monstrous, and its seemingly unending stream of serial killers, perverse collectors, and similarly "called" subjects in whom the apparently innocent "lamb" takes on the sinister connotations of its silent cousins.

"Saint Joan-Marie Le Pen"

If xenophobia is ranked among the premier forms of the modern monstrous in contemporary politics (harking back to an earlier era of anti-Prussian sentiment and opposition to the *fin-de-siècle* immigration of Eastern European Jews into western Europe and America), it comes as little surprise that Joan of Arc has been reenlisted in the 1990's as Jean-Marie Le Pen's aide-de-camp in the war against foreigners on French soil. Claiming to receive his political directives from La Pucelle, Le Pen conjures Joan as an "absolutely extraordinary character . . . a saintly national heroine . . . one of a hundred singularly important personages in the history of the world."[50]

Crusading as a latter-day Saint Joan, Le Pen has discovered political resources in his own Christian name, Jean-Marie, yoking the archetypal virgin saints. *Jean,* the masculine counterpart of *Jeanne,* suggests a twin relation reminiscent of Jeanne and Gilles, while *Marie* carries the obvious connotations of the cult of Mary. A double Virgin, then, trapped in a man's body, or more strangely still, a sensual, feminized Le Pen ventriloquizing the female voice of a national saint, herself famous for dressing like a man. The kinky association of Le Pen with drag fashion and gender bending came glaringly to light in a caricatural way when the supermodel Linda Evangelista brought a lawsuit against Le Pen in 1995, seeking damages for the unauthorized use of her image as Joan of Arc (a photo taken of her by Karl Lagerfeld) on campaign posters.

It was Jean Marcilly, future spouse of Le Pen's ex-wife, who claims to have introduced Le Pen to the potential of Joan of Arc symbology in spring 1984. By 1987, Le Pen was routinely making stump speeches built around hero worship and the chivalresque narrative of combatting cultural decadence, national decline, and Islamic encroachment. Joan of Arc is evoked as the supreme example of national militancy, the figure in whose memory a new offensive against foreign invasion must be launched. In his speeches, Le Pen honors Joan of Arc's transgressive bravery; an "insolent one, who loved France like no one else," who "taught that nothing could be done without conviction or faith," who "brought France back to sovereignty," and who "reminds us that nothing worthwhile is acquired without a fight." Most important, her credo of "loving the English, but the English on their own turf" provides an ideological blueprint for Le Pen's particular brand of national separatism ("France and the French First"); his support for instituting blood right as the principal criterion for citizenship; and his advocacy of an anti-immigration policy propadeutically extending a promise to end unemployment.[51]

A miniature statue of the equestrian Maid stands in Le Pen's family birthplace at La Trinité-sur-Mer, another graces his desk, and, as Philip Gourevitch has noted, "further renderings of modernity's first ultranationalist martyr proliferate in Front offices, in Front publications, and at Front gatherings."[52] The effigies build on a vast history of image appropriationism by the Right and the Left. As for statues in particular, it was the Vichy regime, responsible for making an official national holiday in her name in 1941, that, ironically enough, had three hundred bronze sculptures of Joan melted down during the war in answer to metal shortages. And equally ironically, it fell to Strasbourg's Socialist mayor Catherine Trautmann to protect the city's Joan of Arc statue from defacement by protestors on the day of Le Pen's scheduled rally.

Whether as a magnet of right-wing demonstration tactics, or as a target of anti-Front ire, the Maid's immense symbolic capital has reconsolidated her status in the 1990s, making of her, in Gourevitch's words, a "supreme totem" for such ragtag constituencies as the Pétainists, monarchists, anti-Dreyfusards, Catholics, antiabortionists, skinheads, anti-Semites, and *pieds noirs* comprising France's extreme right wing. The French, he writes, "often describe Le Pen's nativist crusade with the peculiarly Anglo-Saxon word *folklorique,* and pure, defiant, incorruptible, demonized God-and-country Joan is the supreme totem of indigenous folk heroism—much older and more sacred than the tricolor."[53] The potency of Le Pen's mobilization of the Joan legend accounts, at least in part, for Lionel Jospin's call for the "demythification" of Le Penism in 1996. Sensitive to Le Pen's appeals to myths of national glory that play obscenely with history (as in his choice phrase "sublime holocaust" to describe Joan's demise at the stake), Jospin was alert to the deadly consequences of her xenophobic heritage. Two juxtaposed articles in *Le Figaro* attest to Jeanne's diabolical "morph" with the dark side of Gilles de Rais.[54] Published on the day after Le Pen's May Day parade in 1995, the first piece describes a National Front demonstration choreographed to move from Saint-Germain-des-Prés to the Joan of Arc statue at the place des Pyramides. The parade was led by a young girl dressed in a coat of mail, bearing a standard covered in fleur-de-lis. The adjacent article describes the murder of a Moroccan man, hurled into the Seine by a crowd of Le Pen–supporting skinheads. If xenophobia can be said to have assumed a singularly recognizable form in modern-day politics in France, it is the form of Joan of Arc. She is the cartoon sign of a freshly bellicose national character whose hubris echoes the Maid's pronouncements on the last day of her life: "It was I who brought the message of the crown to my King. I was the angel and there was no other. And the crown was no more than the promise of my King's coronation, which I made to him."[55] The egoism that rings in this repetition of the first-person pronoun tells the story of nationalism's partnership with narcissism; honored historically in monstrous epics of patriotic will. Acquitted of its shameful Vichy past and sorry defeats in colonial wars, affirmed by electoral results indicating that close to a third of the people has voted for a Le Pen candidate ("Votez Jeanne d'Arc," meaning "submit a defaced or blank ballot sheet," became the Le Pen supporter's electoral boycott slogan), the newly restored national character represented by "St. Joan-Marie Le Pen" brings radical evil to contemporary stagings of Gallic chauvinism.

Is there a postcolonial Joan waiting in the wings, ready for combat? Though the universal application of Joan of Arc symbolism was readily adapted to the French colonies, the significations were vexed given that

Joan stood for a "last stand" refusal to be colonized, a plea to take back the occupied nation at any cost. Under these circumstances, one might expect to find Joan of Arc reappropriated by proindependence Algerian rebels, but there is scant evidence that this occurred; the Right had overly monopolized her myth by the end of World War II, and besides, the Algerians had their own Joan of Arc in the legendary figure of La Kahina. A seventh-century Berber (possibly Jewish) chieftainess and resistance fighter, La Kahina held the Aurès mountain region against Roman invasion, inspiring modern nationalists to dub her a "Jeanne d'Arc algérienne."[56]

La Kahina surfaces powerfully in Tahar Djaout's recent novel *L'Invention du désert,* in which a writer visits the "chilled cities" of the desert in order to create a fresco of medieval Maghrebian culture. As the narrative alternates between flashbacks to the life of Ibn Toumert, a saintly theologian and hero of early Islam, and scenes from the lives of contemporary imams, masters of "group therapy, politics and the media, the speed of light, and the principle of the multiplex," La Kahina surfaces as a third term, a beacon of pre-Conquest, *Ur*-Maghrebian, Berber *islamité.*[57] The narrator traces Kahina's memory to her lair in the stony, sandy mountain village of Tehouda, a place that "bears witness to passions, festivals, and fires," but which has become "a mirage that has escaped inventory, a site as desolate as a battlefield continually returned to a litter of corpses."[58] Read against the backdrop of Algeria's current political crisis, and recalling that the novel's author was assassinated in 1993 by Islamist hardliners, Tehouda emerges as a territorial double for modern-day Algeria, awaiting deliverance by a latter-day Kahina, but in the meantime, bloodstained by massacres and stripped of official memorials.

I have always denounced terrorism. I must also denounce a terrorism which is exercised blindly, in the streets of Algiers for example, and which one day could strike my mother or my family. I believe in justice, but I shall defend my mother before justice.

ALBERT CAMUS, Stockholm interview, December 14, 1957[1]

Camus's position in the 1950s was one of extreme intellectual and emotional difficulty and tension. He had written about freedom, justice, violence, and revolt in abstract terms and asserted principles that he presented as of both fundamental importance and universal application. He never altogether abandoned this language, and he continued to write about politics in the tone of a severe moralist. Yet his actual positions were political and partisan. The violence of the Hungarian rebels and of the Anglo-French expedition in Egypt raised no problems. It was violence "on the right side"—precisely the logic he had rejected, on grounds of a rigorous morality, in relation to revolutionary violence. Freedom was an absolute for the Hungarians, and their violence in asserting their will "to stand upright" was "pure." The violence of the Algerian Arabs, who thought that they were making the same claim, was "inexcusable," and the nature and degree of the freedom to be accorded to them were matters to be decided by France, in the light of its own strategic needs—a plea which was irrelevant when made by Russia.

CONOR CRUISE O'BRIEN, *Albert Camus: Of Europe and Africa*

Algeria is no longer a Mediterranean paradise. It is neither the homosocial utopia André Gide celebrated at the turn of the century in *Les Nourritures terrestres* nor the never-never land of what Club Med made of the North African coast sixty years later. Gutted and drained by violence aimed at everyone by every kind of warring faction, the nation no longer stands as the emblem of self-determination or successful decolonization. In any event we can be sure that Algeria never stood for the timeless landscape of metaphysical intensity that Albert Camus concocted for his readers at Editions Gallimard in the postwar years. However messy it may have become, Algeria remains a rich and varied terrain for the study of what Edward Said has lately called "a comparative literature of colonialism" with many "intertwined and overlapping histories."

TOM CONLEY, afterword to Réda Bensmaïa's *The Year of Passages*

OUT OF CHARACTER

CAMUS'S FRENCH

ALGERIAN SUBJECTS

The three citations throw into stark relief the fact that Albert Camus's vexed relation to his Algerian *terre natale* remains unfinished business and therefore a necessary part of the agenda in reexamining Camus's reputation as a world-class, cosmopolitical author in the 1990s. The often remarked on, yet no less astonishing phrase from his Nobel acceptance speech in 1956, placing filial piety on the same axis as the defense of a dirty colonial war, provides the context for Conor Cruise O'Brien's scathing exposure of Camus's moral double-standards vis-à-vis Europe and North Africa. It also points up the extent to which critical reception of Camus's work has, until relatively recently, tended to downplay how he compromised his moral stance by taking the French side; focusing instead on the deconstructive metaphysics of his landscapes of absence.[2] Tom Conley's geopolitical positioning of Camus within a Mediterranean dystopia riven by *intellocide* (the assassination of intellectuals deemed symbols of westernization by the Front Islamique de Salut), and the economic ruin wreaked by the morally collapsed, militarily bolstered shell of a postindependence nation-state, underscores how it has now become impossible to abstract Camus's writings from their Algerian backdrop, and more specifically, from the current politics of civil strife.

The Algerian Camus is currently being disputed by Algerian secularists and western postcolonial critics. On one side, we find Algerian exiles and dissidents (many fearing for their lives) who have resuscitated Camus as a universal freedom-fighter who loved the country of his birth despite his misplaced political allegiances. Heralded as a partisan of truce between a Mendès-France Algerian policy and the nascent FLN (National Liberation Front) (this was in 1956 when he agreed to be a go-between in a failed meeting of the "Comité pour une Trêve Civile"), Camus reemerges as a moralist willing to take the heat, one whose defense of justice should remind the West of its obligation not to abandon Algerian advocates of a secular society.[3] It was this "global human rights" Camus, the apostle of an international democracy exercised through consensual mechanisms of world governance, whom I encountered while teaching in the Institute of French Cultural Studies in the summer of 1995. A Kabylian student in the class named Alawa Toumi (then an assistant professor at Bates College), whose research interests included "Women's Movements in Algeria," "Intellectuals and the Resistance," and "Le Fascislamisme," contested my rather flip evocation of Camus's sun-blasted "writing degree zero" as a literary style that whitewashed the colonizer's shadow while neutralizing autochthonous subjects. Toumi's defense of Camus, as it turned out, was rooted in personal stakes: the brother of Khalida Messaoudi, an outspoken feminist activist living underground, who remains high on the FIS's hit list of intellectuals deemed hostile to hard-line Islamicist ideologies of reform, he reinvented Camus as a political operative; a code name for the promulgation of an international democracy movement that would heal the breach between the Islamic world and the West.[4] Distrustful of Western postulates of cultural difference that reinscribe Oriental/Occidental binarisms, he implied that the strategic reappropriation of Camus as an Algerian author on the part of laical Algerians forms part of a larger reaction-formation against the current climate of anti-Westernization and religious censorship. Rather than reject Camus as a traitorous proponent of French Algeria, or at the very least, assimilated *algerianité,* many native Algerians today, he seemed to be arguing, would prefer to lay claim to Camus as part of their own symbolic capital—a star in the firmament of an Algerian literary heritage inclusive of *pied noir* writers. In this cosmopolitan literary bloodline, the names of Mohammed Dib and Kateb Yacine (consecrated postindependence writers) would figure in an indiscriminate jumble of exilic and/or French-identified Algerian-born literary figures, including Jean Amrouche, Mouloud Feraoun, Emmanuel Roblès, Jules Roy, Robert Merles, Rachid Boudjedra, Tahar Djaout, Assia Djebar, Abdelkebir Khatibi, Leïla Sebbar, Jacques Derrida, and Hélène Cixous.

Alawa Toumi's stance made me mindful of a contradictory situation: while the academy has traditionally provided safe haven for oppositional intellectuals, oppositional discourse within the academy, with its paeans to "resistance," has often kept aloof from the politics of human rights. There are many possible explanations for why this is so: taking sides is often intrinsically too complex from a distance; organizations such as Amnesty International or PEN have their own (often parochial) agendas; interventionism contains the risk of backfiring; the institutions monitoring violations often seem complicitous with corporate manipulations of moral capital in a global ethics market. Be that as it may, the recuperation of Camus as a means of resisting *intégrisme* cautioned me against assuming that the "Camus in Algeria" question could be readily dismissed.

But it also failed to relieve my visceral discomfort in rereading his work in the present moment. For critics steeped in postcolonial perspectives, Camus's name triggers not only a deplorable record on the Algerian War that rightly cost him friendships on the Left, but also his systematic nullification of Arab characters, particularly evident in *L'Etranger, La Peste,* and the short stories included in *L'Exil et le royaume.*[5] Dissolving the contours of Algerian cities and coastal landscape into sibilant friezes or projection walls of the European mind, erasing the signs of precursory Algerian secessionism by recording not a trace of the protests and massacres at Sétif in the immediate aftermath of Liberation; and converting the site specificity of a soon-to-be imploding colonial war into a labyrinthine tectonics of European postwar melancholia, Camus presents colonial unease in a metaphysically abstract worldscape.[6]

Sullen, taciturn "Arab" characters emerge as *figurants,* alternately mime and geste stick figures holding up the scenery, or scopic effects, tracking European inquisitors with malevolent diffidence. The short story *La Femme adultère* exemplifies the almost caricatural quality of Camus's rendering of the Maghrebian subject *as* gaze. The Arabs sitting in the bus next to Janine catch the invisible rays of her unfocused desire with their stony "impassive" looks. Shifty observers, they spy while pretending to sleep ("L'autocar était plein d'Arabes qui faisaient mine de dormir enfouis dans leurs burnous"). The driver of the bus seems to "smile with his eyes," but his face remains enigmatically "masked." In a trading town in the interior, a senior Arab merchant haughtily passes the couple as if they were invisible. ("Ils se croient tout permis maintenant," grumbles Marcel). Forming a specular cordon around the phobic Janine, Algerian cyclists appear as giant, menacing burnouses on wheels, zigzagging in wild circles as they close in on their European quarry. The natives are also registered as a barely tangible presence at the end of the novella in the epiphanic space of an "obscure center of her being"; an enemy within that doubles, Janine realizes, as the object of her intense, unaccountable longing.[7] It is no small irony that the strangeness of the Arabs' gaze, as overreaching as their conversation is recessed, grows in direct proportion to the Europeans' refusal to engage with the culture that surrounds them: "The driver says several words to the passengers in this language that she had heard her entire life without ever understanding."[8] Naturally a people seems immured in silence if, when they do speak, nothing is understood!

Though it may be a purely Western obsession with colonial subjects that prompts me to take issue with Camus's ascription of an interiority of naught to the Algerians populating his fictive world, it would seem, nonetheless, that to deny the importance of Algerian subjecthood would be to fly in the face of the classic decolonization literature, which, from Aimé Césaire to Albert Memmi and Frantz Fanon, has affirmed subjectivity claims for the colonized. Making a case for instantiating a colonial subject becomes more plausible provided one eschews universalist models of what that subject might be. On the other hand, surface-depth or inside-outside characterological paradigms, standard practice since French realism, may prove indispensable given their international currency in modern world literature.

Camus aficionados might take issue here with what seems to be a reductive approach to his characterization, alleging, perhaps, that I am applying social realist criteria to produce "positive" fictive types or role models. I emphatically want to disown such normative readings, recognizing as I do that if there is true "genius" in Camus's prose, it lies precisely in its achievement of ontologically benumbed characters, seemingly wrapped in the postwar, prerevolutionary chill of being. My point here is not that the European protagonists should be well-rounded, psychologically transparent figures, but rather, that the Algerian characters should also accede to the complexity of existential characterhood within the terms defined by Camus.

Even if the argument is made that Camus's blunted North Africans are simply extensions of the wounded, mummified personae of their European counterparts (a mummification venerated as part of the high seriousness of the Absurd), their radical decharacterization carries serious political consequences; confirming the negation of a subject people at a time of colonial war. Anticipating Mathieu Kassewitz's *La Haine,* a film made in 1995 about Maghrebian "homies" negotiating cultural disenfranchisement in the Parisian banlieu, Camus reduces his Algerian characters to receptacles of crushing aggression and *ressentiment.* The more celebrated emotions of existentialism—ontological nausea, aborted self-knowledge—are reserved for the Europeans. Edward Said has observed that Camus "exquisitely articulates . . . the massive 'structure of feeling'" incubating within a "metropolitan transfiguration of the colonial dilemma."[9] The emergence of Algerian nationalism, he points out, is gagged and bound; a necessary expense of registering the piercing *Entfremdung* of the colon. In other words, it is the stranger in the Algerians' midst who reverses the path of his own estranging effect as foreign occupier, so that it falls back on himself; forming a narcissistic loop around that eminently seductive, philosophically prestigious figure of the existential antihero—"L'Etranger."[10]

Capitalizing on what Said has characterized as the "waste and sadness" of French imperialism's penultimate gasp, Camus captures the "negative vitality" of settler recalcitrance.[11] Nowhere is this bilious energy more poignantly conveyed than in the portrait of an old-style colon rendered by Camus in his unfinished Algerian epic *Le Premier homme*. Described as "the kind they insult nowadays in Paris, you know . . . of the patriarchal genre," he reenacts Custer's last stand fast-forwarded to the Algerian War.[12] When a nearby farm is attacked (the throats of the parents slit, the daughters raped and murdered), the prefect tells the assembled farmers that it is time to turn a page in the book of history, time to reconsider colonial questions and the manner in which Arabs have been treated. But the old man vows that nobody will tell him what is law in this country. When evacuation orders are given, he empties the wine vats, destroys his crops, and works around the clock to raze every last remnant of his property. Before departing for Marseilles, where he will spend the rest of his days pacing the floors of an efficiency apartment, he advises his Algerian workers to join the revolutionary Maquis. Adopting the myth, popular since *la défaite*, that French national decline is the explicable outcome of devirilization, he predicts that the French will inevitably lose their empire "since there are no more real men left in France."[13] The old colon's grim fate makes a marked impression on the autobiographical narrator of *Le Premier homme*, for this homestead was the narrator's birthplace, the site of a dead paternal legacy. Throughout the novel, the paternal void, and the loss of personal genealogy, undergird the narrator's bizarre affirmation that Algeria has no history.

Though it would be tempting at this point to rehearse in some depth Camus's construction of Algeria as, simultaneously, an impotent, desecrated fatherland and a locus of maternal identification, I will concentrate instead on dissecting Camus's notion of French Algeria as a consummate oxymoron; a cosmopolitan hallucination of hybridity hatched in full view of decolonization. Camus's insistence on seeing one nation where there were at least two, his projection of continental holism in the face of incipient binational antagonism, illustrates the conflict, ever present today, between worldly hybridities and nationalist ethnic and religious particularisms. The conflict is particularly acute in Algeria because French rule prevailed for the longest duration of any colony (1830–1962). The roots of the French nation-state, strengthened by the Napoleonic legacy, had fully taken in Algeria—it was the so-called pearl of the French imperial sweepstake. The Evian Accords signed in 1962 assured France a neocolonial presence in the economic sphere of Algerian affairs after independence. Moreover, the intelligentsia perpetuated French educational and cultural hegemony. As Réda Bensmaïa has noted, Arabization was expected to take hold in the immediate aftermath of the war, but this did not really occur: "On the eve of independence," he writes, "an Algerian literature 'written in French' seemed a contradiction in terms: political independence, it was thought, would be quickly followed by cultural and linguistic independence. Yet since 1962 there has been a flowering of works in French by Maghreb writers."[14] Though the politics of language and censorship today may be precipitating a state of what one Algerian linguist has called *linguicide* (a blackout in cultural literacy in Berber, French, *or* classical Arabic), Bensmaïa's observation points to Frantz Fanon's articulation of the national obstacles to pan-Arabism, that is, to the assertion of common cultural over individual nation:

> Certain Arab states, though they chanted the marvelous hymn of Arab renaissance, had nevertheless to realize that their geographical position and the economic ties of their region were stronger even than the past that they wished to revive. Thus we find today the Arab states organically linked once more with societies which are Mediterranean in their culture. The fact is that these states are submitted to modern pressure and to new channels of trade while the network of trade relations which was dominant during the great period of Arab history has disappeared. But above all there is the fact that the political regimes of certain Arab states are so different, and so far away from each other in their conceptions, that even a cultural meeting between these states is meaningless[15]

With his sensitivity to the "serious ambiguities" arising from the "cultural problem in colonized countries," Fanon apprehended, on the eve of Algerian decolonization, that nationalist discrepancies among Arab states, together with the pressures of global economics, would enable European influence to continue exerting its hold in Arabophone countries.[16] And indeed it has: despite Arabization policies mandating the extirpation of French, despite the importation of English and Russian as technocratic languages under Boumedienne, the virtual "second language" status of French in the fields of education, media, and literary culture contributes to the binational (as distinct from hybrid) character of Algeria's internal political rift.

In Homi K. Bhabha's introduction to *Nation and Narration* hybridity is associated with an internationalism deriving from the Fanonian dictum (enunciated in the same chapter of *Wretched of the Earth*—"On National Culture"—from which I have been quoting): "National consciousness, without nationalism, is the only thing that will give us an international dimension."[17] Bhabha glosses:

> It is this *inter*national dimension both within the margins of the nation-space and in the boundaries *in-between* nations and peoples that the authors of this book have sought to represent in their essays. The representative emblem of this book might be a chiasmatic "figure" of cultural difference whereby the anti-nationalist, ambivalent nation-space becomes the crossroads to a new transnational culture.[18]

Though there is obviously something compelling about the transnational hybridity argued for by Bhabha, the case history of Algeria, both in Camus's day and now (albeit under markedly different conditions), suggests that transnationalism is rendered inoperative by cultural binationalism. Put simply, "chiasmic subjects" will be rent asunder when the claims of conflicting national patrimonies are staked on their bodies. Camus's Algerian crisis brings 1990s utopianism around hybrid identity back to questions of bilateral citizenship and the splitting of patriotic identifications. In Camus's writings, the idealized proto-Braudelian fantasy of "Mediterranean man," a Euro-African subject whose cultural attachments allow him to forget the realpolitik of colonial power imbalance, shatters in the context of the Algerian War, when hybridity is renationalized, rendered schizoid as opposed to culturally composite.

Camus's disavowal of an imminent *post*colonial binationalism is as much a way of writing as it is a clearly outlined set of positions cured over the course of the Algerian revolution. In an introduction to his *Chroniques algériennes,* published in 1958 at the height of the war, Camus deploys a bipartisan rhetoricity operating as a diplomacy of give and take. Consistently the prose moralist, he levies or suspends judgment in equal measure on both sides. Camus condemns torture on the grounds that it is unjust in absolute ethical terms, and counterintuitive because it nurtures the next generation of terrorists. But in the next breath, he pleads the cause of French Algerians abandoned by sectors of metropolitan public opinion, which, in 1958, excoriates the colons as exploiters of a prostituted land. Bent on restoring dignity to his patrimony, Camus honors the settlers of the 1870s—"seigneurs misérables et libres d'un étrange royaume"—patriotic pioneers who tilled the land and shed their blood for France in the war of 1914.[19] This was to become an obsessive theme of *Le Premier Homme,* the work that he was carrying with him in draft form at the moment of his fatal car crash in 1960.

Pursuing a policy of double-pronged redress in the Algerian articles, Camus approves the end of colonialism (and along with it the foreclosure of French dreams of reconquest) but mollifies the other side by ruling out the deracination of Algerian Frenchmen, "who, even if they don't have the right to oppress anyone, maintain the right not to be oppressed in turn, or to dispose as they will of the land of their birth."[20] The distributive grammar of "according this" and "disallowing that," while implicitly crediting a utopian premise that political cohabitation among French settlers and Algerian natives is an eventual outcome of mutual sacrifice, effectively dodges more difficult questions at the core of Camus's ideal of French Algeria: What is the national character of the imperial subject who both loves and despises a semiforeign motherland? What is the cultural identity of the emigrant invested in an expropriated territory yet transnationally acculturated? What is the status of a would-be decolonizer, unable to relinquish assimilationist illusions, including a belief in the implausible politics of benevolent protectionism? How is the hybrid "French Algerian" or "Algerian Frenchman" tenable given conditions, documented by Camus himself, of irreversible economic inequality? And how might a reparations reading of Camus work to rectify the systematic decharacterization of his Algerian fictional subjects?

Conor Cruise O'Brien's *Albert Camus: Of Europe and Africa,* published in 1970, was among the first studies to question Camus's confection of a felicitous French Algerian hybrid. Cutting through the adulation accorded the existentialist Camus during the 1960s, the book offers a clear, hard look at the colonial legacy within the framework of Camus's depersonalized, ethics-driven aesthetics. A maverick intellectual, one of Ireland's great political journalists, the author of a respected study of Edmund Burke, and a significant player in the epic of postwar decolonization in Africa, O'Brien's extraordinary memoir *To Katanga and Back* records the story of his resignation as UN representative in Zaire during the disastrous aftermath of Patrice Lumumba's assassination. Opening with a letter from U Thant, citing UN Staff Regulation 1.5 (dictating discretion after resignation from a top government post), the memoir is full of biting insights into the way in which American Cold War politics took up directly where the European colonial venture in Africa left off.[21]

O'Brien may well have chosen to write a book on Camus because his own biography was so much "of Europe and Africa." With a perspicacity rarely appreciated by literary scholars of Camus (Edward Said being the notable exception), O'Brien points out the glaring contradiction between Camus's signature theme of estrangement and his contrivance of a raceless Algeria in which Moslems and working-class Frenchmen coexist without serious tension in the popular quarters of Belcourt. In addition to demonstrating the naïveté of canonical critics of Camus such as Germaine Brée, who would have us believe that French, Spanish, Italian, Maltese, Jews, Berbers, and Arabs lived together with easy familiarity, "impervious to racial barriers," O'Brien decries Camus's "lamentable Mediterranean solar-myth vein,"[22] most pronounced in *Noces* and "La Pensée de Midi" (a section of *L'Homme révolté*), but discernible early on in his poem "Méditérranée," written during his first year at university. Ideologically nourished by the triumphal modern classicism of Gide, Grenier, and Montherlant, this four-stanza verse treats North Africa as the breeding ground of new gods; avatars of a recrudescent Sparta. In its vision of Greco-Africanism, the poem anticipates Camus's vision of an Athenianized Kabylia, alluded to in his muckraking essay from the thirties, "Misère de la Kabylie." Here, Camus imagines a federated Algeria composed of micro city-states; perfectible versions of a Rousseauesque "douar-commune," in which indigenous self-rule is improved by Enlightenment ideals.

Camus's utopic projection of Algerian democracy shelters another figment of the imagination—pan-Mediterranean man. Caught between his Barrèsian sense of *pied noir* entitlement to Algerian soil and his status as privileged global citizen of a cosmopolis of letters, Camus invented the figure of a nationless regionalist, at home in the world. Pan-Mediterranean man is set up to become the agent of a new world order that would be neither "national nor even continental, certainly neither occidental nor oriental. It must be universal. . . . It is a form of society where the law is above governments, this law being the expression of the general will, represented by a legislative body."[23]

Pan-Mediterranean man is that impossible construct; the hybrid cosmopolitan with territorial loyalties and the conscience of the *Volk*. In a lecture delivered in 1937 at La Maison de la Culture, he argued that

> North Africa is one of the few countries where East and West live together, and in this confluence there is no difference between the manner of the Spaniard or an Italian of the quays of Algiers and the Arabs who are around him. The most essential element in the Mediterranean genius springs perhaps from this encounter, unique in history and geography, born between East and West. . . . This truth of a Mediterranean culture exists and manifests itself on every point: one, linguistic unity, facility of learning one Latin language when one knows another; two, unity of origin, prodigious collec-

tivism of the Middle Ages, the order of knights, order of religious feudalities, et cetera.[24]

To this indifference to difference, Conor Cruise O'Brien proffers a withering riposte:

> The interest of these words—in an early and ephemeral statement—lies in their contradictions. At the very moment when he wishes to affirm the unity of the Mediterranean world, the marriage of East and West, he reveals himself as incapable of thinking in any categories other than those of a Frenchman. Although he rejects Maurras's conception of "the Latin West" with its pro-fascist associations—at this time of Mussolini's invasion of Ethiopia—his own Mediterranean truth reposes on a supposed linguistic unity derived from the similarity of Romance languages: and this in a country of which the majority of the inhabitants were Arabic-speaking.[25]

Several pages later, O'Brien puts an even sharper edge into his conclusion, stating that "when a brilliantly intelligent and well-educated man, who has lived all his life surrounded by an Arabic-speaking population, affirms the existence of a form of unity including the Arabs and based on the Romance languages, it is not excessive to speak of hallucination" (p. 11).

The jury may still be out on how Camusian "unity" should be interpreted. It is certainly a "hallucination" in O'Brien's sense, that is, an extraordinary picture of unreality, a blinkered image of regional identity that leaves out what is Arab or Moslem in Mediterranean culture. But it also presages what Emmanuel Wallerstein, following Braudel (arguably the one who gave academic and historical credibility to Camus's pan-Mediterraneanism), terms "geoculture"—a kind of interstate polity galactically connected to world systems of advanced capital.[26] It may equally well foreshadow what Timothy Brennan has recently dubbed the "new cosmopolitanism" of today's internationalist, "global" writer: "The new cosmopolitanisms," Brennan claims, "model themselves on a nostalgia for 'democracy' as a vision of pluralist inclusion, a diversity in unity, a global progress based on the Enlightenment, however ambivalently."[27]

Whether or not one tries to recoup aspects of Camus's hybrid wish-fulfillment with the help of contemporary models of cosmopolitical citizenship, it seems clear that Camus's political curriculum vitae was at odds with his writing: the former, nursed by antitotalitarianism in the Cold War period, tendered a unity model of culture bolstered by a wildly optimistic faith in franchise (according to Camus biographer Herbert Lottman, "Camus would always believe that Algeria could be saved for France by genuine reforms. He put his hopes in liberalized voting rights for Moslems").[28] The latter, by contrast, portrays *pied noir* consciousness cocooned in trauma and oblivion, locked in the vise of a repressed-memory syndrome that it dare not disturb. In *L'Etranger*, for example, explicit reference to national fracture is repressed; but it fissures the surface normality of everyday life in the form of unaccountable acts: gratuitous crimes, conjugal abuse, domestic and social autism.

French Algerians, like their counterparts, Algerians living under French domination, emerge in Camus's fiction as characters who are "out of character," in the sense of subjectively "out of pocket"—their credit lines used up, their markets exhausted, their "futures" deemed unprofitable. It is this saga of decharacterization that intriguingly informs Camus's thwarted masterwork *Le Premier homme*. Most critics, following cues bequeathed by the author, have assumed that the First Man refers to the dead father of Camus's fictive alter ego Jacques Cormery. Lottman maintains that the First Man was

> Albert Camus's father, who was killed in World War I before Albert was a year old. But it was also Albert Camus himself, growing up in a cultural and historical vacuum accentuated by his family's illiteracy, symbolized by a home without books. "Thus I imagine a first man who starts at zero," he told an interviewer as early as 1954, "who can neither read nor write, who has neither morality nor religion. It will be, if you like, an education, but without an educator."[29]

In the final pages of the novel, the First Man is identified with a "secret part of being," parallel to Janine's discovery of the "obscure part of her being" in *La Femme adultère*.[30] Here, an originary ecoself, unburying itself as it is pulled through the soil by a magnetic force-field hailing from "who knows where," hatches from the Minotaur's sub rosa architecture:

> Something in him that through all those years had been blindly stirring like those measureless waters under the earth which from the depths of rocky labyrinths have never seen the light of day and yet dimly reflect a light, come from who knows where, drawn perhaps from the glowing center of the earth through stone capillaries to the black air of those buried caverns in which glutinous and [compacted] plants find food enough to live where any life seems impossible. (Pp. 278–79)

In what resembles an embryonic dream, the narrator whooshes though the birth canal "yearning to be nobody," yearning for an "immense country," an "immense sea," only to be ejected onto *terra nuova:* "tossed, as if he were the first inhabitant, or the first conqueror, landing where the law of the jungle still prevailed" (p. 279). With "the conqueror" or "colonial First Man" released into the open, the subsequent history of colonialism is compressed into narrative anecdotes. In one anecdote, a fight breaks out between a Frenchman and an Arab against the backdrop of veiled Algerian women whose "beautiful eyes sensual and soft above the white cloth" constitute nonetheless "an invisible menace" (p. 280). In another anecdote, a longing for the oceanic maternal body (the foreclosed motherland?) blends into orgasm with a nameless woman whose desire for eternal youth is revealed as painful folly when she returns "to the foreign country where she was born" (p. 283). Though these anecdotes quickly deteriorate into clichés of being "a stranger in one's own house," they encrypt the mood of colonial panic—a "nameless dread . . . inside these tangled roots that bound him to this magnificent and frightening land"—regnant at the time of *Le Premier homme*'s composition (p. 281).

While granting Camus's disinherited Conqueror his place as the obvious candidate for titular preeminence, I would also submit that beneath the First Man fantasy of the frontiersman who braves a harsh, insalubrious terrain to create a colony (only to lose it when the imperial venture is abandoned by the metropole), there lies a "first" First Man: an under-characterized "person who was there first," a displaced or missing subject. This "first" First Man exerts pressure throughout the novel, as if demanding to be released into characterhood. He is on one level the part of Algerianness that has seeped into the character of the *pied noir* and that surfaces in the odd phrase from the notes: "What they did not like in him was the Algerian."[31] On another level he is the utopian agent of a new world order ("we are the first men—not men on the wane as they shout in the [illegible word] newspaper but men of a different and undefined dawn" [p. 319]). But on still another (and for my purposes more crucial) level, he is an Algerian native, the novel's aborted character par excellence.

Merely glimpsed in the notes and sketches appended to the recently published manuscript, the Algerian character must be built up out of paltry material. He poses a veritable challenge to the reader, inviting hypertextual manipulation, the rearrangement of fragments into a hypothetical linear story of the Algerian freedom-fighter where clearly no such story impinges with authority. In several instances, this missing character bears the name Saddok, an insurgent-terrorist, who may in fact have been based on a real Algerian rebel prosecuted for terrorism—Ben Saddok—whose cause Camus was asked to defend shortly before setting out for Stockholm to accept the Nobel Prize.[32]

Saddok may well have been destined to play an important role in Camus's completed magnum opus. In one snippet of dialogue, Jacques tries to dissuade Saddok from his revolutionary goal of seizing control of the government, by making the argument that Camus had made famous in *L'Homme révolté* about the absolute, corrosive effect of power:

> Yes I hate you. For me honor in the world is found among the oppressed, not those who hold power. And it is from that alone that dishonor arises. When just once in history an oppressed person understands . . . then . . .
> Goodbye, said Saddok.
> Stay, they'll catch you.
> That's better. Them I can hate, and I join them in hatred. You're my brother and we're separated.[33]

Here the schizophrenia of French Algeria is represented through the familial metaphor of divided brothers (part of a nostalgic vision of the friendships that used to exist between French Algerians and "Arabs" before the outbreak of war). In another fragment, fraternal illusions falter, despite efforts to wash away discord in the swimming pool, before the "terrorism-for," "terrorism-against" bottom line:

> "But why get married that way, Saddok?"
> "Should I marry the French way?"
> "The French or any other way! Why subject yourself to a tradition you believe is foolish and cruel?"
> "Because my people are identified with this tradition, they have nothing else, they stopped there, and to part with that tradition is to part with them. This is why I will go into that room tomorrow, and I will strip a stranger of her clothes, and I will rape her to the sound of gunshots."
> "All right. In the meantime, let's go swimming." (P. 313)

If, with Saddok, we are grasping at straws, trying to fill in a characterological void, matters are even harder when all we have to work with is, say, the decontextualized utterance of an FLN commissar: "Yes, I command, I kill, I live in the mountains, under the sun and rain. What do you offer me that's better: laborer in Béthune" (p. 319), or the barest sketch of a terrorist:

> X sees a terrorist fire. . . . He hears someone running after him in a dark street, stands still, turns suddenly, trips him so he falls, the revolver drops. He takes the weapon and trains it on the man, then realizes he cannot turn him in, takes him to a remote street, makes him run ahead of him and fires. (Pp. 297–98)

Is the terrorist killed when X fires? Isn't the terrorist's character the real "X" (in the sense of unknown), of this mininarrative? Is he related to the terrorist whom Camus vowed he would not defend, no matter how justified his acts, if the choice were between the terrorist and his mother? Though the appendices of *Le Premier homme* provide little aid in answering these questions, they do figure the mother as the blank slate against which Algeria's postcolonial future must be projected. "In the last part, Jacques explains to his mother the Arab question, Creole civilization, the fate of the West. 'Yes,' she says, 'yes.' Then full confession and the end" (p. 309). Here, it seems, the narrator confesses to a pessimistic vision of Western civilization's survival in the Islamic world. The creolized Algeria presented here is a far cry from the pan-Mediterranean hybrid imagined in his youth; rather, it embodies a mongrel national subject uninterested in preserving Western mores, or worse, "half-breeds with pointed shoes and scarves who have only adopted the worst from the West" (p. 318).

I will conclude by arguing that Camus's never-never land of French Algeria (an Algeria "made in France"), like so many artificially federated nation-states in the Balkans, was an impossible political artifact. It was an oxymoron in Camus's time, and it remains an oxymoron now, that is, an Islamic nation-state unable to negotiate coexistence with French-identified (and Berber-identified) sectors of its citizenry. Camus's French Algerian subject typifies the "native intellectual" qualified by Fanon as destined to belong to a "race of angels," "colorless, stateless, rootless."[34] "It will be quite normal," Fanon wrote, "to hear certain natives declare,"

> "I speak as a Senegalese and as a Frenchman . . . " "I speak as an Algerian and as a Frenchman . . . " The intellectual who is Arab and French, or Nigerian and English, when he comes up against the need to take on two nationalities, chooses, if he wants to remain true to himself, the negation of one of these determinations. But most often, since they cannot or will not make a choice, such intellectuals gather together all the historical determining factors which have conditioned them and take up a fundamentally "universal standpoint."[35]

Though Fanon himself endorses universal values in prescribing a nationalist project for the native intellectual at the end of his 1959 conference on national culture, this conflicts with what he says in the passage above, where he intimates that default to a "universal standpoint" fails when the subject is forced to choose between two identities. To reject one half of himself, he states, condemns the other half to becoming "a stranger in his own land," that is, to becoming the kin of Camus's fabled *étranger*. The failure of Camus's cosmopolitical hybrid—a vision of French Algeria that collapses in the face of an emergent Algerian nationalism—offers, like the example of Fanon's schizoid native, a kind of object lesson for the future of globalization theory or transnational identity-formation. The lesson is simply this: just as you succumb to the illusion of a "global subject" (who, as Bill Readings would have it, moves in a bureaucratic space of eroded nationalism because the "capitalist system . . . offers people not a national identity

. . . but a non-ideological belonging: a corporate identity in which they participate only at the price of becoming operatives"), nationalism resurges in a different guise, asserting its particularist claims anew, and, in the case of contemporary Algeria, projecting inherited binational schisms onto the hybrid body-politic.[36]

4
CHARACTER ASSASSINATION

RACIAL PATHOLOGIES,

COLONIAL CRIMES:

FANON, MANNONI,

LACAN, PAULHAN

In *Black Skin, White Masks* Frantz Fanon launched a powerful offensive against Octave Mannoni's seminal "psychology of colonialism" elaborated in *Prospero and Caliban* (1950). Accusing Mannoni of sponsoring a theory of native inferiority that, in the colonial situation, took on the character of full-blown cultural dependency, Fanon took issue with Mannoni's approach to the ethics of responsibility in the face of "racialist crimes." At stake for Fanon was something very important, the decolonization of the colonial unconscious.

It is in the context of renewed critical attention to Fanon's engagement with psychoanalysis that I want to situate the reinvestigation of Fanon's bitter attack on Mannoni. Inaugurated in the mid-1980s by Homi K. Bhabha's seminal introduction to a 1986 edition of *Black Skin, White Masks,* the "return of Fanon" has been much in evidence in recent exhibitions, films, academic symposia, and minority discourses. Bhabha reinvented Fanon as a black Lacan whose writings reveal "the ambivalent identification of the racist world."[1] His own writing was profoundly indebted to Fanon's in its conjugation of the language of analysis with political critique. In "Remembering Fanon: Self, Psyche, and the Colonial Condition," he emphasized that "in the colonial situation, everyday life exhibits a 'constellation of delirium' that mediates the normal social relations of its subjects" (p. 137). Evoking the "phantasmatic images of racial hatred that come to be absorbed and acted out in the wisdom of the west," Bhabha constructed the arresting image of "post-Enlightenment man tethered to, *not* confronted by, his dark reflection" (p. 137). "In shifting the focus of cultural racism from the politics of nationalism to the politics of narcissism," he maintained, "Fanon opens up a margin of interrogation that causes a subversive slippage of identity and authority" (p. 146).

Even if the hindsight of ten years prompts a dose of skepticism toward redemptive formulations of "subversive slippage of identity and authority," or "nationalism and narcissism," Bhabha's emphasis on psychoanalytic Fanonism helped relaunch Fanon's oeuvre as a catalyst of post–colonial critique and critical race theory. Henry Louis Gates's promulgation of a "critical Fanonism" (1991) only confirmed this move.[2] If Fanon was remembered only faintly by the mid-1980s as an avatar of sixties activism and as an impresario in the great postwar epic of decolonization, he was now resuscitated by Bhabha and Gates as a writer whose opaque rhetoricity introduced articulations that had no equivalent language in the classic literature of political theory. At the risk of saying unspeakable things (for colonial fantasies are embarrassing, compromising, painful to confess), Bhabha and Gates, via Fanon, forced a deeper confrontation with unspeakable acts of colonial history.

Looking now at the discursive complexity of a text such as *Black Skin, White Masks,* with its imbrications of Sartrean nausea, Lacanian desubjectivation, and nosological technicity, it is difficult to imagine how the work gained mass currency, to fathom the conditions by which extremely dense theory breaks through, crosses over, or conflagrates into an engine of social change. At one level, the answer necessarily lies in that postwar conjunction of intellectual and world-historical forces that allowed French Hegelianism and existentialism to become palatable to a broad readership, but at another level, it may be linked to the mythic status of Fanon himself. Isaac Julien's charismatic documentary, *Frantz Fanon: Black Skin, White Mask,* made for BBC Television and currently circulating sporadically in film festivals and universities in the United States, confronts Fanon's resurgent image as a mythic black hero. Despite its manifest concern to put Fanon's career as psychiatrist, writer, and activist into historical perspective, and despite its refusal to paper over those parts of the Fanonian legacy that have not worn well (his notorious homophobia and misogyny), the film presents, in Julien's signature style, a soft-focus Frantz Fanon whose status as an erotically delectable icon of black masculinity is enhanced by the choice of a handsome actor from the popular British crime series *Prime Suspect* to play his part. Demonstrating how the press of Fanon's larger-than-life reputation undercuts attempts at critical *dégonflage,* Julien's film may itself be interpreted as a symptom of a new wave of Fanon-mania in the 1990s.

If, in the sixties, Fanon's theories of diagnostic social psychiatry and "difficult" textuality were tolerated as part of his architecture of a *tiermondiste* emancipatory humanism, in the eighties and nineties these aspects of his work provoked the most discussion. Gates, Bhabha, Stuart Hall, Kobena Mercer, and Françoise Vergès, all working in divergent directions, were among those who reemphasized Fanon's place in the history of psychoanalysis and psychiatric socialism. Though psychoanalysis itself fell into disrepute in the nineties, attacks on its universalist, Eurocentric foundations and racist blind spots did not seem to obviate the need for psychoanalytically inflected forms of race theory. Indeed, contributions to a recently published volume, *The Fact of Blackness,* distilling proceedings of a Fanon conference organized in 1995 at London's Institute of Contemporary Art, attest to psychoanalysis's usefulness in adducing critiques of racist consciousness.[3] For many, psychoanalysis provides indispensable paradigms for rethinking colonial paternalism, transference, fetishism, negation, sadism, masochism, unconscious drives, and those inversionary structures of identification that give racist shame and guilt psychic form and performative visibility.

In the discussion that follows, I will be examining Fanon's famous attack on Mannoni precisely because it exemplifies many of the pitfalls and virtues of conjugating race and psychoanalysis. It shows, on the one hand, how suppressed colonial histories have been embedded within the conceptual apparatus of psychoanalysis, and on the other, how vital psychoanalysis remains to a nuanced understanding of dependency; whether at the micro level (*colon* facing off against *colonisé*), or the global level (the politics of "dependent" nations within transnational capital flows of debt, technical know-how, and actuarial projection).

Fanon had plenty of good reasons for setting Mannoni up for character assassination, but I would suggest, at the risk of being overgenerous to Mannoni, that Fanon's negative take on Mannoni's theory of indigenous dependency obscures some of the most interesting implications of Mannoni's ethnopsychiatry. Mannoni's Prospero/Caliban paradigm carries the Hegelian dialectic of *Herrschaft* and *Knechtschaft*—or more generally speaking, the problem of psychic servitude—forward historically into Marxist decolonization discourses. From the Caliban-tilted rewritings of the *Tempest* by Aimé Césaire, Roberto Fernandez Retamar, Edouard Glissant, and Jean Guéhenno, to Fanon's *ressentiment*-filled "French Negro," denied Hegelian reciprocal recognition and likened to "those servants who are allowed once every year to dance in the drawing room";[4] to the antimodernization "dependency theorists" of the 1960s (including Colin Leys, Gavin Kitching, Nicos Poulantzas, and Samir Amin among others), the topology of slave consciousness—Caliban's legacy—has given narrative form to colonial cries and whispers.[5] Despite critical efforts to complicate reductive binary models of dependency, and despite attempts to generate pluridirectional paradigms of transnational flow, such binarisms perdure in the "Manichaean delirium" still characteristic of First and Third World systems of exchange.

Mannoni adopted a peculiarly *nachträglich* approach to the apparent "colonizability" of the Malagasy people. Fanon was reacting to some egregiously misguided arguments in Mannoni's book, as in the following:

> To my mind there is no doubting the fact that colonization has always required the existence of the need for dependence. Not all peoples can be colonized: only those who experience this need. Neither are all peoples equally likely to become colonizers, for, as I shall show later, certain other equally definite predispositions are required for that role.

And further:

> Wherever Europeans have founded colonies of the type we are considering, it can safely be said that their coming was unconsciously expected—even desired—by the future subject peoples.[6]

Mannoni's blatant cultural essentialism—his assumption that some peoples have a "natural" predilection for being colonized while others possess the kind of individualist self-reliance that allows them to assume positions of dominance reflexively—was read by an outraged Fanon as an ethnocentric, psychoanalytically credentialed "apologia for colonialism."[7] *"It is the racist who creates his inferior,"* Fanon expostulated, aligning himself with Sartre's famous statement: "It is the anti-Semite who *makes* the Jew."[8]

In focusing on some kind of "colonizable" cultural gene in the "personality" of the oppressed (derivative of native practices of ancestor worship), rather than on the subjugating power of the oppressor, and in locking the Malagasy into a cycle of autocolonization, Mannoni, according to Fanon, relieved the colonizer of his burden of responsibility, allowing him to "forget" the impact of his own injury to native autonomy:

> After having sealed the Malagasy into his own customs, after having evolved a unilateral analysis of his view of the world, after having described the Malagasy within a closed circle, after having noted that the Malagasy has a dependency relation toward his ancestors—a strong tribal characteristic—M. Mannoni, in defiance of all objectivity, applies his conclusions to a bilateral totality—deliberately ignoring the fact that, since Galliéni, the Malagasy has ceased to exist.[9]

Though this last argument may be problematic insofar as it implies that colonized cultures that have "ceased to exist" may no longer lay claim to insurrectionary agency, Fanon zeroes in on the baffling "blame-the-victim" drift in Mannoni's thinking. There is simply no denying that Mannoni's graft of an Adlerian "inferior personality" onto his model of the "dependent" autochthonous subject was fraught with the usual problems of ethnopsychiatric analysis—principal among them the use of universalist personality types. Even if Mannoni hadn't intended any hint of racial denigration in developing the "dependency complex" (as Fanon insisted he had), his Caliban characterology floats in a historical vacuum, insufficiently soldered to the material and economic forces that clearly play a determinative part in the formation of colonial mentalities.

But here one must back up, pausing to ask: Who was Mannoni? Why did Fanon bother to attack him? Why did his theories become a lightening rod for debate in the great postwar epic of decolonization? Mannoni was born in 1899 in Sologne, France, of Corsican parents, and died in 1989. He was married to Maud van der Spoel, a highly distinguished psychoanalyst, clinician, writer, and editor of the important Denoël series, "L'espace analytique," in which Mannoni's more personal books appeared. From 1947 to 1953, Mannoni served as a functionary in the French colonial civil service, rising to the position of director of the Service Général de l'Information in Tananarive, Madagascar. In the wake of the Malagasy insurrection of 1947, brutally suppressed by the French authorities, Mannoni entered a period of crisis. He was demoted and sent back to Paris to an honorific post shortly after delivering a series of radio broadcasts that were critical of French policy. In 1945, during one of his return trips to Paris, Mannoni undertook an analysis with Jacques Lacan that seems to have been fraught with transferential crises. As a member of the Ecole Freudienne de Paris, Mannoni worked closely with Lacan, becoming a regular contributor to *Lettres de l'Ecole Freudienne de Paris, Les Temps Modernes, La Psychanalyse, Scilicet, La Nouvelle Revue de Psychanalyse,* and *Ornicar?* His most celebrated writings included *Psychologie de la colonisation*, first published in 1950 and then reissued in 1964 with *Caliban and Prospéro* prefixed to the title; a Freud monograph of 1968 (published in English as *Freud: The Theory of the Unconscious* (1971), and a collection of essays, *Clefs pour l'imaginaire ou l'autre scène* (1969). Less well known, particularly abroad, were his experiments in personal criticism: *Lettres personelles: Fiction lacanienne d'une analyse* (1951, reprinted as *La Machine* in 1977), *Fictions freudiennes* (1978), and *Nous nous quittons. C'est là ma route. Carnets.* The last work, a selection from his journals written between 1921 and 1958 and published posthumously in 1990, is an extraordinary dream-notebook in which de Gaulle and Lacan compete with each other for the spotlight as patriarchal enforcers of a colonizing psychology.[10] The *Carnets* also include a remarkable passage in which, it could be said, Mannoni discovers the colonial unconscious in a visual impression: a "sharp, clairvoyant eye of the I" that "has behind it a cone of shadow more and more dense, leading to the absolute unconscious of the Subject. And in the absolute unconscious, are the Forces—instincts, tendencies, complexes—that uphold the edifice, make it be, color it."[11] The "Edifice" seems to be located at the base of a pituitary gland of subjectivity (what Bataille would call the pineal eye?).[12] Identifiable as a "cone of shadow," it is remarkably close to a Conradian "heart of darkness," itself something of a colonial cliché alluding to blackness, or the absolute alterity of Europe's projected Other. But what is interesting in Mannoni's rendering is not so much the evocation of darkness, but rather his attention to the psychic color-organ that gives the unconscious its pigmentation—the "Forces" that "uphold the Edifice, make it be, color it." Though Mannoni is quite obviously using the phrase "color it" in the broadest sense to refer to that which endows the Edifice with its defining features, it seems plausible in the context of the *Carnets* to race the term's connotation.

In addition to discovering the racially impacted ontology of the colonial unconscious, Mannoni's intimation of the deeply pathological nature of the colonial encounter prompted a crucial move to autoethnographic elaborations of the colonizer's subjugating consciousness.[13] Scrutinizing the culture of white colons to which he himself belonged, pitilessly revealing the "pauv'con" personality type of which he himself was a prime example, Mannoni made what was for his era a bold and astounding discovery—"le Nègre, c'est la peur que le Blanc a de lui-même" [the Negro is the white man's fear of himself]. Blackness conceived as white self-phobia, or racism diagnosed as a syndrome of colonizer autoimmunization, are ideas that may seem commonplace today, but in the aftermath of World War II, when colonies throughout the Third World who had shed the blood of their conscripts for the cause of European liberation were suddenly wondering why there was no echo of such liberation at home, Mannoni's berating of the colon was nothing short of heretical. His theoretical evolution toward "the decolonization of myself"—even if it assigns "the fact of blackness" the status of incidental cause of internally focused white panic—put the problem of desublimating the colonial unconscious on the agenda for future studies of race and psychoanalysis.

Though Fanon insinuates that Mannoni was trying to get colonial racism off the hook by particularizing it, whereas he wanted to classify it as a universal evil, equal in all places and contexts, Fanon himself, one could argue, was equally committed to creating a taxonomy for the singular perversities of colonial psychopathology. Even in abstracting from the colonial dynamic a globally applicable politics of antiracism, he seems to have shared Mannoni's conviction that Enlightenment liberalism—with its promise of equality and myth of *le semblable*—was an ideological shibboleth designed to shift attention away from the politics of irrevocable difference. In this respect, the racist and the oppressed become strange allies in their common commitment to calling difference by its true name.

If Fanon shared Mannoni's concern to demystify the Enlightenment myth of racial equality, he also seems to have espoused Mannoni's view that the moment of a white man's resolution to exorcise racism coincides with the moment when it is absolutely impossible for a person of color to accept him fraternally; for pretending that the symptom of racism is gone is exactly where the problem of racism may be located. In describing this scenario, Mannoni refers to the *valets de chambre* in an Italian play: at the point where the intermediaries negotiate a successful mediation between their masters, the masters discover the real origin of their quarrel.

Mannoni and Fanon shared a flair for identifying the psychic double-binds of race relations, and it may well be that it was Mannoni's astuteness in psychiatrizing race, coupled with his obtuseness as a political reader of colonial injustice, that "got under Fanon's skin"—literally. Charles Baladier has ascertained that it was Mannoni, ironically enough, who gave Fanon the celebrated title "black skin, white masks." And Jock McCulloch argues quite convincingly that Fanon's imbrications of sociology and psychopathology were disconcertingly close to those of his nemesis:

> At no stage does Fanon really take issue with Mannoni's psychopathology as a descriptive account of the colonial situation; he accepts the prototype of Prospero, while the very title of *Masks* suggests the proximity of his thesis to Mannoni's portrait of Caliban as essentially imitative and dependent.[14]

Seen in this light, Mannoni functions as a paternal imago that must necessarily be killed off in order for Fanon to make his own name. A Martinican, trained in French psychiatry and sent to Algeria as a representative of the French medical corps, Fanon had his own Caliban complex at stake. Conscious of his status as the prototypical "black man in a white mask," Fanon struggled with what he perceived to be a form of alienation unique to An-tilleans—their overidentification with whiteness. Blocked on his own negritude, taking on the white man's phantasmatic othering of the black man, the Antillean subject sees himself in a glass whitely. Unable, to use Hegelian terminology, to "supersede the otherness of itself" and thereby "become equal to itself," unable, that is, to project a black symbolic order, he remains caught in the prise of an aborted mirror stage; his ego shrunken and internally self-abnegating. What this implies is that Fanon needed to jettison Mannoni's "dependent," along with his own conjuration of an emasculated, raceless, Antillean male, in order to make room for that utopian agent of emancipatory consciousness, the virilized Algerian revo-lutionary applauded by Jean-François Lyotard at the height of the Algerian Revolution.[15]

In addition to providing the homosocial Fanon with a "good object" of identification, the figure of the hypermasculated Algerian freedom fighter may have helped resolve Fanon's personal Caliban complex by cre-ating an indirect link between Algerians who had suffered torture at the hands of Senegalese conscripts and Fanon's early recollection of Sene-galese soldiers temporarily stationed in Martinque after World War I. These "blacker" blacks, or second-order "other's others," seem to have formed a bulwark of psychic fear, driving Fanon's compulsion to theorize phobic negritude.

If I find myself indirectly rehabilitating Mannoni's character by imply-ing that it was strategically impugned by an underautoanalyzed Fanon, this interpretive course should be corrected by remembering the transpar-ent ethnocentricity of Mannoni's reading of native character. Fanon devoted an entire chapter of *Black Skin, White Masks*—"The So-Called De-pendency Complex of Colonized Peoples"—to demonstrating the folly of Mannoni's attempt at a Merina version of Freud's *Interpretation of Dreams*. In "the Cook's dream" the subject is chased by an "angry black bull" into a tree. Mannoni interprets the bull as a stand-in for a Senegalese soldier, be-hind whom "lurks the psychologically deeper image of the father."[16] In "Dream of a fourteen-year-old boy, Razafi," a child is "chased by (Sene-galese) soldiers who 'make a noise like galloping horses as they run,' and 'show their rifles in front of them'" (p. 90). Mannoni deciphers this dream as a primal scene; the sound of the horses and the desire to be invisible im-ply, for him, that the child has both "heard and seen" the sexual act. In "Raza's dream," involving a boy who discovers that soldiers have "dis-persed," or "pierced" his homestead, Mannoni interprets the piercing motif as a sign of inadequate paternal protection and of patriarchal menace (p. 93).

Fanon was scathing toward these naively Eurocentric explications: "The enraged black bull is not the phallus. The two black men are not the two father figures—the one standing for the real father, the other for the primal ancestor . . . The rifle of the Senegalese soldier is not a penis but a genuine rifle Lebel 1916."[17] According to Fanon, Mannoni suppressed the real presence of Senegalese military personnel brought in at the time of the Madagascar revolt. Citing the testimony of a Malagasy torture victim who had suffered at the hands of Senegalese conscripts, Fanon mocks the absurdity of ignoring material history for the sake of confirming European projections of a universal unconscious. In Mannoni's hands, ethnographic psychology acts as a foil for the French disciplinary apparatus, a means of disguising political operatives: "Settle down Malagasies, and stay where you belong"—this, in Fanon's view, was Mannoni's endgame.[18]

Whether or not one fully accepts Fanon's thesis that Mannoni's ethnopsychiatry served to neutralize native difference and quell local impulses to revolt, it is clear that Mannoni saw dependency where seasoned ethnographers would infer the logic of the gift. In the famous example of his tennis coach, Mannoni seems deliberately to misassign values of inequality to codes of honor that assume the lender must compensate the borrower for having him in his debt:

> The young Merina who acted as my tennis coach went down with fever. I visited him and as he obviously had malaria I ordered a small supply of quinine to be sent to him. He would never himself have asked me for the medicine, even though he was in great need of it, and he had not been in the habit of seeking favours from me. I used to pay him after every lesson, so that we were quite square each time. Off the courts he would bid me a rather shy good-day whenever we met in the street, but there our relationship ended.
>
> After I had given him the quinine, a change came about. One day, at the end of a lesson, he shyly pointed out to me that his rubber shoes were worn out and that mine, although rather shabby for me, would suit him very well. I handed them over to him readily enough, but two or three days later he came to look for me outside my coaching time and told me, without any trace of embarrassment, that he was in need of cigarette papers. Now at the time cigarette papers could be bought only on the black market, but they were neither scarce nor very dear, and the young Merina earned enough at each lesson to buy several packets of them. There was therefore something incongruous in his request which required looking into. What exactly did it mean?
>
> It meant this: that when I sent him the quinine, my "debtor" did not

see the action simply as a helpful gesture which I had extended towards a sick man. He failed to appreciate its objective and impersonal nature. In fact he did not see it as it really was, but strictly subjectively; he was aware only of the relationship of dependence which was thereby set up between himself and me—not between a tennis-player and his coach, not between a healthy man and an invalid, but between our two selves.

. . . In fact the gifts which the Malagasy first accepts, then asks for, and finally in certain rare cases, even demands, are simply the outward and visible signs of this reassuring relationship of dependence.[19]

If I am tempted to retrieve shards of Mannoni's theory, it is not because I am committed to exculpating him from charges that he reversed the terms of colonial dependency (taking the result of colonial brutality and economic imperialism for the cause), but rather, because I think that in trying to map psychic dependency, he was onto something that he never properly worked out, or, alternatively, that he worked out in a displaced fashion in the context of his psychoanalytic theorization of fetishistic disavowal *(Verleugnung)*. Mannoni may have been extremely myopic in his failure to appreciate fully the political, material, and historical causes of colonial injustice, but he just might have grasped the hallucinatory structure of belied disbelief crucial to the *colon's* ability to wield power in a culture not his own. Pursuing the hypothesis that Mannoni the theorist of colonial dependency and Mannoni the theorist of fetishism are not as separate as all that, I would like to suggest that his famous "Je sais bien, mais quand même" [I know, but . . .]—the phrase by which the fetishist imparts credibility and value to what he knows to be referential false coin—articulates a logic of *dénégation* characteristic of the psychotic aspect of colonial psychology.

To better conceptualize the torsions of this logic, we are perhaps well advised to go back, as Hegel did in *The Phenomenology of Spirit*, to Mme. de Cornuel's witticism: "Il n'y a point de héros pour son valet." "No man is a hero to his valet," Hegel wrote in the chapter "Morality," not, he maintained, "because the man is not a hero, but because the valet—is a valet, whose dealings are with the man, not as a hero, but as one who eats, drinks, and wears clothes, in general, with his individual wants and fancies."[20] The discernible advantage that the underdog obtains almost as an accident of his position as an objectified, negative consciousness carries over into the famous Hegelian dialectic between lord and bondsman:

> We thus achieve an essentially unbalanced relationship in which the bondsman altogether gives up his being-for-self in favour of the lord. The lord uses him as an instrument to master the thing for his own (the lord's) purposes, and not for the bondsman's, and the bondsman acquiesces in the situation and becomes in fact part and parcel of the total objective situa-

tion. This means, however, that the lord cannot get the reciprocal recognition that his self-consciousness demands from a consciousness so degraded and distorted. What the lord sees in the bondsman, or what the bondsman sees in the lord, is not what either sees in himself.

The lord therefore paradoxically depends for his lordship on the bondsman's self-consciousness, and entirely fails of the fully realized independence of status which his self-consciousness demands. . . .

The bondsman in his boundless quaking respect for the lord becomes shaken out of his narrow self-identifications and self-interest and rises to the absolute negativity, the disinterested all-embracingness of true self-consciousness. He becomes the ideal which he contemplates in his lord.

The bondsman has the further advantage that in working on the object he as it were preserves his labour, makes the outward thing his own and puts himself into it, whereas the lord's dealings with the object end in vanishing enjoyments. The bondsman overcomes the otherness and mere existence of material thinghood more thoroughly than the lord, and so achieves a more genuine self-consciousness.[21]

Hegel's consciousness-mastering bondsman, at least in this famous passage of *The Phenomenology of the Spirit,* qualifies as the ancestor of Fanon's black revolutionary, exchanging centuries of reification and debased use-value for advance purchase on the ideal. "Mais quand même . . . " Is this liberatory redistribution of psychic servitude magical thinking? A ruse of fetish logic? Let us go back to the valet and the hero, glossed by Diderot in his didactic narrative *Jacques le fataliste.* In this parable about a man who is no longer master of his own house, the insubordinate valet, on whom the master depends and upon whose whims the master's fate rests, is decreed, by fiat to "be" the subaltern, despite the performative contradiction of his acts. *Dénégation*—the process by which denial is denied—is the machine by which the master upholds the fiction of mastery, the thread on which hangs his charade of governance. Like the fetishist who agrees to suspend disbelief in taking the surrogate phallus to be his true and honorable object of desire, so the valet agrees to abide by the master's law.

The master's charade in Diderot's *sôtie* may be keyed to the buffoonesque performance of the colonial civil servant, adhering to a barely credible script of French national character and nation-ness on a foreign stage, what Mannoni would call "another scene." The foundational illegitimacy of the colonizer's presence, the political crime of usurpation lying submerged and disavowed at the core of the colonial mandate, is profoundly masked by the fetish of state power, embodied in the pageantry of official masquerade. But in order for the masquerade to accomplish itself, it needs to extract a sign of recognition from the native population. Who then is dependent on whom? If the subject people fails to perform "as if" the colonizer were legitimately empowered, if it fails to honor the heraldry

by which a foreign power makes its investments visible, then the whole edifice of the colonial apparatus risks collapse. In the reciprocal game of dependency, in which the colonizer must continually deny his implication in
the paradoxes of *herrschaft* and *knechtscaft,* colonial encounters are both
enabled and threatened by the psychic coil of denegation. "I know I have
no business being here, but all the same . . . "/"I know you have no business
being here, but all the same . . . " Colonial bureaucracy exists by virtue of a
tenuous contract, kept in place by a fetish logic of psychic feints and redi-
rected negatives.

In this context, a developed narrative of the vagaries of colonial *Verleugnung* would lead us by a chain of associations beyond the simple assassination of character (Fanon-Mannoni), to what might be framed as
"assassins without character" (the colon or man without qualities who
commits what Freud would call "a crime from a sense of guilt"). Some
twenty years before, the celebrated French writer Jean Paulhan, son of the
philosopher Frédéric Paulhan, who himself authored a book on character
in the 1890s, began his career in Madagascar, as Mannoni would some
twenty years later, as a member of the French civil service.[22] Though some
of his time was apparently spent gold prospecting, he devoted his principal
energies to teaching and research. Paulhan studied Malagasy language and
did so brilliantly on his exams that he was rewarded with a teaching post at
the Ecole des Langues Orientales. But even as he was accumulating academic honors, he garnered the opprobrium of his French colleagues for
what they deemed to be his excessive identification with Malgache life and
custom. Going increasingly native, taking a Lotiesque pride in passing as
Malgache in native dress, Paulhan retreated from the French expatriate
community ("une bourgeoisie pourrie") into the fold of life with a Hova
family. In his pedagogy, he refused to adhere to the orthodox academic program, encouraging students to investigate their own language and culture
and even preparing courses on psychology to be conducted in Malgache.
Shortly after his arrival in 1908, Paulhan undertook an intensive study
of Malagasy proverbs, called *hain-teny* or "dispute resolving sayings," that
became the basis of a (never completed) thesis. What was distinctive about
the proverbs was the way in which they functioned performatively to enable oppositional propositions to be suspended together in contradiction.
If they sound not unlike Mannoni's psychoanalytic construal of disavowal,
it is perhaps no accident. Certainly in working out the rhetoricity of this *science des mots,* Paulhan seems to have been fascinated by the prospect of a
"primitive" psychoanalysis, inspired at least in part by the concept of primitive mentalities developed by his mentor Lucien Levy-Bruhl.

A fully nuanced account of Paulhan's important place as a forerunner of decolonization psychology in Madagascar would ideally entail close readings of his thesis on the *hain-teny*. For my purposes here, it will suffice to point out that this material provides a precursory version of Paulhan's later work on the logic of locutions—the commonplaces and received ideas that would become the targets of terrorist action in his rhetorical treatise *La Fleur de Tarbes*—even as it reveals a larger puzzle that would situate these Merina proverbs in relation to Octave Mannoni's future theories of colonial disavowal.[23] Like Paulhan, Mannoni would trace the origin of his work to Malagasy proverbs. He used a Merina proverb as an opening epigraph to *Prospero and Caliban* ("Tsihy be lambanana ny ambanilanitra" [Men form one great mat]),[24] and in a later preface to that work, he confessed that it was a *hain-teny* that precipitated his insight into the disciplinary fallacies of ethnographic epistemology:

> For years I have been interested in everything I could find out about that country and its inhabitants, but for a long time I deliberately confined myself to ethnographical rather than psychological studies. However I realized, almost in spite of myself, that there was a background of more disturbing psychological problems behind the ethnographical ones. I found myself taking part either in imagination or in reality in a kind of community life that was quite new to me, and realized with surprise that my own essence was being gradually altered. If for instance I took part in ceremonies concerning the cult of the dead I tried to do it in the spirit of a good ethnographer with questionnaires, photographs, etc.; but I discovered that this cult in its Malagasy form had an equal significance for me, and one which I could not ignore, surround it as I might with the ethnographical bric-a-brac that I was collecting. *I seemed to have unearthed that single root, from which, according to a Malagasy proverb, the branches of the human race divide off like the shoots on a pumpkin plant.* At the same time, driven like everyone else by my own private devil, I carried out various strictly personal experiments which led me to further discoveries, and during my leave in Paris after the end of the war I began a training analysis in the hope of clarifying my ideas.[25]

In this intriguing passage, the "strands of the human mat," rooted in a common race, and intertwined with the psychoanalytic strands of the unconscious, point to a commitment that Mannoni shared with Paulhan, namely, "to penetrate the obscure and imprecise domain of interracial psychology" and to "Get involved in a truly Franco-Malagasy life."[26] And like Paulhan, he would deploy non-ethnographic genres (diaries, dream-cipher, poetry, psychofictions) to translate the suppressed memory of criminality embedded within colonial consciousness. Indeed, Madagascar seems to have functioned as a crime scene for both writers, and as such, a site of particular significance in the annals of prepostcolonial theory.[27]

Though Mannoni may only have committed a symbolic crime—the assassination of native character via dependency theory—Paulhan's sudden and mysterious exit from Madagascar in 1910, together with assorted rumors that surfaced in the press alleging his complicity in a murder, call for a more literal order of interpretation. Many have surmised that he was hustled out of the country to escape prosecution. In his little-known Malagasy novel, *Aytré qui perd l'habitude,* the crime of murder is disclosed without being openly avowed.[28] Published in 1921, the novel is something of a curiosity, an *oeuvre de jeunesse* written in the prose of deconstruction, yet full of semiveiled autobiographical allusions to real people and historical contexts. Indeed, a recent issue of the *Cahiers Jean Paulhan* devoted to his engagement with Madagascar explicitly points to the homophonic resemblance between Aytré and Autret, the latter being the name of an adjutant with a violent, strange temperament who befriended and rivaled Paulhan as they prepared their examinations together in Madagascar.[29]

The narrative follows the aleatory movement of the *dérive,* even as it observes the convention of a story within a story. As the reflexes of the European mental habitus are progressively estranged, a repetition of the habitual together with an accumulation of apparently gratuitous details, aggravates the suspenseful atmosphere of criminality. Traces, stains, enigmatic blots—in short, signs comprising the familiar arsenal of a deferred detection of identity, alternate in the text with allusions to eruptions of native unrest.[30] As in Octave Mannoni's dream notebooks, historical reality is treated as an inexplicable intrusion into the "real" topographies of a racial unconscious.

Maurice Blanchot's brilliant interpretation of Paulhan's text ("Le paradoxe d'Aytré"), focuses tellingly on how the writing itself filters "the event" through narrative folds of the unconscious:

> It sometimes happens to a man that he feels an emptiness in himself, a defect, a lack of something decisive, whose absence becomes, little by little, unbearable. In a short story, "Aytré Who loses the Habit," Jean Paulhan tells the tale of a soldier to whom this happens. Aytré is a sergeant and, with an adjutant who tells the story of the expedition, he leads a column of 300 Senegalese, alongside men of the Fourth Colonial, across Madagascar. Through the adjutant's laziness, Aytré is the one to whom the care of keeping the log of the journey falls. There is nothing extraordinary in this log: we arrive, we leave; chickens cost seven sous; we stock up on medicine; our wives receive magazines, etc. As the adjutant says, that smells of drudgery. But, starting from a certain day, after the arrival at Ambositra, the writing changes, slightly no doubt, in appearance, but, on careful reading, in a surprising and overwhelming way. The explanations rendered become longer. Aytré begins to go into his ideas on colonization; he describes the women's hairstyles, their locks joined together on each side of their ears like a snail;

he speaks of strange landscapes; he goes on to the character of the Malgaches; and so on. In short, the log is useless. What has happened? Aytré has obviously lost the habit. It is as if the most natural things had suddenly begun to surprise him, as if a lack had been brought about in him that he sought to answer by unusual moves, an agitation of thoughts, words, images. And the adjutant is all the more ready to realize that he recognizes in his own uneasiness the trace of a similar predicament. The key to the enigma is easy to grasp. In Ambositra, Aytré met a Mme. Chalinargues, whom he had known some months earlier and whom jealousy pushes him to kill; as for the adjutant, he prepares to keep a sum of money that the same person had handed over to him for her family. In both cases, for both men, something has begun to come undone; the events proceeding from the self have diminished in number: hair done up, judgments on colonization, strange landscapes, all these literary developments signify the same lack; because of it, now beings, behavior, even words can appear only in their insufficiency.

From this little story, it does not follow that literature must necessarily begin with a crime or, failing that, with flight. But that it does imply a caving in, a kind of initial catastrophe, and the very emptiness that anxiety and care measure; yes, we can be tempted to believe that. But let us note that this catastrophe does not fall only on the world, the objects one handles, the things one sees; it extends also to language. That is the paradox of Aytré. In truth, it is easy, or something like easy, to imagine that Aytré, behind the act to which he was driven, found himself lacking and began to translate this lack by an excess of language that would try to fill it. Until then, he was enough for himself; now he is no longer enough, and he speaks to reestablish, by words and by a call to others, the adequacy whose disappearance he feels.[31]

Blanchot deftly suppresses the reality of the crime and focuses instead on the nature of alibi in describing how an "excess of language," construed as a kind of ontic garrulousness, is generated in the wake of an originary semantic catastrophism. Lack, devirilization, and the compensatory function of language—Aytré's central themes according to Blanchot—are comparably worked through in Mannoni's journals. In a dream that Mannoni wrote out in English and committed to his *Carnets*, this paralysis of being is the central motif: the subject falls into mud and is too weak to counter the gravitational force-field. Appeals for help to a native woman who ignores him exacerbate the drama of emasculation. A man comes to his rescue, but the subject's pride is shattered anew when he is hit by a psychic battering ram; a "color bar" (literal sign of the racial barrier conditioning the status quo in the colonies) that crashes through layers of obtuse colonial consciousness to induce a crippling recognition of racist guilt.[32]

Like Paulhan in *Aytré*, Mannoni would encrypt a colonial crime within an impenetrable, psychoanalytic fiction. This roman à clef, entitled *Lettres personelles*, features a colonial civil servant stationed in a colony resembling

Madagascar, who writes letters incriminating the French colonial bureaucratic apparatus to a Kafkaesque "Director" whose character is clearly modeled on that of Lacan. *Lettres personelles* is framed by a fictive preface,
written by a certain "Ph.," a "friend" of the analysand who, in a tone full of
innuendo, drops clues as to how to read the text. Ph. claims to have met a
certain "Octave" just after his return to Paris from a colonial outpost. He
complains of the drudgery of colonial civil service; psychologically un-
moored, he decides to enter analysis. "His analyst was someone who at the
time did not have the grand renown that he has since attained," the narrator informs us.[33] Ph. also mentions that Octave is fixated on a line from
Corneille: "Je suis maître de moi comme de l'univers" [I am master of myself as of the universe].[34] Is this code for a "mastery" complex representing
the flip side of dependency theory? Or, if we take the phrase as a *dénégation*,
so that it means "I'm as much in control of myself as of a runaway train," is
it a delusion of grandeur that turns, on a dime, into dependency on a Bigger
Other? Though Ph. worries that Octave's stories of colonial life will bore his
readers, Octave reassures him that they contain an important edification,
namely, that "we are all colonized."[35] It is as if the novel proleptically an-
nounces Mannoni's autocritique, entitled "The Decolonization of Myself,"
published in 1966 in the British journal *Race* in the aftermath of the Fanon
affair.[36]

In a series of "personal letters" addressed to "Monsieur le Directeur," a
colonial employee copes with an artificial-intelligence machine recently
introduced to improve efficiency in the civil service's bureaucracy. Anticipating the age of cyber, Mannoni invents a Lacanian computer, part
Kafkaesque apparatus (which metes out justice in the penal colony by inscribing the sentences of the guilty on their backs), part deus ex machina of
classical drama, and part Freudian thing, exercising power through a manipulative combination of seduction and threatened abandonment. Responding to the director's invitation to write to him personally, as an
antidote to the impersonality of the Machine, the civil servant becomes a
kind of valet, servicing the Big Daddy of ideological interpellation.

In the colony's *Café Colonial* a familiar cast of sorry characters assem-
bles. One stands out; he is described as a "simian Socrates," a blend of
Balzac's Vautrin and Gide's Proteus. Venaisson, as he is called, is a gay outlaw who has made good in the colonies; canny, corrupt, and charismatic; a
supreme *eiron* with an authoritarian will. "My God," he shouts, at the café
one day. "As if it suffices to screw a native to be called a pederast! But I who
speak to you, I've screwed more than a hundred, and look at me, am I a pederast?"[37] Perplexed at the frankness of the declaration, the narrator floun-
ders: "I had the confused, irksome feeling that Venaisson, in speaking like

this, had just put something very important into question, but I didn't know what," he confides to the director, concluding that it seemed to have some relation to the authority of the Machine. The problem, he reasons on further reflection, is one of an errant negation. What made Venaisson say that he wasn't a pederast?[38] What to do about his stupefying avowal, which preempts an impartial judgment on the part of his listeners? Like a syllogism contradicting itself from within; the problem of Venaisson's disavowed avowal must somehow be neutralized. It is the Machine that must decide his case; the Machine kills him off and gradually takes over the narrative, usurping the patriarchal position formerly occupied by Venaisson.

The novel ends with the triumph of the colonial apparatus, and in trying to sift through its layered subtexts, I find myself crudely aligning Venaisson's "outing" of himself with Mannoni's "outing" of a colonial unconscious, itself visible as a decolonizing *conscience*. "The *Verleugnung* preserves its irrational character, but everything takes place in broad daylight," Mannoni would write in "Je sais bien, mais quand même."[39] This fetishistic ratiocination is the vector in his work where race and psychoanalysis conjoin. In Mannoni's revelation of the mystificatory logic by which colonialism masks its psychic servitude, Mannoni brought the scandal of white unhappy consciousness, however inadvertently, to public view.

Mannoni's revelation of a racial cause at the heart of the psychoanalytic venture becomes more fully apparent when we go back to his signal case history in the "Je sais bien" essay. Here, telephony and telepathy are evoked to describe pathological dependencies embedded in transference relations. The case begins with a telephonic error, committed by Mannoni's receptionist, who, mishearing the name of the caller, leads Mannoni to believe that the message is from a black poet whose social call Mannoni is expecting. Mannoni instructs the receptionist to invite his friend over right away for an aperitif. But when the bell rings, the receptionist informs him: "It is not a black man, it is one of Monsieur's patients."[40] Mannoni says nothing of the racial switch of the subject who comes to visit; he concentrates instead on the analysand's look of satisfaction, and his strange confession: "Je savais bien que c'était de la blague, l'apéritif, mais quand même, je suis rudement content" [I knew of course that the aperitif was a joke, but I was extremely pleased nonetheless] (p. 21). To his surprise, Mannoni finds his own satisfaction matches that of his patient; perhaps because he has so perfectly produced an example of Mannonian fetish grammar with his, "Je sais bien, mais . . . " Thinking the incident over later, however, Mannoni remembers Freud's paper on telepathy in which he unearths the occult aspects of mental life, discovering that "desire acts at a distance on conscious material" (p. 22). For Mannoni, this translates directly into the transference situation at hand, such that the patient, "in reading his mind," knows at some level that Mannoni *did invite him;* responding to his desire to continue the analytic session.

In this "read my desire" parable about transferential love, the black poet is possibly identifiable as the residue of an earlier example used by Mannoni in the same essay, where he sets up a parallel between the mystificatory credulity surrounding the Hopi Katcina dolls and the transgressive force of superstition or magical thinking in the so-called science of psychology. Pursuing this direction further, it would appear that the black poet whose perpetually postponed visit is whited out, so to speak, by the arrival of an unconsciously desired white patient, functions as a distant echo of Mannoni's earlier work on the Caliban typology. The racially charged dependency complex, carried into this 1960s essay on the heels of a suppressed visitor, thus comes back as a remainder of a suppressed colonial unconscious, now seen to be haunting white psychoanalysis's elaboration of a transference/countertransference exegesis. If Mannoni's oeuvre seems worth returning to in the context of reflections on the unreconstructed history of colonial racism within the history of psychoanalysis (and here I am also thinking about the undercritiqued example of Joan Riviere's prototypical "masquerading woman," a Southern propagandist whose overriding fantasy consists of being "raped by a Negro"), it is because his Caliban, like Fanon's, is volatile; capable of resurging at unexpected moments to disturb racially neutral psychoanalytic paradigms.

In addition to race-ing psychoanalysis via the magical thinking of fetishism, Mannoni also seems to have developed a kind of reparations theory to be applied to colonial damages. In studying the Malagasy cult of the dead (which according to some anthropologists he completely misinterpreted), Mannoni was interested in applying Melanie Klein's notion of the internalization of the "good object"; itself linked to the need to make reparations, appease, and thus remain on good terms.[41] Part of what lies behind this focus on repair may stem from Mannoni's own deep-seated desire to make amends for colonial wrongs, the most heinous in his own case being his elaboration of a dependency complex in the midst of a major native uprising!

If a crucial meaning of *Verleugnung* is, as Pontalis defined it, "the denial of reality," it is perhaps no accident that Mannoni made this concept the centerpiece of his work on fetishism. *Verleugnung* became the receptacle for Mannoni's problem with the real, which Fanon had discerned from the start in Mannoni's specious interpretations of Malagasy dreams.[42] Restoring the status of the real to the psychohistory of colonial repression, Fanon would use negation to great strategic effect when he dismantled the psychology of dependency. As a dividend, he symbolically pasted his signature over Mannoni's as the founding father of heroic efforts to "decolonize myself."

One final note: I would conjecture that part of Mannoni's understanding of psychic servitude, crucial to his flawed construction of native dependency, derives from his own experience of master/slave (or to put it more honestly and crudely, "step and fetch it"), while in analysis with Lacan. Consider the following dreams as evidence:

> I have my hair cut and come back to pay. I ask the price of Lacan, who tells me: 160 francs. . . .
> I have the money on me, which surprises me a little. I return to Lacan's place, cross through the house where he has, as a retreat in the garden, his study. A maid tells me he is alone but closes the doors with such precaution that I tell myself: "He must have a woman in there." Lacan appears, he has on a green hat with a ribbon behind, of loud, doubtful taste. I give him the money, a bill falls, I pick it up and give it to him again.[43]

> A dream of a certain "Dr. Fish" to whom I present a serpent. The doctor tells me "to watch out among the 'Colons'" (this is the scientific name—in the dream—of these snakes), it is a poisonous species. . . . I walk *viciously* (in Eng.) on its tail. It doesn't react.[44]

As is so clearly suggested, this "Big Fish," Dr. Lacan, takes obvious pleasure in letting his worm twist on the hook; he both warns the patient about the bite he most surely will receive from the *colons,* but at the same time remains impassive as all efforts to extirpate the evil by battling the colonial serpent inevitably fail. On the basis of dreams such as these, it seems plausible to surmise that dependency theory (including dimensions of its afterlife in neocolonial political economies), contains an obscured origin in the psychic servitude experienced by a colonial civil servant at the hands of his analyst. Cast as the director of a colonial penal colony, Lacan becomes the character responsible for colonizing the mind, while his valet, Octave Mannoni, strives, however pitiably, to become the master of his own house by projecting a dependent characterology onto the native subjects of Madagascar.

METROPOLITAN

MASQUERADES

He takes great pride in his sexuality only in so far as it is a means of appropriating the Other—and this dream other is abolished as such, it is consumed and destroyed: only the Sultan in *The Arabian Nights* has the power to cut off each mistress's head when dawn has come to take her from his couch.

SIMONE DE BEAUVOIR, The Second Sex

It is by writing, from and toward women, and by taking up the challenge of speech which has been governed by the phallus, that women will confirm women in a place other than that which is reserved in and by the symbolic, that is, in a place other than silence. Women should break out of the snare of silence. They shouldn't be conned into accepting a domain which is the margin or the harem.

HÉLÈNE CIXOUS, "The Laugh of the Medusa"

Women haven't had eyes for themselves. They haven't gone exploring in their house. Their sex still frightens them. Their bodies, which they haven't dared enjoy, have been colonized. Woman is disgusted by woman and fears her.

HÉLÈNE CIXOUS, The Newly Born Woman

5 HAREM

SCOPIC REGIMES OF
POWER / PHALLIC LAW

In attempting to interpret Western projections of an "other" eroticism in French colonial fiction between 1870 and 1935, one becomes increasingly aware of the uneasy relationship between postcolonial theory and feminist psychoanalysis. Western feminists from Simone de Beauvoir and Hélène Cixous, to Gayle Rubin, Judith Williamson, and Sandra Lee Bartky have drawn on the language of apartheid, racism, and colonization to dramatize the world-historical situation of women.[1] Economically and socially "enslaved," sexually conquered as "Other," placed under the dominion of a despotic superphallus identified with the Orientalist sultan, their bodies "trafficked," their voices quelled by the "silence of the harem," feminist critics have qualified their subordination to a phallic regime through the language of colonialism.

There are of course some obvious problems that come with this appropriation of Third World discourse for First World universalizing ends.[2] Gayatri Chakravorty Spivak identified many of them years ago in her important piece "French Feminism in an International Frame," pointing out, for example, that what may seem to be an unequivocal gain for women's rights (the outlawing, say, of clitoridectomy) may have adverse effects in a global context, particularly in poorer societies where women who refuse traditional customs may find themselves disinherited, left with neither livelihood nor family.[3]

Spivak alerts us to the "misfiring" of theoretical signifiers in an internationalist context, particularly when those terms blind the reader to cultural and class difference even as they open up to view the history of phallocentric injustice. When, as seen above, Cixous uses the term *harem* as a pejorative expression signaling the censorship of a nonphallogocentric language of female desire, the effect is stirring but blatantly Eurocentric. A harem, strictly speaking, is a gyneceum, a place where women gather and speak to each other, and not necessarily a site of feminine aphasia. Harems can protect and nurture women as well as imprison them; as such they are ambivalent spaces that have always fascinated Western readers.

This all seems obvious now, as does the idea that a culturally atopical, dehistoricized use of the term *colonization* risks weakening or trivializing the term itself. In this regard, V. Y. Mudimbe's revisionist epistemological coordinates of colonial organization are crucial, specifying as they do "the domination of physical space, the reformation of *natives'* minds, and the integration of local economic histories into the Western perspective."[4] Without some memory of where the discursive understanding of colonialism comes from, without some recollection of postwar Marxist debate over decolonization, dependency theory, and economic imperialism, we come dangerously close to papering over the specific conditions of the colonial legacy that gave them their moral significance. These are some of the concerns behind my own attempt to critique the French colonial harem genre from a psychoanalytic, feminist, and postcolonial perspective. While I do not pretend to have escaped in my own theoretical framings some of the very methodological pitfalls that I have outlined here, I hope at the very least to have introduced a measure of critical self-consciousness into the discussion of postcolonial interpretation.

In 1979 Alain Grosrichard published a theoretical account of the seraglio in classical French literature and political thought. Exploring the place of psychosexual phantasms in the Western myth of Oriental despotism (from Racine and Montesquieu to Diderot and Rousseau), his *Structure du sérail: La fiction du despotisme asiatique dans l'Occident classique* is arguably a Lacanian account of the phallus in Oriental costume. Grosrichard discerns a sultan who, like the phallus, incarnates the name of the Father and the body of the Law; takes into himself the monstrous alterity of the Other (phallic power, like the women of the harem, always comes from "elsewhere"); preserves for himself alone the right to unchecked access to *jouissance* (*haram*, "the sacred"); is never fully present (possessed by his possessions, exercising his power through surveillance and scopic mastery); and is implicated in a symbolic order predicated on the signs of castration (the eunuchs). The harem women in this scheme are, according to Grosrichard's reading of seventeenth-century voyage accounts—Baudier, Ricaut, Tavernier, Tournefort—infinite in number, interchangeable in status, and "avid for the phallus in any shape or form."[5] While he ends the book with the image of the despot basking in the radiance of his power, yet over-shadowed by the harem (whose matriarchal concentricity allows for the centrality of the phallus to be kept in place), Grosrichard never really takes his analysis into the harem. As a result, the phallic absolutism of the sultan is never truly put into question; it stands as a monumental fixture of Orien-talist fantasy, allowing the seraglio structure to signify. Though I think one would be hard-pressed to dispense with the phallic paradigm in dealing with the harem, it may be less difficult than Grosrichard's book allows to re-orient the interpretive focus, emphasizing how feminocentrism and the sapphic phantasm inherent in the harem genre leads to a questioning of the phallus in psychoanalysis itself.

While one can say that psychoanalysis shared with colonial ideology the desire to "conquer dark continents" and to conceive the other by con-ceiving otherwise ("le pouvoir de *concevoir autre*"), it also leaned, in order to broaden its conceptual lexicon, on colonial fantasies of *Exote-isme,* a term extrapolated from Victor Segalen's 1908 definition of the *Exote* as a seeker of exogamous desires, rarified debauchery, parasensorial, extraterrestrial loves, outsider eroticisms, psychogeographical *bovarysme,* voluptuous, aes-theticized panoplies of difference and of the *Pseudo-Exote* as sham explorer, or impressionist tourist.[6] In this respect, the exoticist/colonial text, by in-advertently pointing to forms of cultural desire that remain underarticu-lated within psychoanalysis, prompts a rethinking of psychoanalysis itself, revised and adjusted through a cultural lens.

Despite the heterogeneous nature of colonial fiction's authorship and readership, and despite the disparate erotologies and political motivations of its texts, one finds common threads of a colonial unconscious traceable to stories of adventure and romance encountered in the bourgeois nursery: *Mille et une nuits, Bug-Jargal* (Victor Hugo's revolutionary tale of the "royal slave"), Alphonse Daudet's *Tartarin de Tarascon,* and many lesser known works.[7] It is tempting to surmise that the archaic hold that these books placed on the preoedipal Imaginary enabled an originary colonial desire to be carried over into a yearning for colonial mastery. Colonial literature in this sense throws into sharp relief the extent to which a fantasy of colonial mastery structures the competition for phallic domination in any form of eroticism.

Though the harem genre has always been identified with a phallocen-tric paradigm, it has also been the haven of sapphic fantasies, themselves rooted in the dream of an alternative, feminocentric libidinal economy. In colonial fiction sapphism is often so prevalent that one might begin to interpret it in terms of a "haremization effect" that challenges the time-honored interpolation of penis-envy at the heart of the sultan/seraglio model. In the harem, new forms of love, *exote-ic* eroticisms incubate and multiply. The representation of this female socius, sequestered and colonized, but capable of sheltering its secrets nonetheless, invites analysis through the experimental conjoining of postcolonial and feminist theory. In this chapter I will examine, on the one hand, how the sexual fantasies codified in harem texts may be used to construe an antiphallic, gynarchic model of "what a woman wants," and on the other, how the erotics of claustration shape the representation of the French enclosure and domination of North Africa.

In *Totem and Taboo* Freud evoked a primal horde dominated by a patriarch who had secured for himself exclusive property rights over all the women in the socius. Though the story proceeds with disgruntled younger men banding together, committing parricide, and sharing the women among themselves, it is interesting to note that what Freud placed at the psychic origin of civilization was nothing other than a harem. The old man and his seraglio, according to Freud's mythic scenario, functioned as a spur to the world-historical enactment of the Oedipal drama. In the beginning, was a harem . . .

Perhaps more than any other Orientalist construction, the harem survived successive literary and pictorial changes of fashion, bridging broad gaps between nineteenth-century realism, neoprimitivism, and psychoanalysis. Though French surrealism and avant-garde modernism from Apollinaire to Michel Leiris privileged black African and Oceanic cultures over the Maghreb (no doubt because North Africa was already dated, worn thin by Gidean naturism, no longer "primitive" enough), it nevertheless preserved the harem in residual, abstracted form in the pictures of Picasso, Matisse, Duchamp, and Le Corbusier. Picasso painted a fauvist *Harem* in 1906 in which a naked eunuch lies sprawled in a bare room in front of several anguished-looking nudes. Pressed flatly into the walls, their bodies fused with the minimalist interior, the occupants of this gyneceum appear suctioned into a vaginal crevice. Picasso returned to the theme in the fifties and seventies with erotic parodies of Ingres *(Le Bain turc)*, Delacroix *(Femmes d'Alger)*, and Degas *(Degas dans la Maison Tellier)*.[8] Consistently, the old man in the harem, surrogate of the painter himself, is identifiable as a Peeping Tom in old-fashioned European attire, while the women, entwined and exotically costumed, compete in showing this percipient intruder *la chose*. In the rudest terms, the harem is to the architectural anatomy what the female sex is to the woman's body; both signify in unison, spatial zones of pleasure that have no ultimate indicative object.

In its reiterated domestic plan and gendered distribution of spatial drives, the harem has been for centuries easily recognizable as a distinctive *locus sexualis*. A synonym for *transgression* and *taboo* (*bent el haram* means "daughter of sin," "prostitute," and Littré's figurative definition for the French *harem* was "maison de débauche"), the early Arabic word *harîm*, as Malek Chebel points out in *L'Esprit de sérail*, refers to the gyneceum, to the "sexualization of interior space," and to the restriction of male access to the community of women. In contradistinction to the *salem'lik*, or seraglio (broadly, the sultan's palace, a versatile place designating the threshold where male visitors are welcomed as well as the lodgings of the pasha's personal female museum), the full term *harem-'alik*, according to Chebel, refers more specifically to gendered zones of interdiction within intimate dwelling spaces.[9] Similar to the veil (*hidjâb*, "curtain," "that which hides"), a shield or carapace ensuring that a layer of domestic interiority remains stuck on or wrapped around the female body even when it is exposed to public view, the harem, like the metaphorical skin of a building, is a kind of inside on the outside, a concentrate of interiorized interiority, a miniaturized version of the Casbah self-enclosed and circumscribed within the boundaries of the colonial city.

Blurring distinctions between inside (psychic) and outside (the body, the social realm), the harem loomed large in Europe's phantasms as an archaic erotic idea—one man to many women, unchecked sexual domination over totally submissive members of the weaker sex, proliferating penis-envy in a world of women libidinally organized around the sultan. In full-dress pictures of the harem at the beginning of the nineteenth century (Delacroix, Ingres, Gérôme, Alma-Tadema), it was as if the unconscious had secreted itself into spatial and material form. Like its prototypical counterpart, the Parisian *maison close,* the harem was and continues to be a haunting occidental figure of pure *jouissance* made into architecture.

Loti's early novella *Les Trois dames de la Kasbah* emblematizes the sexual spatiality of the harem text. A group of Breton sailors brought to port in Algiers loses its way in the Casbah after a night of drinking and carousing. As they turn in circles, desperate for a place to rest, they hear "Pst, pst!" from behind a bolted door. Three cloistered women lure them into their sanctuary. The conceit of the story revolves around the revelation that a space of chastity, heavily guarded and removed from all contact with the outside world, turns out to be a place of prostitution. The sailors contract syphilis from the women, and after their return to France we learn that "they brought back the Arab contagion with them; their firstborns came into the world covered in sores that were shameful to behold."[10]

Despite the outlines of its plot, *Les Trois dames* is not so much a story about the dangers of harem sexuality as an exploration of the spatial sensation of claustration. Barriers to access are concentrically enumerated: The harem is ensconced within walls and labyrinthine streets of the Casbah, a colonnade protects the courtyard, the courtyard frames a house itself encased in a complex network of iron bars and grills. The only apertures consist of tiny peepholes, "little openings disguised in the thickness of the walls." The women imprisoned within are "plunged in darkness," their eyes "drowned" and their minds fogged over in a cloud of kief. These protracted descriptions of the harem as a multilayered veiled space impart narrative and topological density to the Lacanian assertion that "the phallus can play its role only when veiled."[11] In Lacanian terms, then, Loti's *trois dames,* veiled and encased within multiple protective walls, masquerade as the phallus.[12]

Guy de Maupassant's libertine play *A la Feuille de Rose, maison turque* (written while he was employed at the Ministère de la Marine, financially supported by Flaubert, and performed in a Parisian atelier in 1875 before a select audience including Zola, Edmond de Goncourt, Turgenev, and the disciples of Medan), also illustrates how the harem conceit, as used in soft porn, reinforces the powers of the phallic veil. Though little more than a European brothel in ethnic dress, the harem "swells" the phallic order by suggesting a *locus sexualis* that has no equivalent in Western expression. When the wife of M. Beauflanquer, mayor of "Conville," strays into the harem by mistake, Maupassant plays on the bourgeois confusion between the strangeness of sex and the culturally foreign. "I've heard a great deal about the interior of harems, but I've never had the occasion to visit one," Mme Beauflanquer says to one of the prostitutes. "Ah! she replies, it is the first time that you have ever entered a house."[13] Capitalizing on the subversive affinities between bourgeois home, *maison close,* and harem, Maupassant sustains this coding of eroticism through the device of cross-cultural misreading:

RAPHAELE	(to Mme Beauflanquer): Have you done all the positions?
MME B	No, M. Beauflanquer never changed them.
R	Who is this Beauflanquer? I don't know that pimp.
MME B	Pimp. That must be a Turkish title.
FATMA	Are you good at "rose petal"?
MME B	"Rose petal." *(Aside)* Ah yes, the confiture of Turkey. *(Looks up.)* I've never eaten it. *(The women start laughing.)*
FATMA	She doesn't know rose petal! What then does she do?[14]

Here the veil connotes a secret feminine eroticism (what *is* "rose petal"?) enticingly promised to the European traveler. The cultural supplement of the harem, with its strange dialect, Turkish costume, and décor, acts as an incentive to masculine conquest (we have only to think of Flaubert's braggadocio in recounting his exploits with the courtesan Kuchek-hanem to appreciate the extent to which this psychology was acted out).

It mattered little that actual harems rarely coincided with European male fantasies about them. As Lucie Delarue-Mardrus stated emphatically in her memoir *El Arab: L'Orient tel que je l'ai connu* (1944):

> To begin, let us make ourselves clear once and for all on the subject of the harem, which since eternity has hypnotized the West. The harem is neither the décor of an operetta nor the mysterious realm of all pleasures. *Harîm*, in Arabic, means that which is sacred. Let us translate: the feminine element of the house. . . . Thus, without knowing it, the Roumis [Europeans] all have harems.[15]

And Marc Hélys, alias Leyla, alias Marie Léra, alias Djénane (the heroine of Loti's novel of a Turkish harem, *Les Désenchantées*, 1906) wrote in *Le Jardin fermé* "[T]here was no word more flattering and poetic to Occidental ears than *harem.*" Like the word *odalisque*, "[A]n entire Asiatic poetics resounded in the two syllables of this word . . . hot colors, strange countryside, penumbras forming a halo over searing images: perfume boxes, amorous indolence, feverish passions, tragic pleasures, silent, heavy wall hangings splashed with blood."[16] Where Mardrus emphasized the culturally universal domesticity of the harem, Hélys concentrated on destroying the myth of phallic supremacy, remarking in a chapter entitled "A Parisian Woman in the Harems of Constantinople" on how little the master actually interfered with the lives of his wives and concubines: "Nowhere do women dominate men so much as in this country in which woman's de facto domination is disguised as servility. Woman feels profound contempt for man, a contempt accumulated through the centuries in her soul."[17]

Despite attempts such as these to deflate sexual clichés by presenting the harem as a domestic gyneceum or place of feminine autonomy, it continued to be exploited in Orientalist paintings and colonial fiction as a means of evoking every possible venue of erotic fantasy. Abduction, exhibitionism, voyeurism (between eunuch and captives), bestiality (as when monkeys intervene in lieu of the sultan), sapphism, onanism, masochism (female bondage), and visions of the "dark side" of femininity itself constituted a mosaic of "aberrant" sexual preferences to be grouped under the rubric *harem.*

In Maupassant's salon play, the word functions as a synecdoche of what the West most desires and fears in the Other—polygamy and domesticated prostitution. Cloaked in exoticism, the proverbial male fantasy of multiple female slaves is doubly arousing. M. Beauflanquer is enticed by the invitation to share the Turkish ambassador's personal harem. Acting as eunuch, the pimp Miché didactically informs him: "Understand that these women, who have seen no man other than His Excellency, are used to a certain sexual license." "Yes, but I was made to understand that whomsoever enters a harem risks having his head cut off."[18] Here the castratory threat has an aphrodisiac effect that mingles with the excitement of scopophilic privilege. After paying Miché for his silence, Beauflanquer confesses: "I certainly will be truly glad to know the details of life in a harem."[19] Mired in what Eve Kosovsky Sedgwick has characterized as an "epistemology of the closet," or what I have called elsewhere a "cabinet secret," this motif of breakage and entry once again highlights the erotics of claustration.

The harem, qua space of the master, offers what Lacan described as "possession by the Gaze. . . . this *belong to me aspect* of representations, so reminiscent of property."[20] In Maurice Barrès's *Un Jardin sur l'Oronte* (1922), a deictic rhetoric of sexual showing is used to great scopic effect. The phrases "Ecoute!" [Listen!] and "Ah! si tu la voyais!" [Oh! if you could only see her!], uttered by a Syrian emir as he prepares to introduce a European dignitary to the secrets of his harem, enhance the visual delectation of occluded spectacle.[21] In Loti's *Les Trois dames de la Kasbah,* the titillation of Islamic scopic mastery distracts attention from French colonial surveillance: "It was certainly this solitude of the cloister, that which characterizes Arab dwellings, which revealed all the jealous suspicions, all the wild surveillance of Muslim life."[22]

Harem narratives emerge as the premier literary conduit for "veiled" allusions to France's territorial conquest of North Africa. Though the historic familiarity and formulaic conventionality of harem iconography could make the European viewer feel, paradoxically enough, at ease with the spectacle of radical cultural alterity, there was also invariably a moment when colonial discourse became transparent to itself, revealed as a sickness involving the violent, sadoerotic management of cultural territory and human subjects. For example, in Guy de Téramond's *Schmâm'ha* (1901), the title of which refers to the name of a Kabylian slave-girl who witnesses her French mistress's adulterous affair, the colonial gaze is turned back on the master:

> Léontine had slid into the bed, voluptuously arching herself, abandoning herself to Jean's tender caresses, when suddenly she caught sight of

> Schmâm'ha's eyes glittering in the corner, waiting, an impassive and im-
> mobile spectator to their transports, for permission to leave the room.[23]

Treated like a dog or a piece of furniture, Schmâm'ha is ignored until her
look, which "seems to see nothing," is gradually registered by her employ-
ers in her mimetic passion for the Frenchman. Jean in turn becomes aware
of her mysterious charms and dreams of possessing "this little brown monkey, silent and enigmatic, who would have loved him with the strange ca-
resses of a cat."[24]

This game of colonial mimicry has the effect of rendering European
eroticism strange to itself. After an extenuating scene with his French mistress, Jean wonders to himself whether "the complicity of the flesh is not
the most horrible form of enslavement."[25] Téramond desublimates the
sexual dimension of colonial mastery, inadvertently drawing attention to
the colonial paradigm within the politics of sexual possession.

Albert Memmi *(Portrait of the Colonized Preceded by the Portrait of the Colonizer)*, Octave Mannoni *(Prospero and Caliban: The Psychology of Colonization)*, Frantz Fanon *(A Dying Colonialism)*, and more recently, Malek Alloula
(The Colonial Harem) and Sliman Zéghidour *(Le Voile et la bannière)*, have
each, from the outbreak of the Algerian Revolution to the present, theorized this sexual life of power. Invariably, Algeria "herself" is placed in the
position of the cloistered Muslim woman or slave girl, while France, in the
role of the pasha, looks on with malaise at a feminine dominion teaming
with *ressentiment* toward its metropolitan master. Never certain of his pro-
prietorship, the colonizer, like the Sidi in colonial fiction, must fulfill his
role as a jealous master, enjoining his eunuchs to spy on his female entourage and stirring up intrigue among his consorts so as to anchor their
envy of a rival's access to the phallus in mimetic desire. But these masquerades risk failure. In Charles Géniaux's *Les Musulmanes* (1909) the authority
of the Sidi is depicted as contingent on feminine performances of submissive coquetry:

> The art of depilation, makeup, perfume, unguent, massage, and the bath,
> these must be pushed to perfection, to make of the body a masterpiece,
> nothing was more important if one wanted to reign over the husband's
> heart, he who was still called: Sire, Master. Coquetry, Hanifa proclaimed,
> surpassed even cooking and praying as a necessity of life.[26]

On one level feminine artifice serves to pretend the phallic order into existence, but on another level it undermines its authority. Observing veiled
Moroccan women in the street, the Tharaud brothers drew the familiar
conclusion that the veil ensured rather than impeded feminine liberty:

Once she is in the street, who would recognize this woman under the wool *haïk* enveloping her from head to toe, leaving only the eyes in view? Who could put a name to this unformed thing, where even the most exigent inspection would fail to allow one woman to be distinguished from the another? The uniformity of this clothing gives complete liberty to this wool package: once out of the house, it can travel wherever it wishes to go.[27]

The preponderance of veiling and interior drapery in harem representation illustrates the mutual *tromperie* of sex and culture, already anticipated by Balzac's *La Fille aux yeux d'or*, where a profusion of semitransparent fabrics, fringed curtains, and throw rugs theatricalize the way in which female homosexuality disguises itself behind the appearance of a sultan's harem. In this realist Orientalist work the trappings of the harem operate as a form of cultural camouflage for sapphic desire.

Of the women authors who used colonial fiction as a means of venturing into "dark continents" of feminine Eros, Isabelle Eberhardt is the most well known. Her *Pages d'Islam*, *Écrits sur le sable*, and novellas such as *Rakhil*, *Yasmina*, and *Tessadith* have recently been republished in France and are now beginning to attract serious critical attention. Her collections of tales and journal entries *Notes de route*, *Dans l'ombre chaude de l'Islam*, and *Écrits sur le sable*, originally appeared in Algerian newspapers between 1900 and 1904. Although her critical stance toward many colonial policies make her an atypical representative of *littérature coloniale* (generally motivated by imperialist ideological ends, as in Julien Maigret's series *Vies coloniales* designed to prepare French wives for the civilizing mission in North Africa), Eberhardt's friendship with Resident-General Lyautey and posthumous reception in France garnered her a permanent place in the colonial canon.

Though Eberhardt practiced a kind of ethnographic realism, blending documentary description with poetic, metaphysical evocations of the emotional violence aroused by desert landscape, she refused the "feigned realism" characteristic of French colonial fiction. Eberhardt's attack on commercial Orientalist realism stemmed from her abhorrence of Western decadence and "Ottoman" excess. In a short piece published in 1900 entitled "L'âge du néant" (The age of nothingness), she denounced the stylistics of false appearance associated with Western materialism and the feminine taste for luxury, proposing instead a redemptive North Africanist realism rooted in Islamic faith and the purified nomadic life, a hard and vigorous pastoral.[28] Eberhardt excoriated Western eroticism for its promotion of a sexual license devoid of conviction. Modern society, she claimed, was "avid for pleasure" [avide de jouir] not for the sake of a "divine tremor of *volupté*" but in order to "forget the inexpressible pain of living." Eberhardt condemned civilization for failing to make good on its promise of new forms of *jouissance;* instead of "subtler, sharper, more intoxicating ecstasies," instead of the "divinization of the senses" sought by the free spirit, it delivered only "incurably sterile" decoys of love that left the body unsatisfied, hankering all the more for *jouissance.*[29]

Eberhardt has been resuscitated, however problematically, as an early incarnation of postcolonial feminism.[30] Her novellas focus on the lives of "low-life" North African women: prostitutes, proud daughters punished by their autocratic fathers, rebellious mistresses deserted by their lovers, Kabylian shepherdesses who, though illiterate, maintain a sullen resistance to colonial domination, and nomadic adventuresses in quest of what she calls in the autobiographical short story "La Zaouia" "la jouissance des jouissances."

> Now the drunkenness of my soul in this marvelous countryside, under this incomparable sky and the sublime flights of thought toward the calm regions of speculation, now the sweet ecstasies always mingled with melancholy, the ecstasies of art, that quintessential and mysterious pleasure of pleasures.[31]

The form of this ineffable "pleasure of pleasures" has no precise name; no exact psychoanalytic translation exists for this composite of sexual dissipation, burning desire, and fatalistic submission. Perhaps we might assimilate it to that state of voluptuous inanition that Freud named Nirvana, or the "rest drive," in *The Economic Problem of Masochism.* Catherine Millot has characterized this drive as a "reduction of tensions to degree zero, as a drive in the service of thanatos, as a desire of the body to return to its formerly inorganic state, and as a nostalgia for the state of pure passivity."[32] In addition to calling for "une pensée de bon nirvana" in an autobiographical fragment, Eberhardt, in her tale "Yasmina," names this feeling *Mektoub,* meaning "it is said," "it is written," or "fate." When Yasmina, a young Kabylian shepherdess learns that her *roumi* lover Jacques will be sent away with his military unit, her response is, "*Mektoub* . . . We are all under the hand of God, and we all will die in order to return to him . . . Don't cry *Ya Mabrouk,* it is written thus."[33] Wedding the notion of external destiny to the memory of exquisite passions, *Mektoub* forges a heroic, tragic feminine sexuality.

If Eberhardt translated *Mektoub* into elegiac forms of female desire, Myriam Harry treated it as the nomenclature for Islamic women's fated encounter with Western mores. In *Les Derniers Harems,* a chronicle of the erosion of traditional Muslim practices among women in Egypt, Syria, and Turkey. Registering her astonishment at seeing a young Egyptian girl swimming freely in the ocean, a woman informs her:

The Egyptian woman is conciliatory in character and very fatalistic. She neither revolts nor takes a stand for or against emancipation. She accepts life in
its fashion, "moda," a word that is itself fateful. It was the fashion for her to
veil herself, to bury herself in her hair and her skirts and to remain ignorant.
Now, it is the fashion even among the people to go to school and to show
oneself naked . . . *Mektoub,* another destiny.[34]

In a book published in 1920 entitled *Le Livre des harems* and styled after *The
Arabian Nights* in its chain structure of miniature récits, the woman writer
L. M. Enfrey also evoked *Mektoub* in relation to dream states fusing opiated
passivity with slackness of body. Her insistence on preserving the Arabic
term in French, like Eberhardt's and Harry's, uses untranslatability to designate a psychosexual space of Western nonequivalency. In the story "Fadjera," a prostitute's physical and moral demise is characterized as

> *Mektoub!* this word of moral abandon slides into the midst of the sharpest
> regrets, explains civilization's moments of glory and decadence, fortune
> and ruin. One chants it as if it were a refrain of pain, one pronounces it as if
> it were a magic word, capable of drying the tears of mourning families.[35]

In yet another tale, a young Muslim girl sold into prostitution by her father
slides into "le Mektoub," described as a state of abject passivity.

Enfrey's psychosexual rendering of *Mektoub* diverges sharply from conventional usage. The backbone of Koranic law (the Koran *is* the written will
of Allah and thus a kind of materialized embodiment of the concept), *Mektoub* has been for centuries at the core of Islamic theological discussion.
Strictly speaking, it is the all-powerful sultan, agent of divine Will, who incarnates *Mektoub* by exacting blind submission from his subjects. Enfrey
herself describes one of her traditional sultans as "draped in his costume
of the biblical patriarch, insouciant, immobile, and the *Mektoub* on his
lips."[36] In mixing the principle of absolute obedience to masculine Law
with the voluptuous nihilism of women, Enfrey violates the theological
meaning of the Father's Law, but this violation is itself an interesting (and
fundamentally Western) experiment in the haremization of phallic power.

Variations on the theme of *Mektoub* may be found in almost every text
of Enfrey's harem book. In "La Mélopée de Djamila" a lazy train of amorous
thought is traced from the dream state of the indolent odalisque to collective sighs of pleasure afforded by sapphic embraces:

> The heat is oppressive in the houses, grouped, as if ready to receive benedic
> tion, at the foot of the holy *djemâ.* The mosaic floors of the gardens burn the
> naked feet of the servant girls as they pass. The women lying about volup
> tuously allow their imaginations to wander here and there. Dragonflies ex
> pire over half-opened flowers, soaring in flight, looking for love of every
> kind, scrutinizing every mystery of the caress. It is the enervating hour—

though exquisite—of touching and of kisses from woman to woman; the hour when Fez breathes, in a half-slumber, the voluptuous perfumes of its harems.[37]

Enfrey's gyneceum harbors a utopian dream of sexuality without the phallus. Not only is lesbian desire clearly replacing the older harem trope whereby the sultan/phallus anchors the libido of the female socius, but a countereroticism is articulated. In Enfrey's text, the space of the harem and the sexuality of *Mektoub* form a sapphic "sexterior," both in the sense of "sexually coming out" (*s'extérioriser*, "to bring forth," "to show oneself"), and in the sense of a private interior suffused with concupiscence.

Fostering *Mektoub*—a fatal voluptuousness pegged to a feminocentric libidinal economy—the harem subgenre of colonial fiction may be read as a counternarrative of feminine *jouissance*, deflationary of colonial mastery and the phallic order at one and the same time. Most importantly, *Mektoub* becomes a way of naming the lexicon of psychoanalysis otherwise.

6
ETHNOGRAPHIC
TRAVESTIES

ALIBIS OF GENDER

AND NATION IN

THE CASE OF

ELISSA RHAÏS

In trying to open up certain dead categories and clichés within the framing of culture, realism, a traditional concern within literary criticism, has proved useful when reconfigured as a genre obsessed with the representation of cultural essentialism, be it physiognomical, characterological, racial, national, ethnic, social, or gender-typed. Anchored since the early 1830s in the evidentiary, specifically the descriptivist popular culture of fashion journalism, travel writing, political and military press coverage, institutional reports, and so on, realism has always enjoyed a privileged, if highly problematic, relation to the real, for it is virtually impossible to read descriptions of reality without awareness of the workings of mimetic fallacies (literary conceits for representing the visual textures of facticity) that condition the conventions of historical novels deemed realist.[1]

In reexamining realist narrative technique as it evolves from Balzac and Flaubert to the exoticist canon of obscure colonial novelists, we can begin to grasp some of the shared points of intellectual conservatism between realism and colonialism. Colonial administrations certainly understood the ideological power of colonial fictions, which ordered territorial and psychical conquest into mutually refracting teleological narratives. However, as I hope to show through an analysis of several novels by Elissa Rhaïs, the discursive native subject that emerges in many of these narratives was often capable of undermining colonial norms either by inadvertently capturing a hostile indigenous gaze, or by displacing the boundaries of the cultural stereotype that the realist genre generally served to put in place, or, finally, by splitting or complicating the very notion of a colonial subject, whether authorial, native, or metropolitan.

I am certainly not the first to think colonialism through realism. Timothy Mitchell, in *Colonizing Egypt* (1988), dissected the reality effect of world exhibitions in terms of the problematic scale of their cultural referentiality (at once global and parochial), and their techniques of staging and spectacularity (perspectives ordered by Eurocentric viewing, the optical alienation effect produced by commodified simulations of "Cairo").[2] Antonia Lant has described the "twin realist and fantastic character" of an early cinema infected by "the imperialism of Egyptology."[3] Writing from an Althusserian perspective, John Tagg has noted the socially fixative nature of realism in photographic representation: "Realism sets its subjects in place at the point of intelligibility of its activity, in a position of observation and synthesis which cannot be questioned by the flux of the text and which cannot be thrown into process by the sliding of signifiers that disestablishes social positionality."[4] As a visual codification of the world by a dominant ideology, as a medium that fosters a spirit of surveillance and possessiveness toward the picture, as a mode of image-mediation promising privileged access to (and manipulation of) "truth" (the evidentiary), photographic realism, in Tagg's estimation, also functions historically as a colonization of subjectivity:

> They [photographs] can be taken as evidence. They can incriminate. They can be aids to masturbation or trophies of conquest. They can be emblems of a symbolic exchange in kinship rituals or vicarious tokens of a world of potential possessions. Through that democratized form of imperialism known as *tourism,* they can exert a power to colonize new experiences and capture subjects across a range never envisaged in painting.[5]

Tagg traces the way in which photographic realism consolidates historic definitions of typicality, be it "typical" scenes in foreign locales, or the physiognomical types of native subjects framed as curiosities. Earlier, in his founding text *Orientalism* (1978) Edward Said had similarly characterized the intransigence of Orientalist tropes and typologies—their ability to sink into consciousness as credible stand-ins for reality itself—as "radical realism," and Homi Bhabha following Said in an essay on stereotype and colonial discourse made realism the "third term" in a psychoanalytic scheme conjugating fetishism with colonialism.[6] Bhabha's definition of the stereotype as fetish (a reifying fixer that disavows and abjects difference) encourages the use of a deconstructed realism to unbind the coalition of fantasies and identifications agglomerated in the colonial unconscious. Colonially cultured positions, thus critically undone, appear as tenuous as the sexed positions of heterosexual society criticized by Judith Butler in her revision-ist account of gender identity.[7] In the context of contemporary post-colonialism, this unfixing effect can have unpredictable consequences, leading, for example, to a more open-ended politics of the cultural subject, or to a kind of diasporic utopianism of cultural identifications detached from the lived histories of individuals, or to a reactive recathexis with the stereotype—a conservative return to colonial fetishes.

In framing the topic of colonial realism I am trying to approach such problems as the formation of literary stereotypes; the phenomenon of what Naomi Schor has recently termed "postcardization"[8] in prose and its attendant poetics of cultural fetishism and visual seduction; the allure of "manners and customs" scenography in popular fiction, theater, opera, and early cinema; the status of formulas essential to "the display of peo-ples" (as when singers, dancers, and kief-smokers in Moorish cafés are trot-ted out for ritual inspection); the politics of a racial unconscious embedded in the tropes of local color or the aesthetics of Orientalist colorism; the re-lationship between caricature and cultural identity; the compenetration of ethnic typology and the essence of genre itself; and finally, the historic role of colonialism in the perpetuation of literary realism, itself conceivable as a praxis for freeze-framing and hypostatizing cultural attitudes.

Within the bounds of this chapter my concerns will be more limited to issues arising from the relationship between the historiography of colonial representation and early First and Third World feminism. In looking specif-ically at the work of Elissa Rhaïs, a popular Algerian novelist of the 1920s, I will be asking to what extent fictions and stereotypes of "real" Muslim life may have motivated feminist struggles in France, such that themes of nomadism, political disenfranchisement, and the exploitation of North African women served to dramatize what a later generation of feminists (following Luce Irigaray) would characterize as the "homelessness of women in the symbolic order."[9] The problem of essentialism in the mar-keting of national authors is also typified by Rhaïs's contested reputation as a preeminent Third World woman writer.

Elissa Rhaïs, the "Novel"

The strange case of Elissa Rhaïs poses a mystery for literature and historiog-raphy alike. The principal document concerning her life is a biography sub-titled a "novel" that nonetheless purports to be an authentic, factual account: *Elissa Rhaïs, roman,* published in 1982 by Paul Tabet, her living ex-ecutor (his current position is director of a French cultural foundation that protects copyright privileges). Elissa Rhaïs was the pen name of Leila Bou

Mendil, born in the Algerian resort town of Blidah[10] to a Muslim father and mother of French Jewish extraction.[11] Tabet maintains that she was married against her will to a wealthy Egyptian spice merchant living in Kabylia, who punished her with neglect and confinement when she attempted to resist his jealousy and sexual despotism. Imprisoned in a harem for fifteen years, treated as a pariah by the other wives, deprived of air and exercise, she became bulimic and virtually ate herself to death. Her "awakening" from this nightmare of moral and physical torpor occurred when her husband died and she was able to return to her native city in 1914. Using a small inheritance, she created a local salon where intellectuals gathered. She invented herself as a writer, hiring the son of a poor relation who had received a French education as her personal secretary.

Tabet's biographical narrative charts Rhaïs's literary success with stories recording the bitter plight of North African women: nomadic mothers disinherited and dispossessed, café-chanteuses and *bayadères,* Jewish daughters married against their will, prostitutes and rebellious harem wives. These were her stock characters, and they sold her fiction well at a time when France was preparing to celebrate its centenary of the 1830 conquest of Algeria. *Saâda la Marocaine* (her first novel, published in 1919), *Le Café-chantant, Kerkeb, Noblesse arabe* (1920), *Les Juifs ou la fille d'Eléazar* (1921), *La Fille des pachas* (1922), *La Fille du douar* (1924), *La Chemise qui porte bonheur* (1925), *L'Andalouse* (1925), *Le Mariage de Hanifa* (1926), *Le Sein blanc* (1928), *La Riffaine* and *Petits pachas en exil* (1929), *La Convertie* (1929) went through multiple printings. Reviews in *La Revue des Deux Mondes, L'Intransigeant,* and *Les Nouvelles Littéraires, La Nouvelle Revue Française,* the *Revue Bleue,* and the *Bulletin de l'Afrique Française* bolstered her celebrity and helped to garner fans among the French suffragettes.

Tabet claims that Rhaïs made her first trip to Paris in 1919, where she lived intermittently until her death in 1940. The distinguished roster of visitors to her apartment included Colette, Sarah Bernhardt, Paul Morand, and the Algerian author Jean Amrouche. In 1926, accompanied by her secretary, who she now called her son, she made a triumphant voyage to Casablanca, where she received an official welcome from the French colonial authorities and was given a stipend of six thousand francs to study the condition of women in Morocco. By the early thirties, an American producer pushed to adapt her novel *La Fille des pachas* for the screen (as a kind of companion piece to *Pépé le Moko*).[12] A novella, *Kerkeb, danseuse berbère* furnished the material for an opera libretto with music by the composer Samuel-Rousseau. In 1939 the French government decided to award Rhaïs the Legion of Honor because her novels, in making the colonies seem attractive to French tourists, had performed the invaluable political function of enhancing the civilizing mission.

A problem emerged, however, when a background check was ordered and no evidence was found of any kind of formal education in Rhaïs's past. Indeed, Elissa Rhaïs's novels, exemplary for their authenticity of feminine voice, appeared to have been written by a man. This nephew, or "son," known as Raoul Dahan in Tabet's text, was by his own account the sole author of her fiction, despite the fact that after her death no work was ever published under his name. According to the testimony of Rhaïs's domestics, he had become his benefactress's sexual and literary slave, ironically repeating her own sordid tale of psychological and material imprisonment but in gender reverse order. An accomplice in the production of the Elissa Rhaïs myth (itself much publicized by Plon, the publishing house that launched her career), Raoul became a victim of his own success at narrative cross-dressing.

In an article published in 1984, two years after the appearance of Tabet's *Elissa Rhaïs, roman,* a well-respected critic and bibliographer of North African and colonial literature named Jean Déjeux punctured many surfaces in the Elissa Rhaïs legend as constituted by Tabet.[13] After acknowledging the difficulty of disconfirming the basic outlines of Tabet's version of the story, Déjeux rectifies certain critical errors in his account. Rhaïs's real name was Rosine Boumendil, and she was the daughter of Algerian Jewish parents (on both sides, not just one, as alleged by Tabet). After attending the *école communale* in Blida until the age of twelve, she was married at a young age to a rabbi of Algiers named Moïse Amar, but never incarcerated in a harem, as legend would have it. She had three children by Amar, one of whom died young. Her surviving son, Jacob-Raymond, received a French education and became a staunch supporter of the FLN during the Algerian Revolution. A man of letters in his own right who at one time edited an Algerian Communist newspaper (coauthoring articles with Algeria's premier postwar authors Mohammed Dib and Kateb Yacine), Raymond Rhaïs, as he is known, has always maintained that his mother was the sole author of the Rhaïs oeuvre.

According to Déjeux, Rosine married a wealthy businessman named Mardochée Chemouil (who Frenchified his name into Maurice Chemoul) after her divorce from her first husband. It was Chemoul's nephew Raoul-Robert Tabet (not Dahan), only three years her son's senior, who became her amanuensis after he came to live with the family during his studies at the Faculté des Lettres in Algiers. Déjeux confirms that Raoul acted as scribe; but whether he was the lover of his aunt remains unclear. Elissa

Rhaïs separated from her husband in 1917 and moved to Paris with her two children and adoptive "son." In Paris she apparently did enjoy a brilliant social and literary entrée, successfully playing the card of Muslim Arab woman writer. Déjeux speculates that she jettisoned her Jewish origins out of fear of anti-Semitism, though he does point out that other Jewish writers at the time were able to advance their careers without disguising their heritage. In the late thirties Rhaïs returned to her villa in Blida and died there in 1940 of a sudden illness (not, as Tabet implies, of chagrin over the Foreign Legion debacle). Déjeux makes no mention of any impact she might have had on a burgeoning Third World feminism, but he does bring the controversy over her identity up to the present by referring to the polemic that broke out in *Les Nouvelles Littéraires* after Tabet's television appearance on the literary talk-show *Apostrophes* in 1982. Regardless of whether one can ever ultimately disentangle fact from fiction, the story itself remains of keen historiographical interest insofar as it highlights the travesties that so easily arise from attempts to capture authentic native voices.

Unfixing the Colonial Stereotype

It is not surprising that Elissa Rhaïs's novels fall outside the purview of what French arbiters of literary value commonly refer to as the "readable" *(lisible)*. But it is perhaps this very *unreadability* of Rhaïs's colonial fiction that lends it historical interest as a paradigmatic example of that "forgotten" and rather ignominious genre dubbed *littérature coloniale* by the Lansonistes. The authors that might be said to comprise the archive of colonial literature have for the most part fallen into total obscurity, but they were all descendants of Pierre Loti, of Loti's *Aziyadé*, of course, but also of his lesser-known works—*Le Roman d'un spahi* (1881), *Les Trois dames de la Kasbah* (1884) (later subsumed in *Fleurs d'ennui*), *Suleima* (1882), in which a pet monkey is the predominant figure for an Algerian prostitute-criminal), *Au Maroc* (1890), and *Les Désenchantées* (1906). Loti's strongest immediate influences were Flaubert *(Voyage en Egypte)*, Gautier *(Voyage pittoresque en Algérie)*, Maupassant *(Au Maghreb)*, and the Goncourt brothers (those parts of the *Journal* dealing with the Expositions Coloniales); his epigones included Jean Lorrain, Hector France, Robert Randau, Guy de Téramond, Charles Géniaux, Louis Bertrand, Jérôme and Jean Tharaud, Paul Vigné d'Octon, and Michel Vieuchange among many others. Interestingly enough, a significant number of contributors to the genre were women: Jane Dieulafoy, Marc Elys, Myriam Harry, Clotilde Chivas-Baron, Lucienne Favre, L. M. Enfrey, Lucie Delarue-Mardrus (wife of the French translator of *The Arabian Nights)*, and, of course, Elissa Rhaïs.[14]

Rhaïs's novels, though published in the twenties when modernism, surrealism, and avant-garde experimentation were in vogue, were written in a realist style amounting to a kind of commercialized Flaubertianism. Flaubert, adopting the time-honored literary technique of *ut pitura poesis* in his historical novels, would characteristically evoke exotic urban geography and its "teaming" inhabitants with a lapidary, variegated language. In *Salammbô* he employed a panoptical vertigo, heightened by the spectacle of dead animals (rhopography), anthropological reality effects (place-names, foreign loan words), and splashes of literary technicolor.[15] The same effects can be found in the opening of Rhaïs's *Kerkeb, danseuse berbère:*

> It was the festival of the marabout d'Ellouali, on the neighboring heights of Fez. Around the white cupola of the great saint, between the rocks and aloe, innumerable tents raised their banners. The black, red, or green burnouses of the men swarmed, among the gandourahs of the women, which were white, fringed in shadow. Everyone pushed at the threshold of the funerary kiosk to make their offering to the marabout. Sharp voices intoned the Fatiha. On the edge of the closest oasis, hundreds of sheep were being immolated. Their hacked cadavers hung on carob trees, the oasis ran bloody, clouds of incense rose above the trees. Everywhere there were joyous fires, music. Women let forth their *you-you* and called out to each other in song. . . . Around a waterfall, soldiers equipped themselves for the ritual fantasia. The crowd of pilgrims swelled without end. New groups arrived, scaling the rocky pathways, preceded by flute-players and standard-bearers, and *yaouleds* holding multicolored wax candles destined for the marabout's bier. And over all this, the torrid heat of July, the blinding light of the great Moroccan sky.[16]

Rhaïs thus updated Romantic Orientalism for an age of mechanical reproduction, aping, in this opening passage, the "you are there" sensation conveyed by the moving camera; replacing the image petrifaction of Flaubertian genre painting in prose with a mobile (though equally formulaic) display of peoples, manners, and customs.

In his *Histoire de la littérature coloniale en France* (1931) Roland Lebel, distinguishing colonial fiction from its fin-de-siècle forebears, stressed its reliance on a politically motivated visuality—an optical, nationalistic projection of *élan vital*. Lebel argued that colonial literature was not to be summed up by its treatment of colonial subject matter, but rather, by its "optique nouvelle": "The colonial spirit," he wrote, "is an affirmation of moral energy that affirms itself against decadentism and pessimism; it is a doctrine of action, a school of energy, an act of faith." Where Loti and his successors treated foreign topographies as mere frameworks for description, the colonial writers, according to Lebel, "opted for the colony, assimilating to it as object, as a *milieu naturel.*" No longer did it suffice to "faire beau," he claimed, now it was necessary to "faire vrai."[17]

Rhaïs's novels were marketed as representations of true Muslim life in contradistinction to the false Orientalism of an earlier tradition of literary exoticism. Writing in *Le Journal des Débats* in 1920 Jean de Pierrefeu noted that the "obsessional" aura generated by the vivid colorism of *Saâda* was so strong that the reader would see vestiges of Oriental decor upon looking up from the book. Consistently praised for their "puissance de vérité," that is, their ability to purvey with seeming authenticity the essential "Arab" character (with its putative penchants for violence, jealousy, and self-destruction), Rhaïs's writings did indeed "faire vrai" by filling in the larger-than-life characterological cutouts of Orientalism ascribed by Said to the "radical real."

Whether filled in or not, one could say that the culturally essentializing stereotype grounded colonial fiction (regardless of the author's political persuasions), imposing itself through a variety of devices, from the naming of characters to the description of physiognomies. In *Le Café-chantant* for example, the name of the singer Fouad El Begri ("Lungs of an Ox"), or that of her cohort Fathma Calyptus ("Fathma long-waisted as the Eucalyptus tree"), functions like a concentrate of national character. A great deal of work has been done on the impact of physiognomical theory, fostered by Gall and Lavater, on French realism. The commensurability between facial characteristic and characterological profile, between body type and historic destiny, between physical aberration and psychic flaw, between national costume and cultural identity, forms the bedrock of readerly expectations and has been dissected in the works of canonical realist authors from Balzac to Zola.[18] Rather than rehearse these ideas, I would simply point out the extent to which Rhaïs's use of physiognomy catered to the marketable stereotype. In *Kerkeb,* for instance, the domestic patriarch is described as follows:

> Sid Hafid, the master, is there on the threshold in his white gandourah and yellow leather slippers. He gives orders to the servants in a brutal tone of voice. Sid Hafid is representative of the evolved Moroccan. Long, thin, nervous, a bony face with a beard trimmed into a necklace that trembles at the slightest command, piercing eyes, made up with khol, a hooked nose that bespeaks his sensual egoism, trickiness, and hard pride of race. It is essential that everyone bend to his every word like the camel under the *flissa* of the guide.[19]

Here the strokes of the literary brush—a bony face, a beard that quivers with the issuance of a command, piercing eyes, a hooked nose—serve to "harden and hook" the outlines of character into the type. This use of stereotype recalls Roland Barthes's definition in *The Pleasure of the Text:*

> The stereotype is the word repeated without any magic, any enthusiasm, as though it were natural, as though by some miracle this recurring word were adequate on each occasion for different reasons, as though to imitate could no longer be sensed as an imitation: an unconstrained word that claims consistency and is unaware of its own insistence. Nietzsche has observed that "truth" is only the solidification of old metaphors. So in this regard the stereotype is the present path of "truth," the palpable feature which shifts the invented ornament to the canonical, constraining form of the signified.[20]

Bearing down inexorably on the signifier, the chain of words that coagulates into the type, produces, according to Barthes, a *nausea* that comes whenever "the liaison of two words follows of itself." Though I agree with Barthes that it is this queasiness of the sign that the stereotype evokes in the reader, I would argue that this is precisely what the reader wants in consuming stereotypical literature—the nausea of certainty, of semantic finitude, of what psychoanalysis has described as the fatal attraction of the death drive.

The deathly aspect of the type is eroticized in Rhaïs's tales through costume. The body is arrested in space, materialized in its sartorial envelope, embalmed, as it were (to use an Orientalist analogy), like a prose mummy in an Egyptian tomb. Take, for example, her description of Kerkeb, a quintessentially dissolute harem wife, posed on a red satin couch in the shadow of a sumptuous apartment:

> Of all his wives she was the preferred one, a splendid creature with a saffron complexion, black eyes circled in khol, a chiseled nose, amorous lips half-open to accommodate her ardent breathing. She held on her knees a coffer filled with perfume bottles and aromatic sweets, one of those cases of meticulous, elaborate carving that disciplined sculptors worked on for years in the slums of the upper city. And with no concern for her master's presence, she gazed at herself in a gold-handled, silver encrusted mirror. . . . She took a diadem of brilliants out of the box and placed it in her hair glossy with cumin oil. She admired herself for the last time, satisfied, smiling in the mirror, and lazily got up from the sofa. She was ready. Under the white gandourah her strong body moved freely, her firm breasts, her voluptuous hips around which had just been tied a belt embroidered in black silk, pinned with a giant emerald.[21]

Kerkeb's palpitating belly dancer's body (the guiding trope of the whole story), weighed down beneath piles of *clinquant* that "tie" her identity in place, matches up with many of the 1920s postcards analyzed by Malek Al-loula in his book *The Colonial Harem*. Commenting on the native finery in-sisted upon by the colonial photographers in their female models (usually prostitutes), Alloula speaks of the "ethnographic alibi" that adds, paradox-ically, to the impression of images already adjusted for readability and pur-chase by an Occidental eye.[22]

Alloula's notion of "ethnographic alibi" points up the element of po-tential self-parody in colonial realism by pointing to the juncture where the alibi risks overplaying itself to the viewer. We can see this breaking point most clearly in Rhaïs's fiction when the type veers into caricature and more is revealed about the complex process of native self-marketing under the conditions of colonial image-production than about the local color of autochthonous experience. In *Le Café-chantant,* for example, the Moorish Café is depicted as a gaudy stage set housing a bevy of singers "languishing in nonchalant poses," and "buried under an orgy of satin, ribbons, lace, and jewels,"

> Their vaporous costumes, of sequined muslin and delicate silk stripes, al-lowed furtive glimpses of matte flesh and sumptuous, undulating limbs to shine through.[23]

Here costume and decor suggest the Hollywoodized vamp image of Orien-tal women which many entertainers of the twenties and thirties were in fact incorporating into their stage personae. As Sarah Graham-Brown has noted with respect to the changing image of Egyptian belly dancers:

> This chic, westernized image was curiously mingled with what seemed to be parodies of "Orientalist" poses and costumes. Usually these were costume photographs taken to advertise the appearance of a performer in a particu-lar role. But they add a strange twist to the imagery of women, apparently internalizing some Western ideas of how Middle Eastern women looked.[24]

Extrapolating from Graham-Brown, one begins to see how Rhaïs's real-ism is built on its representation of First World and Third World "looked-at-ness" (the expression is Laura Mulvey's). Thus, while freeze-framing and essentialist stereotyping form an integral part of the colonial realism with which she begins, the net effect is of another kind of realism entirely—the real of image making and its commercial conditions in the context of French colonialism of the twenties.

Multiple realisms converge and clash in colonial literature of the early twentieth century. In the case of Rhaïs's fiction, the tensions are complicated by her status as a North African woman author writing in French for a largely European audience. Though in some sense she clearly subscribed to the flat-tening, mummifying techniques of exotic stereotypification, she also inadvertently fractured the type by recording the traces of westernization on native self-representation. Moreover, unlike most of her European predecessors, she avoided amalgamating exotic peoples in a blur of ethnic and national silhouettes, as exemplified in Théophile Gautier's *A Winter in Russia:*

> Russia, with its immense territory, includes many different races and the type of feminine beauty varies much. One may, however, indicate as characteristic, an extreme fairness of complexion, grayish-blue eyes, blonde or chestnut hair, and a certain *embonpoint* arising from the lack of exercise and the life in-doors, which is compelled by a winter lasting seven or eight months. They suggest the idea of odalisques, whom the Genius of the North keeps confined in the tropical atmosphere of a hothouse. They have complexions of cold-cream and snow, with tints from the heart of a camellia—like those over-veiled women of the Seraglio whose skin the sunlight has not touched. By this extreme fairness, their delicate features are rendered even more delicate; and the softened outlines form faces of Hyperborean sweetness and polar grace.
>
> At this very moment, as if to contradict my description, in the sledge which has just drawn up by the side of my troika, shines a radiant Southern beauty; the eyebrows black and velvety, the aquiline nose, the lengthened oval of the face, the brunette complexion, the lips as red as pomegranates, all betray the pure Caucasian type;—a Circassian, and, for all I know, a Mahometan. Here and there, eyes long and narrow, and rising a little at the outer angle, remind us that, at one extreme, Russia touches upon China; charming little Finns with eyes of turquoise blue, pale golden hair, and tint, pure red and white, contrast well with those handsome Greek women from Odessa, whom you recognize by the straight nose and great black eyes, like those of the Byzantine madonnas. It makes a charming picture,—these lovely heads emerging, like winter flowers, from a mass of furs, which is itself covered by white or black bear-skin thrown over all.[25]

Here the physiognomical pileup technique ultimately slips away from its author's control. Gautier's Russian woman dissolves into a "pale" Arabian concubine, who metamorphoses into a "dark" southern European, who glides into a "possibly Mahometan" Circassian, with affinities to Finnish, Chinese, Greek, and Byzantine models.

Unlike French travelers who went from region to region sampling ethnic body-types much like local cuisines or markets, Rhaïs produced a more nuanced anthropology of the Maghreb. In *Saâda* she noted Algerian racism toward Moroccan immigrants. In *Les Juifs ou la fille d'Eléazar* she alluded to Muslim anti-Semitism. In *Le Mariage de Hanifa* she dramatized the risks of unmarriageability and cultural alienation to Muslim girls who attended French schools. In *La Fille du pacha,* she focused on a noble Arab girl condemned to death for daring to fall in love with a Jewish officer (a triple oppositional play between Arab-Jew, Arab-Westerner, Westerner-Jew). In *Le Café-chantant* she explored the way in which Berber entertainers operated as the ethnic "other" for Arab audiences, and in *Noblesse arabe* she described the rivalry between a local Bedouin girl, in love with the son of her aristocratic landlord, and his designated fiancée brought in from "outside"—a beautiful "*lalla* de harem, un modèle de la race andalouse."[26] *Noblesse arabe* is a particularly complex work insofar as it examines the renomadization of a Bedouin family living in the Algerian city of Tlemcen. It is a Moroccan rather than a French landlord who expropriates their cherished settlement. In this case, Rhaïs explores the sociology of economic, class, and cultural conflict among North African ethnicities, while at the same time implicitly alluding to the history of French territorial and cultural self-implantation.

Though Rhaïs drew heavily on clichés, she used them in the service of social realism. Seeming to follow Frederick Engels, who wrote, "Realism, to my mind, implies, besides truth of detail, the truthful reproduction of typical characters under typical circumstances," Rhaïs, in a sense, redeemed her complicity with the commercialized, patriotic genre of colonial fiction by chronicling the trauma of diaspora and the hardships of everyday life.[27] The opening paragraphs of *Saâda* provide an arresting picture of Spanish and Moroccan immigrants displaced from their homelands and brought to Algeria to work as domestics for the settler bourgeoisie.

> On a freezing afternoon in January 1915, all along the rue du Bey, one of the most tranquil in Blidah, streamed a procession of strangers arriving at the hour of the trains. They were Spaniards for the most part. Women, short and heavy, with an oily complexion, dressed in yellow shawls and loose dresses embellished with dirt-encrusted flounces. Under their arms they carried enormous brown packets, rusty buckets full of cooking utensils, which they supported against their wide hips. Around their skirts, clusters of children squalled, miserable, jaundiced human rejects whose black eyes glittered.[28]

This passage compares favorably with the opening scene of an earlier study of *Les Femmes arabes en Algérie* published by the French suffragette Hubertine Auclert in 1900:

> On entering the terrestrial paradise of Algiers, the first thing that strikes one immediately, under the blue sky, sparkling on the pavement like steel, is the sight of shocking packets of dirty laundry.
>
> These packets move, advance; only then does one discern that they are carried along on dirt-encrusted feet and topped by heads so frayed, decrepit, creviced, and streaked that one hardly recognizes them as human faces; it is the statue of suffering, personifying a race tortured by hunger.
>
> These creatures without age or sex, jostling and exploding in this fairy-tale space, in their no longer white rags and tatters, have just become mothers. An adorable baby is perched on their hips, swaddled in the fold of a *haïk*.

> Wives of the dispossessed, a mouth too many in their tribes, they wander, poor females, everywhere rejected, brutally hunted, insulted in every language by the settlers of all races who installed themselves on their fathers' land.[29]

Though Auclert may have evoked the spectacle of feminine oppression as a goad to legal and social reforms in Algeria, her description of Algerian women as "packets of dirty laundry," ravaged faces, and "statues of suffering" exemplifies First World feminism's symptomatic (and ultimately self-centered) tendency to construct "Third World Woman" as a flattened, negated subjectivity.[30] Chandra Talpade Mohanty has pointed out that "colonization almost invariably implies a relation of structural domination, and a suppression—often violent—of the heterogeneity of the subject(s) in question." She articulates the way in which contemporary First World feminism recolonizes the other (despite good intentions to do otherwise) by constructing "a composite, singular 'third world woman'—an image which appears arbitrarily constructed, but nevertheless carries with it the authorizing signature of Western humanist discourse."[31]

Saâda shares with Auclert's *Les Femmes arabes* a use of stereotype for humanitarian ends, but *Saâda* nuances social typicality, entering the psyches of abused, impoverished women. When Saâda's husband fails to find work and becomes an alcoholic, she turns to prostitution and develops a taste for vice. Worst of all, by the standards of the text's Islamic normative frame, is her studied indifference to the stigma of social shame:

> Saâda thus did nothing to hide her crime . . . she refused even to pull her djellbala over her shameless nudity.
> . . . Every day she would go with another client. She sold herself to whosoever came along, without hesitating or haggling over the price, tasting in her debasement a bitter pleasure, as if drunk on vengeance. She was happy to let the jet of filth fall back on those she considered to be the authors of her fall.[32]

In a fit of crazed lust and dejection, Saâda's husband rapes a child and is taken away for punishment. Poverty, prostitution, and rape—this chain of depredations set against the backdrop of Oriental nomadism becomes a universalized allegory for woman's oppression and psychic homelessness.

French Feminism and the Colonial Stereotype

Though Saâda's story read today from a postcolonial perspective seems to call for interpretation as an allegory of France's political "rape" of North Africa, French feminism in the twenties tended to ignore this reading in favor of the universalistic one. At one level it can be argued that this universalism was justified insofar as French women in their failure to obtain the vote in the postwar period became the political "Third World" not only of the West, but also, as Steven Hause and Anne Kenney have shown, of the Third World:

> Of the five European "great powers" that went to war in August 1914, only France had not given women the vote by 1919. With the enactment of integral suffrage laws in the United States and Canada in 1920, the equal political rights of women (at least in the law) had become an unmistakable characteristic of Western civilization. Indeed, Western imperialism exported this equality. The British soon implanted it in East Africa and South Asia. Ataturk encompassed it in his westernization of Turkey. By the 1930s, while the French Senate stood intransigent, women were voting in Palestine, parts of China and several Latin American republics. Women voted in Estonia, Azerbaijan, Trans-Jordan, and Kenya but not in the land of Jeanne d'Arc and the Declaration of the Rights of Man. This contrast was widely noted in France. The Buisson report covered it in detail and the Barthélemy Report reiterated the argument. By 1919, suffragists found it "humiliating to think that a daughter of the country of the Revolution" still had to beg rights granted to women in "backward" countries.[33]

Hause and Kenney alert us once again to the uneasy relationship between French feminism and the colonies.[34] Not only was there the unpleasant mirror effect of political "backwardness" that complicated the identification of First World feminism with Third, but there was also the fact that First World feminism simply could not see how women of the colonies might define their liberatory struggles in a path conflicting with the goals of European empire. This is not to suggest that all French feminists, whether on the left or right, wholeheartedly endorsed *la mission civilisatrice,* but it is probably safe to say that in this period of invoking Enlightenment principles in the service of the rights of women, it was assumed that what was in the best interest of French feminists would be in the interest of women of all nationalities. And of course, in many instances, this is often how North African feminists presented the matter themselves. Tabet notes the voluminous correspondence that Rhaïs received from Tunisian, Algerian, and Moroccan women, many of them indicating their solidarity with Western feminism's stand against a patriarchal social order. It hardly mattered that Rhaïs's representation of pashas and sultans nourished Western clichés about Oriental despotism; the bottom line for many North African (and Middle Eastern) feminists of the twenties was release from the oppressive strictures of family, religion, marriage practices, the veil, and so on.[35]

This said, it is hard to imagine that First World feminism's instrumentalization of colonial typologies fully masked the significant political contradictions between global panfeminism and colonialism. Just as the World War II vocabulary of democracy, resistance, and liberation helped to fuel the FLN on the eve of the Algerian Revolution, so the rhetoric of feminism led logically to the questioning of colonial domination. And it must be remembered here that the interwar period during which the majority of Rhaïs's fictional works were written was a volatile period in colonial history, one in which nascent Algerian nationalisms burgeoned. The Jeunes Algériens movement (anti-Muslim, assimilationist, in favor of extending suffrage to pro-French Algerians) emerged after the 1919 Jonnart reforms alongside the Islamic, pan-Arab, nationalistic Reformist Party of Ben Badis, which competed in its turn with the Etoile Nord Africaine, an ancestor party of the FLN advocating secular nationalism.

Not surprisingly, First World feminism's vision of nationalism was highly selective in its myopic Eurocentrism. Whether in fiction or in the staging of political demonstrations, indigenous self-determination movements simply failed to figure. As Lisa Tickner notes with respect to the suffragette pageants in Britain (themselves "colonially mimetic" of official state ritual), there was a profound (though ill-perceived) irony attached to the spectacle of colonial and commonwealth unity, whereby the suffragettes unwittingly recolonized the world through images that sought to decolonize women worldwide:

> In order to give substance to their claim for international representation the suffragists were obliged to draw on the rhetoric of national identity. All the national costumes, tokens, music and assorted cultural signifiers that could be mobilized (some of them of fairly recent origin) were pressed into service. Scottish pipers, Welsh choirs, Irish harps, joined the fern tree (New Zealand), the kangaroo (Australia), the maple leaf (Canada), the springbok (South Africa) and the elephant (India) among the colonial and international contingents. In lieu of a history of their own, women turned to an accumulated language of symbolic identities, much of it claiming ancient authority but in fact a fairly recent development along with the nation-state. Boadicea was for them not the embodiment of "an ancient past beyond effective historical continuity" as she was for British nationalism, but like Joan of Arc a type of militant femininity. If all invented traditions attempt to use history as the cement for group cohesion as Eric Hobsbawm has argued, then the women's use of historical components was no more and no less selective that those of the discourses to which they were opposed.[36]

Tickner highlights the political dimensions of cultural masquerade whereby European feminists embodied the mythic personae of nation-states or impersonated the larger-than-life inspirational identities of legendary women (Mary Queen of Scots for the royalists, Joan of Arc for the militants in both England and France). Writing in 1898 in his antifeminist tract *La Femme dans les colonies,* Pétrus Durel inveighed against the French woman who neglected her duties as wife and mother, choosing instead to "reread history" with an eye to resurrecting Joan of Arc or Jeanne Hachette as icons of imminent feminist victory.[37]

Feminist victory was not to be claimed by Elissa Rhaïs; her humanization of the brittle codes of social realism and attention to feminine disenfranchisement was lost when her credentials as a Third World woman writer were discredited. And yet, in hindsight, her writing invites less dismissive interpretations of Third World exoticism, focusing on the literary "value" of exoticist costumes and mise en scènes. Were they simply strains of Orientalism, nexes of essentializing mythologies and stereotypes, theme parks for Western identity-staging? Or did they operate as sites of global feminist history? Following the drift of this last question, one might reemphasize the way in which gender masquerade was encrypted within Rhaïs's ethnographic travesty, displacing a confession of "bitextuality" (or double-gendered copyright) into the ethnographic alibi provided by colonial realism. In a café scene in *Saâda,* an unknown youth who goes by the name of "Sid Moussa" is introduced by the Sheik into the male circle of hashish smokers *(haschaïschïa):*

> Blushing "Sid Moussa" advanced toward the assembly, extending a hand to each one, pronouncing not a word, hardly looking up.
>
> This did not prevent them for a second from guessing that "Sid Moussa" was a woman. The light touch of the fingers alone sufficed in averting them. Closer up, physically, they smelled the *odor di femina.*
>
> Despite this, not one of them flinched or signaled their protest to Sid Kaddour with an indiscrete allusion. They respected their sheik. They also knew him to be experienced and wondered whether he might not have had some secret reason for daring an initiative that would otherwise seem imprudent.
>
> This woman whom he had introduced among them was certainly out of the ordinary. The very fact that she had asked or consented to penetrate here testified to that. In any case, she possessed a splendid body, which their instinct ferreted out beneath the burnous, and eyes to drive you mad.[38]

We might have guessed: Saâda has entered the text (much like Eberhardt in real life), disguised as a young man. She penetrates the inner sanctum of male privilege for some "secret reason," traceable, perhaps, to the enigma of authorship surrounding the name Rhaïs. Was Raoul merely the scribe, transmitting the oral tradition of harem tales told to Leila when she was a prisoner of her husband, or was he a consummate ventriloquist of female voice? Was Rhaïs a bisexual narrator? Did it matter that the novels may have been written by a man if, for female readers at the time, they rang true as the creations of an authentic Third World, feminine voice? The splitting of Rhaïs into a s/he ultimately leads one to read this scene from *Saâda* as a message in a bottle, a "sign" sent by Raoul to the reader alerting her to the fact that the appearance of gender identities should never be trusted.

Read critically, the story of Rhaïs's reception turns into a parable about the interpretation of the colonial stereotype in which cultural and gender travesty use each other as alibis of authorial identity. For all we know, the novels could have been written by a French colonial officer—the mere fact that such doubts prove difficult to dispel on the basis of the writing alone points to the fundamental unreliability of time-honored notions of historical narration, authentic voice, and national literature. Without such notions, the historiography of literary history will have to be rewritten, but do we have any choice? Just as traditional gender terminology recedes under the onslaught of challenges to "compulsory heterosexuality" (to be replaced by more tentative articulations of sexual identities or by nothing at all), so the language of culture and national type becomes increasingly impossible to employ in good faith. What remains for the critic is the search for a nonrelativistic lexicon that defines itself self-reflexively as a symptom of historical vision.

7

ACTING OUT
ORIENTALISM

STEREOTYPE,

PERFORMATIVITY,

THE ISABELLE

EBERHARDT EFFECT

In considering the status of Orientalism as a theatrical conceit in turn-of-the-century feminist performance, I want to continue situating discussions of performativity and the stereotype that in their turn beg certain questions about the appointment and settling of identity. It has struck me that in the concern to escape stale gender epistemologies, with their heterosexist contraries and psychosexual clichés, a frangible alternative rhetoric has been ushered in figuring sexual identity as a conditional performativity that leaves only a ghostly and sometimes ghastly trace of the stereotype behind in the wake of its performances. Mutable sexualities, body parts semiotically open to erotic opportunity, sexed bodies recast as morphologically plastic and phantasmatically unbound—such parsings, grafted from the language of Judith Butler's chapter "The Lesbian Phallus and the Morphological Imaginary" in *Bodies That Matter,* while eschewing an outright utopianism of gender possibility, nevertheless rekindle great expectations for a genuinely gender-troubled future.[1]

There has been considerable confusion surrounding the status of the term performativity in Butler's work. Despite its celebrity in relation to her writing, the term, interestingly enough, did not figure in the index of *Gender Trouble,* where *parody* was the preferred word and did much of performativity's work. In Butler's later work, performativity emerges as a concept coinciding with the French sense of "une belle performance," that is, an obtained result, an act accomplished on bodies in readiness (and here agency seems psychoanalytically curtailed, as it is in poststructuralism). The ordinary-language philosopher J. L. Austin had of course employed the term to refer to how locutionary exchanges are driven by circumstantial motivations and intentions, the conditions by which speech-acts either misfire or hit their mark. Implicitly transposing these rules of language to gender, Butler, it seemed, wanted to preserve the framework of discursive constraint on meaning-production (where constraints are produced by normative prohibitions and the Law), while steering clear of a full-blown rehabilitation of subjective agency and intentionality.

Of course, the immediate purchase of the term performativity is on the realm of theatricality, but Butler has often seemed committed to taking the performance out of the performative:

> In no sense can it be concluded that that part of gender that is performed is therefore the "truth" of gender; performance as bounded "act" is distinguished from performativity insofar as the latter consists in a reiteration of norms which precede, constrain, and exceed the performer and in that sense cannot be taken as the fabrication of the performer's "will" or "choice"; further, what is "performed" works to conceal, if not to disavow, what remains opaque, unconscious, un-performable. The reduction of performativity to performance would be a mistake.[2]

Performativity was thus linked to the "citationality" of cultural norms and practices, and to the psychic prohibitions and exclusions that regulate the normative visibility of the symbolic order; its connection to "living theater" was more or less disavowed, except in the arena of queer politics, where "theatrical rage" was recognized as a vital strategy deployed against the "the killing inattention of policy-makers on the issue of AIDS."[3]

Butler's reservations toward theatricality were shared by Eve Kosovsky Sedgwick. In her discussion of queer performativity in Henry James, underscoring "the obliquities among *meaning, being* and *doing,*" Sedgwick warned against the domestication of the term through reductive determinations of

> whether particular performances (e.g. of drag) are really *parodic and subversive* (e.g. of gender essentialism) or just *uphold the* status quo. The bottom line is generally the same: kinda subversive, kinda hegemonic. I see this as a sadly premature domestication of a conceptual tool whose powers we really have barely yet begun to explore.[4]

With this caveat against taming the mental constructs for thinking sexuality Sedgwick upped the ante in the intellectual quest for alternatives to exhausted dyads and oppositionalities. But in dismantling historically resilient gender ontologies with an eye to accomplishing more than a simplistic resistance to gender essentialism and less than a naively redemptive vision of sexual polysemy, Sedgwick, like Butler, still left open the question of the hinge that keeps identity signification in place. A nagging anxiety about how referents ultimately come to bear meaning (that follows learning of the arbitrariness of signifiers or the nonorignary nature of the Transcendental Signified) accompanies the prospect of reading sexual semiotics adrift in psychic prohibitions and identifications. The materialist grounding of phantasmatic signification—acknowledged as essential by Butler and Sedgwick alike—often remains elusive on the level of interpretative history.

My hypothesis in this chapter is that part of what allowed turn-of-the-century sexuality to perform itself along Sedgwick's axis of "meaning, being, and doing" was its mediation by the culturally exotic stereotype. Psychoanalytically, the stereotype is akin to Freud's notion of "character types," assigned explicit importance in the essays: *Psychopathic Characters on the Stage* (1905–6), *Character and Anal Eroticism* (1908), *Some Character-Types Met with in Psychoanalytic Work* (1916), and *Libidinal Types* (1931). In the second of these essays he wrote:

> Among those whom one tries to help by means of psychoanalytic treatment, one very often meets with a type of character in which certain traits are strongly marked, while at the same time one's attention is arrested by the behaviour of these persons in regard to a certain bodily function and of the organ connected with it during their childhood. I can no longer say on what precise occasion I first received the impression that a systematic relationship exists between this type of character and the activities of this organ, but I can assure the reader that no theoretical anticipations of mine played any part in its production.[5]

In this account, the character-type makes itself embarrassingly evident. Undoubtedly sensitive to anti-Semitism's strategic use of physiognomical stigmas and types, Freud is understandably wary of legitimizing facile conjugations of bodily feature with personality trait. But the character-type refuses, as it symptomatically does, to go away.

A rather underrated staple of critical discourse that may be ripe for theoretical revisitation, *stereotype,* as we all know, is a term deriving from the history of printing referring to the metal plate made from a mold of composed type. An early example of technology's impact on textual representation, the stereotype retains the semantic residue of the materiality of its origin even within its more figurative usage as a synonym for the commonplace, hackneyed, or conventionally "settled in form." The notion of *imprinting,* whether visual or discursive, remains a key to understanding the negative reputation of the stereotype as that which stamps the complex subject with the seal of reductive caricature and/or bad habit. It was in this way that Oscar Wilde employed the term in his bitter reproach to Lord Alfred Douglas in *De Profundis:* "My habit—due to indifference chiefly at first—of giving up to you in everything had become insensibly a real part of my nature. Without my knowing it, it had *stereotyped* my temperament to one permanent and fatal mood."[6] The association of the stereotype with "permanence" and "fatality" implies that the stereotyped character is flawed, even deviant, insofar as it contains a groove of moral decadence veering toward the death drive.

Wilde's reference to his "stereotyped temperament" encapsulates a drama of ego destitution and volitional subjugation. In an essay concentrating on the way in which stereotypes are "intercepted" in the graphic, slogan-slashed art of Barbara Kruger, the late Craig Owens also reminds us that "to imprint (stereo-*type*) the image directly on the viewer's imagination, to eliminate the need for decoding," is tantamount to visual "subjection."[7] A tool of paranoid surveillance, according to Owens's Foucauldian ascription,

> A form of symbolic violence exercised upon the body in order both to assign it a place and to keep it in place, the stereotype works less through persuasion (the goal of traditional rhetoric: ideological adherence, consent) than through deterrence—what Jean Baudrillard calls "dissuasion." It promotes passivity, receptivity, inactivity—docile bodies. This effect is achieved primarily through intimidation: the stereotype poses a threat. (P. 194)

Though this passage calls for a nuanced reading of the stereotype's moral and physical damage to the subject, what I would like to pick up on here is not so much the repressive effect of the stereotype's overlegibility (explored in interesting ways by Roland Barthes in terms of how stereotypical iterations, conceived as deadening repetitions of intellection, "repress" and thereby produce textual bliss), but rather on the problematics of *posing* implicit in Owens's assertion that the "stereotype poses a threat." Inadvertently or not, Owens signals the performativity of the stereotype, its theatrical flair for striking a pose, assuming a guise, pretending an identity into existence. As Owens observes in another essay dedicated explicitly to the problem of posing, "the subject poses as an object *in order to be a subject*" (p. 215). This formulation, it would seem, lies at the heart of the essentialism versus parodic gender performance debate insofar as it illustrates the lack of clear boundaries between the two camps. Though essentialism in feminist theory privileges crystallized, transcendent stereotypes, while its performative counterpart supposedly emphasizes typological dissolution and resignification, the two discourses are, so to speak, joined at the hip by their mutual reliance on a subject that makes itself *be* by enacting objectification.

The enactment of objectification can be seen at work quite self-consciously in the way in which French feminism mobilized Orientalist stereotypes to fashion novel sexual identities that functioned as props on which to hang a pose. "Monstrous superhuman figures," to borrow Mario Praz's terms, were excavated from cultural history; women such as Sémiramis, Thaïs, and Cleopatra, whose erotic appetites were legendarily matched to their thirst for political authority. Sémiramis was an Assyrian queen who rebuilt Babylon with fortresses, fabulous palaces, and suspended gardens. She became famous in ancient history for her successful military campaigns throughout Asia and the Middle East. Revived in the eighteenth century as the subject of plays by Crébillon and Voltaire, celebrated as a romantic heroine in Rossini's opera of 1823, Sémiramis, not surprisingly, resurfaced at the turn of the century in a 1904 dramatic production written by the decadent author Joseph Péladan (famous for his fin de siècle taste for androgyne and lesbian protagonists) that received ecstatic reviews in women's journals of the period such as *Fémina*. Like Péladan's *Sémiramis*, Anatole France's *Thaïs*, first published in 1890 and adapted for the immensely popular opera by Jules Massenet in 1894, played on the hieratic, historic grandeur of the female stereotype by exploiting the full regalia of Orientalist decor. In this kitsch anticlerical conversion story about a fourth-century Egyptian courtesan and a hypocritical holy man who falls under her spell while diverting her from the path of sin, Thaïs is featured as an actress, seducing her riveted audience on the Alexandrian stage. Clothed in heavy gems, and presented to the viewer as an image graven in stone, she embodies the stereotype made pure performative, at once fetishized and mobilized in conceptual and visual space.

The immense prestige of the historical stereotype embodied in these Orientalist phallic women made them ripe for feminist reappropriation. In Britain, for example, a feminist Thaïs emerged in suffragette circles in the teens and twenties with the revival and retranslation of *Paphnutius*, a medieval play written by Hrotsvit von Gandersheim.[8] As emblems of national character, these stereotypes conferred the ideological adhesive of nationalism onto a nascent women's movement built on fragile coalitions and disparate class interests. In the context of Parisian identity politics, where the political was defined more personally and the salon or stage prevailed as the chosen arena of activism, Orientalist stereotypes were used as a means of partially or semicovertly outing sapphic love. Colette's outing of her erotic partnership with the marquise de Belboeuf in *Rêve d'Egypte* may be seen, in this regard, as of a piece with Mikhail Fokine's choreographed renditions of *Cléopâtre* (based on Théophile Gautier's short story "Une Nuit de Cléopâtre") and *Shéhérazade* in 1908 and 1910, respectively, for the Ballets

Russes. Both productions featured the celebrated lesbian performer Ida Rubenstein in the major role.[9] Rubenstein's exotic features (she was Russian Jewish), great height, thin, androgynous body, and imperious manner made her a favorite for Orientalist roles in which sadomasochistic scenarios prevailed. Peter Wollen has traced the origin of her Orientalist mystique to the beginnings of her acting career in St. Petersburg, "where she was first introduced to Fokine by Bakst because she wanted dance lessons in order to play the part of Salome in her own production of Oscar Wilde's play."[10] He also notes that she eventually would perform Salome's Dance of the Seven Veils when it was transposed to *Cléopâtre*, making her entrance "on the shoulders of six slaves," and removing each veil (increased to twelve) in an elaborate striptease. What is particularly interesting in the case of Rubenstein and Colette is the use of Orientalism as an erotic cipher, a genre of theatricality in which acting "Oriental" becomes a form of outing, and outing is revealed to be thoroughly consonant with putting on an act (each flips into the other unpredictably).

An important fin de siècle paradigm for this acting/outing slippage may be found in Pierre Loti's *Aziyadé* (1879), already encountered in chapters 5 and 6. Though dated, the work provides a prime example of Orientalist decadence devolving around the treacly romance of a British naval officer whose heart is stolen by a Circassian slave. The mise en scène is formulaically embellished with *turqueries,* just as his Far Eastern novel *Madame Chrysanthème* avails itself of stylistic *japonisme,* or *Le Roman d'un Spahi* of a black African fetish discourse. *Aziyadé* is the earliest of his colonial novels, earning him the dubious title "Pimp of the Sensation of Difference," bestowed by his revisionist successor in the aesthetics of tourism, Victor Segalen. Set in Salonika and Istanbul during the waning of the Ottoman empire, *Aziyadé* is suffused with an atmosphere of imperial belatedness; what Mario Praz in *The Romantic Agony* characterized as "the long Byzantine twilight, that gloomy apse gleaming with dull gold and gory purple, from which peer enigmatic faces, barbaric yet refined, with dilated neurasthenic pupils . . . a period of anonymous corruption, with nothing of the heroic about it, . . . devoid of any virile element."[11] Like Remy de Gourmont's *Lettres à l'Amazone* (written for that leading figure of lesbian salons in Paris, Natalie Clifford Barney), and Pierre Louÿs's "Chansons de Bilitis" (poems about a Turkish high priestess of Lesbos), *Aziyadé* functioned as an underground script for the initiate, interpreted improvisationally in salon skits and "real life," as when two Western-educated Turkish women, Nouryé and Zennour Noury-Bey, purportedly snared Loti in his own sequel by posing as Aziyadé reincarnations, returned in the flesh from a fictional tomb. (Loti went along with the ruse, half believing in the revisitation of his dead mistress, and using the episode to great effect to structure his subsequent Turkish harem novel *Les Désenchantées)*.

Just as it would be for Parisian sapphic circles, the art of cultural camouflage was important to Loti's self-fashioning as both textual and (auto)biographical figure. A naval officer from Brittany, he was famous for having himself photographed in the local costumes, both masculine and feminine, of the foreign territories he visited, including China, Japan, the South Sea Islands, North Africa, West Africa, and the Middle East. He even extended this fascination with exoticist drag to the Moorish interior of his own home at Rochefort, transformed into a kind of domestic stage-set modeled after the Turkish apartment that *Aziyadé*'s central character appoints for himself in the Istanbul Casbah. Loti also gave vent to theatricalized Orientalism when, in order to gain his idol Sarah Bernhardt's attention, he "had himself carried in to Sarah, as Cleopatra was carried in to Caesar, wrapped in a carpet."[12] Not only was Sarah Bernhardt celebrated for her role in Victor Sardou's *Cléopâtre*—which she played into her seventies—but she, like Loti, had herself photographed in character, stretched out on a divan with jeweled girdle and arm-bracelets, an adoring female attendant at her knee. One could say that Loti's grand gesture, his trying to "be" Sarah, by "being" Sarah Bernhardt "being" Cleopatra, embodied a kind of portmanteau Orientalism crossing bisexual and bicultural identifications.

The histrionic quality of Orientalist posing, common to art and life in Loti's case, points to a performative reading of *Aziyadé* in which the narrative is read as a scenography written in order to be acted out. Each diegetic sequence is built up around visually suspended tableaus, thrown up like so many expendable scrims and flimsily interconnected by diacritical ellipses. A sense of theater is also given characterological specificity through the conceit of a central narrator whose name is shared by the author (Loti was the pen name of Julien Viaud), and the protagonist, who "passes" as a Turk under the alias Arif-effendi. The dissolution and fragmentation of authorial and characterological integrity lends the novel a modernist aspect: there is no essentialist core to Loti's persona; in fact he continually refers to the emptiness within, to a self filled up with *eski,* the Turkish word for existential vacuity and ennui. Loti's protagonist clings to seeming Turkish so as to avoid the more difficult metaphysic of "being" nothing, nothing, that is, but a fleeting coalescence of what Alan Sinfield has termed "expressivity effects." In his social deconstruction of Shakespearean character criticism Sinfield writes,

> I have been trying to exemplify a way of reading in which speech and action in a fictional text may be attributed to characters—understood not as essential unities, but as simulated personages apparently possessing ade-

quately continuous or developing subjectivities. But, beyond that, the presentation of the dramatis personae must be traced to a textual organization in which character is a strategy, and very likely one that will be abandoned when it interferes with other desiderata. To observe this is important, not just as a principle of literary criticism, but because it correlates with a repudiation of the assumption that reality, in plays or in the world, is adequately explained by reference to a fixed, autonomous, and self-determining core of individual being. Rather, subjectivity is itself produced, in all its complexity, within a linguistic and social structure.[13]

Sinfield signals the extent to which the very notion of character, like its more degraded cousin, the stereotype, is a fixing in flux; a stamp of the real flimsily appended to strategic, contingent, semiotic subjectivities. Character itself emerges as stereotype in drag.

Loti's sham Turkishness highlights the theatrics of passing crucial to the performance of national and sexual character. In the novel, the protagonist wavers between the successful cultural plagiarist traveling through the Casbah unremarked, to the inauthentic native who, on catching sight of himself in a mirror, perceives a risible figure resembling "a young tenor, ready to break into a passage of Auber."[14] This failed cultural pass is intertwined with the failed heterosexual pass. When Loti tries to test Aziyadé's love by "playing the sultan," forcing her to suffer his liaison with another Turkish woman, his cultural masquerade backfires as he finds himself rendered impotent by the courtesan's Europeanized dress. This masculinist demise, coinciding as it does with his inability to carry off the part of despotic pasha, implies that Arif-effendi's staged harem is really a convenient disguise for Loti's homoerotic closet. Aziyadé herself, childlike and subservient, emerges as the travestied stand-in for Loti's young servant Samuel, with whom he savors "the vices of Sodom" in the brothels of the red-light district. Falling asleep on a boat with Samuel by his side, the narrator has a wet dream signaled by the sudden eruption of enemy fire. This fantastic episode, along with the book's allusions to cruising, trysting, and the procurement of boys, add up to what Roland Barthes, borrowing Loti's phrase, characterized as the novel's element of "pale debauchery." "Pale outing" may in fact be the more appropriate expression, particularly insofar as it shadow-plays what Barthes himself was doing through his reading of Loti. Famous for his reticence on the subject of his own sexuality, Barthes came as close to publicizing his open secret by "bringing out" (in D. A. Miller's words) the gay innuendoes of Loti's writing and culturally staged persona. Loti's Turkophilia gives a new twist to Said's characterization of the colonial traveler's perception of the Orient as a "living tableau of queerness."[15]

I do not mean to imply that Loti's Turkish act was merely a decoy for that which was erotically not quite "out" (after all, Loti was perhaps only acting "out," that is, not really outing himself, but only appearing to do so), but rather that acting and outing are mutually implicated in exaggerated truth claims, claims to being "true to type." Acting and outing, as ontological strategies, commonly rely on essentialist typologies of enacted being that are thrown into definitional crisis by the wild mimeticism of affect. Perhaps it is this inflation of affect that helps to explain why campy Orientalist scenarios have always been and continue to be good value within gay drama; their overacted quality points to the way in which nonconformist sexual identity must perform its way into existence, more often than not through the transformation of originally conservative models.

Orientalism, as a nexus of extravagant psychic investments and layered semblances of the type, evolved into feminist and lesbian camp for a number of other more obvious reasons. Not only were women empowered or accorded sexual license through association with the dominatrix characterologies attached to exemplary princesses, queens, seductresses, or women leaders of the East, but, more interestingly, their agency was enhanced by "being" these avatars both on stage and off.[16] Ida Rubenstein, Sarah Bernhardt, Mata Hari, Colette, Lucie Delarue Mardrus, Renée Vivien, and others expanded the performative parameters of the historic stereotype by moving their larger-than-life thespian personae into the choreography of erotic everyday life.

In the case of Renée Vivien (Pauline Tarn), the author of several lesbian cult books and translations of Sappho, whose short life was mythically commemorated by Nathalie Barney and Colette among others, the art of "being" Sappho seems to have done as much for the legendary quality of her persona as anything she wrote or transposed.[17] Her Sappho, according to Jean-Paul Goujon, was "Asiatic" and exotic, inhabiting a Lesbos that never forgot its contiguity to Smyrna.[18] This conflation of Greece and the Orient was of course particularly common in turn-of-the-century art, literature, opera, dance, and theater; syncretistic otherness was the fashion, spawning a wild hybridity of styles—Egypto-Greek, Greco-Asian, biblical-Moorish—that would eventually be taken over by Hollywood. The particularism of the Orientalist stereotype was important nonetheless. In Vivien's case, a "real," living Turkish woman anchored her exoticist fantasies. Goujon has recently unearthed evidence of her epistolary (and ultimately consummated) romance with Kérimé Turkhan-Pacha, an "emancipated" woman from Constantinople who had originally written to Vivien as a literary fan. Erected as the proverbial "Captive Princess" on the shores of the Bosporus in Vivien's prose fragment *Le Jardin turc* (1905–6) and apostrophized as the "brown Mistress" and "My Sultana" in subsequent love poems, Kérimé, according to Goujon, played Orientalist double to Natalie Barney in Vivien's erotic pantheon. The heady mix of fantasy and tourism that sealed the Vivien-Kérimé love affair spilled over into Vivien's financial sponsorship of Nouryé and Zennour Noury-Bey, the same Turkish women who had pretended to incarnate Azyiadé in the hopes of enlisting Loti's help in evading their respective harems. Informed by Kérimé of their escape from Constantinople and struggle to survive in Paris, Vivien furnished them with an apartment and living allowance, thereby securing a place for herself as a character in the as-yet-unwritten sequel to Loti's *Désenchantées*.

In addition to allowing Vivien to extend her fanciful construction of a Hellenic Paris-Lesbos into the psychoterritory of the Orient, Kérimé may have also played a central role in the Barney-Vivien quest for the "gynandromorph" defined by Barney's feminist biographer Karla Jay as "a higher, more perfect being, which would re-establish the principle of Femaleness in the universe."[19] In Natalie Barney's fantastic, rhetorically extraterrestrial "biography of a soul," *The One Who Is Legion, or A.D.'s After-Life*, the gynandromorphic principle is ethereally manifest in a succession of what Terry Castle has identified as "apparitional lesbians."[20] Identities "on loan," persons whose posthumous correspondences are retrieved from the "dead-letter office" in the hopes of constituting a "herstory," these transubstantiated shadow women form a great chain of being whose essence approximates an androgyny purged of its diametric opposition to masculinity. At one point in the novel the problem of how to generate a feminocentric characterology that eschews singular, individual identities is fascinatingly considered; diverse theoretical gambits are themselves performed in an invocatory, interrogative voice:

> Put down every wanderer found in our catacombs, fix them by some familiar trait, and so learn to know and govern our ghosts, our lovers, our low-characters, our martyrs and saints, and any that we might encounter in this journey through ourselves. Surprised that authors had established no manner of dealing with even their fictitious personages, should we not definitely adopt the play-writer's method of giving a name to each *dramatis persona*—the drama here consisting in their divergences and conflicts—their combined chemistries. But what of their simultaneous claims and antagonisms?[21]

The response to this incredulous question is negative; there is no fixing trait or character-name adjudicating among "simultaneous claims and antagonisms." When alternative systems for classifying the multivalent female soul are tested—musical composition, color-codes, orthography—the confusion only worsens. In the end the narrator reverts to a composite of stereotypes including the siren, the sphinx, and St. Joan, to be appointed communal "sponsor" or surrogate for the soul after "she" has committed suicide.

Barney's phantasmatic, Swedenborgian soul-mate appears in hindsight to be a precursor of the transcendental female subject invented by Luce Irigaray—contradictorily essentialist and antiessentialist, singular and multiple, at one and the same time. In this light, it is all the more interesting that Barney resurrects the stereotype at the end of her novel as an antidote to the complete derealization of character attempted at the outset; antiessentialism is thus curtailed by the return of the type.

In a more down-to-earth vein, Cléo de Mérode's memoir *Le Ballet de ma vie* charts the predication of the feminine subject on the exotic stereotype and its subsequent fanning out into exorbitant character. Cléo's improbable name helped to overdetermine the mythic creature she became; christened "Cléopâtre-Diane," she joined Orientalism to Hellenism in her stagecraft and publicity images. A celebrated belle epoque *cocotte* whose erotic inclination, like that of her famous rival Liane de Pougy, was deeply feminocentric, Cléo began her career as a precocious star of the Paris Opera ballet corps. The winner of *L'Illustration*'s beauty contest, her image was mass reproduced. In the realm of high art she became a favorite model for painters, sculptors, and photographers (Nadar among them). It was costumed as an Egyptian dancer in *Aida,* so the legend goes, that she seduced Leopold II, king of Belgium. In 1900 she clinched the Orientalization of her performance profile (much like Ida Rubenstein and Ruth St. Denis), with "la danse Cambodgienne," the hot attraction of the Exposition Universelle's *Théâtre Asiatique.* Toward the end of World War I, she amplified her Orientalist repertory with the role of "the Sulamite" in Charles Cuvillier's *Judith courtisane.* Here she performed an Egyptian dance with hieratic steps against a black décor, dressed in a dramatic gold tunic and black velvet cape designed by Paul Poiret.

Mérode's signature performance as the Cambodian dancer was intended to rival Sibyl Sanderson's interpretation of Thaïs, witnessed by Mérode early on in her career while a "rat d'Opéra" on the set. Sanderson's rendering of Thaïs exfoliated around her, emerging in Mérode's account as a catalyst of Orientalist characterology. In the choreography, the pairing of roses with the mask of comedy points to the kind of punned relationship between performance and sex already evident in the acting/outing paradigm:

Still a child but already tall, I also appeared in *Thaïs,* where I danced a decorative intermezzo with some of my companions. We played the part of
novice actresses, following the courtesan, and we balanced ourselves
around her waving roses in one hand and a mask in the other. . . . And Thaïs
was Sibyl Sanderson! The beauty of her plasticity, the shapeliness of her postures, the powerful charm that exuded from her person and her act attracted
the admiration of all.[22]

In this picture of young dancers impersonating the role of courtesans' disciples in anticipation of the courtesan's role that many of them would
eventually play in "real life," character is enhanced by the transmission of
admiration, rapture, and the thrill of bodily proximity to the diva, generating waves of affect that would, for many, translate into the sapphic bonds
of the Parisian city of women. Cléo's ties to Paris-Lesbos were guaranteed by
the presence of her lifelong companion Marie Briot, a retired theater pro-
fessional who had been part of the circle of Louise Balthy, a celebrated lesbian demimondaine known for her "ugly" chic.

Cléo de Mérode was mythologized by her era as one of the great feminine stereotypes of Paris 1900, a stereotype compiled in large measure
from the Orientalist performances of famous actresses: Sarah Bernhardt's
Cleopatra, Sibyl Sanderson's Thaïs, Rose Caron's Salammbô, Mme Héglon's
Delila, Loïe Fuller's pseudo-Eastern veil dance, Sada Yacco's Salome. Identification with these female icons was sealed by the hallowed ritual of torch
passing whereby the novice takes into herself the stereotype of the big, exotic, feminine Other offered by the diva.

The expanded notion of performativity and performance that emerges
from early feminist theater history has been recognized by a number of critics, most notably Sue-Ellen Case, who sees Natalie Barney as a preeminent
forerunner of the contemporary woman performance artist. Barney, Case
observes,

> invented the practice of women performing for women, which was to be-
> come important in feminist theater in the 1970's; she introduced images of
> lesbian sexuality; she conceived of improvisatory performances relating to
> the talents of women performers; and she created theatricals which oc-
> curred in her private, domestic space, but which were intended as formal,
> aesthetic works and even found their way into published dialogues. The
> personal theater of the salons and private theatricals paved the way for a
> new art form in this century, which has created an important intersection of
> feminism and theater—women in performance art.[23]

Case's concern to develop a feminist history of performance, while highly
useful, presents in this particular instance an unproblematized view of

role-playing, role models, and feminist identifications with the enabling stereotype. In his psychoanalytic dissection of the colonial stereotype, Homi Bhabha argues that "the point of intervention should shift from the *identification* of images as positive or negative, to an understanding of the *processes of subjectivication* made possible (and plausible) through stereo-typical discourse."[24] Though it is not entirely clear what these "processes of subjectivication" fully entail, it seems that for Bhabha, the stereotype, like the fetish, embodies an image-repertoire of deadening repetitions (around, say, race or gender) that ultimately produces alienation from the psychi-cally surinvested system of representations within which it is codified. Bhabha recoups the stereotype as the bad object of colonial mimicry by al-lowing it to return as a good object of subjectification, shattering politically fixed colonial subjects into a multitude of refractive, potentially emancipa-tory subject positions.

Bhabha's complication of the identification paradigm as applied to race and cultural identity lines up well in many respects with Judith Butler's performative reading of gender-imitation within the morphological Imag-inary, but both theorists avoid fully recognizing the psychic recalcitrance of the stereotype as a constricting component of gender and cultural iden-tity. Disavowed, the stereotype rebounds reavowed, as that which gender destabilization pins itself on as a point of departure or referent of resig-nification. The irrepressible coherence of characterology embedded in the stereotype introduces a kind of psychic ossification that reassimilates sub-jective novelties into the *doxa*. The stereotype, I would maintain, is the Achilles' heel of performativity, or better yet, the "Cleopatra's nose" (to use Lacan's Pascalian trope for "le je ne sais quoi" in "The Freudian Thing") of historical subjectification.[25]

How then do we escape the prison-house of stereotypes in the field of identity politics? I don't think we can, but it is perhaps the desire to do so that motivates one of the more astonishing episodes in feminist perfor-mance history—the acting out of what I will call the "Isabelle Eberhardt complex." In looking at this complex, I will argue, subjectification occurs not so much, as Bhabha affirms, through a "shift *from* identification," but rather *through* a radical identification *with* nothing, nothing but the stereo-type drained of its recognizable identity markers: its "Europeanness," its "femme-ness," its metaphysics of presence.

Eberhardt's larger-than-life biography, modeled quite self-consciously by Isabelle herself after Loti's Orientalist fictions, exerted and has contin-ued to exert an extraordinary hold on the Occidental feminist imagin-ary (see chapters 5 and 6). Her life story, recounted first by executors and would-be publishers Victor Barrucand, Robert Randau, and René-Louis

Doyen, and emphatically retold in more recent times by Rana Kabbani, Annette Kobak, Denise Brahimi, Edmonde Charles-Roux, Lesley Blanch, and Paul Bowles, illustrates a compulsion to repeat symptomatic of the stereotype. Eberhardt was the illegitimate daughter of a Slavic anarchist named Alexander Trophimowsky, who had an affair with Isabelle's mother after he was hired as the family tutor. Gifted in Oriental languages and fascinated by Islam, he taught Isabelle and her brothers Arabic. From 1897 on, Eberhardt traveled to North Africa, eventually adopting the name Si Mahmoud Essadi, converting to Islam, and getting herself inducted into the Sufi brotherhood of the Qadriya.[26] Cross-dressing as an Arab man, she pursued the rough pleasures of nomadic travel, casual sex, and drugs. A self-destructive streak matched the dark flashes in her destiny. Though her short stories and newspaper articles in the Algerian press garnered her a following in North Africa and abroad, she also enraged local colons who were probably behind an assassination attempt that she survived (but not without an augmented sense of morbidity), only to die in 1904 in a freak desert flood at the age of twenty-seven.

One could say that Isabelle Eberhardt fell masochistically in love with death. In one tale, an anonymous male character sings "an ancient song in which the word for *love* alternated with the word for *death*."[27] A beautiful Jewess is impaled in the street after falling prey to the charms of a cruel Sidi in "The Magician," a dancer, abandoned by a French conscript, turns to self-wasting alcoholism and prostitution in "Achoura," a young woman commits suicide when forced into a repulsive arranged marriage in "Taalith," and throughout her journals, a solitary global adventuress restlessly moves on from shelter to shelter, "vagabonding" in body and spirit. "Vagrancy is deliverance," she wrote: "To be alone, to be *poor in needs,* to be ignored, to be an outsider who is at home everywhere, and to walk, great and by oneself, toward the conquest of the world."[28] In virtually all her stories, women bind themselves as she did, to a nihilistic credo of addiction, moral abnegation, and poverty. Here one could say that the degree zero stereotype performed by Eberhardt—that of a gender-dispossessed, deculturated woman inserted into the violent landscape of colonial history—fulfilled the Wildean ascription of "bad habit" or fatal groove.

Eberhardt's biography has been acted out by successive generations of feminists. In the twenties and thirties Lucie Delarue-Mardrus not only paid tribute to Isabelle's memory through a visit to her grave in Ain-Sefra, but she also "interpreted" the Eberhardt script in her self-staging as "la Princesse Amande." Immortalized in the memoir of her amanuensis Myriam Harry (written in what Wayne Koestenbaum would call "diva prose," a writing at once "florid, self-aggrandizing, imperial, amusing, banal, pathetic, full of trashy cadences"), Lucie is introduced in Harry's *Mon amie Lucie Delarue-Mardrus* in a Carthaginian amphitheater, overseeing the rehearsal of one of her own plays.[29] Interestingly, it is the offstage theatricality of her Orientalist identity performance that upstages an account of her play:

> The actors from the French theater, beturbaned and draped in Tunisian fabric, in keeping with their instinct for the stage, were smoking, like Oriental gentlemen, narghile pipes, svelte as jets of water. Lucie Delarue-Mardrus—baptized "the Almond Princess" by her husband—came and went, hieratic and silent on the arm of Jeanne Delvaire, inspecting, with her discerning eye, the little kingdom of Shéhérazade.[30]

Alternately cast in the part of Shéhérazade and Salammbô, sporting an opal ring, "set à la byzantine," that had been worn by Sarah Bernhardt in *Cleopatra* and *Lorenzaccio,* Lucie arouses awe and jealousy of her seductiveness in her self-appointed scribe. Throughout her life, as recounted by Harry, Lucie continued to play the role of Orientalized doyenne of the lesbian elite. She organized parties and tableaux vivants drawing on her husband's acclaimed erudition as an Arabic scholar (he translated *Mille et une nuits* and published a popular study of the queen of Sheba); she authored Egyptophilic texts constructed around morbid femmes fatales (the novel *Amanit)* and dedicated verse to Eberhardt evoking her "bedouin coat" as a kind of sacred mantel of transvestism sanctioning future feminist explorations into the shadowy regions of bisexual biculturalism.[31]

The "Eberhardt complex" was similarly at work in Henriette Célarié's visit to Eberhardt's final dwelling. As soon as she crossed the threshold of the narrow barrack, stooping under a hand of Fathma, Célarié started to "be" Eberhardt, "imagining" herself "leaning on the parapet, awaiting the hour when the local mullah would announce that the sun had disappeared on the horizon and that the fast could be broken." Eberhardt's ghost—a phantasm of Islamic melancholia—inhabits Célarié; she is left overpowered by a sense of Eberhardt's "anguished, demoralized spirit," "tortured by piteous regrets," and the vagaries of her "savage and unsatisfied heart."[32]

The dark epiphanies of the Eberhardtian lady traveler also informed the biography and writings of the Australian journalist Ernestine Hill. Meaghan Morris has determined that in Hill's death-driven panoramas, typically found in her travel narrative *The Great Australian Loneliness* (1937),

> a very strong relation is established in these texts between death and the historical mission of travel-writing (narration as well as description). This is partly a matter of their chosen "landscape": death is a dominant figure in

the scenic history of a colonizing struggle to conquer the land, the sea, and the natives. In their expansionist commitment to Australia's brave white future, Hill's texts are not apparently concerned with any intimations of an absolute "death of history"—except for Aborigines. They are histories of death: not only because of the colonial scene, but because "history" is conventionally represented as a narrative of the dead (the past, or the passing).[33]

Whether it is Hill's desolate outback or Paul Bowles's "sheltering Moroccan sky" (in which Bowles, who translated Eberhardt into English, augured the suicide of his wife, Jane Bowles), there is a drama of ego destitution expressed through Eberhardtian mimesis. *The Sheltering Sky* (1949) rewrites the Eberhardt legend in the key of existentialist colonialism. When Port, the principal male character, dies midnovel of the plague, his beautiful American widow Kit is abducted by a caravan of camel-drivers. Like Eberhardt, Kit dons the costume of an Arab youth, and like Eberhardt, she learns to "love rape" at the hands of her captors within a landscape of masochism.

Whatever the reason (the trope of female bondage?) Eberhardt's cult status has been firm in feminist and lesbian circles and continues to this day, rendered most interestingly by Leslie Thornton's art-house film *There Was an Unseen Cloud Moving* (1987).[34] Thornton takes the miraculous bones of Eberhardt's story and splices it with sepia-toned stills from the colonial archive, both then and now. North African wonders such as the Casbah, Mecca, or desert dunes are intercalated with early cinema clips of flying carpets and exotic dancing, creating the impression of "an unruly fetishism of the exotic object," to borrow Mary Ann Doane's terms in relation to another ironic Orientalist film by Thornton, *Adynata* (1983).[35] In this feminist *vita nuova* writ large, vignettes of Isabelle's unconventional upbringing, sex and drug exploits, and religious mysticism (played by different actresses with an East Village look) alternate with excerpts from educational films (with their inimitable acoustic cues) featuring camel convoys and geography maps. The net effect is a performative history, both personally and politically regressive to an age of innocence, in which bits of intentionally stilted acting thwart viewer identification with a "role model." The various Isabelles fall in and out of character, tugging blasphemously at their veils, improvising hippie dialogue, declaiming their passions with camp exaggeration. In this way, the avant-garde techniques of disjunction, dissociation, and disavowed seduction function, to borrow Craig Owens's phrasing, "to mobilize the spectator against the immobility of the pose."[36] The plurality of Eberhardts undermines character essence. Like Lady Macbeth in Alan Sinfield's reading, Eberhardt is "compounded of contradictory stereotypes" and therefore becomes "a character who is not a character."[37]

This "character who is not a character," this stereotype that is a virtual subject stymied in its ideological "prise" by the mobilized spectator, is nonetheless residually and resiliently a cultural referent that "passes" for itself through a history of what Butler, in her phenomenological vein, referred to as "essence fabrication," "sedimented acts," and "corporeal stylizations."[38] Stereotypes, both cultural and erotic, are generated by and through the frozen inventory of gestures constitutive of theatrical meaning. Though the sheer performativity of this inventory can serve to unsettle identity (easily unmasked as "nothing but an act"), the rehearsed cultural referentialism of the performed type, together with its excessive affect, function to create politically strategic points of semantic connectivity among the blurred procedures of *acting, outing, being, doing, passing,* and *meaning*. Simultaneously subversive and hegemonic, unfixing and status quo, stereotypes render sexual identity politics legible through adhesive, situationally motivated fictions of culture.

8 CLEOPATRA'S NOSE

CHARACTEROLOGY

AND THE MODERN SUBJECT

IN BELLE EPOQUE PARIS

My hypotheses here will be somewhat sweeping and tentative: I am con-
jecturing that the hyperproduction of "new" feminine identities during
the turn of the century helped precipitate the invention of a gender-neutral
modern subject. The fin-de-siècle proliferation of wildly aggrandized, historically invested, exotically inflated character-types, together with French
society's fascination with female performers and feminine performativity
both on stage and off, rendered characterology suspect. As the trope of theatricalized role-playing—with its campy, over-the-top stereotypes and diva
antics—became increasingly typed as feminine, feminist, or queer, character-analysis itself, I am suggesting, was phased out as a slightly fantastical,
old-fashioned methodology. As Terry Castle has perspicaciously shown in
The Apparitional Lesbian, the "fantastic" nature of lesbian characters, fre-
quently transposed to distant historical periods or costumed settings (she
cites Woolf's *Orlando* and Sylvia Townsend Warner's *Summer Will Show)* often led to their being dismissed by critics as quaint or caricatural. While
Castle addresses only indirectly the problem of characterology as a code of
representation of particular importance to women, her work invites further speculation on how feminist characterology might be used to rewrite
the "heroic" history of the modern subject.

In reviving character-analysis, the purpose is not to rehabilitate an
essentialist vision of unitary subjectivity or continuous consciousness;
There is no complicity here with the backlash against poststructuralist theorizations of the character-less or de-moralized humanist subject. Rather, I

am pursuing an intuition that characterology is relevant to recent theoretical debates over the definition of identity, identification, and gender performativity. I am also interested in exploring the hidden stakes of the abandonment of character analysis by Freud, Lacan, and others: was there, for example, a sublated gynophobic "cause" to this turning away from character-critique; or, were the themes that displaced it—object relations, defense mechanisms, the character of the ego, the unperformability of the unconscious, the promotion of an ethics of *jouissance* over and against an Aristotelian morality of character—simply more intellectually compelling as frameworks for analyzing the complexified subject? And allowing that this was the case, is there something to be gained by restoring to these abstracted discourses of subjectivity a social and historical etiology of character-performance or character-identity?

In the previous chapter's discussion of sapphic theatricality in turn-of-the-century Paris, I examined the reappropriation of Orientalist stereotypes. The problem of character—positioned as the high cultural version of the stereotype—was interpreted as both enabling and reductive; enabling insofar as the subject was enhanced through a surplus of affect, reductive in sofar as the subject was simplified through typology, settled into conventionalized "character grooves" of stifling overdetermination. I ended on an equivocal note, arguing, on the one hand, that the stereotype initiates a dereification of the subject as it veers into camp, on the other, that the stereotype remains the Achilles' heel or "Cleopatra's nose" (an expression borrowed from Lacan) of performativity theory, the stamp or residue of the real that patrols subjective boundaries, reasserts social regulation, and repeals adventures into unperformed or unnamed sexualities. Though I do not propose now to resolve these contradictions, I want to return to the problem of character, activating it as a means of reinserting the historic performativity of feminine identity into theorizations of the subject. In what follows, I examine the fluorescence of exemplary feminine character-types of the belle epoque, attending to how they altered the feel of modernity, even as they panicked modern culture into neutering the terms of subjectivity.

The Belle Epoque Woman—too easily projected as some kind of monolithic amalgam of essentialist types, seems a logical place to start in investigating the devaluation of characterology, primarily because she epitomized newly attained heights of exorbitant ontology and ego-display. A parade of larger-than-life female stereotypes showered the belle epoque with aura. The Courtesan, the New Woman, the Amazon, the Demimondaine, the Orientalist, the Socialite, the Streetwalker, the Suffragette, the Religious Enthusiast, the Femme Fatale, the Actress, the Cyclist, the Bourgeoise, the Colonial Civil Servant's Wife, the Coquette, the Fashion

Plate, the Adulteress, these reified identities were subject to further declension in works such as Paul Bourget's *Physiologie de l'amour moderne* or Jean Lorrain's *Une Femme par jour*. Belle epoque character-types embodied the historical hybridity of 1900, captured by Paul Morand in his book *1900* as an impression of pastness plastered onto an emergent streamlined aesthetic, of perverse, decadent, "sterile" sexualities molded into new technologies of visual formalism.

The year 1900 witnessed the emergence of what might be called an *écriture demimondaine,* with the "demi" referring to the milieu of "high society by half" as well as to the literary palette of halftones (mauve, rose, flesh-colored gauze) contouring and costuming the bodies of courtesan subjects. Stylistically negotiating late naturalism, Baudelairean aestheticism, and modernism, this writing of and about the demimonde may be located in narrative renderings of subcultural milieu. In Emile Zola's *Nana,* for example, the backstage world *(les coulisses)* is bathed in a sallow afterlight and peopled by fantastic, semi-invisible bodies. It is perceived as a space of oppressive sexuality by Muffat, as he staggers up the back stairs of the theater in search of Nana:

> The room was empty, and, under the flare of the gas, a solitary chamber pot stood forgotten among a heap of petticoats trailing on the floor. This room afforded him his ultimate impression. Upstairs, on the fourth floor, he was well-nigh suffocated. All the scents, all the blasts of heat, had found their goal there. The yellow ceiling looked as if it had been baked, and a lamp burned amid fumes of russet-coloured fog. . . . And he shut his eyes, and drew a long breath, and drank in the sexual atmosphere of the place. Hitherto he had been utterly ignorant of it, but now it beat him full in his face.
>
> . . . At the end of the corridor was the dressing room belonging to Simonne and Clarisse. It was a long, ill-built room under the roof, with a garret ceiling and sloping walls. The light penetrated to it from two deep-set openings high up in the wall, but at that hour of the night the dressing-room was lit by flaring gas. It was papered with a paper at seven sous a roll, with a pattern of roses twining over green trellis-work. Two boards, placed near one another and covered with oil-cloth, did duty for dressing-tables. They were black with spilt water, and underneath them was a fine medley of dented zinc jugs, slop-pails, and coarse yellow earthenware crocks. There was an array of fancy articles in the room—a battered, soiled, and well-worn array of chipped basins, of toothless combs, of all those manifold untidy trifles, which, in their hurry and carelessness, two women will leave scattered about when they undress and wash together amid purely temporary surroundings, the dirty aspect of which has ceased to concern them.[1]

This freeze-frame of the empty dressing-room littered with soiled, broken toiletries, each guarding the impression of fleeting bodies tossed about in illicit transactions, finds its corollary in Nana's character. Part guttersnipe, part diva; part common prostitute, part actress; part master mistress, part lady of Gomorrah, her image resonates in the interstitial spaces of the social in-between. The "Nana-effect" is heightened further through the deafening repetition of her name at the races (a kind of mantra warding off French national decline and defeat), and finally, through her survival as the notorious star of Zola's most scandalous fiction.

Looking back to the 1870s and 1880s, Marcel Proust capitalized on the already assimilated aesthetic of "Nana-ness" in constructing Odette's ambivalent character. Like Nana, Odette's aura is typified by excess and in-betweenness: to Swann, her profile appears "too sharp," her skin "too delicate," her cheekbones "too prominent," her features "too tightly drawn," her eyes "so large they seemed to droop beneath their own weight," straining the rest of her face and making her "appear unwell or in a bad mood."[2] As in the case of Nana, Odette's persona is pulled back from the signs of ostentation that mark her profession. The pile of signifiers marking the *grande horizontale*—an expensive carriage, ruinously extravagant jewels—falls away to reveal the girl of good family whom one has known all along (the same but not quite). Odette's ambiguous origins also serve as the driving force of the endlessly self-revising storied structure of the *Recherche* itself:

> I had difficulty in believing that she was a courtesan, and certainly I should never have believed her to be an ultra-fashionable one, had I not seen the carriage and pair, the pink dress, the pearl necklace, had I not been aware, too, that my uncle knew only those of the top flight. But I asked myself how the millionaire who gave her her carriage and her house and her jewels could find any pleasure in flinging his money away upon a woman of so simple and respectable an appearance. And yet, when I thought of what her life must be like, its immorality disturbed me more, perhaps, than if it had stood before me in come concrete and recognisable form, by being thus invisible, like the secret of some novel or some scandal which had driven out of the home of her genteel parents and dedicated to the service of all mankind, which had brought to a bright bloom of beauty and raised to fame or notoriety, this woman the play of whose features, the intonations of whose voice, reminiscent of so many others I already knew, made me regard her, in spite of myself, as a young lady of good family, when she was no longer of any family at all.[3]

The "not right" genre to which Odette's troubling aspect is yoked (and which resonates in the famous last line of "Un amour de Swann," when Swann exclaims, "To think that I've wasted years of my life, that I've longed to die, that I've experienced my greatest love, for a woman who didn't appeal to me, who wasn't even my type!")[4] is didactically explored through meditations on the hook, or characterlogical cause, of seduction within feminine beauty. Odette embodies a beauty symptom that both confirms and disturbs the previous chain that Swann has learned to recognize and embellish with code. In a variant from the twelfth *cahier* of *Du côté de chez Swann*, the sight of Odette's face perceived from afar on the Méséglise path after she has become Mme Swann, prompts a disquisition on the character of feminine beauty. At first blush, beauty seems to be a "quality," or "superlative," culled from faces serialized in memory, but on second study, it is recast as a dormant fantasy of the not yet imagined—a blonder than blond Liane de Pougy, a yet more mysterious Mona Lisa, a still more supple Botticellian Prima Vera.[5] In the *esquisse*, Proust complicates the paradigm of fin-de-siècle beauty when the sublime, fantastical woman of his dreams is voided by the sudden appearance of a washerwoman who usurps the narrator's attention entirely and unexpectedly. This intrication of the unexpected within the fabric of the type complements the previously elaborated aesthetic of beauty as that which is *extra to surplus*.[6]

The literary taste for late realist, physiognomically marked character-types fostered a boom in egeria, whose personalities conflated histrionic female legends with contemporary social types. Cleopatra–Sarah Bernhardt, Salome–Ida Rubenstein, Salammbo–Rose Caron, Sémiramis–Mme Segond-Weber, Sappho–Emma Calvé, Thaïs–Mary Garden, Salome–Olive Fremstad, these composite characters crystallized into portmanteau identities, often with a feminist-Orientalist or lesbian-Orientalist profile. Around 1900 the preoccupation with the character of feminine eroticism, so strongly thematized in the novel from Zola to Proust, was further enhanced by the increasing sophistication of publicity. While there had always been press attention accorded social and political elites and avatars of the stage or society, the turn of the century witnessed enhanced media interventions in the production of personae. Supplementing the mass diffusion of literary memoirs, courtesan autobiographies, and theatrical reviews in women's magazines, a nascent entertainment industry began to capitalize, internationalize and technologize the marketing and management of national stars. It was once again Marcel Proust who registered through his narrator Marcel the sentimental impact of the publicity machine's star production on the budding fan:

> But if the thought of actors preoccupied me so, if the sight of Maubant coming out of the Théâtre-Français one afternoon had plunged me into the throes and sufferings of love, how much more did the name of a "star" blazing outside the doors of a theatre, how much more, seen through the window of a brougham passing by in the street, its horses' headbands decked with roses, did the face of a woman whom I took to be an actress, leave me in a state of troubled excitement, impotently and painfully trying to form a picture of her private life.

I classified the most distinguished in order of talent: Sarah Bernhardt, Berma, Bartet, Madeleine Brohan, Jeanne Samary; but I was interested in them all.[7]

As Proust accurately records, no one succeeded in syncretizing character-acting with identity-performance more effectively than Sarah Bernhardt. Bernhardt in the role of Cleopatra typified the kind of feminist personification of historic legend that in its turn became magnified into a social phenomenon. In Jean Lorrain's literary sketch "Les Amoureuses de Cléopâtre" (Cleopatra's lovers), the description of Sarah-Cleopatra stalked by her lesbian entourage records how going to see Sarah implied an initiatory experience in gynosocial bonding:

> We are going to see them again, lolling about in the alleyways of Bondy Street, ready to lay siege on the loge where Sarah would return after each act, exhausted, practically bloodless, and staggering under the unbelievable weight of the brocaded fabrics and precious stones of a barbarous princess: at each new performance of the grand fantastic one, her fans reappear from God knows where, all recognizable from their hair, curled and henna-dyed à la Titus, a suit-jacket open over an olive-cloth vest, all with a deadly pallor under their androgyne hairstyles, their eyes cruel and fixed between eyelashes drenched in mascara.
>
> They are as legion as demons, and despite being disconcerting in their half-masculine outfits of crude material, they are very fin de siècle, forming a strange but complementary note in the sumptuous, bohemian interior that is crazy Sarah's open house.[8]

Lorrain lards this account with an anecdote about an Austrian princess besotted with Sarah, who uses her sickly body to play a cadaver in one of her plays. When Sarah scratches the woman's face by accident, her victim marches off proudly to exhibit the scar to her friends at five o'clock tea. Dubbed by Lorrain the "Cleopatra of tomorrow," Sarah is portrayed as a savvy manipulator of her position in the lesbian pantheon.

Sarah appears equally regal, byzantine, monstrous, and inspiring to women in Elizabeth de Gramont's belle epoque memoir *Au temps des équipages*:

> An unexpected treat was in store for us in London: Sarah Bernhardt's season. We spent five afternoons and five evenings running in the theater at which she was acting. I saw her in *Tosca, Fédora, Théodora, La Dame aux Camélias, Phèdre*. Sardou suited her better than Racine. She was a Romantic of the style of 1875. Sarah was no column, but a richly Byzantine arabesque. She needed pearls in her hair, orchids, trains to her dresses, daggers, and leopard-skins. When I saw her in London, she was physically still extremely seductive. With her ruffled fair hair, that daughter of Jerusalem looked like a priestess who from Solomon's temple had gone over to that of Baal. Her voice was of gold, her eyes of precious stones, her suppleness feline. She was

the incarnation of the feminine serpent unfolding the coils of her voluptuousness throughout the world, in turn a princess of Byzantium, a Floren-
tine adventuress, a consumptive courtesan; in sum, she was all those who,
dowered with an arsenal of allurements, triumph over men and events.[9]

The accent on Sarah's byzantine allure, erotic prowess, and demonic
changeability of character—all common stereotypes of Jewishness associated with her by her contemporaries—are in de Gramont's admiring account part of the readily interpreted Orientalist code-language of
turn-of-the-century sapphism. As Peter Wollen "Fashion/Orientalism/the
Body") and Michael Moon ("Flaming Closets") have emphasized in their
readings of successive stagings of *Shéhérazade*, Orientalism from the belle
epoque on has played as a subcultural form of gay performativity.[10]
Though Bernhardt was never officially outed, her exotic roles, coupled
with her celebrated transvestic performances in *Hamlet, L'Aiglon,* and
Lorenzaccio, rendered the "Sarah Bernhardt type" a crucible of identification among the amazons of 1900.[11]

Natalie Barney, perhaps the most famous salon lesbian of the belle
epoque, began her career with a sonnet dedicated to Sarah commemorating the historic "gender trouble" created by her production of *Hamlet* in
which she played both Hamlet *and* Ophelia.

> . . . You render us inconstant to nature, to the laws;
> I love a woman, as much as I love the Dane,
> I love that you are you and everything at the same time!
>
> [Tu nous rends inconstants à la nature, aux lois;
> Tantôt j'aime une femme, et tantôt le Danois,
> Je t'aime d'être tout et d'être toi quand même!][12]

The line "you render us inconstant to nature" captures the way in which
Bernhardt's performance was received as authorization of a socially pro-
hibited sexuality. Enmeshed within a complex psychic paradigm of narcissism and same-sex love, the type that is "Sarah" emerges as a prefiguration
of the "gynandromorph"—a characterology of "thirdness" invented by
Barney and Renée Vivien to denote a gender transcendent of stereotypical
masculinities and femininities.

Natalie Barney made Sarah's third-sex performativity the site of her
own acting out when she performed her courtship of the famous fin-de-
siècle courtesan Liane de Pougy, dressed as a Shakespearean page. In Liane's
semifictionalized account of their romance, *Idylle saphique*, "Flossie" (as
Natalie is called) prostrates herself at Liane's feet in the theater box in order
to palpate her body as it registers "the golden voice of the great Sarah utter-
ing the priceless philosophy of bitterness and irony that is Hamlet's."[13] The

fairy godmother of their passion, Sarah Bernhardt enables the page and his lady to work out the erotics of submission and "queening" that not only gave their love its character, but also pointed to the complex problem of erotic identity's indebtedness to being "in character."

The problem of "erotics in character" is consciously posed here in relation to Judith Butler's speculations on the "gendered character of the ego." Butler, of course, is not using the word *character* in the theatrical sense, but rather to connote manner or bodily ethic as applied to "sexed positions." But it is my sense that the ego's gendered character is indissociable from the performance of character-typologies; theatrical meaning and dramatic history mediate the ego's identifications. I want to put the theater of characterology back into the story of how subjective agency is formed.

Butler rereads Freud's *The Ego and the Id* in an attempt to explore the relationship between object-cathexis, identification, and melancholia, specifically the "question of ungrieved and ungrievable loss in the formation of what we might call the gendered character of the ego."[14] Freud, as she points out, had by his own admission originally underestimated the importance of melancholic identification: "It may be said," he wrote in *The Ego and the Id,* "that this identification is the sole condition under which the id can give up its objects. At any rate the process, especially in the early phases of development, is a very frequent one, and it makes it possible to suppose that the character of the ego is the precipitate of abandoned object-cathexes and that it contains the history of those object-choices."[15] Camouflaging the object as a way of taking its place, the ego acquires the "character" of that which is pathologically mourned, that is, preserved in the psyche as a loss.

For Butler, same-sex desire constitutes the lost object of gender-identification. Nowhere is this process more evident than in drag performance, which

> exposes or allegorizes the mundane psychic and performative practices by which heterosexualized genders form themselves through the renunciation of the *possibility* of homosexuality, a foreclosure which produces heterosexual objects at the same time that it produces a domain of those whom it would be impossible to love. Drag thus allegorizes *heterosexual melancholia.*[16]

Butler's model of heterosexual melancholia works well to uncover the disavowed "queer-envy" of heterosexuality and the sadness of society's homosexual foreclosures. Her theory is also important in its revision of Freud because it insists on gender as a significant dimension of the ego's character. Extrapolating a bit, I would say that for Butler, the character of gender is theorized litotically, through the negative affirmation of lost or repudiated objects simultaneously incorporated and denied. Gendered character *is*, insofar as it is not what it is not; it is the remainder of disputing disavowals, and its signs are shifters of ambivalent identification; slippages between being and seeming, having and being, having and losing, taking in and giving up; placing here and loving somewhere else, doing and meaning, acting and outing.

Going back to Freud's essay, however, one finds further grounds for drawing out the theatrical side of the ego's identification with dispossessed genders, for according to Freud, the ego "ravishes" the id, convincing it to relinquish the object by acting as the object's stand-in. This mimetic "character" of the ego is articulated in performative terms, terms that evoke, astonishingly enough, the ego's rape of the id: "When the ego assumes the features of the object, it is forcing itself, so to speak, upon the id as a love-object and is trying to make good the id's loss by saying: 'Look, you can love me too—I am so like the object.'"[17] Now, admittedly, this is a highly masculine model of ego-identification. But taken theatrically, one can say that the ego engages equally in the feminine masquerade. Functioning as a defense mechanism by masquerading as the prophylactic of loss, pretending to be a character (the lost object) that it is not—much like the standard stage actor throwing herself into a role, or the woman of Joan Riviere's famous essay assuming the socially expected farce of womanliness—the ego's character is thus "ethically" defined by being seductively "in character."

Turning again to belle epoque gender performativity, one could say that a kind of melancholia hangs over the way women threw themselves into theatrical roles, enacting them histrionically, valiantly exposing the seams between being and acting, seeming and passing, as if by exposing the rift between genders desired and genders disavowed, they affirmed the magnificent leap of faith required to be, "fantastically," in a gendered place that society has normatively foreclosed.

In Colette's vignette of Mata Hari it is the pathos of her relative *failure* to pass as an Eastern hetaera that lends her identity the splendor of a melancholic ruin:

> She was a dancer who did not dance much, yet at Emma Calvé's, before the portable altar that she used as a background, supported by a little group of coloured attendants and musicians and framed in the pillars of a vast, white hall, she had been sufficiently snake-like and enigmatic to produce a good effect. The people who fell into such dithyrambic raptures and wrote so ecstatically of Mata Hari's person and talents must be wondering now what collective delusion possessed them. Her dancing and the naive legends surrounding her were of no better quality than the ordinary claptrap of the current "Indian turns" in the music hall. The only pleasant certainties on which her drawing-room audiences could count were a slender waist below breasts that she prudently kept hidden, a fine, supple moving back, muscu-

lar loins, long thighs and slim knees. Her nose and mouth, which were both thick, and the rather oily brilliance of her eyes did nothing to alter—on the contrary—our established notions of the Oriental. It should be said that the finale of her dance, the moment when Mata Hari, freed of her last girdle, fell forward modestly upon her belly, carried the male—and a good proportion of the female—spectators to the extreme limit of decent attention.

In the May sunshine, at Neuilly, despite the turquoises, the drooping black mane of hair, the tinsel diadem and especially the long thigh against the white flanks of her Arab horse, the color of her skin was disconcerting, no longer brown and luscious as it had been by artificial light but a dubious uneven purple. Having finished her equestrian parade, she alighted and wrapped herself in a sari. She bowed, talked, was faintly disappointing.[18]

Mata Hari's Orientalism—a cultural affect of foreignness—signifies the incorporation and psychic preservation of what is ruled out by classic femininity: *sapphism, prostitution,* and *feminism.* These phantasmatic identifications are both given up and preserved within the ego in the form of stilted character. With its simultaneous erection and disaggregation of the Mata Hari legend, Colette's depiction invites us to read the narrator's final "disappointment" as a symptom of the kind of melancholia that typically surfaces in relation to Western feminist Orientalism; the blatantly falsified exoticism of Mata Hari's "Asiatic" persona draws attention to the virtual unperformability of her gendered character.

Natalie Barney also lionized Mata Hari as a larger-than-life historical prototype. Barney's commitment to the retrieval of great women in history, like that of her lover Renée Vivien, may be seen not so much as a quest for role models (which is how feminist criticism's use of heroines and historic archetypes usually gets typecast), but rather as the working through of gender melancholia. Similarly, Renée Vivien's most important poem, *Souveraines,* treats historical feminine figures as afflicted with some version of gender melancholia. As Karla Jay notes,

> An octave is devoted to each of these women's achievements, but the summation spoken by each woman is the same: "The fatal star of Beauty / I was not happy." According to Vivien, no matter how beautiful the woman is and no matter what she has accomplished, the exceptional woman is always unhappy.[19]

Vivien's rewriting of the legends of Lilith, Vashti, Andromeda, and Henry VIII's fated wife Ann Boleyn featured them as rebels prepared to choose death or infinite punishment over submission to masculine law. Feminist characterology in this instance deploys the exemplary biography to reveal the "becoming a character" aspect of gendered character.

Like Vivien, Barney plundered history for female types, but her types were always more ontologically hyphenated with the amazons of 1900, most of them friends, lovers, or members of her coterie. In an early volume of sonnets, *Quelques portraits-sonnets de femmes,* published in 1900 with illustrations by her mother, the artist Alice Pike-Barney, Sarah Bernhardt and the dancer Eva Palmer reincarnate the classical muses of song and movement. Liane de Pougy moves ghostlike through the character-frames of Flaubert's Salammbô and the Greek deity of the hunt, Diana. In "Salammbô" the lines "Des jeunes voluptés, où l'ennui vient s'asseoir / Pour lamenter sans fin la mort de ta caresse" [Youthful pleasures, where ennui comes to sit / To endlessly lament the death of your caress] mourn the expiration of *jouissance.*[20] In "Chant d'Endymion," dedicated explicitly to Liane, an acute wish for effacement of self in the other also ends with a memorial to spent passion: "Ta voix, ta douce voix, musique enchanteresse / Qui fait oublier que le spasme d'amour a fui / Et que même la lune tombe dans la nuit!" [Your voice, your sweet voice, musical enchantment / Making one forget that the love spasm has vanished / And that even the moon falls in the night].[21]

Liane-Diane, the prostitute-goddess, was for Barney a truly original character in her gynocracy. One of the few purely French courtesans of the highest order (her rivals La Belle Otero, la Cavalieri, and Cléo de Mérode were all foreign born), she enjoyed an apotheosis as France's national icon. Dubbed "un Tanagra d'exportation," her elegant thinness and arresting features gave her body trademark status in patriotic craft and costume design. Her personal style was both nostalgic and modernist, a blend of Louis XVI and Coco Chanel. She was in many respects the prototypical modern sex worker, mindful of charging exorbitant fees to the wealthiest men of Europe for her services. Offenbach's librettist Henri Meilhac purportedly paid Liane eighty thousand francs just to contemplate her in the nude. But Liane confounded narrow stereotypes of prostitution; her credo of independence, financially nurtured by her investment-conscious mentor, Valtesse de la Bigne, made her a model New Woman, and yet she was far from immune to gender melancholia. In a letter to Barney, disillusionment with her profession mingles with the a deeper crisis of identity:

> You see then, I'm forgetting my work, my new duties and they break my heart. Here, I am the mistress of a clubman who smokes fat cigars and spends his days and nights gambling . . . I wait for him in my bed, unable to sleep, feverish, unable to dream, saddened . . . in a painful materiality. However, the courtesan in me ought to be content for he has just given me a necklace of the white pearls I love, worth one hundred thousand francs. Well, my little one, I suffer on all sides with all of my being. I suffer by wanting to die.
>
> Why this dividing of myself?
> Why am I not whole like these men, like women?
> Where does my sadness come from, my revolt, my pain?[22]

Liane de Pougy was the highly successful author of *Idylle saphique* and *Mes cahiers bleus,* and her lifelong correspondents included Jean Cocteau, the erudite Academician Salomon Reinach, and the poet Max Jacob. Her erotic proclivities were openly lesbian. Though she married a Rumanian prince and died a canonized saint, for Natalie Barney, her most ardent lover, Liane remained an archetypal amazon whose demeanor and physical mold marked her as "a true original"; mythic, fabulous, self-conflicted, yet in sync with the zeitgeist of 1900. As Jean Chalon recounts:

> Natalie took Liane to her favorite couturieres, the Callot sisters, who studied Mlle de Pougy and then gave her verdict: "It's easy to see what becomes you. Never wear anything but green or white. In addition, your long neck should always emerge from a simple, square, low neckline that accentuates your head, the long line further carried out by your body in diaphanous floating materials that go on forever. You are a true original. We will design some exquisite things for you."
>
> Natalie: "It's true you are an original. You're lucky to have your own particular style, whereas so many people go to so much trouble to invent one. You, my Liane, are like a fairy, a siren, a far-off princess. The Callot sisters are right: long dresses, precious jewels, you are made for necklaces, chains, rings."[23]

It is perhaps no accident that Natalie cast Liane in the part of fairy, siren, and far-off princess in her poems and literary portraits. As she wrote in her *Souvenirs indiscrets,* the two of them were constantly in costume, even when passing an intimate evening alone. Part of *becoming a character* or of being a gender *in character* seems to have been bound up in the performance of genders at the limit of the unperformed (original), or campily brought back from the dead and reprojected into modernity.

Natalie Barney's most successfully fashioned character-type was herself. In "Portrait of the Author by the Author in the Guise of a Preface," her prefatory text to *Nouvelles pensées d'une amazone,* Barney cast herself as the "Amazon" aka "Natalie-Natalis." Jealous, seductive, dedicated to free love, gynophobic (averse to traditional femininity), proud, melancholic, the amazon emerges as the quintessential character of the lesbian 1900:

> This haunting by the double being or the androgyne obsessed Goethe, who thought he found it in the "amazon Natalie."
>
> And Gourmont, who in his *Letters to the Amazon* named me "Natalie-Natalis," did he have the intuition, did he or did he not know—that Goethe called his amazon Natalie?
>
> This third, this disparate one, this singular, this isolate, this one without equal, this odd-one-out, this solitary among the coupled, this enclosed outsider, is generally represented as Seducer and not as victim of the state of freedom.

For such beings, it seems less hazardous to produce oneself *(se produire)* than to reproduce.[24]

The miraculous propulsion of a true-life personage into a theatricalized, gendered identity was surely among Barney's most significant projects. Her persona inspired myriad fictional portraits: "Flossie" in Liane de Pougy's *Idylle saphique*, Laurette Wells in Lucie Delarue-Mardrus's *L'Ange et les pervers*, Valerie Seymore in Radclyffe Hall's *Well of Loneliness*, Claudine of Colette's numerous *Claudine* novels, and Evangeline Musset in Djuna Barnes's *The Ladies Almanack*. In her turn, she immortalized and aggrandized her lovers and fellow amazons—Liane, Renée Vivien, Colette, Romaine Brooks, Lucie Delarue-Mardrus, Mathilde de Morny, Una Troubridge, Emma Calvé, Elizabeth de Gramont-Tonnerre, Mata Hari, Oscar Wilde's niece Dolly Wilde, a Chinese lover named Nadine Wong, a Turkish lover Nimet Eloui-Bey. The practice of literary cross-indexing—what might be called the lesbian "Who's Who" effect—fanned out into memoirs and published correspondences written by and about women. The overall result was a heightened feminist characterology, which, while it may have led on the one hand to a cultural investment in character-criticism, on the other may have triggered the anticharacter tendency within modern psychoanalysis.

I will conclude with a cursory look at Freud and Lacan on the issue of character, bearing in mind the operative assumption that, as the belle epoque waned in the late teens and twenties, the taste for bloated character-roles entered its twilight years and became associated with a kind of childishness; an old-fashioned propensity for period costume; a decadent, comedic Shakespeareanism or kitsch Orientalism. The auxiliary effect of character-acting's decline was a certain devaluation of feminist and queer performativity that really had to await the sixties for its open revival.

Though, as we have seen, Freud was concerned with character-types in *The Ego and the Id,* he assigned explicit importance to the concept in *Psychopathic Characters on the Stage* (1905–6), *Character and Anal Eroticism* (1908), *Some Character-Types Met with in Psychoanalytic Work* (1916), and *Libidinal Types* (1931). In the last essay, he sorted character typologies—the erotic, the narcissistic, and the obsessional—according to the predominance of anal, oral, and genital drives. This kind of triage works as a computation system—a little bit of genital combined with a pinch of oral, and you have x-personality. The result is Freud at his most reductive.

For my purposes, the earlier work offers more promising theoretical material, perhaps because it was formulated within the historical frame of the belle epoque. In *Psychopathic Stage Characters,* Freud was primarily interested in the stage as a showcase for the acting-out of neurosis, and he foregrounds Hamlet as a character whose visible resistance to unconscious repression makes him an exemplary "subject of analysis." He ends the short essay criticizing Hermann Bahr's play *Die Andere* for its apparent use of a neurosis that fails to elicit audience identification with the subject of analysis, in this case a woman in the grip of what we might now call sexual addiction. The essay signals the importance of dramatic characters as spectacular projections of ego-formation and attempts to define the conditions under which audience identification misfires or reaches its mark.

In *Character and Anal Eroticism* Freud opened up the question of the ego as a defense against the impulses of the id, arguing that, in Richard Wollheim's words, "a triad of traits—orderliness, parsimony, and obstinacy—could be regarded as the product of a sustained reaction formation against the pleasures of the anal zone or the satisfactions to be won from retaining, expelling, and playing with, the faeces."[25] In Wollheim's view, the essay's negative reception led Freud to abandon the defense theory of character-formation. Freud argued later in his career that the ego is weakened by excessive defense. Is it an accident that excessive defensiveness was habitually singled out as a defining feature of femininity, of the weak-egoed subject par excellence? Is it pure chance that as Freud gave up on the theory of the ego's defense, it was a woman analyst and translator of Freud, Joan Riviere, who took it up in her work on "womanliness as a masquerade" and "jealousy as mechanism of defense" in the 1920s? Or that another woman writer, the American feminist Laura Jackson Riding would analyze the New Woman in terms of a cosmetic defense theory, in which "accentuated appearance" is read as a mode of psychically protective self-fashioning? Is it again pure coincidence that the male analyst most famous for reviving character-analysis in the twenties was Wilhelm Reich, Freud's renegade disciple, and that Reich's idea of "character armor" was habitually associated with the "passive-feminine" character? While this is not the place to plot this psychoanalytical history in detail, what emerges from the Freudian turn away from defense (construed as the ego's theatrical attempt to fool the id into forgetting its losses), is a typecasting of the feminine as defensive, and constantly warding off lack.

If early psychoanalysis feminized character-analysis by foregrounding defense, this did not, paradoxically enough, prevent it from degendering the modern subject. In Freud's writings on character, the problem of the feminine ego was never posed as such, and he seemed oblivious to the manifestation, in his own era, of women experimenting with differently gendered characterologies. The spectacle of hyperinflated feminine identity-performance is submerged within neutered paradigms of egoic mimicry.

Following Freud, Lacan evinced disinterest in "defense" and had remarkably little to say about character, though its absence is arguably crucial to his theorizations of the unconscious. Lacan tracked the sublation of character into the "ethics" of the subject's "enjoyment" *(joie)*. In his "Preliminary Interventions on Balint," presented in the seminar of 1953 (a reading of Balint's book *Primary Love and Psycho-analytic Technique)*, Lacan criticizes the "puritanical moral ideal" that he discerns lurking behind Balint's depreciation of libidinal types in favor of an object-relations approach. What interests Lacan is the defense of pleasure within the moral construction of the subject:

> Character controls man's relations to his objects. Character always signifies a more or less extensive limitation of the possibilities of love and hatred. So character signifies limitation of the capacity for love and enjoyment. The dimension of enjoyment *(joie)*, which is extremely extensive, goes well beyond the category of *jouissance* in a way that one should spell out. Enjoyment *(joie)* implies a subjective plenitude which well deserves being expanded on.[26]

In the opening of the ethics seminar (1959), Lacan refers to the gulf between the Aristotelian notion of character (defined in terms of good and bad habits, the science of character), and the terms in which psychoanalysis defines itself: that is, trauma and its persistence.[27] The term *character* disappears from the *Ethics*, but remains operative, implicitly, in the idea of a nonpuritanical, yet ethical *jouissance,* positioned, like the unconscious, beyond representation. Unlike the unconscious, whose clues are difficult to trace, character possesses detectable marks or traits; it is therefore tautological and overobvious. Perhaps for this reason, it was phased out of the Lacanian subject; character was too representable, too literal, too visible, and too moralistic in a Victorian sense of that term. It is interesting to note here that Walter Benjamin had similar objections to character when, in what he deemed to be his finest essay, "Fate and Character" (1919), he emphasized that the physiognomically based, or "mantic" character reading of the moderns (for him, a fancy form of fortune-telling) represented a debased version of the ancients' determination of fate through morally neutral abstract principles.[28]

To do proper justice to the claim that the "disappeared" character of the Lacanian subject has some distant, but causal, connection to the effacement of feminist characterology, a more careful and rigorous analysis of Freud and Lacan's writings would be necessary. But I will nonetheless end with the speculation that, by inventing the notion of an unconscious that "speaks us," and by laying out the analytic conditions of the unconscious's unrepresentability, Lacan contributed to the degendering of the ego's character. Somewhere in this process, the acutely sexed identities of women character-types in the belle epoque seem to have lost face.

VIRTUAL

COLONIES

[H]er great serpent, the black Python, was wasting away; and for the Carthaginians the serpent was both a national and private fetish. It was believed to be born of the earth's clay, since it emerges from the earth's depths and does not need feet to move over it; its progress recalled the rippling of rivers, its temperature the ancient, viscous darkness full of fertility, and the circle it describes, as it bites its own tail, the planetary system, Eschmoûn's intelligence.

    . . . From time to time Salammbo approached its silver-wire basket; she drew aside the purple curtain, the lotus leaves, the birds' down; it stayed constantly rolled up, stiller than a withered creeper; and from looking at it she ended by feeling a kind of spiral in her heart, like another serpent slowly coming up into her throat to choke her.[1]

THE DANCE OF
COLONIAL SEDUCTION

FLAUBERT AND

THE LINE OF DESIRE

In this passage from *Salammbô* Flaubert's striking image of the doubled serpent portrays a creature coiled listlessly on itself to signify an ailing national fetish, unwinding in reverse iterability into the body of a woman
whose contorted dancing will exorcise "the spiral in her heart" now threatening to choke her to death from within.[2] This reverse iterability takes the
form of a jackknife image if one sees the juncture where national and female fetish cross as opening out into mirror trajectories of signification.
The line of fate that inscribes the threat to Carthage posed by the rebellious
Barbarians shadows the twisted line of fate belonging to Salammbo, daughter of Carthage's king Hamilcar, and victim of ravishment by Mâtho, the
colossal Barbarian captain. Together these lines describe a pattern of serpentination linking, allegorically and conceptually, the classic scene of seduction in colonial narrative to the whorls and circuities of the colonial
gaze.[3]

I intend to look specifically at descriptions of Oriental dancing that
seem designed to compete with the allure of visual representations promising direct access to the colonial real.[4] The colonial real, as it slides toward
the literary genre of colonial realism, designates the place where tourist
narrative and realist Orientalism (as featured in Balzac's *La Fille aux yeux
d'or* or *La Peau de chagrin)* not only join each other, but also coincide with
the sign of the real that interpellates the subject at the blindest spot of his or
her identity in national space. Though there are obviously many ways to
ramify this notion of the colonial real, for now it must stand as an experi-

mental term mediating between psychoanalytic and historical accounts of the colonial subject (colonized and colonizer alike), whose positionality is a phantasmatic construction of literary texts, themselves firmly anchored in the sociopolitical history of nineteenth-century French colonial life in North Africa.

The representation of exotic dance scenes in French realist and naturalist literature provides fertile ground for examining the way in which the female subject of colonial domination was used to figure a visual fantasy of direct contact or a haptic encounter with the real. From the trotting out of bayadères, to ceremonial performances by daughters of the court, to the commercialized acts of belly dancers and striptease artists (as in the *stéréoramas mouvants* featured at the World's Fair of 1900), such scenes have always served to structure the formulaic spectacles of opera, ballet, cabaret, and film.[5] In the novel, as well as in painting, sculpture,[6] and photography, these production numbers or entertainment set-pieces are particularly susceptible to psychoanalytic dissection because of the way in which they reveal the reification of cultural attitude in psychical, phantasmatic space. What interests me is the way in which the rhetorical repetitions of undulation and serpentination encrypt what Lacan would call the "line of desire" cathecting colonial looking to its exoticist visual object. Scopophilia, cultural voyeurism, and the market-propelled techniques that produce canonical images of colonial "reality" seem commonly driven into the shape of that "interior 8" which, in this instance, maps out an aesthetic of colonial desire. I want to investigate the bizarre formalism of this colonial desire as a way of understanding the seductive call within the history of colonialism and postcolonial theory alike, of a "reenchantment industry" (the expression is Ernest Gellner's) that continues to seem profoundly reliant on late Orientalist figurations of eroticized tourist attractions.[7]

I draw my fascination with the serpent-figure not from any hackneyed psychology of the serpent-phallus, nor from the even more overused repertory of biblical images of evil, but rather from the art historian Leo Steinberg's analysis of Picasso's "Women of Algiers" paintings of 1954 and 1955.[8] I will dwell extensively on the terms of Steinberg's interpretation because his language, though ostensibly more concerned with aesthetic than with cultural questions, provides highly suggestive categories for rethinking cultural vision.

Steinberg begins by exploring Picasso's "life-long obsession with all-sided presentment," his appropriation of techniques "developed within the Renaissance system of focused perspective . . . of harmonizing an ideal of omnispection with the logic of a fixed point of view."[9] Among these techniques he notes the *figura serpentinata:*

> In a note to Vasari acknowledging the gift of a drawing, Aretino (1540) praises a certain nude which, "bending down to the ground, shows both the back and the front." He was describing a figure of hairpin design, a variant of the *figura serpentinata.* Its elastic anatomy serves Mannerist art for the simultaneous display of front and back without recourse to repetition, external propos or the aid of witnesses. It incorporates both views at once in a jack-knifing spine lengthened only by one or two extra vertebrae.[10]

I have already noted a similar kind of hairpin kineticism characterizing the love-dance performed by Salammbo and her serpent:

> [T]he python fell back, and putting the middle of its body round her neck, it let its head and tail dangle, like a broken necklace with its two ends trailing on the ground. Salammbo wound it round her waist, under her arms, between her knees; then taking it by the jaw she brought its little triangular mouth to the edge of her teeth, and half closing her eyes, bent back under the moon's rays.[11]

This obvious paroxysm of feminine *jouissance,* at once kitsch and high art in its decadent aestheticism, curiously imbricates perspectival twists and mirror effects, suggesting that desire pictures itself through waving, bending lines. The python circles the woman's neck and is coextensively wound by Salammbo around the waist; this inverted and self-inverting encirclement, in which snake slides into female body and vice versa, is compounded by the jackknife image of arching back: the snake "falls back" to initiate the ritual, and at its closure Salammbo "bends back" under the moon's rays.

The wavy line of movement that Steinberg identifies as a motif of Picasso's modernist Orientalism, as seductive as the snake charmer's meandering melody, or the curls of smoke rising from the hashish-smoker's narghile in nineteenth-century Orientalist tableaus, is of course grounded in the long and complex decorative history of the Moorish arabesque, but it also possesses another aesthetic genealogy that may help to explain the psychology of colonial visual pleasure, with all its attendant ideological consequences for skewing the iconographic power relations of East and West. As Ernst Gombrich reminds us in *The Sense of Order: A Study in the Psychology of Art:*

> It was William Hogarth who first suggested that the pleasure he found in what he called the "line of beauty," the wavy line, derived ultimately from our searching mind and eye: "The serpentine line by its waving and wind-

ing at the same time different ways, leads the eye in a pleasing manner along
the continuity of its variety, if I may be allowed the expression; and which
by its twisting so many different ways, may be said to inclose (tho' but a
single line) varied contents."[12]

There is a "having one's cake and eating it too" aspect to Hogarth's line of
beauty, for it satisfies epistemological hungers ("the searching mind and
eye") *and* the appetite for visual seduction ("leads the eye in a pleasing
manner") at one and the same time. The same conjunction of intellectual
curiosity and visual drive can be found in Lacan's appositely formulated
notion of the "interior 8" or "line of desire," which he claims emerged from
his attempt to draw the "topology of the subject":

> You can obtain it [the topology] from the interior 8. Bring the edges to-
> gether two by two as they are presented here, by a complementary surface,
> and close it. In a way, it plays the same role as complement in relation to the
> initial 8 as a sphere in relation to a circle, a sphere that would close what the
> circle would already offer itself as ready to contain. Well! This surface is a
> Moebius surface, and its outside continues its inside.
>   . . . This image enables us to figure desire as a locus of junction between
> the field of demand, in which the syncopes of the unconscious are made
> present, and sexual reality. All this depends on a line that I will call the line
> of desire, linked to demand, and by which the effects of sexuality are made
> present in experience.[13]

Lacan's Möbius surface loops the loop of inside and outside, knotting the
pulsation of demand with the sinuations of mediated looking so that they
fuse into a common thread of desire whose path reiterates yet again the
figura serpentinata.

Though an abstract, logically abstruse way of characterizing an optical
trick for capturing all-seeingness or subjective multisidedness in a single
line, Lacan's line of desire, concerned as it is to make manifest the "effects
of sexuality," may be brought "down to earth," so to speak, as a depiction of
the form of the scopophilic gaze as it targets the object of seduction. This
seems to be part of what Leo Steinberg is getting at when he locates the
figura serpentinata in the art of the pinup, itself derived from the conventional, age-old posture of the sensual (usually female) figure rotated on its
axis, projecting, as he puts it, "well-being, self-admiration or erotic entice-
ment."[14] "Pin-up models posing for calendar art," Steinberg affirms, "tend
to work up a *figura serpentinata,* and their photographer, if he has a sense of
craft, knows just how much expository rotation is wanted to meet the
terms of an 'eyeful.'"[15] A still version of the dancing body, which likewise
seeks to expose itself simultaneously from front to back, the pin-up model

as "eyeful" underscores how the image of sensuality gathers itself up and delivers itself over as a "filling" repast for the scopophilic gaze. And epistemologically, this gaze often perceives itself self-consciously as a serpentine form.

Let us go back for a moment to Flaubert's dancers, specifically to the Salomé of his short story "Hérodias," in which the Tetrarch's temptress performs for the price of John the Baptist's head: "Her eyes half closed, she writhed her body above her waist and undulated her belly with a wave-like motion that shook her breasts; and her face remained impassive, and her feet never stopped."[16] Salomé finishes this medley of serpentinas by spreading her legs and arching her body back so far that her chin brushes the floor. As critics have long surmised, this scene was inspired by the "bee dance" or striptease of Flaubert's favorite courtesan Kuchuk Hanem, of whom he wrote to his mistress Louise Colet:

> To go back to Kuchuk. You and I are thinking of her, but she is certainly not thinking of us. We are weaving an aesthetic around her, whereas this particular very interesting tourist who was vouchsafed the honors of her couch has vanished from her memory completely, like many others. Ah! Traveling makes one modest—you see what a tiny place you occupy in the world.[17]

This passage is interesting for a number of reasons: first, it illustrates the way in which the serpentine figure goes from being a rather literal evocation of the gyrations of a dance to a metaphorical way of talking about the epistemological limits to knowing culturally "other" subjects. "We are weaving an aesthetic around her," says Flaubert to Louise, thereby making transparent the process by which the appearance of the seductive object is attached, as if by a figure eight, to the hermeneutics of aesthetics and sexual fantasy.

A second interesting aspect of Flaubert's statement lies in his taking cognizance of "the tiny place you occupy in the world." Flaubert's tourist seems situated here in a frustratedly fixed occidentalism that is nonetheless in the process of insistently trying to wrap its vision around the world. Here the serpentine figure seems to embody the yearning for global perspectivalism, the tourist's hunger for an "eyeful" of cultural alterity balanced on the head of a Eurocentric pin. Once again Steinberg's language, in relation to Picasso's "cutting loose" of vision through the use of "circumspicuous or circumambient sight, of visual rays bent around corners," seems uncannily apt in its unwitting conjugation of visual curiosity with colonial desire.[18] Depicting Picasso as an image-fetishist who "paints a figure as though he had toured it to collect impressions of its various aspects" (p. 190), Stein-

berg then goes on to place him, "entwined with his passions," in a cartographic imaginary replete with a kind of narrative coda describing the history of colonial conquest:

> Closer still [to Picasso's radical simultaneities] are those splendid projec-
> tions whereby geodesists, cosmographers, and mathematicians have for
> centuries rendered the world's sphere on a plane surface—gnomonic,
> quincuncial, and homolographic projections, discontinuous and kidney-
> shaped map projections with their distortions, repeats, and disjunctions.
> These ingenious summaries of the sphere on the plane are the natural ana-
> logue for Picasso's manipulations of the human image. Granted that Pi-
> casso's heuristic impulses are not pure but entwined with his passions, he
> treats the body as those maps treat the globe, treats it like a cartographer
> processing data, and again like the global ruler in the Age of Discovery
> whose *mappa mundi* unfurls a circumnavigated world. (P. 192)

The cosmographer-cartographer, like the colonial observer of Orientalist
dancing, steers a serpentine course between the desire for *dépaysement* (the
loss of fixed national self-reference), and the will to dominate and domesti-
cate foreign territory through unitary (Western) perspectivalism.

In Flaubert we see some of this effect in the opening of "Hérodias,"
where the female body is displaced to the landscape. In this passage, Salomé's dance of seduction is foregrounded by a panoptical, geomorphic
survey of the ground itself:

> The citadel of Machaerous rose up toward the east of the Dead Sea, on an
> outcrop of basalt in the form of a cone. Four deep valleys surrounded it, two
> on the sides, one in front, the fourth behind. Houses were piled up against
> its base, in the circle of a wall that undulated, following the unevenness of
> the terrain, and by means of a zigzag route through the rock the town was
> connected to the fortress whose walls were 120 cubits high with numerous
> corners, crenellations on the edge, and here and there towers that appeared
> like fleurons on this crown of stones suspended over the abyss.[19]

It is not just a question of phallic towers and plunging valleys that code this
vision of the Oriental world in a field of sexual desire, but more specifically
the belly dance in the territory: the undulating wall, the zigzagging path
that sculpts the rock-face (the verb *taillader,* "to cut," encompasses the
word *taille,* in turn connoting the undulating waist of the dancer)—these
figures of speech point to the way in which Orientalism, via the figure eight
of serpentination, plants a palimpsest of seduction inside the viewer's cran-
ing outlook toward the East.

Though I have been deliberately taking Steinberg's topic-specific discussion of Picasso's serpentination out of context, bending his rhetoric to
frame a theorization of the colonial gaze, I feel somewhat justified in doing

so because of the rich implications of Steinberg's apparently throwaway analogies between global visual projection and Picasso's representational strategies for treating the female nude. Commenting on Picasso's nudes of the 1940s, Steinberg deploys tantalizing concepts of corporeal "vagrancy" and "translocation" as if the woman's body constituted a world map of nomadized territories, encampments of exile, and ambient land masses:

> The female body undergoes new kinds of revision. Its "commonplaces" serve as exponents of vagrant aspects. A dotted bosom becomes the prefix to any aspect soever, so that frontal figures as they bend over sprout breasts at the shoulder blades. . . . Yet the body coheres; there is neither Cubist dismemberment nor schematic disjunction. These figures work, and Picasso's draughtsmanship makes their irrational translocations seem genuinely informative about the rotundity of the object observed. Could a cartographer do it? Could he make the world's other side present to the imagination by entering Pacific islands on the Atlantic?[20]

Steinberg's omnipotent cartographer remaking the world according to whim by "entering Pacific islands on the Atlantic" parallels the privileged spectators of Oriental dance numbers who "translocate" portions of the female anatomy, as if in an effort to map their bodies according to their own inner topographies of exoticist longing. Flaubert characterizes Azizeh (one of Kuchuk Hanem's rivals), as a corpus whose head might break off from her skeleton and float away like some imperiled peninsula: "Her neck slides back and forth on her vertebrae, and more often sideways, as though her head were going to fall off; terrifying effect of decapitation."[21] Even more to the point is Edmond de Goncourt's description of belly dancing at the Universal Exposition of 1889, in which the lower quarters of the dancer's body migrate like pieces of relocatable urban fabric from one "quartier" (pun intended) to the next.[22] "The belly dance performed by a naked woman interests me," Edmond writes, "making me aware of how her feminine organs move house, of how the parts of her belly change neighborhoods" [me rendrait compte du déménagement des organes de la femme, du changement de quartier des choses de son ventre].[23] This nomadism of the female sex is anticipated in a prior scene where de Goncourt recounts how he came to see Gustave Courbet's pornographic sketch of a truncated female sex entitled *The Origin of the World* (the work was putatively commissioned by a Turkish bey for private delectation and eventually ended up, as Linda Nochlin recently discovered, in the personal collection of Jacques Lacan):

> [The art dealer] de La Narde says to me: "Do you know this one?" And he unlocks a painting whose exterior panel shows a village church in the snow, and whose hidden panel is the picture painted by Courbet for Khalil-Bey, a

female belly with a black and prominent mons Venus, over the narrow opening of a pink cunt. Faced with this painting, which I had never seen before, I was obliged to make honorable amends to Courbet: this belly is as beautiful as the flesh of a Corregio.[24]

In this episode, the suspension in space of a disembodied "origin of the world," recalls Steinberg's analysis of Picasso's formalist nudes whose "task is to make exiled space present in effigy."[25] The "romance" of exile (tourism) and fetishized erotic display (the effigy) come together in Steinberg's phrase, which could serve as the caption to a cultural interpretation of de Goncourt's translocated belly, itself a fetish symbol for the spellbinding visual appeal of the colonized female sex.

Like the world of the sultan's jealously guarded seraglio, turned out of its private quarters for European viewing, Courbet's exposed, depersonalized genitalia afford Edmond de Goncourt a vision "bent around corners," a line of perception leading directly to exclusive recesses of colonial desire. It is perhaps for this reason that he uses the pretext of a sociological flânerie through the mock "rue du Caire" at the Exposition to unveil a number of saucy revelations about his personal experience with "Moorish" prostitutes.

Here a remark suggested by my nights with Moorish women in Africa. It is hardly explicable, this dance, with its furious unleashing of the belly and bum, in women who in coitus have the least pronounced movement, a barely perceptible *rolling,* and who, if you ask them to spice this movement up with some of the *pitch* of our European women, reply that you are asking them to make love like dogs.[26]

Edmond's deception over the lovemaking capabilities of Arab women implies that their dancing offers better sexual value for the money: coitus emerges as low-energy choreography; it is dance minus the serpentination (not enough *tangage,* or pitching about, he complains). A similar idea can be found when he praises a Saxe porcelain chamber pot on view at the "exposition des Arts de la femme" for its "snaking form" ("une forme plus contournée, plus serpentente"), "more amorous even than the secret parts of woman."[27] With characteristic misogyny, de Goncourt ingeniously and perhaps unwittingly inverts the traditional interpretation of belly dancing as a thinly masked performance of the sex act, by configuring the sex act as a poor second set to the dance.

Edmond de Goncourt's privileged ranking of dance may be more fully understood when one recalls the erotic value of money as it was used in the staging of belly dance numbers either on site in North Africa or in European music halls and brothels. Catering to male tourists who would presumably make an evening of it by trysting with a prostitute, the dance would invariably reach an "interactive" climax when spectators would come forward to "reward" the performers. Théophile Gautier records this moment in his *Voyage pittoresque en Algérie* (published in 1845) after describing "la danse moresque" in what by now has become a familiar language of serpentination—"perpetual undulations, twisting loins, shaking hips, body in an impossible spiraling rotation, body like a caterpillar upright on its tail, neck bent back."[28] The scene continues with the appearance of a black factotum who holds a candle up close to each part of the dancer's body, as Gautier says, to "face, throat, arm, or something else." This inspection, reminiscent of the slave-market painting by Gérôme, has the effect of assigning a financial rating to each lineament, and there is a strange erotic frisson that comes of turning people into property that may be part of the secret "kicks" inherent in even the most bureaucratic form of colonial domination. Like the ghostly agent of colonial mimicry in Homi Bhabha's ascription, the attendant shadowing the dancer encourages her purchase with obsequious grins.[29] And as this figure of doubled serpentination loops its loop, we have the "interactive" finale: spectators plaster gold pieces on the sweaty body of Zorah (the most African of the dancers, and therefore the favorite among Gautier and his companions), "on her forehead, on her cheeks, on her chest, on her arms, and finally, on the spot that they admired most."[30] This "money shot" was and continues to be a stock-in-trade convention of the belly dance. In 1919 we find a similar scene in Elissa Rhaïs's best-selling colonial novel *Saâda la Marocaine:*

> One heard the clicking of the gold and silver coins that the spectators made ring for the bayadères. One saw handsome caids rise to their feet, pull glittering louis from their pouches, moisten them with saliva, and stick them onto the dancers who were lucky enough to please them.[31]

For the spectator normally confined to voyeurism because of the distance from the stage conventionally required by the dictates of spectacle, this ability to touch a live performer with coin affords a particularly transgressive thrill (it remains today a standard trope of striptease acts worldwide). I would argue that the promise of such a touch—a magical Midas touch rendering transparent the transmogrification of sex into money—provides a key to understanding the peculiar attraction of the belly dance as performed under Western eyes. In addition to serving as an objective that motivates the serpentine visual foreplay of the colonial gaze, and in addition to "dangerously" confusing art, ethnographic spectacle, prostitution, and erotic performance, this on the money/on the body moment in the dance holds out what every colonial traveler or modern-day tourist seems to desire, namely, the chance of being "touched" by what one sees; of experiencing a palpable collision with the real. It was this vital though bitter-tasting touch of the real that Flaubert seemed to be after with the dancer Kuchuk-Hanem (as he explained didactically to Louise Colet):

> You tell me that Kuchuk's bedbugs degrade her in your eyes; for me they were the most enchanting touch of all. Their nauseating odor mingled with the scent of her skin, which was dripping with sandalwood oil. I want a touch of bitterness in everything—always a jeer in the midst of our triumphs, desolation even in the midst of enthusiasm.[32]

Evoking the erotics of disgust—the "nausea" of archaic (anal-erotic) drives—Flaubert's encounter with the colonial real matches up with Maupassant's equally acidulous pleasure in the spectacle of women dancers performing "unnatural acts" on members of their own sex. Intrigued with the dance as a visual translation of cryptolesbian sensuality (much like Walter Benjamin in relation to the sinuous forms of art nouveau), Maupassant added the serpentination of sexual deviance to the Flaubertian idealization of cultural eccentricity.[33]

To conclude, I would simply argue that there is something about the way in which serpentination is recapitulated in the discourse of postcolonial theory that makes one wonder whether a "wavy line" of disavowed colonial desire haunts even the most rigorous, well-intentioned efforts to unmask the colonial gaze. A case of this eerie return of the repressed within theory itself can be found in Malek Alloula's provocative, original analysis of early-twentieth-century harem postcards. *The Colonial Harem* (published in France in 1981 with the subtitle *Images d'un sous-érotisme)* is avowedly an exploration of the "multiform violence" buried in what Alloula ascertains was "a right of (over)sight that the colonizer arrogates to himself."[34] Alloula wants "to return this postcard to its sender" by theorizing the hidden history of colonial domination unconsciously recorded in the cards. But with all due respect to Alloula, and as a number of critics have noted, the layout of his book retraces the sinuous path of the colonial gaze that he has dedicated himself to dismantling. As the text moves along with its accompanying images—women shrouded in heavy muslin up to their eyes, women behind bars, women taking tea, women smoking pipes, women lounging, women dancing—there is progressively more nudity. First a breast is partially exposed, then by the middle of the book the chest is fully bared, and finally by the end the striptease of the torso is complete. Round tattooed breasts are compared to untattooed pendulous breasts (as if once again in the slave market), and the final image, perhaps most disturbing of all, is a picture entitled "Arabian woman with the Tachmak" in which the bosom, bifurcated by a long black veil, become entirely aestheticized, placed in a formal arrangement around the garment. The woman's eyes stare back directly at the camera, as if to say "Terminus, the *figura serpentinata* stops here." This book, like so much postcolonial theory, proceeds recursively like a dance of seduction: a critically sophisticated one, no doubt, but a teasing, undulating dance nevertheless that makes of the critic a colonial tourist.

[B]lack film *noir* is a light (as in day*light)* cast on black people.
  MANTHIA DIAWARA, *"Noirs* by *Noirs:* Toward a New Realism in Black Cinema"

10 THE LANDSCAPE
OF PHOTOGENY

"MOROCCO" IN

BLACK AND WHITE

What is the status of blackness in noir? How has race erupted into formalist issues of whiteness within modernist art practice, disturbing categories of disinterested aesthetic interpretation? As Manthia Diawara has shown in his essay on the appropriation of classic Hollywood film noir by black American filmmakers of the 1980s, the use of chiaroscuro is far from being ideologically neutral. Extrapolating from several decades of work by feminist film theorists who have explored the close psychological fit between deadly heroines and dark-lit cinematography, Diawara asserts: "From a formalist perspective a film is *noir* if it puts into play light and dark in order to exhibit a people who become 'black' because of their 'shady' moral behavior."[1] Even if a critic may want to back off insisting on strictly coded equivalencies between historic racial representations and the color of light and form, it seems imperative, particularly in the present era, to confront the aesthetics of whiteness and colorlessness with its disavowed racial unconscious.

Diawara interrogates the racial valence of noir in a film genre ostensibly concerned with psychological darkness and the emotional densities of light rather than with scenarios of raced characterology. In so doing, he sets an example for blatantly decontextualizing problems of filmic formalism. The implicit justification behind this crossover move is that it resets the critical boundaries of aesthetics and politics: in this case, Diawara complicates the binary racial paradigm of black and white by reconfiguring it as noir and light.

Diawara's conjugation of unlike discourses is similar to the strategy I have adopted in attempting a postcolonial critique of site spectacularity. I am interested specifically in trying to theorize a connection between the aestheticized politics of *rayonnement* (the export of Enlightenment ideas and culture to colonial or postcolonial territories) and the subliminally political aesthetics of photogenic landscape. In common parlance the word *photogenic* refers to that which is artistically suitable for being photographed, as in a face or figure. By implication, the photogenic subject is automatically understood to be a person. But what happens when the subject is not a person but a place? A site or a landscape? Exploring the subject of site photogeneity has lead me to speculate about whether places can be analyzed as photogenic on their own terms, that is, as visual lures that do not depend necessarily on anthropomorphic analogies to "giving good face." Beauty, to paraphrase Leo Bersani and Ulysse Dutoit, has its own light; a traitorous illumination; a "spectatorial lighting up . . . analogous to Judas's treacherous 'lighting up' of Jesus as the one accused of being the self-proclaimed Messiah."[2] While beauty's light does not depend on human subjects, it often records the treachery and violence done to them, as in the case of the subject of colonial history, consistently "disappeared." In the context of French colonial history, place is often a displacement of a disappeared person, to wit, the famous pictures of Egyptian monuments taken in the 1850s by Flaubert's travel companion Maxime du Camp, who systematically deleted local humanity or included a single native figure to give scale to the site.

The work of Jean Epstein and Edgar Morin on photogeny *(photogénie)*, outlined in Epstein's writings on close-ups and filmic ontology in the 1920s, and in Morin's *Le Cinéma ou l'homme imaginaire* (1958), makes it apparent that the early movie camera—the cinematograph—played a key role in defining the particular photogeny associated with the visuality of modernity and the colonization of place, both optical and bureaucratic.[3] Morin noted that the first cinematographers thrust themselves on the world and became tourists, much like the first colonial settlers. The images delivered by these cinematographs exerted their fascinating hold on the viewer because of the particular way in which their technology understood photogeny, literally the "genius of the photo" or what Morin refers to as "image charm," in the sense of spell, enchantment, visual seduction. Taking his cue from Epstein, a 1920s avant-garde filmmaker and theorist, Morin saw photogeny as cinema's *prise de conscience,* the moment when it recognizes its own powers of visual enthrallment. Photogeny emerges as an ethics of visual reflexivity, involving the spectator's apperception of the magical realism of quotidian representations, the legendary embedded in the everyday, and his/her own obliquity as subject of representation. Morin distinguished between photographic and cinematic photogeny on the grounds that the latter, in its reliance on a deprivatized viewing space, enhances the alterity and strangeness of the image.

In 1920 the filmmaker Louis Delluc related the term *photogénie* to the banal beauty exuded by the faces of certain actors on screen. It mattered little whether the light was poor, the cameraman hysterical, the director a sadist, or the scenario abominably stilted: if the actors were photogenic, Delluc argued with barbed irony, any film could be salvaged. Delluc sought to disengage an aesthetically redemptive photogeny from the "monotone quintessence," visual clichés, and insufficient mastery of "the algebra of light," characteristic of an early French cinema overly indebted to photographic stills and postcard images.[4]

Though Delluc stigmatized facile photogenic beauty, he was nonetheless concerned with safeguarding its seductive powers, concentrated, it appears, in the match between high-modernist design and erotic lighting.[5] In tune with contemporary apologists for the erotics of modern primitivism (Apollonaire and Picasso among many others), Delluc heralded the sophisticated visual appeal of light on dark skin. He was careful, however, to maintain this aesthetic at a safe distance from what he thought to be the prosaic arena of publicity and commercial image-production characteristic of tourism. Instead of faces that appeared as bland screens "over which feeling played its tricks," he pressed for sculptured, masklike visages set on top of bodies clad in minimally patterned clothing, what he called "visual dresses." Delluc's vision of the photogenic relied upon an aesthetic of classic modernism: ocean liners, airplanes, and railroads were photogenic by virtue of "the geometry of their structure"; in costume design, black and white uniforms beguiled the eye while transcending the false consciousness of period costume. Extolling the photogenic potential of flesh, Delluc also provided a kind of inadvertent authorization for *cinéma colonial;* celebrating the way light played on matte skin tones, he singled out meridional complexions or the sinuous bodies of women of color, as in René Le Somptier and Louis Nalpas's Orientalist film *La Sultane de l'amour.*

Some years later Roland Barthes reprised the notion of photogeny. Like Delluc, Barthes focused on the aesthetics of sexual light; unlike Delluc, however, he refused to exclude popular visual culture or soft porn from the realm of photogeny. Relocating the photogene in the photograph, Barthes analyzed how "threadbare visual legends" get turned into ready cash in relation to the particular kind of pleasure yielded by baron von Gloeden's famous photos of Neapolitan *ragazzi* posing as classical ephebes. The hot visual appeal of von Gloeden's pictures resided for Barthes in the "blue-black gaze"—the bruised yet appealing light that showers the sun-darkened bodies of boys. Such visual erotics recall Lacan's notion of the "filigreed gaze" of the painter, which, in seminar XI, he describes as an autographic "play of light and opacity" secreted on the canvas.[6] In von Gloeden's pictures, as seen by Barthes, the gaze of the photographer appears as an iridescent smudge, connoting the "sublime blur" of art and sex:

> Whereby these little Greek gods (already contradicted by their blackness) have rather dirty peasant hands with big rough fingernails, worn feet that are none too clean, and very visible swollen foreskins—no longer stylized, i.e., tapered and reduced: uncircumcised is what they are, and one sees only that: the baron's photos are at once sublime and anatomical.[7]

Malek Alloula noted a comparable mark of the gaze in the "tawdriness" associated with soiled bodies and tacky garments of the postcarded harem girls collected in his book *The Colonial Harem:* "This tawdriness that keeps reappearing is beyond the control of the postcard," he writes. "It is its original sin, its mark of infamy, in sum, its signature at the bottom of a counterfeit."[8]

This racially freighted idea of dirty light and menacing patches of shadow can be extended to the particular photogeny of colonial landscape in film noir. Josef von Sternberg's *Morocco* (1930), Jacques Feyder's *Le Grand Jeu* (1934), Julien Duviver's *La Bandera* (1935) and *Pépé le Moko* (1936) (set in Algiers), the ever-classic Michael Curtiz film *Casablanca* (1942), Hitchcock's postwar version of *The Man Who Knew Too Much* (1955), and more recently Bernardo Bertolucci's fey adaptation of Paul Bowles's *The Sheltering Sky* (1990) all capitalize on Morocco's star quality—a noirish photogenicity rivaled only perhaps by San Francisco, Berlin, and Hollywood.

Shadows, arrayed in complex decorative patterns against bands and wedges of intense light (von Sternberg's *Morocco)* or sprayed in dark technicolor blue around a minaret at nightfall (*The Man Who Knew Too Much)* emerge as a visual specialty of Morocco movies. Morocco's cities and desert expanses were revealed as historic marvels, the visual legend of film. By the early 1930s the film crew had become such a commonplace appearance in the Moroccan landscape that Wyndham Lewis would dedicate an entire section of his jaundiced travelogue *Journey into Barbery* to a pastiche of what he called "film-filibusters," industry magnates who "send their troupes (not troops) merely to afford their sham-sheiks a Hispano-Mauresque photographic setting." Stating that these sham-sheiks were nothing better than shadow figures at one material remove from the "thin reality" of the cinematic screen, Lewis inadvertently captured the ghostly atmospherics peculiar to the construction of "Morocco" as Orientalist commodity, screen place of screen-memory, and virtual colony.

More recently, Rachid Boudjedra's 1980 magic realist novel, *Les 1001 années de la nostalgie* (A thousand and one years of nostalgia), grimly satirizes the commercial photogeneity of postcolonial landscape. A North African desert town is transformed by the arrival of a foreign film crew equipped with fabulous sets simulating the dream-décors of Sheherazade's tales. The inhabitants become exotic extras, unable to recognize themselves, while the once familiar landscape around them is subjected to cosmetic surgery, enhancing the "face" of Islam: the sky bandaged with bluer than blue, the sun covered in cellophane, the old mosques asticated with counterfeit decoration, and a seascape replete with quays, docks, and sailors implanted in the sand like some worn bad cliché of a desert mirage. These stagings, morbidly culminating in the use of recently assassinated residents to play the role of cadavers, are realized in the name of the cinematograph, itself described as the benignly demonic agent of a kinder gentler recolonization ("une recolonisation en douce").[9]

The photogene, emerging from a theoretical montage of Delluc, Barthes, and Boudjedra, is an affair of black and light. Consider, for example, the photosensitive way in which the colonial novelist and filmmaker Jean d'Esmé evoked the carbonized landscape, "brutal light," and "black fortifications" of Senegal while on location for his 1938 epic *Sentinelles d'empire:*

> Soot-colored land, paved with black stones, flat, calcified, devastated like an incinerated landscape; in the distance, two mountain peaks resembling two enormous blocks of coal to which the brutal light gives a sinister sheen; further still, at the flaming horizon, an abrupt black wall over Dakar.[10]

D'Esmé seems to have been particularly conscious of filming Africa as a brilliantly lit epidermis. Writing about *Peaux-noires,* a film made during a year of travel through Cameroon, Chad, Ubangi-Shari, the Congo, and Gabon, he claimed to have sought "not to express Africa's soul, but rather, simply, to show her face."[11]

As the notion of photogeny is transferred from face to place, from flesh to building skin or wrinkled desertscape, from racially marked body to film noir, the problem of what gives a site its sex becomes entangled with the more difficult political and aesthetic problem of identifying what is noir in the aesthetics of noir. Put slightly differently, what (or who) is *black* in the shadows of the high-gloss landscape? These questions are particularly pertinent in relation to some of the aesthetically sensitive films made in the 1920s and 1930s. Marc Allegret's *Le Voyage au Congo* (1925–27), for example, capitalized on the art value of African bodies. Filmed on site in the company of his lover and mentor André Gide (whose bitter exposé of colonial injustice in the Congo earned him the wrath of many literary admirers), the film, in hindsight, might be seen as a precursor of Leni Riefenstahl's album of aestheticized Nubians or Mapplethorpe's photographic eulogy of black masculinity. Each of these artists, in their way, depended on a dermographic photogeny that submerged and obscured the racial politics of black and white in the high-art aesthetics of black and light.

A photogene, appropriately enough, refers to an impression retained on the retina of the eye after the object itself has vanished, an afterimage. Most avant-garde and surrealist filmmakers of the 1920s, committed to capturing dream consciousness or the ubiquity of ghosts and phantasms in everyday life, exploited this visual conceit repeatedly. In the context of colonial representation, the psychological photogene acquires historical meaning in a master-narrative of European imperialism, technological incursion, intrigue, and espionage. Native subjects are noticeable as absences: shadows that glance off the side of a pyramid or mosque, anonymous geometries arranged as infill for the marketplace scene, milky traces of overexposure. Their belated appearance concentrates new significance on the psychic and mechanical techniques of afterimaging crucial to the projection of colonial vision.

The hegemonic facescape of the colonizer in the desert and the scapegoating of native faces provide examples of what Gilles Deleuze and Félix Guattari dubbed *visagéité:* to designate regimes of "face-ness" or face-production. "Visage-ification" is what gives legibility (and therefore power) to human bodies. Faceness operates semiotically through the system *mur-blanc-trou-noir* (white-wall-black-hole). As the agent of subjectification, faceness stamps out the terrifying specter of the inhuman (the *Visage-bunker,* or mask of dead white meat).[12] For Deleuze and Guattari, the face of power is a colonizing force (one thinks of those futurist canvases in which rays of light irradiate from the giant head of Mussolini, beaming down over Italy), as well as a visual gold standard of Christian racial orthodoxy:

> The face is not a universal. . . . it is the white man himself, with his large
> white cheeks and black eyeholes. The face is Christ. . . . If the face is Christ,
> that is to say, the average white man, the first derivations, the first typolog-
> ical swerves *(écarts-types)* are racial: yellow man, black man, men of the sec-
> ond and third category. They too are inscribed on the wall, organized
> around the hole. They must be Christianized, that is to say visage-ified.[13]

Deleuze and Guattari argue that racism does not just proceed through the exclusion or othering of strangers, but equally through the disturbance created by the other's nonidentity with whiteface. For white Europeans, the "crime" of people of color has traditionally been their possession of visages that are simply not legible *as face*. Deleuze and Guattari deterritorialize the aesthetics of the portrait and the picturesque by revealing their ideological collusion with Christian pedagogy. That is, they show how photogeny's techniques for mesmerizing the spectator with facescapes can be complicitous with racist visuality.

Though Delluc was certainly blind to the colonial implications of photogenic landscape, his close associate Jean Epstein theorized its significance as an episteme of psychic eruption and territorial breakdown in ways that suggest postcolonial applications. Aerial perspective, close-ups of shifting landmasses, facescapes of character and place—these linchpins of avant-garde sublimity, however far they may seem from any specific colonial agenda, may be adduced as part of the strutwork supporting imperial vision.

In a film entitled *Photogénie* (1925) that was subsequently destroyed, Epstein translated the technics of visual mastery into a sublime cinematic metaphysic capitalizing on the mesmerizing effects of light, magnification, and scale. Epstein regarded the cinematograph as an instrument of the fourth dimension—a tool that, by "laminating time" (showing time to be subject to technological manipulation), rendered it commensurable with space. The spatialization of temporality was crucial to his aesthetic of photogeny; for Epstein, the photogene was lodged in a cinematic representation that, like virtual reality, seemed to implant the camera's eye within the viewer's body:

> When a character is going to meet another, I want to go along with him, not behind or in front of him or by his side, but in him. I would like to look through his eyes and see his hand reach out from under me as if it were my own; interruptions of opaque film would imitate the blinking of our eyelids.[14]

Epstein's *kino-eye,* not unlike that of Dziga Vertov, Sergei Eisenstein, Salvador Dalí, and Luis Buñuel, was most tangible in the close-up, where physical touch joined the visual image in an electric moment of contact: "Close-up, close-up, close-up," he wrote. "Not the recommended points of view, the horizons of the Touring Club, but natural, indigenous, and photogenic details" (p. 95). In prose that conjures up Bataille's essay on the big toe, Barthes's discursus on the zoom-lensed face of Greta Garbo, or Lacan's theory of the captation of the image, he wrote: "A close-up of an eye, is no longer an eye, it is *an* eye: that is to say, the mimetic décor in which, suddenly, the character of the gaze appears" (p. 140). Epstein was fascinated by the way in which an inanimate object, say a revolver, could, when enlarged in *gros plan,* turn into a "personnage-revolver," that is, a "character," capable of signaling suicidal impulses, criminal desire, even remorse. The term for close-up in French—*gros plan*—translates literally as "big plan" or "map." For Epstein, the *gros plan* turned the screen into a relief map squirming with everyday objects coming alive. Stark seascapes or landmasses vertiginously filmed from above became expressive faces; the sky itself turned plastic and morphic when placed in the eye of the cinematograph, a material to be used in visual construction. Epstein wrote that if cathedrals were built in stone and sky, then films could be made from photograph and sky (p. 190).

Mobile microscopy combined with subliminal telescopy produced a new kind of photogenic landscape—the *kinetic flesh-land.* In the 1922 essay "Langue d'or," Epstein imagined the human face bathed in an electrocuting shower of light, "cooked, recooked, corroded, cured, brushed, and embossed with the colors of passion."[15] The shock produced by the mutant magnified detail was comparable to the trauma of a wound or the psychic reaction to seismic upheaval. In the style of futurist prose poetry, splicing human faces with geomorphic contours and eruptions, he communicated the effect of photogeny in a psychoanalytically familiar language of splitting and cutting:

> Muscular preambles ripple beneath the skin. Shadows shift, tremble, hesitate. Something is being decided. A breeze of emotion underlines the mouth with clouds. The orography of the face vacillates. Seismic shocks begin. Capillary wrinkles try to split the fault. A wave carries them away. Crescendo. A muscle bridles. The lip is laced with tics like a theater curtain. Everything is movement, imbalance, crisis. Crack. The mouth gives way, like a ripe fruit splitting open. As if slit by a scalpel, a keyboardlike smile cuts laterally into the corner of the lips.[16]

Epstein's metaphor of photogenic eruption materialized in one of his first films, *La Montagne infidèle* (1923), a documentary recording a volcanic explosion at Mount Etna. In a 1926 lecture based on the film, Epstein cast Mount Etna as an earthwork of sublime terror, a monument of site photogeneity galvanizing the surrounding Sicilian landscape:

> Sicily! The night was an eye full of the look. In front of us: Etna, giant actor releasing its spectacle two or three times a century, and whose tragic fantasia I had come to film. . . . No tragic actor of the theater ever knew a storm of such proportions, the earth suffering, but dominated, crackling with its call . . . Etna, telegraphing the extreme shaking of disaster . . . spreading its deadly postexplosion pall . . . grilled leaves, naked trees, lava spreading like broken plates.[17]

Seeking, perhaps, to rescue the sublime from the banal by defining it cin-emtographically (thus founding a new cinematic ontology that would be-come the basis for postwar film theory from André Bazin to Jean-Luc Godard), Epstein relied nonetheless on a tradition of the aesthetic sublime that calibrated momentous philosophical shifts of ground with images of earthshaking metastasis. One thinks of Empedocles, the pre-Socratic philosopher who died by throwing himself into Etna's inferno to show, in defiance of Socratic wisdom, that instead of exiting the cave, one should plunge in ever further, thus privileging terrestrial immanence over tran-scendence. One thinks of Voltaire's interpretation of the Lisbon earth-quake in terms of a fundamental questioning of the beneficence of God; of Edmund Burke's prefiguration of the terrifying aesthetic sublime in the Dublin floods of his youth; of Bataille's trip of horror to Mount Etna with his consumptive, masochistic mistress Colette Peignot (Bataille wrote that "this ascension of Etna had an extreme significance for us . . . we were ex-hausted, and in some sense ex-orbed [*exorbités*—our eyes popped out of our skulls] by a strange, disastrous solitude: it was a moment of rupture in which we were leaning over the gaping wound on the crack of a star where we were breathing").[18] In a more recent context, one thinks of Robert Smithson's *Spiral Jetty* in conjunction with some of his art-critical earth-works of the 1960s, writings that conflate intellectual and topographical fault-lines:

> Oceanic depths in these maps submerge the continents of prose. Equators
> spill onto shores of misplaced thought. Where do these maps start? No
> place. . . . Continental critical drift merges and sinks into different photo-
> graphic seas. Swamps of "isms" develop around reproductions of art. . . . de-
> tails of paintings stick out of intellectual lava flows.[19]

Finally, as someone who experienced the Los Angeles earthquake of 1994, I can't help thinking of the vacuous sublimity of those clips, taken by super-market surveillance cameras, that were endlessly played on television to il-lustrate the force of the quake. Like cinematographs dispatched by God to venture where no human eye would dare to go, these surveillance cameras remained vigilantly on location throughout the disaster, recording shaking countertops and toppling grocery shelves, generating new televisual fodder for the eminently recyclable myth of moral apocalypse in the Southland.

If Epstein's sublime photogeny ends the century with this flickering image of a supermarket floor strewn with soapboxes and biscuit containers, nevertheless it is in this surveillance from above that the colonial and nat-ural photogene found, and perhaps still finds, its most characteristic form. We might then see the collapsed shelves of supermarkets or the fleeing shadows of bank robbers as the suburban equivalents of the wasted battle-fields of war and nuclear assault (theorized by Paul Virilio), or the terrain of the colonies, subdued and surveyed by aerial cartography, as landscapes of photogeny in which disaster, shock, and metaphysical ruin have been visually encrypted.

Jean (1877–1952) and Jérôme (1874–1953) Tharaud, French travel writers of the 1920s and 1930s who produced a stream of popular accounts of historic Moroccan cities, judged the impact of aerial shots so profound that it prompted them as writers to try to compete in prose. Hypnotized by the outlines of distant landmasses, they figured the earth as a field of fili-greed shelters covering over the unreal. Their chronicle of an airplane voyage around the world, *Paris-Saigon dans l'azur* (1932), begins with a hallucinatory recollection of their former teacher, the geographer Vidal de la Blache, promenading his spindly fingers over the map of the globe, fondling the world like a giant fetish. ("The whole universe seemed to be held alive in his hand. It seems that from up above, I will see the fingers of the old professor walking on the world.")[20]

Faithful colonial servants, the Tharauds traversed North Africa at the invitation of Maréchal Lyautey (the chief colonial administrator of Morocco), generating copy for the burgeoning French tourist industry, as in *Algiers to Marrakech by Automobile,* or books devoted to the historic cities of Fez, Rabat, and Marrakech. Born and raised in the Limousin, near Oradour, a town whose inhabitants were burned alive as the German army retreated during World War II, the Tharauds promoted conservative values through a redemptive vision of the French countryside. A typically French Catholic quest for a new spiritualism is evident in their inclination toward sentimental regionalism, their disciple-like following of the great avatars of patriotic pastoral (Charles Péguy, Maurice Barrès), and their "Arabophilic" fascination with the spiritual grandeur of Islam. Their tender spot for the landscape of a static biblical Orient often created a conflict of ideological interest: on the one hand they endorsed the project of empire; on the other, they were chagrined by the scarring of territory caused by industrialization. Surveying Iraq by plane, they expressed horror at what the landscape told them:

> "Baghdad!" Of these syllables nothing remains—the fabulous tale has come undone, the Orient fallen into dust, abandoned by the English to the void. . . . It is a Baghdad of petrole, "la Baghdad de *l'Anglo-persan-oil-Company.*"[21]

Baghdad marred the crusade for aerial landscape of geometric epiphany such as those afforded by the cities of Persia. Equaling Baghdad, for the Tha-rauds, the Cambodian temple of Angkor Wat was the ne plus ultra of site seduction, the analogue to Versailles in the harmonious order of its parterres. Soaring past it, only to swoop down close, they recounted an experience of sublime terror: the looming temple was "a cinematograph running toward you from the depth of the screen, growing larger and larger, seeming almost to submerge you, then suddenly distancing itself again, vanishing into phantasmagoria."[22] In this curious description, Angkor Wat is cast as a redoubtable foreign monument masquerading as a movie camera. Surging up in *gros plan* (literally "in your face"), the camera fixes the airborne viewer in an unnerving reverse gaze; but the passenger's fear of being caught on film by the other is soon quelled as the plane veers back on course. The latent imperialism of aerial vision thus reasserts itself over Indochina's greatest architectural treasure.

In this aeronautic worldscape the Tharauds struggled to dissipate the fear that came of seeing landmarks of a great non-European civilization suddenly rise up. In their travel book on Marrakech, they responded to a similar struggle by using narrative *leveling* techniques. They invented a degree-zero topography—or if you will, a kind of ecoabsolutism—evacuating human subjects, essentializing culture and space, and distracting the reader from the politics of colonial eminent domain. North Africa's photosensitive empty spaces are evoked to heighten a sense of the civilizing mission as an epic, expansionist project (a stadium for cultural and theological *rayonnement)*, while shadows are deployed to black out the real, obscuring lingering impressions of an anomalous European presence.

Fond of the panorama, a conceit characterized by Marie Louise Pratt as the "promontory description" or "Monarch-of-all-I-survey" scene, the Tharauds modernized nineteenth-century narrative techniques of visual mastery, substituting aerial photography as the mediatic equivalent of painterly perspectivalism.[23] Here, they fulfilled Jean Epstein's dream of a truly modern photogeny. Fulminating against the deadness of picturesque landscape in film ("the landscape film is, for the moment, a big zero. . . . The picturesque in cinema is zero, nothing, negation"), and summoning futurist technology to render "landscape's dance," with "cinematic vivacity," Epstein wrote: "I yearn for a drama aboard a merry-go-round, or more modern still, in airplanes. The fair below and its surroundings would be progressively confounded. Given centrifugal force, vertigo, and rotation, the tragedy would be photogenically enhanced tenfold." [24] The final vignette of the Tharauds' book on Marrakech embodies this centrifugal movement insofar as textual form would allow:

> And so it is, that suddenly as if by a miracle I escape from all this monotony, and I take off in the air. An airplane bears me aloft, while myriad gazes track-

ing us from below seem to tie us to the earth like the tail of a kite. Soon the encampment assumes the aspect of a box of toy soldiers unwrapped on a table. Everything becomes still. I no longer distinguish the whiteness of tents squashed on the plateau or the minuscule brochette of horses and mules attached by cord. Soon even every trace of human life disappears. . . . I have beneath my eyes something that makes me think of a piece of anatomy, with its arteries, veins, and lesser vessels.

. . . But what are those needle-points of light that I see there, stuck into the pelt? It takes me a moment to realize that this porcupine hail consists of thousands upon thousands of date tree trunks crowned by palms surrounding Marrakech. The city unveils herself in her gardens. The immense caravanserai of earth and dried mud, which gives so strong an impression of rubble, of the ruined and indecipherable, when one peregrinates by foot or mule in its streets, shows itself from a bird's-eye view to be a handsome design without error, with its courtyards and terraces, its rectangular spaces, its alternating whites and blacks; a real fantasy of the geometer or applied draftsman. Ah! the unique sensation of being able, virtually, to raze the terraces, open up this secret life of Islam to the naked eye! But hardly has this illusion had time to lodge inside the spirit, than the book is closed, the machine landed, and one's moment as a bird gone forever.[25]

An exhilarating vertigo motivates this passage, yet this technovision projects a brutal wish to see a corrected, modernized, razed Morocco—a land of Islamic mystery opened up to Western use, camera ready, its organs delivered over after surgical intervention. The use of scale, another cinematic value championed by Epstein, heightens the effect of a dominated frontier; the miniaturization of horses, mules, and nomads turns Morocco momentarily into an infantilized territory littered with toys.

With theological intensity Morocco unveils her face only to occlude the bird's-eye viewer with an overpowering light (and here it is hard not to think of Lacan's famous example of Zeuxis's bird-tricking trompe l'oeil grapes). In this way, the photogene slips from its function as agent of visual publicity to be recast as an ethical headbeam that puts the colonial viewer back in his or her place—that is, out of the picture.[26]

Where the Tharauds eradicated the indigenous sublime through aerial opticality, the far more successful writer André Malraux used the metaphysics of elevation to indulge a European fantasy of site projection that involved imaging a city where none could be found. In 1934, shortly after winning the Goncourt Prize for *La Condition humaine,* Malraux set out to find the lost city of the queen of Sheba, an exploit that was part publicity stunt, part Orientalist dreamwork. Inspired by literary renderings of Sheba's visit to King Solomon in Judea, stirred by essays in the *Bulletin de Géographie* that hypothetically situated Sheba's city of origin in pharaonic Egypt, biblical Sinai, Palestine, Syria, and Yemen, Malraux resolved to rescue this dead urban treasure from obscurity using Western technologies of aerial excavation. Saint-Exupéry was his first choice of pilot, but after the literary aviator turned him down, he convinced Edouard Corniglion-Molnier to be his guide.

Eventually collected under the title *La Reine de Saba: Une aventure géographique* (1934), Malraux's articles adopted the narrative structure of epic adventure and colonial hubris. The Icarian plane occupies the hero's position, surging forth as a miracle of "whiteness . . . an apparatus that is the West itself."[27] Strident occidentalism is a leitmotif of the mission: when the government of Yemen creates a diplomatic fracas over the fliers' failure to request air rights, Malraux responds indignantly that a Frenchman in pursuit of honorable discoveries is answerable only to a nation as powerful as France (pp. 96–97). Such conceits of nationalist supremacy are reinforced by the rhetoric of sexual conquest. As the airplane pursues its course over the Arabian desert, scouring the area of Yemen between the cities of Sana'a and Mareb, the queen of Sheba's imaginary body is increasingly displaced to a landscape of photogeny. Viewed from above, the threatening spectacle of the *informe* gives way to shapes of explicit castratory menace: Medusal dunes, shark-toothed mountain ranges, the wounded, strafed terrain of the steppes, shock-inducing desert expanses of "geological solitude," dark, ominous hatchings outlining the Valley of the Tombs. Swooping down, the plane enacts its powers of inquisitorial master; the "prodigious spectacle of a dead city" (a dummy capital near Mareb thought to be the possible location of Sheba) is gradually brought into line with European modernism as Malraux compares what he perceives of the ruin—its tubular columns, oval towers, and chunky ramparts—to the blocky white architecture of Mallet-Stevens (p. 78). As if to reinforce the stamp of European projection on this mythic desert town, Malraux included drawings by the architect-urbanist André P. Hardy featuring imaginary reconstructions of Sheba's temple in the style of French modern; its grids, pyramids, and colossal towers drawn up, as it were, out of the contours of the desert, like some ancient antecedent of Le Corbusier's *formes courbes* projected for the littoral of Algeria between 1931 and 1934.

Imagined out of the aerial vision of this "vast, virtually white spot, a beachhead of colossal stones in the middle of the sand,"[28] this antique "ville radieuse," subordinating Middle Eastern building types to the codes of white modernity, inevitably conjures up Le Corbusier's abstracted colonial landscape. Though it may seem crude to interpret Corbusian whiteness as a Western sublimation of North African vernacular, the texts and illustrations of his Algerian project appear to warrant a critical perspective dealing with the racially marked subtexts of urban formalism. Like Malraux and the Tharaud brothers, Le Corbusier made his appraisal of the territory by air: "The airplane reveals to us a miracle of wisdom, of knowledgeable and salutary order; above, opening up like living shells is the fragrant greenery of the gardens. The elegant design of the arcades in the middle of the country of Thirst reveals a true civilization."[29] In the various projects for Algiers, aerodynamic futurism and relief-map design were harnessed in the service of "urban biology"—a plan for a new Mediterranean capital set along the sinuous striation of an autoroute. With pedagogical intent, *La Ville radieuse* mobilized aerial vision to unblock passageways into old Algiers that were barred to the outsider. In one drawing an airplane loops stylishly around a minaret in the M'zab desert; the caption comments approvingly on how the "plane discovers the city's secrets." The image of interiors pried open for inspection was enhanced by the jumble of tourist postcards—pictures of veiled women in archways and walls—that Le Corbusier used to make a personal album of "suggestive documents." The implicit justification for such violations of private space may be found in sketches and captions praising the *barbares* for their ingenious solutions to urban dwelling.

In adapting the white stucco wash of local Algerian architecture to the "whiter than white" transparency of the European *unité d'habitation,* Le Corbusier captured the photogeneity of local color and put it to use in a formally glamorous, decolorized aesthetic of modernism. Arguably, this colonial implant inserted in the corpus of European architecture, could be read as an avenging antibody (a suppressed noirness) that is only manifesting itself now within the postcolonial politics of Third World urbanism.

The Martinican author Patrick Chamoiseau's *Texaco* grounds the politics of postcolonial territoriality in the landscape itself. A barren landmass of oil derricks belonging to the American oil conglomerate becomes the site for the foundation of a new town, baptized "Texaco" when a postcolony of squatters occupies the site. They pass symbolically from the equivalent of the stone to the iron age, building first in mud, then in fiber cement, and finally in heavy-duty *beton.* From *zone-vide* petrolscape to permanent settlement, Texaco—unlike Boudjedra's mythic North African town robbed of its identity by the movie camera—emerges as an earthwork of Afro-Caribbean enfranchisement whose photogeny is cast in the *style art brut.*

A landscape of cement bunkers, Texaco concocts its strange, austere beauty out of a creolized urbanism in which sex, race, and power have been intermarried and placed in what Edouard Glissant would call "a state of eruption," itself a "burst in modernity."[30] Here, as in the notion of a more generalized photogeny that I have tried to construct, the sex of buildings or the racing of landscape resides in displaced or abstracted visual significations rather than in literal transfers of the raced, sexed body to the nonfigurative visual subject. The literal approach is evident in many of the works of art and media exhibited at the Pompidou Center's 1995 show, "Féminimasculin: Le sexe de l'art," in which phallic and vulval morphologies have a cartoonish referentiality. Sigmar Polke's photograph of rifted mountain cliffs, for example, reveals a striking intention to accentuate the landscape's resemblance to a clitoris. While I would not necessarily want to exclude images of this kind as examples of photogenic—in the sense of sexed or sexy—landscape, I would also like to stress that photogeny should not perforce be tied to visual one-linerism or mimetic anthropomorphism. Part of the interest of this investigation of the dark spaces of noir, or the faces of landscape, or the aerial perspectives and cartographic configurations of imperial vision, has been to explore more mediated strategies for defining nonfigurative visual seductions in a postcolonial moment when all identities—whether of buildings, landscapes, or societies—have become subject to the unsettling mirages of photogenic representation.

Digression on "la place du Maroc." The city and the interior, the city and the country, are not alone in their intersection: such intersections can be found in a far more concrete form. There is, for example, the place du Maroc in Belleville: when I discovered it one Sunday afternoon, this melancholy mass of stone tenements became for me, not only a Moroccan desert, but also, and especially, a monument of colonial imperialism; a topographic vision crossed with allegorical signification, but for all that, it never lost its place at the heart of Belleville.

WALTER BENJAMIN, *Das Passagen-Werk*

IMPOTENT EPIC

THE CRISIS

OF LITERARY TOURISM

IN THE AGE

OF MECHANICAL

REPRODUCTION

Walter Benjamin's resituation of "French Morocco" to the Parisian metropole describes the complex relay of place, demography, community, national style, and cultural identity subsumed by imperialism in the public realm in France and North Africa beginning in the 1870s and continuing through to the present. This "little Morocco in France," marking the presence of colonized North Africa in France itself, auguring mass *pied noir* immigration to France in the wake of the Algerian War, and presaging the increasing ghettoization of Maghrebians in the banlieux and *bidonvilles* of contemporary French capital cities, forms a piece with myriad comparable countermonuments to the colonial legacy, from the razed summits of Kabylian villages to the phenomenon of the *harkis*—Algerians who fought for France—consigned to legal and territorial no-man's-land to this day.

Though his perspective is anticolonial, Benjamin's depiction of "la place du Maroc" as a space of national hybridity physically and psychically migrating through modernity sits on an extended literary tradition of writing North Africa and the Middle East as crossover regions of exoticism, tourism, ethnography, and European modernism. From the nineteenth-century belletristic travelogues of Chateaubriand, Gustave Flaubert, Théophile Gautier, Pierre Loti, Alphonse Daudet, Guy de Maupassant, Jane Dieulafoy, and Isabelle Eberhardt, through to the early-twentieth-century chronicles of Louis Bertrand, André Chevrillon, Michel Vieuchange, Jean Lorrain, Robert de Flers, Maurice Barrès, Myriam Harry, Henriette Célarié,

Elissa Rhaïs, Colette, the Tharaud brothers (and, on the Anglo side, Edith Wharton, Wyndham Lewis, and George Orwell), a sense of belatedness in the face of encroaching mass tourism infuses a consistent oscillation between nostalgia for tradition and the obligatory recording of European incursions into the fabric of Moroccan everyday life. As Edith Wharton wrote, on visiting Morocco in 1917:

> These drawbacks [lack of petrol, weather constraints] were more than offset by the advantage of making my quick trip at a moment unique in the history of the country; the brief moment of transition between its virtually complete subjection to European authority, and the fast approaching hour when it is thrown open to all the banalities and promiscuities of modern travel.
>
> Morocco is too curious, too beautiful, too rich in landscape and architecture, and above all too much of a novelty, not to attract one of the main streams of spring travel as soon as Mediterranean passenger traffic is resumed. Now that the war is over, only a few months' work on roads and railways divide it from the great torrent of "tourism"; and once that deluge is let loose, no eye will ever again see Moulay Idriss and Fez and Marrakech as I saw them.
>
> In spite of the incessant efforts of the present French administration to preserve the old monuments of Morocco from injury, and her native arts and industries from the corruption of European bad taste, the impression of mystery and remoteness which the country now produces must inevitably languish with the approach of the "Circular Ticket." Within a few years far more will be known of the past of Morocco, but that past will be far less visible to the traveller than it is to-day. Excavations will reveal fresh traces of Roman and Phoenician occupation; the remote affinities between Copts and Berbers, between Baghdad and Fez, between Byzantine art and the architecture of the Souss, will be explored and elucidated; but, while these successive discoveries are being made, the strange survival of medieval life, of a life contemporary with the crusaders, with Saladin, even with the great days of the Caliphate or Baghdad, which now greets the astonished traveller, will gradually disappear, till at last even the mysterious autochthones of the Atlas will have folded their tents and silently stolen away.[1]

Melancholia, concentrated in the lingering image of native peoples flushed out of their homelands by the invading tourist hordes and "silently stealing away," to a somewhere as yet to be identified, emerges as a constant of the genre, alongside the familiar cultural narcissism and possessiveness of the Western traveler convinced of his or her unique access to exotic vision.

French Orientalist "protectorate" prose, often intended to buttress the morale of those engaged in executing the civilizing mission, alternates with dismay at the recession of indigenous customs in the face of westernization. By the early twentieth century, literary travel writing is conflicted, self-doubting, and often bent on indicting the very industry on which it is premised. In Louis Bertrand's *Le Mirage oriental* (1910), for instance, tourism is excoriated both for "sequestering" the traveler in a European cocoon of "civilization" (food, plumbing, ready-to-wear exotic attractions) and for bringing about the "debacle of local color" by fostering a local economy based on peddling, pimping, harassment, the commercial exploitation of ruins, and the spoliation of nature.[2]

The best-selling travelogues of Jean and Jérôme Tharaud (see chapter 10) typified the coordinates of this self-hating genre. Technically organized around the visually framed presentation of cities, urban monuments, pilgrim sites, and dramatic set-pieces of folkloric urban and rural everyday life, their texts, as we have seen, call out for interpretation in terms of their active competition with the photographic or cinematic image. Colonial reality emerges as postcarded or reified in space, enhancing commercial value in the metropolitan sphere of mass culture. The Tharaud brothers created a modernist Orientalism that joined a technocratic colonial ideology to the "timeless" scenography of antiquity, biblical legend, and Gothic sublimity. The municipal fortifications of Rabat appear as "fantastically" high unified walls, animated by furtive, murderous apparitions dressed in white, gliding silently along the enshadowed ogives. "It all seems timeless," they remark, "as if belonging to no age of the world. A diffuse emotion fills the heart and slows the pace: one looks, one advances no more; one thanks life for this privileged moment, time suspended on its course, poetry arrested there, and this reverberation of the city, fabulous magician, it too an instrument of dream."[3] In describing Fez the Tharauds spliced the modern approach to the city (in a motor car that scatters servants and chickens in its disruptive path) with a shopworn topos of architectural and cultural fixity:

> Considerable luxury, no invention. In architecture, as in everything else, the Fassi follows tradition. Too lazy to conserve, too untalented to invent, what he does today is exactly what he did yesterday. In our European cities, varieties of style ceaselessly oppose past and present beneath our eyes, constantly reminding us of vanished tastes and modes of existence. Nothing comparable here. The same thought, virtually an instinct, re-creates the same thing in the same place. In Fez there is only one age and one style, that of yesteryear, today, and tomorrow. Here the miracle of arresting time has been accomplished.[4]

As Edward Said, among others, has pointed out, Morocco, like other places in the West's Orientalized Orient, was represented as a kind of living historical museum of ancient civilization, a blunt cliché of cultural stasis that allowed it to be translated into an extension of "la France classique," defined by the Moroccan critic Abdelkebir Khatibi in his *Figures de l'étranger dans la littérature française* (1987) as a national *doxa* composed of "courtly language," "charismatic power," and "theological nationalism."[5] Assimilating Morocco to French classicism—a supreme carrier of cultural capital and linchpin of national pride—was of course a skillful way of promoting policies of associationism, an evolving colonial civic and educational program that, like assimilationism, effectively usurped the cultural identity of its subject peoples.

If there were specific tensions within France itself between the cosmopolitan universalism of a pasteurized *culture française* and the parochial nativism of Barrèsian regionalism (as argued in Barrès's *Les Déracinés)*, these tensions were exacerbated to some extent by the politics of cultural export. Though Morocco belonged to a Braudelian, pan-Mediterranean culture, its profound religious, linguistic, and social alterity and internal cultural diversity rendered its incorporation within the institutions of *francité* difficult and often impossible. Budding *pied noir* culture, itself a *métissage* of nationalities, social classes, and ethnicities (Italian, Spanish, Jewish) was a far from ideal conduit for transmitting Frenchness. By all accounts, between 1912 and 1925, the head of the Protectorate of Morocco, Resident-General Hubert Lyautey, negotiated the tensions between universalism and regionalism, assimilation and separatism, modernist urbanism and preservationism, French elitism and Moroccan political hierarchy with remarkable savvy. The history of these negotiations emerges *en filigrane* throughout the Tharauds' books on the capital cities of Fez, Rabat, and Marrakech (Casablanca, developed as a *ville nouvelle* by the French, was not chosen on account of its relative insignificance as a historic capital; by the same token, Tangiers was historically too European to count as an authentic Moroccan city).

The Tharaud brothers' Moroccan oeuvre affords examples of an exoticist spectacularity that refuses to see while exploiting visual and verbal pyrotechnics to the hilt. I have undertaken a portion of that reading in the preceding chapter, but here I want to examine the Tharauds' production of colonial sites in order to assess the impact of topographic stereotypes on French national consciousness, the politics of settler territorialism, and the legacy of what Frantz Fanon called the "pathology" of colonialism.

The Banality of Travel Writing

The Tharauds' writings represent an attempt to remobilize the genre of literary travelogue in an age of film and cheap photographic reproduction. Since travel writing was already thought to be freighted with touristic banalities by the mid–nineteenth century, it is not hard to imagine that by the early twentieth century it was even more in danger of teetering on the verge of obsolescence. Visual documentation of exotic places delivered what Anne Friedberg has dubbed "virtual tourism" more effectively than literature or painting.[6] The travelogue was reduced to the status of glorified caption to the album, of subtitle to the silent film, of commentary to the talkie. As if aware that its eventual destiny would have to be a Hollywood film, *The Sheltering Sky* (1949) opens with a series of establishment shots: Port opening his eyes, Port looking around the room and falling back on pillows, Port tracking "the apathetic designs stenciled in indifferent colors around the walls, the closed window of red and orange glass," followed by "Cut!" (a chapter break), and then pan to the Café d'Eckmühl-Noiseux, where "a few Arabs sat drinking mineral water; only their fezzes of varying shades of red distinguished them from the rest of the population of the port."[7]

How the Tharaud brothers instrumentalized the essential failure of their chosen genre of literary photographic realism (much like Bowles a generation later with his photogenic, existentialist colonialism) is part of the story of how colonial ideology—itself a distinct form of unmodern jingoism—retooled itself compensatorily so as to accommodate the demands of what Paul Rabinow has characterized as urban "techno-cosmopolitanism" or "middling (in the sense of technocratic) modernism."[8] Underlying the problem of the leaden predictability and banality of tourist writing is the equally problematic banality of critical writing about tourist writing. Though Marie Louise Pratt has credited the academy with trying to "decolonize knowledge" by discomposing many of the repetitions and derealizations of Euroimperialist banality, it is not clear whether such efforts have prevented the recolonization of knowledge within these same critical strictures.

> Redundancy, discontinuity, and unreality. These are some of the chief coordinates of the text of Euroimperialism, the stuff of its power to constitute the everyday with neutrality, spontaneity, numbing repetition (Livingstone, Livingstone . . .). In recent years that power has become open to question and subject to scrutiny in the academy as part of a large-scale effort to decolonize knowledge.[9]

Georges Van Den Abbeele, in *Travel as Metaphor,* has been even more self-conscious about the extent to which criticism becomes part of the problem under critique. Noting that banality has been endemic to travel writing since the Renaissance, he observes that

> the very banality or banalizing of travel to be found in literature both veils and unveils its importance for Western culture. . . . But if one grants the banality of the genre commonly associated with innovation, the question that needs to be raised is whether the commonplace quality of the metaphor of travel does not at some point constitute a limit to the freedom of critical thought.[10]

Van Den Abbeele discerns that there is a certain chic to "liking banality," which mirrors the good/bad taste of enjoying the much-maligned practice of tourism, but he also implies that travel literature banality is part of the more serious problem of the subject's inability to travel beyond a mental habitus. Like Dean MacCannell, whose groundbreaking work on the semiotics of tourism in the early seventies opened up the question of "who's zoomin who" in the touristic encounter, Van Den Abbeele explores the elisions between travel patterns and the closures or "terminal destinations" of consciousness.[11] While it may seem drastic to posit consciousness shrinking as the paradoxical result of horizon-expanding tourism, it does seem justified in the light of an outpouring of postcolonial criticism around travel literature that seems to repeat itself to death. As Meaghan Morris has argued with respect to certain tendencies in cultural studies, "In this kind of analysis of everyday life, it seems to be *criticism* that actively strives to achieve 'banality,' rather than investing it negatively in the object of study."[12] Morris raises the question of what it means when banality becomes an end unto itself within academic criticism, a kind of radical chic version of "*épater* the canon" and its high-art cultural values. Extending her critique, one could say that traveling theory, though essential to revisionist understandings of travel writing and the ongoing practice of tourism, also seems to have the banality-effect as part of its critical ambit. The solution to this problem is far from clear, but it is perhaps by investigating the formation of urban clichés that visual stereotypes of site and place can be somewhat released from the curse of psychic redundancy.

Colonial Goncourts

Under the charismatic sway of Péguy, Lucien Herr, Jean Jaurès, and Romain Rolland at the Ecole Normale Supérieure, Jérôme Tharaud embraced socialism, attended discussions lead by Jean Grave, anarchist author of *La Société mourante et l'anarchie,* and enlisted ideologically as a Dreyfusard. In 1896 he took a holiday trip to Algeria, experiencing, like André Gide, a Virgilian idyll complete with sexual initiation in the arms of an Arab servant boy. After failing the agrégation, Jérôme attempted to launch himself as a writer, contributing short fiction, already coauthored with his brother, to Péguy's *Cahiers.* After four years of peregrination working as a tutor in central Europe, Jérôme crossed enemy lines in the Dreyfus affair when he agreed in 1905 to become the personal secretary of Maurice Barrès. The Tharauds' allegiance to Barrès was handsomely rewarded when Barrès helped them obtain the Goncourt Prize in 1906 (only three years old at the time) for *Dingley: L'illustre écrivain,* a mediocre fictional biography of Kipling. Barrès had recently returned from a voyage to Greece and was writing his *Voyage de Sparte* (1906). An account of his grand tour through Egypt, Lebanon, Syria, and Iraq, *Une Enquête aux pays du Levant* was published on the eve of his death in 1923. Barrès's fascination with race, religion, and "oriental mystery" left its mark on the Tharauds' literary style and racial imaginary. Despite a budding anti-Semitism (full-blown after 1914) they returned again and again to scenes of Jewish life and custom in *Bar Cochebas notre honneur* (1907), *Quand Israel est roi* (1921), *L'An prochain à Jerusalem* (1924), *Causerie sur Israel* (1926), *La Rose de Sâron* (1927), *Petite Histoire des Juifs* (1927), *Quand Israel n'est plus roi* (1933), *Le Chemin d'Israel* (1948). Their involvement with North Africa began in 1911 when the Orientalist painter Etienne Dinet (himself a convert to Islam) persuaded them to take up the cause of the Muslim population in Algeria. Despite the fact that North Africa vied for their attention with other global attractions—Indochina, Spain, Syria, West Africa, France—they devoted a trilogy to the study of Islam, entitled *Les Mille et un jours de l'Islam* (respective volumes in 1935, 1938, 1941). Intoxicated by the passion of Islam, and worried at the prospect of its erosion through a colonial mission without faith, they returned from an initial visit to Algeria and wrote *La Fête arabe* (1912). This "epic of the failure of the marriage between Islam and French civilization" was denounced as scandalously pro-Arab and "defeatist" by much of its World War I French readership. According to their biographer Jean Bonnerot, while the book had "the allure of a plea for the ancient Arab race sacrificed to foreign mercantilism, it was above all, through a study of racial and religious conflict, a poem of the desert and an album of landscapes."[13] The phrase "album of landscapes" grounds my argument about the critical centrality of the photographic album in their exploration of literary equivalents to photography.

Though it was reproached for using a "fatigued palette" derivative of Fromentin, Chateaubriand, Flaubert, and Gautier, *La Fête arabe* launched the Tharauds' Moroccan venture, for it so impressed Lyautey that he arranged for them to be officially invited to his "court" in Rabat.[14] When they became familiar with Rabat, Lyautey sent them to Marrakech, which in 1918 was still being conquered by the French even as they were fighting a European war. The visit spawned a series of works devoted specifically to Moroccan cities: *Rabat ou les heures marocaines* (1918), *Marrakech ou les Seigneurs de l'Atlas* (1920), *Fez ou les bourgeois de l'Islam* (1930). It is these works that make the Tharauds important in a discussion of imperialism in the public sphere; they went beyond the Moroccan travelogue to write "Morocco" as a set of historic loci in the process of transformation by colonial urbanization. The Tharaud brothers bequeathed a vision of Morocco contoured along the familiar lines of a colonial epic, yet strangely afflicted by an anxiety induced by the defamiliarizing effect of modernity doubled in a non-European context. This anxiety of modern place was further enhanced by their phobia of image-production in the age of new media.

Powers of the Image

How to recover the game of the past? To relearn not only how to decipher or rework the images imposed on us, but to make others of a radically different order? Not only to make other films or better photographs, not simply to relocate the figurative in painting, but rather, to put images into circulation, in transit, in travesty; deforming them, making them red hot, freezing them, proliferating them? To banish the boredom of Writing, to relieve the signifier of its privileges, to dismiss the formalism of the nonimage, to thaw its contents, and to play, in science and pleasure, in, with, against the powers of the image.[15]

In a presentation on the photogenic paintings of the artist Fromanger, Michel Foucault evoked the image frenzy induced by the mass circulation of photographic images and apparatuses between 1860 and 1900. For Foucault, this was a wild, promiscuous period in the history of image-production: photographs fed on book illustrations, paintings cannibalized the photographic aura, pictorial photography preempted the painterly landscape of sentiment, artistic singularity lost out to cheap photographic copy, high-art puritanism eroded. The desire of the image was rampant, seemingly congruent with the cruising locomotion of people in quest of nonexclusive identity and anonymous sex: "Thus images ran around the world under fallacious identities. Nothing repulsed them more than staying captive, self-identical, in *a* painting, *a* photograph, *an* engraving, under the sign of *an* author."[16] According to Foucault, few regretted this wild migration of genres, styles, and media with the exception of a few "jealous painters, and of course Baudelaire." He reminds us that in his salon of 1857 Baudelaire had written: "If photography is permitted to supplement some of art's functions, they will forthwith be usurped and corrupted by it, thanks to photography's natural alliance with the mob. It must therefore revert to its proper duty, which is to serve as the handmaiden of science and the arts."[17]

For Walter Benjamin ("A Short History of Photography") Baudelaire's position was crucial to understanding the complex relationship between literature and the image:

> One thing, however, both Wiertz and Baudelaire failed to grasp: the lessons inherent in the authenticity of the photograph. These cannot be forever circumvented by a commentary whose clichés merely establish verbal associations in the viewer. The camera is getting smaller and smaller, ever readier to capture fleeting and secret moments whose images paralyse the associative mechanisms in the beholder. This is where the caption comes in, whereby photography turns all life's relationships into literature, and without which all constructivist photography must remain arrested in the approximate. Not for nothing have Atget's photographs been likened to those of the scene of a crime. But is not every square inch of our cities the scene of a crime? Every passerby a culprit? Is it not the task of the photographer—descendant of the augurs and haruspices—to reveal guilt and to point out the guilty in his pictures? "The illiteracy of the future," someone has said, "will be ignorance not of reading or writing, but of photography." But must not a photographer who cannot read his own pictures be no less accounted an illiterate? Will not the caption become the most important part of the photograph? Such are the questions in which the interval of ninety years that separate us from the age of the daguerreotype discharges its historical tension. It is in the illumination of these sparks that the first photographs emerge, beautiful and unapproachable, from the darkness of our grandfather's day.[18]

On one level Benjamin appears to be making the kind of "this kills that" argument that Victor Hugo made about architecture and the book: namely, that the book renders the teaching walls, or "speaking architecture" of Gothic cathedrals, obsolete. Benjamin alleges here that with the advent of small portable cameras, and an increased access to photographic reality, photography has made verbal commentary gratuitous. At another level, however, he appears blithely unconcerned with the literary artist's image-envy (or, as in the case of Baudelaire, photographic paranoia). He invalidates trite "verbal commentary," only to reinstate an essential literary supplement to the art of photography by conceiving a new role for the caption. The caption becomes a hermeneutic modem—deciphering visual rebuses, negotiating the aporia of empty spaces, projecting, through a kind of superreading, the crime that has deserted its scene and left no visual trace. In Benjamin's scheme, it seems, the caption-writer challenges the image-reading competence of the photographer (who henceforth succumbs to the "death of the author" syndrome) and heralds an age of photographic postliteracy in which not being able to read images vies with lexical illiteracy on the scale of disabled modern skills. By glorifying the caption and effectively recasting the caption-writer as Super-reader, Benjamin provides a "new and improved" mandate for the used-up, burned-out, cliché-hobbled travel-writer. Prompted to devise interpretive strategies of detection and suspense for the documentary image, the caption-writer emerges as the avatar of photographic postliteracy.

In their effort to fight the losing battle against photogenic seduction in visual media, the Tharaud brothers qualify as would-be Benjaminian caption-writers. One of their techniques was to admit the superiority of the enemy. In some instances they openly avowed their exhaustion in continually having to generate the kind of illustrative copy that Benjamin would associate with commentary. Midstream in a description of a sumptuous apartment in Fez, they break down:

> Nothing is more bizarre than the contrast between the luxury of the room where we were (ceilings of cedar, bees nests, incrustation of mother-of-pearl, plastered stucco, brilliant zelliges . . . *but I am quite tired of endlessly enumerating the elements of this rarefied décor whereby words make the rounds without showing anything*), nothing was more surprising than the contrast between the refinement of things and the vulgarity of the entertainment.[19]

As this passage indicates, there was something laborious about verbal characterizations of material reality once the photograph had stepped in to convey visual information with genuine accuracy and efficiency. This sentiment resonates in a number of statements throughout the Tharauds' early novel *Dingley: L'Ilustre écrivain*. In this anomalous work, the biographical theme of Kipling's commitment to empire is intertwined with the narrator's avowal of his inferiority complex vis-à-vis the documentary image. When Kipling/Dingley writes home to his wife from the front of the Boer War, he refers enviously to his friend Melton Prior's success as a war photographer: "Thanks to him, the last shopowner in London, Paris, and New York will have an exact idea of the carnage. Never before has one seen in such a gripping manner humans and beasts immobilized by fear or scattered to the four winds."[20] He then goes on explicitly to bemoan the limitations of the man of letters in the face of the new medium: "Unfortunate men of letters! Photographers offer them formidable competition. Even the most picturesque phrase has less expressive force than one image from a penny-book. Will we soon be reduced to writing psychological novels about French adultery or Slavic morals?"[21]

Kipling at the Movies

There is probably a chapter of colonial history that could be written on the French reception of Kipling. For the British, he was infuriatingly enduring, as George Orwell wryly observed: "During five literary generations every enlightened person has despised him, and at the end of that time nine tenths of those enlightened persons are forgotten and Kipling is in some sense still there."[22] The Tharauds' contemporary and fellow travel-writer André Chevrillon (1864–1957), a specialist of English literature (following his uncle Hyppolyte Taine), published a long article on Kipling's "poetry of imperialism" in *La Revue de Paris* that very likely inspired *Dingley*. Chévrillon spent considerable effort in his article exploring the relationship between national identity—specifically the grandiosity of Englishness—and the politics of empire. In a way that would suggest that India was to Kipling, what Morocco would become to the Tharauds, Chévrillon evoked Kipling's performative cities of empire:

> And above all, the Empire, the completed Empire, the Colonies, the Dominions, each marshalled in its turn, with its light, its landscapes, its peculiar, memory-laden scents. . . . In *The Song of the English,* when the dead have spoken, bearing witness to the laying down of their lives, when the sons have vowed to serve, all the great cities of the Empire stand forth and proclaim themselves: Bombay, noisy with the roar of a thousand factories, with the babel of all nations in her bazaars; Calcutta, born from the river mud—"death in her hands, but gold"; Madras, whom Clive had kissed on mouth and eyes, once crowned above all other queens, still dreaming of her ancient glory; Victoria, where West changes to East, the well-forged link in the tested chain of Empire, and all the others, rising in turn and making obeisance to the old mother, gray-haired England, who greets her children.[23]

Dingley is a paean to just this kind of mystical, oedipalized patriotism; its plot, such as it is, revolves around Dingley/Kipling's ability to rouse the English people with his war reporting, despite the impediment of photographic realism. But photography is not the only visual medium that the hero must overcome; cinema is also presented as a rival art.

For Sara Suleri, the "colonial dischronology of imperial time" in *Kim* contributed to Kipling's construction of a cinematic India, an India that would haunt the BBC screenplays of Paul Scott's *Raj Quartet* in the 1980s and resurface as "the cinematic twilight of the Raj" bathing Andrew Harvey's New Age spiritual travelogue, *The Hidden Voyage* (1993). In Suleri's interpretation of Kipling's narrative technique, in which she emphasizes "the cutting of discursive corners," we see an instance of cinema's early implication in the conventions of colonial fiction, what Suleri calls the "cinematic animation of the Indian sublime."[24] Extrapolating here, one could say that the Tharaud brothers' personifications of Moroccan city life qualify as a "cinematic animation of the Moroccan sublime." In describing the municipal walls of Rabat they adapted filmic techniques of tracking, panning, and close-ups to the text. They trail the reader-tourist into an impasse, where a group of women kneel on the steps of a tomb before a dazzling wall. As the viewer prepares to look inside, they explicitly invoke the sense of being in a film:

> Was I in this popular quarter, about to witness the showing, on this luminous screen, of one of those cinematographer's films that, even in the most distant outposts of the Maghreb, constitutes the delight of passersby? Ah! But it was something quite different! A rising curtain, certainly, but a curtain rising on invisibility and madness.[25]

In *Dingley,* a text published so early that it represents a kind of film history curiosity in its representation of the early camera—the Tharauds' film-envy manifests itself in a particularly interesting way: patriotic fervor is invoked to overcome the writer's inferiority complex in the face of the aesthetic power of the filmic image. The quest for imperial victory is thus curiously intertwined with the will to vanquish the cinematic medium.

The extended scene in which the cinematograph is associated with the national enemy portrays Dingley's guilt over his failure to obtain a stay of execution for a heroic Boer insurgent, Lucas de Toit, after the British victory. After the Boer hero meets his death, Dingley is overcome by malaise. In an effort to break his "state of burdensome ennui," he enters a music hall, only to encounter war footage showing Lucas de Toit's death by firing squad:

> When he walked in one Sunday toward four in the afternoon, the spectacle was reaching its end. On the cinema screen, stretched out in front of the stage like a giant trap made for capturing images, marched the portraits of the commanding generals in South Africa. . . . Each one stayed there, immobile, for several seconds, in the middle of the circle of light projected on

the screen, in the postures, smiling, disheveled, relaxed, or solemn, in which the photographer had surprised them. And the crowd greeted all of them, victors or vanquished, with the same favor, because they were all equally respected as representatives of the British forces.

Suddenly a tent appeared. Under the tent a shadow moved. Dingley recognized Lucas du Toit. The Boer held in his closed hand the short pipe that he, Dingley, had seen burning; the same mud was on his boots, and on his shoulders was a worsted overcoat that he had seen him sleep in often. Immediately, the young man, as he had seen him in the night by the light of a lantern in the dynamited farm, the man who had been his master, substituted himself in his spirit for this trembling phantom. Faster than the images that passed on the glass of the lantern, other images, other memories, pressed themselves into his memory, carrying him a thousand leagues from this feverish room. For several minutes he lived so intensely on the starry Veld that he was dazzled by the clap of the curtain where suddenly everything was effaced, like a man who wakes with a jump and sees the full moon through the window.[26]

Here the cinema is endowed with the demonic power of bringing back the dead to haunt the conscience of the living. The rest of the episode describes how Dingley attempts to evict the ghost of Lucas de Toit and thus break the spell of cinema's supernatural power to project history "live":

The same silence that reigns in the desert was in this room on pins and needles, where one heard no other noise than the hissing of the projector, and where no light shone except the rays of the magic lantern.

A fiery salvo burst into the aisles, the two men toppled face forward; the hall became a conflagration of light; frenetic hurrahs and jingoistic refrains filled the music hall, and the fracas of the orchestra, which furiously unleashed the famous ditty:

Forward, soldiers of the queen,
For Britain and for the Empire!

We will be the masters of the world!

The novelist became conscious of the fact that, through its enthusiasm, the crowd gave its manifest approbation to his own patriotic resentment of the insurgent Afrikaner. The day when, in the park of Dossieclipp, sacrificing a movement of personal sympathy to the interests of the Empire, he had closed his ears to a wife's pleas, he was in agreement with his nation. Not that he had ever really doubted these feelings for a minute in his tranquil certainty of possessing the most accurate instinct for the deepest feelings of the English spirit. What did misinformation or the discord of a day matter? He held the most decisive power over this public; that of guiding it over the paths that he himself had chosen. Finished the days of spiritual despondency, with the adventures of his London hooligan, he would ignite raw, strong, brutal emotions, of the kind that they had just experienced on seeing this sort of hero executed on the screen, but with a different kind of power! for the life of the cinema is precarious and impoverished, and for a long time to come, a well-constructed narrative, with all its old energy accumulated in words, will dominate the game of this technology![27]

To the reader's surprise, Dingley exorcises Lucas de Toit's ghost through recourse to a grotesque barbarism of the mob. Perhaps the only way to justify so distasteful a moral turn is to read Dingley's resort to bloody-minded jingoism as a last defense against new technologies of representation. Lucas de Toit is forgotten; it is the war film (and by implication, the superior power of cinematic image-production) that is really on trial. To rescue the colonial epic and the "old energy" of literary propaganda that has been drained away by film, Dingley will sacrifice compassion. Curiously, the future agenda of colonial literature is defined through an antimodern condemnation of new media. In this way, the Tharaud brothers may have unconsciously allegorized colonialism's uneasy relationship to technological modernity in its newer colonies in North Africa.

Civilization and Its Discontents

In its fraught negotiation of modernity-within-colonialism, the Tharauds' oeuvre offers illuminating parallels to Resident-General Lyautey's struggles to create "French Morocco."[28] Like Lyautey, they were loyal representatives of the French state, contributing to the colonial mission a grandiose vision of French destiny in the colonized territories. And yet, like Lyautey, they were not insensitive to the crimes of modern urbanism, specifically the demolition of Islamic art and culture that came in its wake.

Concern for preservationism may be found in their earliest work on Algeria, La Fête arabe. The novel revolves around the fortunes of a visionary colonial doctor who bemoans the "backwardness" of North African Islam, attributing Algeria's lack of intellectual renewal to the combined effects of Turkish invasions and the fanaticism of the mullahs. He dreams of an enlightened colonialism crowned by the creation of an "imaginary city" that would embody all the virtues of oriental modernism. Elected mayor of a small town on the edge of an oasis, he attempts to realize his dream, devising a theme park for tourism, a city mimetic of the Greco-Roman images encountered in children's literature. If, as he admits, the overt picturesqueness of the town approaches visual banality, so be it; commerce and a sense of elegance will redeem the packaging. Years later when the narrator visits the town his deceptions begin on de-embarking from the train; he encounters brute poverty unleavened by pastoral charm. Quarantined in dreadful encampments, the nomads have disappeared. The depopulated city has become "formless," a mosaic of *terrains vagues* punctuated by vestigial ruins of ransacked local architecture. Five or six Arab boys set on the narrator, competing for his cases. As they vanish down an asphalt strip he wonders whether he has stumbled into a destitute corner of Europe. Glimpsing the old village, with new construction next to it, he cannot figure out why detritus and disrepair have mushroomed everywhere. On the main square a Hôtel de Ville resembling a Swiss chalet reminds him of bleak hotels in Asnières. An abominable clock has been crudely jammed into the tower of a minaret. He then recognizes a man from his last visit, Benvenuto Mammo, who boasts that the town has become a true *ville française*. Epitomizing the failure of this colonial experiment is the loss of tourism:

> For years now the tourists had abandoned this dishonored vacation spot. Each traveler was a suspicious individual in the eyes of the local rabble. Bags would be searched on the pretext of checking for contraband. If tourists so much as leafed through a Baedaker, municipal agents would distrustfully move forward.[29]

As *La Fête arabe* draws to its close, we learn that the narrator's mistress, a native whom he had saved from an undesirable marriage, has betrayed him to two brothers who are planning his assassination. She herself is murdered by a perfidious French conscript. The narrator's sole consolation lies in his Eberhardtian existence as a nomad dedicated to living the desert sublime. The book ends with a "lament to Arab destitution."[30]

In choosing, in their subsequent career, not to write about Casablanca, a new town that became the site of what the sociologist Janet Abu-Lughod would diagnose as "urban apartheid," the Tharauds pursued their commitment to writing a timeless epic of North Africa.[31] After *La Fête arabe* they turned their attention to cities possessed of a distinguished patrimony, old cities such as Rabat or Marrakech that lent themselves to what might be called "protectorate" prose. According to Paul Rabinow, protectorate style, as distinct from conquerer's style, referred to neoclassicism joined with neo-Moorish vernacular motifs; it was "the style of the protector who had already vanquished."[32] Protectorate prose, as I am loosely transposing the term, combines European exoticism's habit of recording vernacular expressions or scenes from the everyday life of the other, with benign snapshots of colonial modernity. One sees this style clearly in evidence in the book on Marrakech, where they evoke, for example, the saccharine picturesqueness of "les petits métiers charmants" alongside the "magic" modernism of venerable French institutions: the post office, the bank, the café:

> Ah! that he might come immediately, the humble, genial painter of this old familiar Orient! All these artisanal vocations await him. . . . In among this childlike bustle, under the trellis of reeds whose light and shadow would be the delight of the photographer, a prodigiously lively crowd circulates. . . . Certain European establishments take their place in this delirium. The post office with its crown of banners, the hardware store, the bank, the ice store and the Café de France, the bicycle shop, the carriages for rent with their Spanish coaches, all these things from another world seem equally baroque as the magic circles, and the director of the bank and the newspaper man, wilder even than the sorcerer![33]

The way in which the Tharauds came to write monuments and urban scenes for a tourist public cohered well with French urban policy, as Paul Rabinow elaborates it:

> By strict restoration of the individual buildings and of the site itself, the French turned these "artistic vestiges of a shining civilization" into monuments. The groundwork was laid for tourism, the museumification of Moroccan culture and a new historical consciousness. A city-wide policy of architectural control over Moroccan construction was instituted, and was applied also to French construction. The goal was to avoid a pastiche of Algerian "moorish" styles, characterized as "world's fair décor," as well as the individualism of suburban kitsch.[34]

The Tharauds created a normalizing language of power by using nostalgia for old Morocco to temper the effects of Europeanization. Wavering between the use of local color (the recording of folkloric customs and sights) and the use of a classical, paternalist rhetoric of place redolent of Virgil and Volney, their descriptions registered the impact of modernity while "protecting" and preserving Morocco as a living museum. In crafting this kind of literary tourism, in commercializing site-representation for mass consumption, they helped re-inter the apparition of cultural vandalism that their own early work had served unerringly to record.

Normalization. Compensation? To answer this question is to ponder the extent to which the French colonial project—and its generic literary expression, the colonial epic—formed part of a psychic paradigm in which a post-*défaite* (1870) national consciousness of military inferiority spawned the compensatory need for imperial self-aggrandizement. National anxiety, seemingly heightened by confrontation with technological moder-

nity, resulted in the imperative to control the diasporic flux of images produced by new media. The optically driven prose of the Tharaud brothers
constitutes what is perhaps the sole legacy of importance bequeathed by
two presently obscure hack writers; loyal foot soldiers in the production of
colonial vision, whose patriotism was duly rewarded by the Académie
Française.

12 POSTCOLONIAL CYBERPUNK

DIRTY NATIONALISM

IN THE ERA OF

TERMINAL IDENTITIES

In thinking about how to define the emergent theory and praxis of post-colonial cyberpunk—a term I am coining to refer not only to futurist writing from formerly colonized nations, but also to experimental minority fiction and its proliferating cognates, posturban grunge, apocalypse narrative, electronic transnationalism, extreme criticism—I will begin by taking up the issue of "time-lag" famously developed by Homi Bhabha in *The Location of Culture,* a concept that may well have had something to do with postcolonial theory's resistance to injecting itself with contemporaneity. Consistently in Bhabha's densely theorized arguments, the temporality of modernity becomes a way to think postcoloniality.[1] But to what extent is postcoloniality stubbornly antimodern, reverting to a melancholic *mauvaise conscience* conditioned by the age of empire? How does one keep postcolonial theory from becoming imbricated in the kind of conservative postmodern nostalgia (evinced in high-gloss films topically and atmospherically evoking the age of imperialism) promoted by the culture industry and (to some degree) the academic marketplace as well?

When Bhabha critiques Benedict Anderson's representation of colonial racism as "outside of history," that is, "part of an archaic acting out, a dream-text of a form of historical retroversion that 'appeared to confirm on a global, modern stage antique conceptions of power and privilege,'" he nevertheless retains the notion of retroversion as symptomatic of the kind of "time-lagged" signification that he sees being written out in postcolonial modernity.[2] "Time-lag," Bhabha insists italically several pages on, "keeps alive the making of the past."[3] Can one ever really keep retroversion from becoming retrograde? Insofar as it tended to focus on the heyday of empire, postcolonial theory, particularly in its early iterations, often seemed frozen in a twilight temporality coinciding with a time when subjects were "real" emancipatory subjects, imbued with a sense of indigenous identity. The Martinican writer Raphaël Confiant confessed that for a long time the prospect of writing a science fiction novel seemed anathema to him; tantamount to relinquishing legitimacy as an Antillean writer. When commissioned to write *Bassin des ouragans* (1994), "a novel of today," he struggled against his own ingrained aversion to linguistic presentism:

> I had a shock this year. The Italian editors of the Thousand and One Nights series—which launched the ten-franc book—decided to publish modern authors. They proposed that I be the first. The text had to speak about today . . . It was the first time in my life that I wrote the word *television* in a text! This word, exactly like *computer* or *AIDS*, was absolutely foreign to my imagination. I was born in the fifties, my universe inhabited by sugar plantations, smoking distilleries, Hindu ceremonies . . . I'm infused with the Martinican society of that time. It is extremely difficult for me to write about the contemporary period.[4]

Postcolonial literariness and postcolonial subjectivity, despite their flirtation with poststructuralist paradigms, often project a redemptive longing for transparent meaning, oral and narrative tradition, wholeness, homeliness, civil equality, collective agency, and focused political anger. While there is clearly much to commend in this adherence to traditions of emancipatory humanism, too often it is used to grant criticism permission to ignore the strange intellectual flora and fauna of cyberculture, specifically the screen subjects characterized by Scott Bukatman as "terminal identities." As a result, and at least until quite recently, postcolonial theory and aesthetic practice often seemed time-lagged in the sense of quaintly periodized.

Cybercrit appears to capture the ontologically nihilist bent of poststructuralist theory's aftermath, mobilizing ghostly, derealized selves within a dirty realist, sleaze, or pulp tradition (a mixture of dystopian fiction, comics, graffiti, porn, fanzines, slash and snuff movies, spy movies, film noir, New Wave boredom, hacker white-collar crime, electronic conversation, channel surfing, flight simulation, military paranoia, cowboy culture, posturban pastoral, surveillance cameras, urban guerilla warfare, immaterial capital, eco-apocalypse, survivalism, cyborg erotics, technical imaging, "smart" technology, virtual subjects, etc.). Does postcolonial cultural production sit in a preterit time zone, worlds apart from this techie futurism? Or is it in fact well equipped to theorize the new forms of colonialism that cyber has helped spawn—multinational power brokering, world debt finance, transnational speculation, and so on?

This last question is obviously to some extent purely rhetorical since, as many have noted, cyberpunk is rife with postcolonial scenarios that highlight the anachronicity of the future. Philip K. Dick's inaugural cyberpunk novel *Do Androids Dream of Electric Sheep* (1968) is suffused with dated aura: "In a giant, empty, decaying building which had once housed thousands, a single TV set hawked its wares to an uninhabited room."[5] Intergalactic colonialism prevails in *Do Androids;* in the postnuclear era most of Earth's population has migrated to Mars, which markets itself as a comprador haven, much like the French and British colonies in Africa used to do, promising enrichment, social caché, and a retinue of servants.

A junk-bond genre, cyberpunk refashions and retrofits traditional sci-fi narrative conventions to accommodate the economic and political fallout of corporate colonialism. In Cynthia Kadohata's marginally cyber, postapocalyse Los Angeles novel, *In the Heart of the Valley of Love* (1992), corporate colonialism and its backlash, acute Japan-bashing, are ironically historicized:

> A cloud landed one day on top of the tallest building in Los Angeles, the Natsumi Hotel. The hotel, built by one of the wealthiest women in Japan and named for her daughter, was the source of considerable controversy when it opened two decades earlier. *Natsumi* means "summer." Twenty years ago, hatred of Japan was so fierce that the City Council actually debated whether they could force the hotel to be called the Summer Hotel. But reason prevailed and it was called Natsumi.[6]

In the "twenty years later" of 2052, national chauvinism has waned to the point of indifference; citizens just accept the postcolonial condition of economic imperialism.

With its historically white, male, First World bias, cyberpunk recodes and reinforces economic imperialism through epistemes that rely on the capitally enriched subject-positions of electronic information access. "A standing joke about cyberspace," Scott Bukatman reminds us, "is that, in an era of ATMs and global banking, *cyberspace is where your money is.*"[7] Cyberpunk fiction never strays too far from the money, charting the narrative paths of individual hackers and corporate conglomerates according to the vagaries of a blind, egoic, overblown drive to materialism.

As a form of postmodernism deeply imbricated (as Fredric Jameson noted at the outset) in "the cultural logic of late capitalism," cyberpunk emerges as an obvious target of derision for postcolonial political and aesthetic praxes. Internet identities are inethical subjects insofar as they allow for identities without accountability: you can "be" who you want to be, cruise whom you want to cruise, assume any cultural or gender alibi you may desire, "pass" as a leader of resistance through counterfeit samizdat. But while there is clearly a lot to question, demystify, and dehype in cyberpunk, I would argue that its ironic screening of the subject can in some instances lead to a productive critical unmasking of complacent selfhood, capitalist fantasy, multicultural masquerade, racial phobia, or civic dysfunction within the so-called public sphere of the postnation.

Synthetic, prosthetic, and medically futurist, cyber identities—as Donna Haraway projected in her famous "Manifesto for Cyborgs"—are capable of combining transsexuality with transraciality in their imaging of a composite, queer, "multiculti" body, made out of grafts and surgical implants of ethnic or racial features. In this sense, they are the quintessential "hybrid" postcolonial subjects, exposing phobias and fantasies around sexual deviance, androgyny, miscegenation, and racelessness.

The sexuality of cyborgs was among the first themes to attract notice in cybercriticism. Haraway wrote: "The cyborg is a creature in a post-gender world; it has no truck with bisexuality, pre-Oedipal symbiosis, unalienated labor, or other seductions to organic wholeness." Haraway also celebrated the aesthetics of cyborg sex, which "restores some of the lovely replicative baroque of ferns and invertebrates (such nice organic prophylactics against heterosexism)."[8] At about the same time that Haraway was fantasizing a cyberutopia of sexuality "uncoupled from organic reproduction," sex and character were sublated in cyberpunk film and fiction. Describing the canonical cyborg film *Blade Runner* (1982), Janet Bergstrom noted that the "delirium" induced by the film's atmospherics could be traced to the match between visual disorientation and contrived characterlessness. Set and narrative trump each other as motors of plot, while androids and replicants obfuscate reassuring signposts of sexual difference, lamely replaying what is left of them in scrambled combinations.[9]

Transgendered cybersexuality, while it is not the principal focus of discussion here, "implants" itself within postcolonial conceptions of nation and race as part of the politically charged relationship between diaspora and transnationalism, pigmentation and desire, and, most controversially, hybridity and miscegenation. In William Gibson's classic *Neuromancer* (1983) the barman and his clients have transnational bodies. Ratz is pieced together with the hardware and detritus of cold-war contraband. Lonny Zone's whore has an uncertainly raced tan, and an African mercenary inverts the terms of colonial mimicry, his crisp naval uniform genuflecting to the tribal markings on his face:

> Ratz was tending bar, his prosthetic arm jerking monotonously as he filled a
> tray of glasses with draft Kirin. He saw Case and smiled, his teeth a webwork
> of East European steel and brown decay. Case found a place at the bar, be-
> tween the unlikely tan on one of Lonny Zone's whores and the crisp naval
> uniform of a tall African whose cheekbones were ridged with precise rows of
> tribal scars.[10]

The cyborg's transracial, transnational body conjures forth an identity no
longer split between First and Third World, between metropole and native
home, but rather, a body so fragmented that its morphology is a diaspora.

The same diasporic morphology can be discerned in cybercities, con-
figured according to capital flows, corporate transfers, black-market sub-
cultures, human warehousing, and identity by-products:

> Friday night on Ninsei.
> He passed yakitori stands and massage parlors, a franchised coffee shop
> called Beautiful Girl, the electronic thunder of an arcade. He stepped out
> of the way to let a dark-suited sarariman by, spotting the Mitsubishi-
> Genentech logo tattooed across the back of the man's right hand.
> Was it authentic? If that's for real, he thought, he's in for trouble. If it
> wasn't, it served him right. M-G employees above a certain level were im-
> planted with advanced microprocessors that monitored mutagen levels in
> the bloodstream. Gear like that would get you rolled in Night City, rolled
> straight into a black clinic.
> The sarariman had been Japanese, but the Ninsei crowd was a gaijin
> crowd. Groups of sailors up from the port, tense solitary tourists hunting
> pleasures no guidebook listed, Sprawl heavies showing off grafts and im-
> plants, and a dozen distinct species of hustler, all swarming the street in an
> intricate dance of desire and commerce.
> There were countless theories explaining why Chiba City tolerated the
> Ninsei enclave, but Case tended toward the idea that the Yakuza might be
> preserving the place as a kind of historical park, a reminder of humble ori-
> gins.[11]

As temporal space, Ninsei is both anachronistic (a historical park) and
prophetic (the dissolution of personhood). As physical space, it exemplifies a kind of postnational, hologrammatic, ash-can cosmopolitanism reminiscent of American Ashcan school paintings of working-class life at the
turn of the century, or dirty realist Chicago prole novels by Nelson Algren
in the forties.

Cyberculture has the unnerving habit of transcoding technology into
another race that breeds with other human races and ethnicities. In the
Hong Kong remakes of the French film *La Femme Nikita, Black Cat I* and *II*,
the protagonist is a transracial cyborg, that is, an Asian-American woman
who has been surgically implanted with a "search and destroy" microchip.
Working for the CIA ("she is our instrument, our best weapon"), Black Cat

has been programmed to eliminate Russian hit men (ordered to assassinate Boris Yeltsin), who themselves have been enhanced and bulked up with radioactive material. Sporting a black tube dress and spike heels, Black Cat performs amazing kung fu moves at high voltage, while repeatedly rescuing her emasculated fellow agent Robin, the only other Chinese-American character in the film. There is no romance between them in the movie; bionic, bicultural, transracially and technologically crossbred, Black Cat emerges as the resolutely single avatar of a postgendered world order.[12] Her eros is sublimated into the hard-edged miracle of her athletic high style. Metastacizing software, she is the streamlined heiress to the early (1933) futurist, protocyborgian images of fashion-conscious femmes fatales decked out in

> illusionistic, sarcastic, sonorous, loud, deadly, and explosive attire: gowns that trigger surprises and transformations, outfitted with springs, stingers, camera lenses, electric currents, reflectors, perfumed sprays, fireworks, chemical preparations, and thousands of gadgets fit to play the most wicked tricks and disconcerting pranks on maladroit suitors and sentimental fools.[13]

In *Black Cat,* fashion, as weapon, bodily extension, and seductive foil, acts as a kind of genetic interface mediating race, technology, and desire. And of course, as Mark Dery reminds us, "Hollywood morphing and borging" have "real-world analogs":

> Genetic engineering, wherein DNA sequences from one organism are introduced into another to produce "transgenic" plants and animals, is a sort of morphing. The virus-resistant mouse created at Ohio University in 1992 by injecting a human gene that promotes interferon production into a fertilized mouse embryo is a morph. So is the genetically altered pig created at the Princeton-based DNX Corporation by injecting clones of human DNA into fertilized swine eggs, yielding a pig that produced human hemoglobin. . . . But morphs aren't confined to high-tech labs; they're all around us. . . . Borgs, likewise, are not confined to sci-fi films. In cyberculture, the body is a permeable membrane, its integrity violated and its sanctity challenged by titanium alloy knee joints, myoelectric arms, synthetic bones and blood vessels, breast and penile prostheses, cochlear implants and artificial hips. The Utah arm, the Boston elbow, and the Otto Bock hand—lifelike prostheses activated by electrical current in the form of electromyographic (EMG) signals coming from the amputee's stump and surrounding muscles—have attained mythic status in modern medicine.[14]

Though *Black Cat* may well belong to an entrenched class of true-life transgenic "morphs and borgs," a theoretical language of postcolonial cyberpunk is very much still in the making. Perhaps one of the obstacles to creating it lies in the fact that this language joins up all too easily with its predecessor, a nineteenth-century colonial lexicon of race, which, as Robert Young has noted, embeds the "fascination with people having sex— interminable, adulterating, aleatory, illicit, inter-racial sex,"

> half-blood, half-caste, half-breed, cross-breed, amalgamate, intermix, mis- cegenate; alvino, cabre, cafuso, castizo, cholo, chino, cob, creole, dustee, fustee, griffe, mamaluco, marabout, mestee, mestindo, mestizo, mestize, metifo, misterado, mongrel, morisco, mule, mulat, mulatto, mulatta, mu- latress, mustafina, mustee, mestezoes, ochavon, octavon, octoroon, puchuelo, quadroon, quarteron, quatralvi, quinteron, saltatro, terceron, zambaigo, zambo, zambo prieto.[15]

Young's ABC of "Malthusian" racial declensions seems disturbingly proximate to the postcolonial counterlexicon of cultural and racial admix- tures, including Edouard Glissant's *antillanité*, referring to pan-Caribbean "transversality," and Antonio Benitez-Rojo's equally archipellagan con- cept of cultural and religious "supersyncretism" (a counterweight to the englobing *americanismo*). While this postcolonial discourse of hybridity foregrounds historical migration and diaspora, fractal consciousness, and differential cultural fusion, it is nonetheless hard to keep clean from the legacy it represses, namely, phobic projections of miscegenation. Cyber- punk desublimates hybridity's colonial past, its slave narratives and racial hallucinations.

In Lance Olsen's up-to-the-minute *Tonguing the Zeitgeist* (1994), the colonial drama plays itself out in the way in which certain genes colonize identity from within:

> Uriah was one-eighth Japanese. Mostly he was Irish. There was also a dash of Native American in there, some French, some Spanish, more Iranian than he'd care to admit, Brazilian, Danish, Hungarian, even a pinch Polish too, which was great, the Poles being a romantic breed, gallantly if fruitlessly charging the Russian tanks on horseback during the Second World War. The Japanese genes were bullies, though, when it came to Uriah's appearance and cultural identity. His dark brown eyes were Japanese eyes, his light brown skin Japanese skin, his silky black hair kept knotted atop his head, Japanese hair.[16]

What is curious about this passage is that it conjugates racial subjectivity *without* reference to the cyborg. Why, one wonders, does the author refrain here from fabricating a transracial cyborg especially given that he begins the novel evoking a rock star diva named Quyntifonic who releases images of ghoulish creatures from her holographic head and who is worshiped by fans whose outré, tasteless fashion statements boast cosmetic mastec- tomies, AIDS maquillage and glued-on electrodes? Possibly, the idea is to show the extent to which cyborgian hybridity parodies diversity, merely recycling the way many North Americans perform their personal ethnic breakdowns ("I'm part Irish, part Jewish, part German, part black . . . "). Deconstructing the masquerade of high-punk multiculturalism, *Tonguing the Zeitgeist* also exposes that staple of sci-fi racism, anti-Asian white panic. The familiar melting-pot trope shears away at the apparition of the dreaded "Japanese gene."

Cyberpunk's obsession with racial phobias often spin into fantasies of racelessness. In William Gibson's chapter "Colored People" (referring to the name of a tattoo and body piercing parlor in his recent novel *Virtual Light,* 1993), the reader is exposed to the representation of a man with missing limbs (a cyborg forsaken by his prosthesis?), whose bodily surface has been subjected to what one might call "race-losigkeit," a condition of racelessness or race-loss:

> The first thing Rydell saw when he got out of the Patriot in the alley off Haight Street was a one-armed, one legged man on a skateboard. This man lay on his stomach, on the board, and propelled himself along with a curious hitching motion that reminded Rydell of the limbs of a gigged frog. . . . His face, as if by some weird osmosis, was the color of dirty concrete, and Rydell couldn't have said what race he was. His hair, if he had any, was covered by a black knit cap, and the rest of him was sheathed in a black, one-piece garment apparently stitched from sections of heavy-duty rubber innertube.[17]

In the relatively rare examples of cyber-sci-fi novels written by authors of color, the motif of racelessness enhances the unfocusing of identity. In Octavia Butler's *Parable of the Sower* (1993), a millennial L.A. novel set in 2024, the reader infers that the novel's protagonists are inhabitants of an African-American and Latino community not far from the fortressed city walls, yet there is no explicit mention of race. Pigmentation has been obscured by the mandatory uniform of filthy clothing that citizens must don if they want to avoid being beaten up, since anyone who is clean is assumed to have the enormous wealth required to circumvent drastic water shortages. It is not until we learn that a predominantly Caucasian town nearby has been selected for management by a corporate triumvirate of Japanese, German, and WASP interests (known as KSF, or Kagimoto, Stamm, Frampton and Company), that the African-American identity of the first-person narrator is confirmed. A survivalist, and leader of the besieged township of Robledo, Lauren Olamina has the pigment-signifier *melanin* encoded in her name, but the color-code has been lost. Her identity as a black woman has yielded to her identity as a weepy cyborg, whose "scrambled neurotransmitters" have led to broken emotional immune systems, specifically a condition of hyperempathy causing her to bleed uncontrollably at the spectacle of suffering.[18]

If here, racelessness inheres in a narrative autism on the subject of identity, so it does in Cynthia Kadohata's *In the Heart of the Valley of Love*. Francie and her Aunt Annie, the two female protagonists, are billed as Japanese-American on the book jacket, but this is the most Asian-less Asian-ness imaginable in what is marketed as an Asian-American novel. Explicit allusions to racial characteristics have been intentionally sidelined, displaced to leitmotifs such as skin diseases or tattooing. Auntie Annie, like her acquaintance the black-market water-supplier Max, suffers from an ailment referred to as "derma-what-do-you-call-it."[19] Heading to Tattoo City with her boyfriend Mark, Kadohata's main character renders the tattoo the site of displaced racial anxiety: "I felt very nervous to be getting a tattoo," she says. "I picked up a book on Egyptian art and riffled through it, barely seeing. I looked at my wrist, at the pictures, at my wrist. I'd never realized how thin my wrist was. 'Those Egyptians sure had a way with coffins!' I said, in a tweety voice" (p. 126). The faintly perceptible Orientalism of the Egyptian design that Francie will transfer to her wrist acts as a distant reminder of the racial identification that Francie has forgotten, misrecognized, or given up. The fact that the tattoo is only a decorative bracelet allows racial identity to remain profoundly disavowed, relegated to the psychic topsoil of "only skin-deep": "Of course it hurts!" the tattoo artist Carl tells her. "But it's not ego-wrenching pain, darling, it's way down there on your wrist, and it doesn't have anything to do with your soul at all" (p. 127).

The racelessness of Kadohata's narrative exerts the pressure of its absence on the contours of her futuristic urban tableau, merging with the "low visibility" of barely perceptible shapes and forms produced by heavy smog.

> The sky was black between the clouds. Giant forms we could barely make out lurked on both sides of the highway at one point. Along many freeways in Southern California, huge steel and paper-mâché animals, people, cartoon characters, or *things* had been built to entice people to stop at restaurants, gift shops, or gas stations. One place had built dinosaurs; another, further north, had a thermometer sixty feet tall. Both those had been built before the turn of the century. Visibility was so low it wasn't safe to drive, so we pulled over and parked next to a monstrous hand with a teacup on the tip of one of its fingers.[20]

Kadohata's "things"—"giant forms" of indeterminate animal, human, or technological species-being—remain racially opaque. As the smoke-and-mirrors figure of a repressed racial unconscious, the theme of colorless race recalls a moment of the famous Lacanian footnote in Frantz Fanon's *Black Skin, White Masks*. Most "critical Fanonists," to borrow Henry Louis Gates's term, focus on the first part of the note where Fanon charts the colonial psychodynamics of racial identification in relation to the mirror stage:

> When one has grasped the mechanism described by Lacan, one can have no further doubt that the real Other for the white man is and will continue to be the black man. And conversely. Only for the white man The Other is perceived on the level of the body image, absolutely as the not-self—that is, the unidentifiable, the unassimilable.[21]

Gates, Homi Bhabha, Kobena Mercer, Rey Chow, and Diana Fuss, among others, have used this passage to understand the place of racial pathology in the formation of the subject; here the "real," or *objet a* flashes into view as a negational blackness, race-ing the traumatic fissuring of the (white) subject.[22] While it is fairly obvious why this passage is important, further along there is an equally provocative articulation of the experience of racelessness in the black Imaginary that has been relatively understudied. Fanon begins with a consideration of "Negro deliriums," clinically called heutophany or heutoscopy, "the liberation of the body image." He then goes on to interpret this "loss of body image" as characteristic of the Antillean child. "When Antilleans tell me they have experienced it (the mirror hallucination), I always ask the same question: 'What color were you?' Invariably they reply: 'I had no color.'"[23] This construction of the whited-out mirror stage may be read on one level as a record of the Antillean's bad faith, his disremembrance of negritude, his psychic cathexis with the white oppressor. On another level, however, it looks like a futurist projection of subjectivity beyond race, an out-of-body experience in which the subject watches himself "fade" or slip away; the flesh petrifying into marmoreal, technologically alien body parts; his identity discomposing into ethnic fragments that fail to accrue to a racially marked self. An amnesiac, race-divested subject, whose mirror stage is plagued by a dysfunctional Symbolic order, Fanon's Antillean, like the hero of cyberpunk, watches dispassionately as selfhood is sucked out of its body and carried off in a maelstrom of indeterminate matter. This is precisely the kind of existentially and historically escapist fantasy in which cyberpunk as a form of representation excels.

A colonizing genre with a future anterior temporality that extends the time line of the time-lag, cyberpunk encompasses the disinheritance of subject formation, the wastage of city-states, the decadence of empire, the recrudescence of slavery, and the psychoses of eugenics.[24] But in rendering the subject extraraced (Gibson's transnational cyborgs) or "race-los"

(Kadohata's decolorized Asian-American characters), cyber also effects discomfiting slippages among transracial utopias, the racist history of miscegenation, and the politically irksome fantasy of no-race. Of course, it was to be expected that cyber would unmask categories of racial identity, since it disturbs and invalidates identity all the time with its visualizations of posthuman beings, ontological alibis, stealth egos, hacker souls, prosthetic locomotion, armed psychic defense, screened communication and delirious ethics. But while cyberidentity may remain profoundly antipathetic to the emancipatory "identity politics," flush with agency, that is the subject of much contemporary postcolonial theory, I predict that postcolonial theory and aesthetic practice will "cyberize" themselves quite soon (if they haven't already), pushing the envelope of the politics of global subjectivity as they place the diaspora on-line.[25]

13 NOMADOLOGIES OF TOMORROW

THE DELEUZEAN

WORLDSCAPE

The general framework of this concluding chapter concerns globalization's impact on the self-imaging of nation-states. It is becoming increasingly apparent that transnational interstate economies are "colonizing" individual nation-states, rendering them quasi-obsolete even as they preserve the integrity of their differences for marketing purposes. In the sphere of cultural production, this kind of multinational nationalism or consumerist national particularism proves compatible with new iterations of corporate millennialism (to wit, Britain's projected billion-dollar Millennial Dome). The millennium, as many have already noted, is one of the greatest marketing ploys in history.

As millennial hype cuts across national boundaries, further weakening discrete, recognizable forms of national identity, transworld aesthetics and cosmic projections of an alien nation become more and more visible. This upmarket, New Age flirtation with alien-ness provides the backdrop to projects that overtly engage with a space-age formal vocabulary: magmas and blobs, astral abstractions, Afrofuturism.

For race aliens, that is, members of minority populations historically excluded from public forms of national self-representation, there are strategic reasons for appropriating and remotivating the visual vocabulary of elsewhere, up, out, and beyond. For a number of years now, black performers and artists have been experimenting with reclaiming the alien: Afrofuturism, from Sun Ra and George Clinton, to the recent videos of John Akomfrah and the Black Audio Collective, has launched its own distinctive space race, replete with miracles of teleportation, data thievery, and digitized race memories.

Afrofuturism taps into the zeitgeist's anxieties over the precariousness of the here and now, or even more specifically, the uncertainty of what it means to be human under conditions of economic oppression and environmental or genetic mutation. It is surely no coincidence that a spate of recent novels and art projects have taken on the task of picturing the face of the posthuman, exploring the provisionality of humanoidness by cloning primates who are all-too-human. Turner Prize runner-up Christine Borland rescued and recast mutant heads—some of them clearly morphs of monkey and human—from a clinical museum in Germany where they were no doubt used as teaching aids in courses on eugenics and the master race. A nouveau-Darwinian ape-man stars in Peter Høeg's book *The Woman and the Ape,* where the narrative crescendos in scenes of interspecial lovemaking.

> She waited for disgust to flood through her from top to toe. But it never came. Something else came instead—more desire, a need, pressing, beyond all question of pride and submission.
>
> "Please," she said.
>
> Erasmus entered her with a kind of sensitive ruthlessness, along the golden mean between pain and sensual delight, and as he did so, she bit his earlobe, gently but deeply, until on the tip of her tongue she felt the first metallic hint of blood and her nostrils were filled with a scent, a savanna of scent, a continent of scent, of animal, man, stars, glowing embers, air mattresses and burnt rubber.[1]

The sexual ecstasy of phylogenic crossover, rendered experientially as epiphanic flight into a new "empire of the senses" (a "continent of scent"), occurs in a mock Garden of Eden, a forest in central London originally conceived as a "horticultural machine, . . . a *drug* of a garden, a landscaped hallucinogen."[2]

The chemically induced defamiliarization of the European metropolis also proves crucial to the dystopic portrayal of London in Will Self's novel *Great Apes:*

> Past the Guinness Trust block of flats at the road's mouth there's a procession of rancid eateries and fast-food joints. Fish follows chicken, chicken follows fish—each factory-fed on the other. Global geography is discombobulated here so that the Far East precedes the Near East and Indo-China and India trade places, again and again and again.[3]

Where Høeg concentrates on mapping a secret zone of the posthuman fantastic within city walls, Will Self uses a reconfigured continentalism drawn by the patchwork residency of London's immigrant communities as the setting for unhatching a mutant race. In Self's London, the ontological state known as "chimpunity" is explored in a virtual world inhabited by primates with career ambitions, everyday habits and routines "just like us," only with fewer sexual hang-ups, since they don't object to sex with family members or mating in front of the children before breakfast. Speaking in English inflected by a "pant-hoot," a "HooH'Graa," an "euch-euch," and a "huu?" Self's alpha males research the farthest reaches of the human, investigating reproductive transactions between animate and inanimate matter. In a work titled *A Chimp Who Mated an Armchair* cited by the chimp-doctor Zack Busner (who specializes in studying apes suffering from the delusion that they are human), the reader is invited to conjure up the strange progeny of primates and domestic architecture: chimp-chairs or buildings with simian morphologies, bodies cut into primatological sections or plans, blurred boundaries between inert object and live form. Though the land of apes is far afield from the sci-fi spacescapes of Afrofuturism, both function as nomadological territories spawning a future imperfect race of alien nomads.

In an essay entitled "Off-White," Arjun Appadurai surmised: "The violence that surrounds identity politics around the world today reflects the anxieties attendant on the search for nonterritorial principles of solidarity."[4] Appadurai's vision of a postnational condition comprised of deterritorialized subjects—refugees and migrants who create transnational communities regardless of national boundaries or official language, diasporic enclaves refusing to be assimilated by their adoptive countries, ethnonationalist mobilizations of capital and information—seems to echo, however indirectly, Gilles Deleuze and Félix Guattari's call for "philosophical reterritorialization," a refaulting of global outlines estranging the universality of national democracies and enabling citizens to experience "becoming-other."[5]

Deleuze and Guattari's presciently postnational vision of deterritorialized subjects, associated in *Anti-Oedipus: Capitalism and Schizophrenia* with the "body without organs," the "desiring machine," "genic decoding," vectors of partial objects and flows, and gerundive ontologies ("becoming-another-sex," "becoming-god," "becoming-a-race,"), conjugates otherness with futurology.[6] What results is a post-nation-state, populated by citizens whose tribal loyalties and patriotic memories are subjectively intact but continentally adrift.

While Jean-François Lyotard has offered a vivid articulation of the perspectivally upended "scapeland" or burrow in his essays on the inhuman—the mole's myopic tunnel as seen by a bird, "the earth seen from the moon for an extraterrestrial"—Deleuze and Guattari were unique in inscribing the terms of a shifting worldscape on projections of a radically denational-ized subject.[7] With its millennial and sixties-style revolutionary inflec-tions, their writing foretold a postnational condition that lined up eerily with sci-fi visions of extraterrestrial conquest:

> In imperial states deterritorialization takes place through transcendence: it tends to develop vertically from on high, according to a celestial compo-nent of the earth. The territory has become desert earth, but a celestial Stranger arrives to reestablish the territory or reterritorialize the earth.[8]

Though this passage, in context, functions somewhat allegorically as part of their critique of the *imperial spatium* in ancient Greece, it alerts us, nonetheless, to the way in which Deleuze and Guattari used the "celestial Stranger," as a means of expanding parameters for thinking the world. The radical globalism of their geophilosophy—crucial to why one might be tempted to envision the next millennium as turning on a "Deleuzian cen-tury," invites us to look for signs of postnational futures in the territorially unbounded genres of cyberfiction.

In cyber-fi, the monuments, street plans, and characters that prover-bially function as psychic ledgers of urban identity (triggering emotion at the mere utterance of place-names—Moscow, Mexico City, Paris, Cape Town, Berlin, Los Angeles, Jerusalem, Cairo, New York, Beijing), are sup-planted by shapeless cartographies. The traffic embankment, sealed off from view by metal splash guards, strewn with wreckage, and harboring a crash victim for whom nobody whizzing on the motorway will stop, in J. G. Ballard's *Concrete Island,* typifies the genre's technologically wasted, con-tourless no-man's-land.

Lunar and lunatic, stepped and iced over, deforested and scavenged, warped and melted down, this *smooth space,* as defined by Deleuze and Guattari, delivers catatonia and rush, and is identified with the "'moved body' going from one point to another in a striated space."[9] Smooth space aligns the aerodynamic whoosh of the war machine with the locomotion of displaced nomads who have learned to stay put in flight. The deterrito-rialized terrain of nomadology, by now a consecrated fetish of architec-tural fantasy, is plotted rhizomatically in Deleuze and Guattari's *Nomadology: The War Machine* in terms of a riotous, hectic polity. The state apparatus has withered away, yielding political ground to "the pack," "warriors of indiscipline," who question honor, practice blackmail, and adhere to a "volatile sense of honor" (p. 13). Planar, immanent, syntag-matic, and connective (or "recombinant" to use William Gibson's updated terminology), smooth space, like Ballard's traffic island, is "indefinite and noncommunicating," a "local absolute" (pp. 53–54). The culturally abstracted subjects of geophilosophical smoothness take the *"pledge of hegira* or emigration" (p. 50).

In the proliferating genres of postcolonial cyberpunk and Afrofuturism, I would argue, we find what is perhaps the most compelling example of a Deleuzian nomadology of tomorrow, spatially driven and urbanistically attenuated. The alien quality of Ballardian industrial parks, low-tech aesthetics, and ecogenocide takes on enhanced political resonance in Third World cinema and fiction. Consider Kidlat Tahimik's *The Perfumed Nightmare,* a 1977 cult film about a Filipino jeepny driver whose childhood idealization of the American space mission (he is founder of the Werner von Braun fan club), crumbles under the weight of Paris in the throes of so-called urban renewal, "the ugly poured-concrete masses of the new supermarkets that fall into traditional *arrondissements* like meteorites from the future."[10]

Another example is found in the subversively priced ten-franc novel *La Savane des petrifications* (The petrified savanna), a satire of racial politics in the postcolony by the Afro-Caribbean writer Raphaël Confiant. The narrator is a Martinican author monitoring his culture's glacialization under the North American influence of cable TV, while a French academic, in search of black orality, becomes mired in the cultural and linguistic complexities of modern *créolité*. The novel's title page, featuring a small screen with the letters "CNN" blocked against a wavy background, conjures up the smooth space of the airwaves. In Confiant's fiction, the parched topographies of tropical *doudouist* fiction converge with the technologically scarified landscape of postcolonial cyberpunk. Here, Creole vitalism becomes the pendant to Afrofuturism; asteroids are replaced by the molten magma of the earth's core; and virtual subjects, instead of releasing themselves into outer space, incubate "in the mangrove swamp of virtualities," thereby going to ground.[11] In a related vein, modernity, in the form of ecoalienness, is parodically portrayed in pitched battle with traditionalism on the desiccated Algerian plain of Tahar Djaout's novel *L'Invention du désert* (The desert's invention), wherein the wrath of the imams ("the omega of hadj's rites, the symbolic lapidation of Satan") is impotently directed at an incinerator spewing polymers, bottles of Pepsi, bits of steel and plastic into the wasted desert surround.[12]

Alien-ness of a biotechnological order receives a postcolonial twist in Amitav Ghosh's *The Calcutta Chromosome: A Novel of Fevers, Delirium, and Discovery* (1995). The ID card of a vanished employee, its "plastic laminate warped and melted along the edges," its "lettering mostly illegible," and its photograph "vanished under a smudge of soot," shows up on the computer screen like a viral intrusion.[13] Interfering with the workings of Lifewatch systems ("a small but respected non-profit organization that served as a global public health consultancy and epidemiological data bank"), this errant ID ensnares Antar, an Indian techie who works for the company as a programmer, in a mystery leading back to the days of empire.[14] His quest to retrieve L. Muragan reveals that, prior to his disappearance, Muragan was on track to discredit the British claim to malarial cure, billed as the "cold fusion" of the colonial era. Spirtualists, gurus, ghosts, and supernatural coincidences now encumber the story of Sir Ronald Ross's scientific victory with Orientalist claptrap that cannot be dismissed or rationally explained away, despite the fact that it is stored in a data bank and technologically managed. As Antar probes the Lifewatch files for clues to deciphering the codes of viral afterlife, he stumbles instead on reincarnation rituals that double as technological experiments in controlled destiny. He also uncovers the face of the future human in the vector where genetic coding is crossed with digital engineering. Antar meets his own decomposing cadaver, technically imaged on the screen in future time, in the guise of a leering posthuman hologram.

Where Amitav Ghosh figures the beyond of postcolonial identity by combining Orientalist spiritualism with DNA cyber-fi, the African-American jazz novelist Nathanael Mackey uses music as the race alien's preferred medium.[15] In Mackey's epistolary novel *Bedouin Hornbook* (1986) the titles of musical compositions are inspired by covert signals from another realm of consciousness. The work called "Eventual Elegy," part of the longer oeuvre "Aggravated Assent," is said to originate "millions of years ago, the ambiguous verdict of a galaxy-wide dispute between conscious and mechanical forces."[16] One of the band's players, a character known by the moniker Jarred Bottle, is featured as hailing from "interstellar space," a "test-tube baby" who has been "unalterably, involuntarily forwarded, as by a conveyor-belt" (p. 171). Jarred Bottle's theme song, "I Can't Get Over You," is vested with the key to extraterrestrial ontology. No simple love lament, it functions as "a shorthand treatise whose namesake brooding had to do with an ontic, unbridgeable distance, a cosmogonic, uncrossable gap" (p. 170). If Jarred Bottle's creations suggest a fleet of black spacewalkers exploring alternative subjectivities in cosmic hot-spots of future time, other members of the band experiment with backward temporal travel. In a piece called "The Slave's Day Off" archaic memories of slave experience are dredged up and delivered to a present-day avant-garde California musical gig thanks to the "hyperhistorical," "archival coefficient" provided by Sun Ra's Afrofuturist "Omniverse Arkistra" band (p. 83). Music similarly performs the work of healing and analysis in the opus titled "Bottomed Out," inspired by subliminal racial messages beamed through the billboards of San Francisco. In an advertisement for whipped cream and cake, the trauma of slavery is accessed through scrambled references to whipping, sexual subordination, and substance abuse:

> The billboard carried an ad in which a piece of cake was pictured sitting on a plate. It was a piece of devil's food cake beneath a mound of whipped cream, on top of which sat a glossy red cherry. At the base of the ad were the words "Top your favorite bottom with real whipped cream." We stared, not knowing exactly what about the ad had gotten Penguin worked up. . . . "Can't you see it?" he answered. "It's the same oppressive meal they've always dished out. Only now they're trying to pass it off as dessert."
> . . . He made the point that one couldn't help hearing echoes of "deserve" in the word "dessert," that one was being invited to buy into something he termed "saccharine abuse," being invited to endorse a code of "justified injustice." . . . The rest of what he had to say turned largely on the words "top" and "bottom." Their use in the ad, he argued, was loaded with the meanings they brought from the S/M world, whose parlance, as you no doubt know, equates "top" with "dominant," "bottom" with "submissive," "top" with "actor," "bottom" with "acted on," "top" with "master," "bottom" with "slave." It was the S/M ruse of consent he found so offensive, he explained, especially given the ad's white-over-black theme or insinuation. (Pp. 184–85)

Exemplary deconstructors of white society's racial unconscious, paranoid and projective in their worldview, the protagonists of Mackey's *Bedouin Hornbook* pay a dreamy homage to George Clinton's heroes of astrofunk, those cosmonauts of deep space mining black holes, preparing the next Big Bang, and negotiating the condition of "thrown being" or perpetual flight.

Illustrating Greg Tate's surmise, "Ironically, one of the things that's allowed black culture to survive is its ability to operate in an iconoclastic way in regard to the past; the trappings of tradition are never allowed to stand in the way of innovation and improvisation," *Bedouin Hornbook* recasts alienation as a term that carries the memory of African dispossession into modernist forms of African-American culture.[17] In this respect the novel could be placed on a continuum alongside the websites, installations, and videos of the artist Renée Green. Funk is enshrined in a kind of media lab in *Import-Export-Funk-Office*, while music memory links, prompting mnemonic investigation of the embrace of technoscience by black performers of the seventies, prevail in a paper that Green delivered at a conference in Germany called "Loving the Alien: Diaspora, Science Fiction, and Multikultur." The vestigial image of an album cover featuring "Herbie Hancock in a spaceship bubble flying over a purple spacescape on the album called *Thrust*" spikes a pileup of associations: ethereal drums, silver clothes, the Apollo Space Mission, Star Trek's lone female astronaut Uhura (whose name means "freedom" in Swahili), and on and on.[18] These ganglia of impressions prompt reflections on the relevance of seventies funk to obsessions of the late nineties: "alien within/blood relations/germ warfare/ becoming Alien/loss of control" and so on. Afrofuturism is also the genre of choice in Ralph Lemon's choreography for *Geography,* performed in 1996 at the Brooklyn Academy of Music. A rhizomatic work of African dance, subjecting traditional African drum rhythms and steps to the breakage and spin of American modern dance, *Geography* is nomadized still further by Nari Ward's techno-*bidonville* set designs of distressed, washed-out scrims and shimmering walls of recycled bottles and by D. J. Spooky's overtly Deleuzian score.

Afrofuturism has perhaps come up with its most distinctive version of rhizomatic art and Deleuzian smooth space in the form of *paraspace,* an idea developed by the African-American sci-fi writer and semiotician Samuel R. Delany to conjure a life-world of effaced nationalism, blunted characters, and psychic extremes.[19] As Scott Bukatman has noted in relation to William Gibson's outlaw regionalism, the zones of paraspace

> represent the libido of the technocratic city. . . . To map the city through the language of psychoanalysis might indicate its status as subjective projection—or, and this seems more accurate—it might represent the very usurpation of subjectivity through urban configuration.[20]

The "usurpation of subjectivity through urban configuration" only partially applies to Delany's black sci-fi epic *Dhalgren* (first published in 1975), which locates its characters in a space between urban dysfunction and psychological projection. *Dhalgren's* protagonist, the Kid, suffers from a malevolent environmentalism that could trendily be described as spatial-deficit disorder, but which clearly resembles old-fashioned urban paranoia:

> What makes it terrible is that in this timeless city, in this spaceless preserve where any slippage can occur, these closing walls, laced with fire-escapes, gates and crenellations, are too unfixed to hold it in so that, as from a moving node, it seems to spread, by flood and seepage, over the whole uneasy scape.[21]

In a brief discussion of *Dhalgren,* I want to examine the conceptual and political stakes of the "uneasy scape"; emphasizing the worldscape over the netscape (the former is a virtual space with distinctly urban scar tissue, the latter, by contrast, is a retail wall). At first reading, cyberpunk appears to delocalize urban sites and wipe out historical memory. Likewise, smooth space may appear aggressively antiurban as it renders visible markers of the city blurred or illegible. But I would suggest that in Delany's paraspatial fiction, a raced worldscape emerges—one that seems to echo Deleuze and

Guattari's theoretical vision in its engagement with history. Class and race warfare are visualized through futurological landscaping. The worldscape registers the emergence of a predominantly black survivalist culture that redefines the hegemonic contours of the traditional urbs:

> "There *are* a thousand people—perhaps—in this city."
> "I did meet one family who—"
> "There are many others. And most of them, as Paul Fenster keeps reminding us, are black."[22]

In *Dhalgren* the inhabitants of the city of Bellona learn that they have been cursed by their own private blitzkrieg, while the rest of the country— New York to Los Angeles—has apparently been spared. Though occasional newspapers get through, an informational impasse renders citizens primally obtuse: The question, "what happened?" remains intractable. The phenomenal world emits signals, but the populace has knowledge only of a lobotomized *cause* of urban fear:

> "But do you *know* how terrible it is to live inside here—" she gestured at the green walls—"with everything slipping away? And you can hear everything that goes on in other rooms, in the other apartments? I wake up at night, and walk by the window, and I can see lights sometimes, moving in the smoke. And when the smoke isn't so heavy, it's even worse, because then the lights look like horrible things crawling around . . . This has got to stop, you know! Management must be having all sorts of difficulty while we're going though this crisis. I understand that. I make allowances. But it's not as though a bomb had fallen, or anything. If a bomb had fallen, we'd be dead. This is something perfectly natural. And we have to make do, don't we, until the situation is rectified?" She leaned forward: "You don't think it *is* a bomb?"[23]

Forced to submit to the mental strain of extreme hypotheticals, the characters of *Dhalgren* trivialize their unthinkable misfortune, treating it as an aberrant form of the everyday. A coping function, raw nerve-endings waving wildly, has become a communal reflex. Domestic routines continue as before in sections of semiabandoned apartment buildings not yet turned over to squats. The poet Mr. Newboy seems only dimly aware that half of his house has been trashed and looted; informed by Management that part of his home is off-limits, he simply doesn't venture there anymore.

In *Dhalgren* the middle-class home is the site where the emergent worldscape erupts most visibly. In the chapter "The House of Ax," the Richards family plans a move to an apartment in the same building exactly resembling the layout of their old one, only in reverse. Though violent, druggy Scorpions have occupied the floor below (the Scorpions are a lumpen warrior-hipster class arrayed in dog collars, chains, and switch-

blade wristlets), the Richardses seem unable to process the fact that they are
homesteading in a survivalist enclave. Their relocation involves a painstak-
ingly slow transfer of domestic effluvia, helped along by an odd-job man
with literary pretensions, the Kid. The Kid moves freely between the porn-
and-scavenger demimonde of the Scorpions and the middle class. Like the
smooth social paraspace of Bellona, where everyone is skidding, Kid's persona has lost its class bearings. He reviles the Richards family because it is
not paying him, but takes refuge in Mrs. Richards's maternal care.

The farcical ordinariness of apartment life vanishes when the Richards
children—June and Bobby—decide to bring a rolled-up carpet to the new
place.

> Out in the hall, June screamed: a long scream he could hear empty of all
> breath. Then she screamed again.
>
> Mrs Richards opened her mouth without sound; one hand shook by
> her head.
>
> He dashed between the television and the tables, out the door.
>
> . . . The rug lay on the floor, the last foot sagging over the sill in the
> empty elevator shaft. The door nudged it, went *K-chunk,* retreated, then be-
> gan to close again.
>
> "Mom! Bobby, he fell in the—"
>
> *K-chunk!*
>
> "No, oh my dear God, no!"[24]

Bobby has stepped back into a blind elevator shaft. The *K-chunk* sound is the
phonic announcement of urban panic shattering the psychic fortress of denial. Relying on Scorpion help, Kid descends into the death-shaft and trawls
up his final movable item. Bobby's disfigured corpse is delivered over the din
of Dragon Lady's pitiless roar: "YOUR SON IS DEAD, LADY!" The Richardses cope
with Bobby's death with surreally sunny socializing, abandoning the body
to putrefaction in the old downstairs apartment. Kid, by contrast, becomes
delusional, subject to hallucinations and blackouts. After initially suspect-
ing foul play by Bobby's sister, vulnerable to her brother's threat to "out" her
as a secret porn addict, Kid falls prey to a terrifying conviction that the death
was "accidentally" committed by the city itself:

> Because that means it's the city. That means it's the landscape: the bricks,
> and the girders, and the faulty wiring and the shot elevator machinery, all
> conspiring together to *make* these myths true. And that's crazy. . . . Do you
> think a city can control the way people live inside it? I mean, just the geog-
> raphy, the way the streets are laid out, the way the buildings are placed?
> (Pp. 249–50)

Kid's friend Tak interprets this evidence of city-murder as proof that Bellona has been trapped in science fiction. "Huh?" says Kid. "You mean a

time-warp or a parallel universe?" "No, just . . . well, science fiction. Only real. It follows all the conventions" (p. 372). Delany mines the cliché of a lurking middle-class phantasm—a premise in films like *Escape from New York* or *Safe*—that these streets have become so mean, we're no longer projecting cyberpunk's worst urban fear, we're it!

Exploring the mental warp and woof of urban dwelling as a heightened self-consciousness about acting out sci-fi, the narrative folds, in a Deleuzian way, like a Leibnizean pleat or Möbius strip: inside and outside, here and there, fantasy and fiction, subject and city, ripple, as if illustrating the formula that Kid discovers in a manuscript distilling Wittgenstein, Lévi-Strauss, and Chomsky: "A particularly parametric work of careful, crystalline catalysts in lingual synthesis."[25] Though apparently meaningless, these "lingual syntheses" might be said to apply quite aptly to the porn-driven, retrofuturist, industrial vernacular spoken by the Scorpions ("That naugahyde rimmer of rusty Chevrolet nineteen-fifty-two exhaust pipes! I hope the next time she sucks off a number she rips his foreskin in her bridge work!").[26]

If *Dhalgren* experiments with linguistic sex and violence to capture posturban zombification, it also defines Bellona libidinously as a "saprophytic city" (an organism that feeds on decay), a place where you can have your fantasy and eat it too.[27] The fantasies that prove particularly edible in Bellona center on the "fascinating and psychotropic detail" of group sex, and on black people: "A lot of people came into the room. Coffee, chocolate, and tamarindo faces, hands, and shoulders swung by, turning, as chains from long or stocky necks swung under several hairdos of beach ball dimensions."[28] Blackness is satirized as alien junk food, and fetishized in jet vinyl crowned with celestial naturals. The black technobody remains a staple of Delany's experimentation with futurological subjectivities.[29] In the eighties he would valorize matte black in the semiotics of Afrofuturism:

> From the beepers, the Walkmen, the Diskmen, through the biggest ghetto blaster—the stuff put forward as portable is not chromium. It's black. With the exception of the silver CD (which, to become functional, must be slipped into its black-encased digital reader), this is a very different set of signifiers from the sparking bus bars, the quivering dials, and the fuming beakers of science fiction imagery.[30]

Though Delany cautions that "when one talks about 'black youth culture as a technological culture,' one has to specify that it's a technological culture that's almost entirely on the receiving end of a river of 'stuff,' in which the young consumers have nowhere near what we might call equitable input," his fiction approves a riskier approach to Afrofuturist identities.[31]

Taking on Negro grotesques from repressed memory (best personified by the jocular, ironically named, unrepentant black rapist George Harrison), he jumbles them up with half-breeds, hippies, race-baiters, and white supremacists, creating scenarios in which the conventions of speculative fiction are used to complicate paradigms of racial subjection. Thwarting the reader's potential desire for a "blacker" novel,[32] *Dhalgren* trumps the race card by desegregating neighborhoods, depicting good interracial sex, banalizing racist epithets, and confounding vital statistics—"for somewhere in this city is a character they call: The Kid. Age: ambiguous. Racial origin, same. True name: unknown."[33] Consistently, references to racial identity are erratically introduced: "Five were sitting on the steps. Two leaned against the wrecked car at the curb. Why am I surprised that most of them are black? The flower-children, whose slightly demonic heirs these are, were so emphatically blond, and the occasional darky among them such an emphatic mark of tolerance!"[34] In a sequel novel, *Trouble on Triton: An Ambiguous Heterotopia* (1976), skin color fails to be processed racially by a super-Aryan interplanetary visitor named Bron:

> Two people were coming up the center of the road. From braided hair to crusted boots, they were the dirtiest people Bron had seen since Fred.
> One kept digging a middle finger under the lens of some goggle-like things perched on her nose. (The dirt, however, wasn't black or gray but sort of brownish.)[35]

Sending up racist clichés, Delany defamiliarizes the historic normativities of skin color. Like Ismael Reed, Octavia Butler, Ursula Le Guin, Nathanael Mackey, Renée Green, and the London-based Black Audio Collective, Delany seems more interested in unraveling the psychic underpinnings of alien-ness within color coding than in confirming the preordained contours of a racist world.

I will conclude by suggesting that, far from being simply displaced into literary urban form or commercialized as New Age Others (as in Orson Scott Card's *Xenocide* and *Ender's War*), Delaney's race aliens remind us that "African-Americans, in a very real sense, are the descendants of alien abductees," even as they become the organic fiber of the nomadological worldscape, part of the deep space that is impossible to detect but that holds up the atmosphere, part of the air that is breathed or not breathed, part of the wildly black market of its absent economy, part of the global compass set to readjust worldview.[36] Delany's astrocentric novel, *Trouble on Triton,* captures the imperial state's free fall from transcendence to immanence, as it becomes reterritorialized in its turn. Earth's hubris shrinks when perceived from the solar system's "outer Mongolia." Galaxies out-

flank planetary orbits, continents become indistinguishable loci of memory, cultural landmarks lose their hegemonic grip on the world map, and
cities shrink to minuscule dots, vanishing from sight altogether:

> The Taj Mahal—would he get to see it after all? He must ask Sam how far
> away it was—that was much more interesting than Boston. But though he
> knew all about the clay-pits to the south of it and the story of the queen who
> died in childbirth buried within it, he wasn't sure which continent it was
> on—one of them beginning with "A." . . . Asia? Africa? Australia?[37]

As the letter *A* skids along the names of continents, so Bron, in the process
of completing a High Surveillance Mission, speeds from point to point in
space. Viewed from where he sits, the earth's surface resembles the tessel-
lated abstraction of the Deleuzean worldscape, "a horizonless milieu that is
a smooth space, steppe, desert or sea."[38]

NOTES

Preface

1. The bibliographies of each of these authors is extensive. I will signal here a few texts that have been particularly crucial to the French case: Charles-André Julien's *Histoire de l'Algérie contemporaine* (Paris: Presses universitaires de France, 1979) and *L'Anticolonialisme en France de 1871–1914* (Paris: Press universitaire de France, 1973); Charles-Robert Agéron's *Politiques coloniales au Maghreb* (Paris: Press universitaire de France, 1972); and Abedelmalek Sayad's *L'Immigration algérienne en France* (1976; Paris: Editions Entente, 1984).

Intoduction

1. Pierre Nora, introduction to *De l'archive à l'emblème*, vol. 3 of *Les Lieux de mémoire: Les France*, ed. Pierre Nora (Paris: Gallimard, 1992), pp. 15–16. Unless otherwise noted, all translations are my own. Original French text is included where it is deemed particularly instructive.

2. Jean-Christophe Bailly and Michel Deutsch, "Le Fantôme du national," *Libération*, June 17, 1993, p. 6.

3. Significant contributions in this direction include Abiola Irele's *The African Experience in Literature and Ideology* (London: Heinemann, 1981) and Christopher Miller's essay "Literary Studies and African Literature," in *Africa and the Disciplines*, ed. Robert H. Bates, V. Y. Mudimbe, and Jean O'Barr (Chicago: University of Chicago Press, 1993).

4. James Clifford, "Of Other Peoples: Beyond the 'Salvage' Paradigm," in *Discussions in Contemporary Culture*, no. 1, ed. Hal Foster (Seattle: Bay Press, 1987), p. 126.

5. Homi K. Bhabha, "Interrogating Identity," in *Institute for Contemporary Art Documents* 6 (London, 1987) p. 5.

6. Gayatri Chakravorty Spivak has equally well evoked this partitive subjectivity, inserting herself into an expository essay on "who claims alterity" as the caste Hindu, Marxist feminist subject of "internal colonization. See "Who Claims Alterity?" in *Remaking History*, ed. Barbara Kruger and Phil Mariani (Seattle: Bay Press, 1989).

7. André Malraux, *Picasso's Mask* (New York: Holt, Rinehart and Winston, 1976), pp. 166, 170.

8. Jean-Paul Sartre, preface to Frantz Fanon's *The Wretched of the Earth*, trans. Constance Farrington (New York: Grove Press, 1963), p. vi.

9. Jim Berkley, "An Elegy for the Era of High Theory," graduate seminar paper, UCLA, 1995.

10. Peggy Kamuf addresses deconstruction and institutional politics in *The Division of Literature; or, The University in Deconstruction* (Chicago: University of Chicago Press, 1997).

11. Henry Louis Gates, Jr., *The Signifying Monkey: A Theory of African-American Literary Criticism* (New York: Oxford University Press, 1988), p. 46.

12. See Jacques Derrida, "Racism's Last Word" and "But, beyond . . . (Open Letter to Anne McClintock and Rob Nixon)," trans. Peggy Kamuf, in *"Race," Writing, and Difference,* ed. Henry Louis Gates, Jr. (Chicago: University of Chicago Press, 1985), pp. 329–38 and 354–69 respectively. See also Anne McClintock and Rob Nixon, "No Names Apart: The Separation of Word and History in Derrida's 'Le Dernier Mot du Racisme,'" in *"Race," Writing, and Difference,* pp. 339–53.

13. Jacques Derrida and Geoffrey Bennington, *Jacques Derrida par Geoffrey Bennington et Jacques Derrida* (Paris: Seuil, 1991); Jacques Derrida, *Le Monolinguisme de l'autre* (Paris: Galilée, 1996).

14. Report cited in Jacques Derrida, "Géopsychanalyse 'and the Rest of the World'" (1981), in *Psyché: Inventions de l'autre* (Paris: Editions Galilée, 1987), p. 327.

15. Derrida, "Géopsychanalyse," p. 327.

16. Ibid., p. 329.

17. See Anne McClintock, "'No Longer in a Future Heaven': Nationalism, Gender, and Race," in *Becoming National: A Reader,* ed. Geoff Eley and Ronald Grigor Suny (Oxford: Oxford University Press, 1996), pp. 260–85. See also Benedict Anderson, "Exodus," *Critical Inquiry* 20 (1994): 327.

18. Jenny Sharpe, "Is the United States Postcolonial? Transnationalism, Immigration, and Race," *Diaspora* 4, no. 2 (1995): 185. For Sharpe the crucial issue is "the relationship between the diasporic identities we call 'postcolonial' and the globalization of consumer culture."

19. Philip McMichael, "The New Colonialism: Global Regulation and the Restructuring of the Interstate System," in *A New World Order? Global Transformations in the Late Twentieth Century,* ed. David A. Smith and Jozsef Böröcz (Westport, Conn.: Greenwood Press, 1995), p. 37.

20. Alain Finkelkraut, "Wounded," trans. Linda Asher, *New York Times Magazine,* June 8, 1997, p. 49.

21. The anti-Eurocentric position is succinctly laid out by Ella Shohat and Robert Stam in their introduction to *Unthinking Eurocentrism: Multiculturalism and the Media:*

> Endemic in present-day thought and education, Eurocentrism is naturalized as "common sense." Philosophy and literature are assumed to be European philosophy and literature. The "best that is thought and written" is assumed to have been thought and written by Europeans. . . .
> Although neoconservatives caricature multiculturalism as calling for the violent jettisoning of European classics and of "western civilization" as an area of study, multiculturalism is actually an assault not on Europe or Europeans but on Eurocentrism— on the procrustean forcing of cultural heterogeneity into a single paradigmatic perspective in which Europe is seen as the unique source of meaning, as the world's center of gravity, as ontological "reality" to the rest of the world's shadow. Eurocentric thinking attributes to the "West" an almost providential sense of historical destiny. Eurocentrism, like Renaissance perspectives in painting, envisions the world from a single privileged point. It maps the world in a cartography that centralizes and augments Europe while literally "belittling" Africa. The "East" is divided into "Near," "Middle," and "Far," making Europe the arbiter of spatial evaluation, just as the estab-

lishment of Greenwich Mean Time produces England as the regulating center of temporal measurement. Eurocentrism bifurcates the world into the "West and the Rest" and organizes everyday language into binaristic hierarchies implicitly flattering to Europe: *our* "nations," *their* "tribes"; *our* "religions," *their* "superstitions"; *our* "culture," *their* "folklore"; *our* "art," *their* "artifacts"; *our* "demonstrations," *their* "riots"; *our* "defense," *their* "terrorism."

Unthinking Eurocentrism: Multiculturalism and the Media, ed. Ella Shohat and Robert Stam (New York: Routledge, 1994), pp. 1–2.

22. Marc Fumaroli, *L'Etat culturel: Essai sur une religion moderne* (Paris: Editions de Fallois, 1991), p. 293.

23. Ibid., p. 33.

24. Philippe Dagen, "La nouvelle droite émue par l'esthétique nazie," *Le Monde,* March 27, 1997, p. 35.

25. Philippe Dagen, "L'Art contemporain sous le regard de ses maîtres censeurs," *Le Monde,* February 15, 1997, p. 25.

26. See Marc Fumaroli's long essay, "Le Génie de la langue française," in Nora, *De l'archive,* pp. 911–73.

27. Kristin Ross's *Fast Cars, Clean Bodies: Decolonization and the Reordering of French Culture* (Cambridge: MIT Press, 1995) exemplifies the tendency in contemporary French studies to examine the hidden institutional stakes of schools of French thought. The most controversial interpretive thrust of the book concerns her reading of structuralism as a kind of excuse to forget history. The "messy" side of class struggle, urban apartheid, and the torture of Algerians, was, Ross implies, rendered semi-invisible by France's obsession with Americanization. This obsession manifested itself in the fetishization of gadgets, hygienic appliances, mass media, fast cars, and, in general, the designer visuality of modernity. For Ross, structuralism and Annales school history *(longue durée)* are guilty by association since, as positivist methodologies, they contributed to the ahistorical, technophilic postwar ethos.

28. See, for example, Ann McClintock et al., eds., *Dangerous Liaisons: Gender, Nation, and Postcolonial Perspectives* (Minneapolis: University of Minnesota Press, 1997); Arjun Appadurai, *Modernity at Large* (Minneapolis: University of Minnesota Press, 1996); Partha Chatterjee, *The Nation and Its Fragments: Colonial and Postcolonial Histories* (Princeton: Princeton University Press, 1993); Andrew Parker et al., eds., *Nationalisms and Sexualities* (New York: Routledge, 1992); Etienne Balibar and Immanuel Wallerstein, eds., *Race, Nation, Class: Ambiguous Identities* (London: Verso, 1991); Homi K. Bhabha, ed., *Nation and Narration* (London: Routledge, 1990); Paul Gilroy, *There Ain't No Black in the Union Jack: The Cultural Politics of Race and Nation* (Chicago: University of Chicago Press, 1987); Benedict Anderson, *Imagined Communities: Reflections on the Origins and Spread of Nationalism* (London: Verso, 1983).

29. David Hume, "Of National Characters," in *Political Essays,* ed. Knud Haakonssen (Cambridge: Cambridge University Press, 1994), pp. 78–79.

30. Etienne Balibar, "The Nation Form: History and Ideology," in Eley and Suny, *Becoming National,* p. 137.

31. Ibid., p. 90.

32. See Grégoire, *Rapport sur la nécessité et les moyens d'anéantir les patois, et d'universaliser l'usage de la langue française,* appendix to Renée Balibar and Dominique Laporte, *Le Français national* (Paris: Hachette, 1974), pp. 198–215. Balibar

and Laporte's book offers a fascinating account of the fit between national character and national language as it germinated during and after the Revolution. The work also contains an illuminating introduction by Etienne Balibar and Pierre Macherey.

33. Jacqueline Rose, *States of Fantasy* (Oxford: Oxford University Press, 1996), p. 62. Rose quotes Linda Colley, *Britons: Forging the Nation, 1707–1837* (New Haven: Yale University Press, 1992), p. 112.

34. George Orwell, "England, Your England," in *A Collection of Essays* (New York: Harcourt Brace Jovanovich, 1953), p. 253, as cited by Michael Gorra in his useful concluding chapter "Notes towards a Definition of Englishness," in *After Empire: Scott, Naipaul, Rushdie* (Chicago: University of Chicago Press, 1997), p. 158.

35. This lecture served as the basis for Derrida's subsequently published book *Le Monolinguisme de l'autre.*

36. Ernest Gellner, *Nations and Nationalism* (Ithaca: Cornell University Press, 1983), p. 123.

37. Ibid., p. 125.

38. Tom Nairn, "Scotland and Europe," in Eley and Suny, *Becoming National,* p. 80.

39. Gellner, *Nations and Nationalism,* p. 138.

40. Ibid., pp. 140–41.

41. In the estimation of Susan Buck-Morss, Hegel (in his *Philosophy of History*) was blamed unfairly for a nationalism that he never truly espoused. Nation, she reminds us, comes from *natio,* meaning "where you are born," but for Hegel, nationalism was dissociated from birthplace and affixed instead to a rational modern Protestantism, to a Germanic spirit imbued with and indebted to the Protestant ethic. Thus Hegel's theory of the state was not based on territorial nationalism but rather on categories of reason and positive law. How else, Buck-Morss asks, could he root for Napoleon while the city in which he was writing was being invaded by Napoleon's troops? (Susan Buck-Morss in private conversation).

42. Ernest Renan, "What Is a Nation?" trans. Martin Thom, in Eley and Suny, *Becoming National,* p. 50.

43. In an illuminating essay "Currying Favor: The Politics of British Educational and Cultural Policy in India, 1813–54," Gauri Viswanathan charts how the need to forge an upright, decent, exemplary model of English character stemmed from the dissolute way of life enjoyed by servants in the East India Company in the early nineteenth century. English literature served a moralizing function in India, drawn on as a source from which idealized Englishness could be extracted; it was then used to graft a model of the ideal Anglo-Indian, schooled in Eng. Lit., and tempered into becoming the perfect colonial subject. In McClintock et al., *Dangerous Liaisons,* pp. 113–29.

44. For a useful discussion of J. G. Fichte's insistence on the importance of original language to the vitality of the nation (articulated in his *Addresses to the German Nation,* a lecture of 1808), of Wilhelm von Humboldt's adumbrations in the 1820s, and of Giuseppe Mazzini's reworking of similar claims in the context of the Young Italy movement of the 1840s, see David Lloyd, *Nationalism and Minor Literature* (Berkeley and Los Angeles: University of California Press, 1987), pp. 63–66.

45. See Fredric Jameson's hotly disputed, highly influential "Third-World Literature in the Era of Multinational Capitalism," *Social Text* 15 (fall 1986): 65–88.

46. If multinational character is the result of global economic pressure from

without, there are comparable adjunct pressures from within. As Balibar reminds us, referring to the pivotal work on immigration of Gérard Noiriel, "[S]ince the end of the nineteenth century, 'French identity' has continually been dependent upon the capacity to integrate immigrant populations. The question arises as to whether that capacity is today reaching its limit or whether it can in fact continue to be exercised in the same form" ("The Nation Form," 137).

47. André Green, *Le Discours vivant. La conception pychanalytique de l'affect* (Paris: Presses Universitaires de France, 1973), pp. 219–70.

48. On these themes, see Lisa Lowe's chapter "Imagining Los Angeles in the Production of Multiculturalism," in *Immigrant Acts* (Durham: Duke University Press, 1996), pp. 84–96.

49. Donna Haraway, *Modest_Witness@Second_Millennium. FemaleMan_Meets _OncoMouse (TM). Feminism and Technoscience* (New York: Routledge, 1997), p. 261.

50. Lawrence Grossberg, "History, Politics, and Postmodernism," in *Stuart Hall: Critical Dialogues in Cultural Studies,* ed. David Morley and Kuan-Hsing Chen (London: Routledge, 1996), p. 167–68.

51. Roger Caillois, "Mimétisme et psychasthénie légendaire," in *Le Mythe et l'homme* (Paris: Gallimard, 1972), p. 33.

Chapter One

1. Elizabeth Constable offers a theoretically nuanced interpretation of the connections between cosmopolitanism, anti-Semitism, Orientalism, and nationalism in Barrès's thought in *"Ce bazar intellectuel:* Maurice Barrès, Decadent Masters, Nationalist Pupils," in *Perennial Decay: On the Aesthetics and Politics of Decadence* (Philadelphia: University of Pennsylvania Press, 1998).

2. Diane Rubenstein, "The Normalien and the Pathographic: Foucault, Althusser, and the Bicentennial Imaginary," University of California Humanities Research Institute, Irvine, 1996, photocopy.

3. Maurice Barrès, *Les Déracinés* (Paris: Gallimard, Folio, 1988), p. 85.

4. The phrase "the village that died for France" is an adaptation of Patrick Wright's title: *The Village That Died for England: The Strange Story of Tyneham* (London: Jonathan Cape, 1995).

5. In his preface of 1904 to *Un Homme libre* Barrès recalled: "We all came together, mistraliens, proudhoniens, young jews, neo-catholics and socialists in the famous *Cocarde.* ... I never stop laughing when I think that this motley team worked out the foundations of nationalism, and not only political nationalism, but a wide-sweeping French classicism" (Maurice Barrès, *Romans et voyages,* vol. 1 [Paris: Editions Robert Laffont, 1994], p. 92).

6. Pierre Mille, *The French Novel,* trans. Elisabeth Abbott (Philadelphia: J. B. Lippincott, 1930), pp. 142 and 148 respectively.

7. Barrès was elected deputy of Nancy in 1889 and retained his seat in the legislature until 1893.

8. Maurice Barrès, *Le Jardin de Bérénice* (Paris: Librairie Plon, 1921), p. 52.

9. [Cette cosmopolite qui n'a ni son ciel, ni sa terre, ni sa société, c'est une déracinée. Dans la bréviaire des idéologues, pour exprimer son bohémianisme moral, si étrangement compliqué de délicatesses, faudra-t-il pas que par un trait un peu grossier, mais significatif, nous l'inscrivions sous le vocable de *Notre-Dame du sleep-*

ing-car] (Maurice Barrès, *Trois stations de psychothérapie* [Paris: Perrin et Cie, Libraires-Editeurs, 1891], pp. 46–47).

10. Ibid., p. 50.

11. Maurice Barrès, *Le Culte du moi*, in *Romans et voyages*, vol. 1. See Barrès's own interesting commentary—*Examen des trois romans idéologiques*—on the three novels comprising this trilogy: *Sous l'oeil des barbares, Un Homme libre, Le Jardin de Bérénice.*

12. Barrès, *Les Déracinés*, pp. 240–42.

13. Ibid., pp. 243–44.

14. Ibid., p. 350.

15. David Carroll, *French Literary Fascism: Nationalism, Anti-Semitism, and the Ideology of Culture* (Princeton: Princeton University Press, 1995). See in particular chap. 1, "The Use and Abuse of Culture: Maurice Barrès and the Ideology of the Collective Subject," pp. 19–31.

16. *Le Monde des Livres*, in *Le Monde*, December 1, 1995, pp. 1–10.

17. Roger-Pol Droit, "Les d'Artagnan du concept," in *Le Monde des Livres*, p. 9.

18. Nicolas Weill, "Paul Celan de retour à Paris," *Le Monde des Livres*, p. 2.

19. Eric Fottorino, "Le Vieil homme et l'infante," *Le Monde des Livres*, p. 3.

20. Tahar Ben Jelloun, "Khair-Eddine ou la fureur de dire," in *Le Monde des Livres*, p. 2.

21. Lanson, *Etudes d'histoire littéraire* (Paris: H. Champion, 1929), p. 89.

22. Ibid., p. 90.

23. Gilles Deleuze and Félix Guattari, *Mille plateaux: Capitalisme et schizophrénie* (Paris: Les Editions de Minuit, 1980), p. 25.

24. Ibid., p. 31.

25. Jean Paulhan, *Les Fleurs de Tarbes ou la terreur dans les lettres* (Paris: Gallimard, 1990). Paulhan takes his title from a sign posted at the entrance of the public garden of Tarbes: "It is forbidden to enter the public garden without flowers in hand." For Paulhan, this rather ingenious proscription encodes an incitement to floral theft. He is interested in releasing the hidden or asphyxiated "countersense" of language.

26. Marc Augé, *Non-places: Introduction to an Anthropology of Supermodernity*, trans. John Howe (London: Verso, 1995), p. 22.

27. Jacques Hassoun, *Les Contrebandiers de la mémoire* (Paris: Syros, 1994), pp. 61, 68, 101, 118.

28. Jean Bernabé, Patrick Chamoiseau, and Raphaël Confiant, *Eloge de la créolité*, bilingual edition, trans. M. B. Taleb-Khyar (Paris: Gallimard, 1989), pp. 114, 109, 97–98; emphasis added.

29. Edouard Glissant, *Poétique de la relation* (Paris: Gallimard, 1990), pp. 23, 26, 43.

30. Patrick Chamoiseau, *Texaco* (Paris: Gallimard, Folio, 1992), pp. 336–37.

31. Paul Gilroy, *The Black Atlantic as a Counterculture of Modernity* (Cambridge: Harvard University Press, 1993), p. 3.

32. Deleuze and Guattari, *Mille plateaux*, 35.

33. Gilroy, *Black Atlantic*, p. 37.

34. André Gide, "A propos des *Déracinés*," *L'Hermitage*, December 1897, in *Prétextes* (Paris: Mercure de France, 1929), p. 51.

35. Gide, "A propos des *Déracinés*," p. 54.

36. Gide, *Prétextes*, p. 72.

37. Ibid., p. 76.

38. Ibid., p. 119.

39. Georges Perec, *Espèces d'espaces* (Paris: Galilée, 1974), p. 34.

40. Simone Weil, *L'Enracinement: Prélude à une déclaration des devoirs envers l'être humain* (Paris: Gallimard, Folio, 1949), p. 14.

41. Claude Ollier, *La Mise en scène* (Paris: Garnier-Flammarion, 1982), p. 102.

42. Gaston Bachelard, *La Terre et les rêveries du repos* (Paris: Librairie José Corti, 1948), pp. 290–322.

Chapter Two

1. For a useful overview of Joan's biography, including nuanced accounts of historical contexts in which aspects of her biography were revived and represented in art, politics, literature, music, and film, see Marina Warner, *Joan of Arc: The Image of Female Heroism* (New York: Vintage Books, 1982).

2. For more on Dreyer's film, see Robin Blaetz, "'La Femme Vacante,' or The Rendering of Joan of Arc in the Cinema," *Post Script* 12, no. 2 (1993): 63–78, and "Retelling the Joan of Arc Story: Women, War, and Hollywood's *Joan of Paris,*" in *Literature/Film Quarterly* 22, no. 4 (1994): 212–21.

3. For an informative review of the film, see William Johnson, "From the Journals of Jean Seberg," in *Film Quarterly* 4 (summer 1996): 35–38.

4. Theresa Hak Kyung Cha, *Dictée* (Berkeley: Third Woman Press, 1995), p. 1.

5. For a brilliant essay on Cha's *Dictée* that addresses the problem of dictation in relation to interpellation, see Lisa Lowe, "Unfaithful to the Original: The Subject of *Dictée,*" in *Writing Self Writing Nation* (Berkeley: Third Woman Press, 1995), pp. 35–69. My thanks to Tamara Ho for alerting me to this essay as well as to the three others in this collection (all devoted to *Dictée*), by Hyun Yi Kang, Elaine H. Kim, and Shelley Sunn Wong.

6. Etienne Balibar, "Subjection and Subjectivation," in *Supposing the Subject,* ed. Joan Copjec (London: Verso, 1994), pp. 8–10.

7. In her preface to *Supposing the Subject* Joan Copjec argues that:

> in psychoanalysis the subject is not hypostatized, but hypothesized—that is, it is only ever *supposed:* we never actually encounter it face to face.
>
> We have, in fact, for a long time now—since the beginnings of modern science— been dwelling in the graveyard of the subject. For modern science, as we know, established itself on a thorough exclusion of the subject, an effacement of all authorial traces from every text deemed to be scientific. In recent years these exclusions have been renewed by waves of "sappers" who have reassured us, over and over again, that nothing of the subject remains alive in our modern world. Structuralism, deconstruction, historicism—so many of our contemporary discourses have announced the death of the author, the end of man, the deconstruction, atomization and demise of the subject, that one cannot help but be struck by the very thoroughness of its effacement.
>
> Psychoanalysis has theorized and named exclusion as radical as this: it calls it *foreclosure.* What is absolutely, thoroughly eliminated from the symbolic will never, like the repressed, return there, but it does return in the real. In other words, psychoanalysis argues that the subject, eliminated from all its own statements, deconstructed, appears in the real, or: the subject discovers itself *in* its very effacement, *in* its own modern graveyard. This is the secret solidarity between science and psychoanalysis, the reason why the latter historically follows the former. (Pp. xi–xii)

8. Cha, *Dictée,* p. 117.

9. Charles Péguy, "Que Jeanne d'Arc ne fut pas proprement un Chevalier," (from *Cahier*, September 24, 1911), in *Morceaux choisis* (Paris: Gallimard, 1928), p. 235.

10. Ibid., p. 237. Péguy goes on to salute Joan of Arc for her "professionalism" in mastering the hierarchies and techniques of saintliness, "the armature and bone structure of the saintly métier" (p. 238). Here his language seems to anticipate my reading of Joan's sense of calling as an example of the militancy of the ego.

11. Judith Butler, "Conscience Doth Make Subjects of Us All," *Yale French Studies* 88 (1995): 25.

12. Ibid., pp. 12, 16.

13. See Daniel Paul Shreber's *Denkwürdigkeiten eines Nervenkranken* (Memoirs of my nervous illness), trans. Ida Macalpine and Richard A. Hunter (Cambridge: Harvard University Press, 1988); and Sigmund Freud, "Psycho-analytic Notes upon an Autobiographical Account of a Case of Paranoia (Dementia Paranoides)" (1911), in *The Standard Edition of the Complete Psychological Works of Sigmund Freud*, ed. and trans. James Strachey (London: Hogarth Press, 1953–74), vol. 12. For a comprehensive, suggestive reading of Shreber's text and Freud's case study in the light of recent theoretical work on interpellation and national psychosis, see Eric L. Santner's *My Own Private Germany: Daniel Paul Shreber's Secret History of Modernity* (Princeton: Princeton University Press, 1996).

14. Louis Althusser, "Ideology and Ideological State Apparatuses (Notes towards an Investigation" (1969), in *Lenin and Philosophy and Other Essays*, trans. Ben Brewster (New York: Monthly Review Press, 1971), p. 179.

15. For further elaboration of this story, see my source for this information, Elizabeth Roudinesco's *Jacques Lacan & Co.: A History of Psychoanalysis in France, 1925–1985*, trans. Jeffrey Mehlman (Chicago: University of Chicago Press, 1990), pp. 108–9.

16. Jacques Lacan, "Ecrits 'inspirés': Schizographie," in *De la psychose paranoïaque dans ses rapports avec la personnalité suivi de premiers écrits sur la paranoïa* (Paris: Editions du Seuil, 1975), p. 366.

17. Ibid., p. 367.

18. Ibid., p. 378.

19. David Halperin, *Saint Foucault: Towards a Gay Hagiography* (New York: Oxford University Press, 1995), p. 71.

20. Georges Bataille, *Le Procès de Gilles de Rais* (Paris: Société Nouvelle des Editions Pauvert, 1979), p. 47.

21. See Maurice Heine's numerous essays on Sade in *Le Minotaure* as well as Paulhan's "defense" of Sade's oeuvre recently republished in *Le Marquis de Sade et sa complice ou les revanches de la pudeur* (Paris: Editions Complexe, 1987).

The twin causes of erotic liberty and political liberation were present when in 1957 the publishing house of Pauvert was barred by the French censors from diffusing Sade's *Oeuvres complètes*. Bataille, Cocteau, Breton, and Paulhan were called to testify on behalf of Sade. Their defense was made primarily in terms of ratifying Sade's works as an antidote to "la philosophie molle." Jean Paulhan presented Sade as the forefather of Nietzsche and Freud, heralding him as a revolutionary thinker who gave expression to the corporal rhetoric of sexuality.

22. Dr. Augustin Cabanès, *Le Cabinet secret de l'histoire* (Paris: A. Maloire, 1900).

23. The most prepossessing of all these studies from a literary point of view is Panizza's, particularly the section on criminal psychopathological typologies (*Psy-*

chopathia criminalis [Paris: Ludd, 1993], a translation of *Génie und Wahnsinn* [Munich, 1891]). Seeming to anticipate twentieth-century instances of the psychiatrization of repression, he ironically entered the term *la mania antigouvernementalis* into the lexicon of terms used to describe the mental condition of political subversives.

24. Havelock Ellis, *Studies in the Psychology of Sex* (New York: Random House, 1933), 1:125. Ellis treats Gilles de Rais as "the classic example of sadism in its extreme form." Following F. H. Bernelle's 1910 Thèse de Paris entitled *La Psychose de Gilles de Rais*, he speculates that it was his reading of Suetonius that gave Gilles ideas for many of the abominations carried out. He also links his legend to folkloric phantasms of vampires and werewolves.

25. For an ethnographic approach to the Gilles/Bluebeard legend see the essay by E. Sidney Hartland (a Scottish folklorist famous for his altercations with James Frazer): "The Forbidden Chamber," in *Folklore* 3 (1885), as cited in *Encyclopedia Britannica*, 11th ed., s.v. "Bluebeard."

26. Huysmans's account of Gilles de Rais's first murder in the series of "épouvantables holocaustes," culminates with a description of blood transformed into ink. J.-K. Huysmans, *Là-bas* (Paris: Gallimard, 1985), pp. 193–94.

27. Péguy, "Jeanne d'Arc," p. 219.

28. Ibid., pp. 243–44.

29. See Jean Paulhan's *Les Fleurs de Tarbes ou la terreur dans les lettres* (Paris: Gallimard, Folio, 1941). Paulhan's intimation of a regime of linguistic Terror refers to the returning of language to its "primitive" rhetorical roots—that is, to a "state of nature" or condition of raw persuasive, expressive power. Gradually domesticated through centuries of courtly usage and literary convention, the "letter" has lost its ability to inspire awe or terror. Paulhan seeks to restore redoubtable sublimity to language, even if this means unleashing its power of horror.

30. See Eric Walter, "Vies et maladies du docteur Marat, le thème morbide dans le discours biographique," in *La Mort de Marat*, ed. Jean-Claude Bonnet (Paris: Flammarion, 1986), pp. 335–72.

31. Pierre Klossowski, "Le Marquis de Sade et la Révolution," in *Le Collège de Sociologie,* ed. Denis Hollier (Paris: Gallimard/Idées, 1979), p. 392.

32. Péguy, "Jeanne d'Arc," p. 7.

33. As cited by Yves Hersant in his notes for Huysmans's *Là-bas*, p. 376.

34. George Frederick Drinka, *The Birth of Neurosis: Myth, Malady, and the Victorians* (New York: Simon and Schuster, 1984), p. 171. According to Freud, the term *invert* was rather misleadingly applied to the homosexual who "feels he is a woman in search of a man." Referring to the Greek paradigm of ephebe and older man, he argued for a kind of latent bisexuality or hermaphroditism in the pederastic invert:

> As soon as the boy became a man he ceased to be a sexual object for men and himself, perhaps, became a lover of boys. In this instance, therefore, as in many others, the sexual object is not someone of the same sex but someone who combines the characters of both sexes; there is, as it were, a compromise between an impulse that seeks for a man and one that seeks for a woman, while it remains a paramount condition that the object's body (i.e. genitals) shall be masculine. Thus the sexual object is a kind of reflection of the subject's own bisexual nature.

Sigmund Freud, *Three Essays on the Theory of Sexuality,* trans. and ed. James Strachey (New York: Basic Books, 1975), p. 10. Gilles de Rais's veneration of an abstract, idealized Joan of Arc becomes explicable according to Freud's interpretation of inversion.

35. Michel Tournier, *Gilles & Jeanne* (Paris: Gallimard, Folio, 1983), p. 149.

36. Jules Michelet, *Joan of Arc,* trans. Albert Guérard (Ann Arbor: University of Michigan Press, 1974), p. 3.

37. Ibid., p. 101.

38. Ibid., p. 116.

39. The mystical, socialist context in which Péguy placed Joan of Arc did not prevent his fascist son Marcel from producing his father's early play *Jeanne d'Arc* (1897) for the collaborationist stage in 1941.

40. Reinach's argument takes into account the prodigious sums of money that Gilles spent on luxuries, pomp, and entertainment. He suggests that Gilles was framed by kin outraged by his expenditure of the family fortune. He also maintains that the threat of excommunication was used effectively to extort Gilles's confession. See the section on Gilles in Salomon Reinach, *Cultes, mythes et religions* (Paris: Ernest Leroux, Editeur, 1912), 4:276.

41. Maurice Barrès, *Autour de Jeanne d'Arc* (Paris: E. Champion, 1916), p. 73.

42. Charles Maurras, *Jeanne d'Arc, Louis XIV, Napoléon* (Paris, 1937), p. 30, as cited by Warner, *Joan of Arc,* p. 261.

43. Léon Daudet, *Souvenirs et polémiques* (Paris: Robert Laffont, 1992), p. 359.

44. Gabriel Jacobs, "The Role of Joan of Arc on the Stage of Occupied Paris," in *Vichy France and the Resistance: Culture and Ideology,* ed. Roderick Kedward and Roger Austin (London: Croom Helm, 1985), p. 107.

45. Avital Ronnell, *The Telephone Book/The Telephone Call* (Lincoln: University of Nebraska Press, 1989), p. 9.

46. Michelet, *Joan of Arc,* p. 80.

47. Louis Althusser, *L'Avenir dure longtemps suivi de les faits* (Paris: Stock/IMEC, 1992), trans. by Richard Veasey as *The Future Lasts Forever* (New York: New Press, 1993).

48. For an analysis of Althusser's crime, exploring its pathographic symptomologies, see Diane Rubenstein, "The Normalien and the Pathographic: Foucault, Althusser, and the Bicentennial Imaginary," University of California Humanities Research Institute, Irvine, 1996, photocopy.

49. Slavoj Žižek, *The Sublime Object of Ideology* (London: Verso, 1989), p. 101. Žižek deals with Kantian ethics and radical evil in "The Unconscious Law: Towards an Ethics beyond the Good," in *The Plague of Fantasies* (London: Verson, 1997), pp. 213–41.

50. Pierre Jouve and Ali Magoudi, *Les Dits et les non-dits de Jean-Marie Le Pen: Enquête et psychanalyse* (Paris: Editions de la Découverte, 1988), p. 62.

51. Extract from speech delivered by Le Pen on May 10, 1987, before the statue of Joan of Arc in Paris, cited by Christophe Hameau, *La Campagne de Jean-Marie Le Pen pour l'élection présidentielle de 1988* (Paris: Travaux et Recherches Panthéon-Assas Paris II, 1992), p. 81.

52. Philip Gourevitch, "The Unthinkable: How Dangerous Is Le Pen's National Front?" *New Yorker,* April 28 and May 5, 1997, p. 110.

53. Ibid.

54. "Le Pen: Chirac c'est Jospin en pire" and "Mort d'un Marocain: Des skinheads recherchés," *Le Figaro,* May 2, 1995, p. C7.

55. *Joan of Arc in Her Own Words,* comp. and trans. Willard Trask (New York: Books and Co., 1996), p. 143.

56. Pierre Montagnon, *La Conquête de l'Algérie: 1830–1871* (Paris: Pygmalion, 1986), p. 31.

57. Tahar Djaout, *L'Invention du désert* (Paris: Seuil, 1987), p. 57.

58. Ibid., pp. 32–33.

Chapter Three

1. Herbert R. Lottman, *Albert Camus: A Biography* (New York: Doubleday, 1979), p. 618. A variant of this statement was made in the form of a comment to Emmanuel Roblès: "If a terrorist throws a grenade in the Belcourt market where my mother shops, and if he kills her, I would be responsible if, to defend justice, I defended terrorism. I love justice, but I also love my mother" (p. 577).

2. A recent book by Wolf-Dietrich Albes, *Albert Camus und der Algerienkrieg* (Tubingen: Max Niemeyer Verlag, 1990), overturns this tradition of deconstructive readings. Albes seems to interpret Camus's entire philosophy of the Absurd as a product of colonial guilt.

3. Herbert Lottman writes: "For Camus the war was criminal and stupid. He hoped to obtain the agreement of the French Government, the FLN, and Messali Hadj's movement—which Camus wrongly considered to be of equal importance— for the civil truce scheme. In coming to Algeria he also hoped to make contact with the nationalists, without daring to hope that he would actually be able to meet representatives of the FLN!" (*Albert Camus*, p. 571).

4. For more on Messaoudi, see her *Une Algérienne debout. Entretiens avec Elisabeth Schemla* (Paris: Flammarion, 1995).

5. Camus's altercation with his friend, the Algerian author Jean Amrouche, illustrates the truly nasty side of Camus's position taking. On January 11, 1958, Amrouche published an article in *Le Monde* (that had been refused by *L'Express)* entitled "La France comme mythe et comme réalité. De quelques vérités amères." Amrouche asserted that France had forgotten the evils of the colonial system in its dream of a universal mission. He insisted that one could no longer maintain "the traditional ambiguity between liberal humanist rhetoric *[le dire]* and colonial, racist acts *[le faire raciste et colonialiste]*." In his view, the French Left and Right were bedfellows on the Algerian question. The Left served as an alibi for the chauvinist rightist majority, while the French Communist Party pusillanimously supported French Algeria. Amrouche saw independence as the only possible historical outcome of the war. Shortly afterward, he was denounced for his "excesses" by Jacques Huergon, a former Latin professor of Camus's at the University of Algiers. Camus congratulated Huergon: "I was 100 percent in agreement with you in what you have written on Amrouche" (as recounted by Olivier Todd, *Albert Camus, une vie* [Paris: Gallimard, 1996], pp. 710–11).

6. Conor Cruise O'Brien's reading of *La Peste* (*Albert Camus: Of Europe and Africa* [New York: Viking Press, 1970]) reacts strongly against Camus's semierasure of the Algerian city and its inhabitants. Camus should have either created a completely nonspecific site, he argues, or avoided the implied substitution of Arabs for Germans in his portrayal of an occupied city.

7. Albert Camus, *La Femme adultère,* in *Oeuvres complètes d'Albert Camus* (Paris: Gallimard and Club de l'Honnête Homme, 1983), 4:112, 115, 120, 123, 126, 128 respectively.

8. Ibid., p. 115.

9. Edward Said, *Culture and Imperialism* (New York: Knopf, 1993), pp. 184–85.

10. Conor Cruise O'Brien supplies a brilliant reading of the "aloneness" of the stranger in Camus's short story "L'Hôte." He points out that in the final published version, the story ends with the words "Daru looked at the sky, the plateau and beyond the invisible lands which stretched down to the sea. In this vast country which he had loved so much, he was alone" (quoted in *Albert Camus*, p. 85). The original manuscript stopped with the Arab walking to prison; there was no reference to threats.

The second version ends: "YOU BETRAYED MY BROTHER. YOUR SCHOOL WILL BURN AND YOU WITH IT. Daru looked unseeing at the light springing from the surface of the plateau. In this vast country, which had been his, he was alone."

The third version ends: "In this vast country without which he could not live—with which he made one—which remained his only native land" (ibid., p. 85)

Comparing the three versions, one observes the "love of country" gradually giving way to the alienation of solitude. The native land attenuates to the point where it becomes alternately a "light" (presumably of the white heat of native anger), and "invisible," a vacant blur merging with the sky.

On the theme of loneliness in the homeland, see also the section "Meursaults 'Fremdheit' als Bedrohung der kolonialen Gesellschaft Algerien," in Albes, *Albert Camus.*

11. Said, *Culture and Imperialism*, p. 185.

12. Albert Camus, *Le Premier Homme* (Paris: Gallimard, 1994), p. 167.

13. Ibid., 167–68.

14. Réda Bensmaïa, "1962, November. After Eight Years of War, Algeria Becomes Independent," in *A New History of French Literature*, ed. Denis Hollier (Cambridge: Harvard University Press, 1989), pp. 1018–19. Bensmaïa also notes Memmi's change of heart on the Arabization question when he wrote in the anthology *Ecrivains francophones du Magreb* (Francophone writers from the Maghreb) (1985), "Without ceasing to believe that the Arabic tongue will ultimately find the place it deserves, I have had to admit that the inertia of custom is more powerful than logical or sentimental expectation" (p. 1019).

15. Frantz Fanon, "On National Culture," in *The Wretched of the Earth*, trans. Constance Farrington (New York: Grove Press, 1963), pp. 216–17.

16. Ibid., p. 217.

17. Ibid., p. 247.

18. Homi K. Bhabha, *Nation and Narration* (New York: Routledge, 1990), p. 4.

19. Camus, *La Femme adultère*, p. 123.

20. Albert Camus, "Avant-propos," in *Chroniques algériennes*, 1939–1958, in *Actuelles*, vol. 3 (Paris: Gallimard, 1958), p. 28.

21. Conor Cruise O'Brien, *To Katanga and Back: A UN Case History* (New York: Simon and Schuster, 1962).

22. O'Brien, *Albert Camus*, p. 67.

23. Albert Camus, "Démocratie et dictature internationales," in *Ni victimes ni bourreaux*, in *Actuelles*, vol. 1 (Paris: Gallimard, 1965), pp. 340–41.

24. Quoted in O'Brien, *Albert Camus*, pp. 8–9.

25. O'Brien, *Albert Camus*, p. 9.

26. Immanuel Wallerstein, *Geopolitics and Geoculture: Essays on the Changing*

World-System (Cambridge: Cambridge University Press, 1991).

27. Timothy Brennan, *At Home in the World: Cosmopolitanism Now* (Cambridge: Harvard University Press, 1997), p. 38.

28. Lottman, *Albert Camus,* p. 356.

29. Ibid., p. 7.

30. In this section I will quote from *The First Man,* trans. David Hapgood (New York: Vintage Books, 1995), p. 278.

31. Ibid., p. 317.

32. According to Lottman, the case of Ben Saddok was the last time Camus would consider an appeal by friends on the left:

> The dilemma arose during the prosecution of Ben Saddok (accused of the killing of a prominent Moslem not committed to the rebellion who had been Vice President of the Algerian Assembly). The defense attorney wrote to Camus to say that his client had carried out a political act, and that he was appealing to Camus as author of "Réflexions sur la guillotine" despite the attorney's connection with political causes that Camus opposed.... Camus agreed to make a plea for Ben Saddok if the defense attorney guaranteed that no publicity would be given to the letter he would address to the court.... He even drafted a letter for the court in support of Ben Saddok, which his editor quotes as if it had actually been sent, but he apparently left it in draft prior to his departure for Stockholm. On his return he told the defense attorney that he had intended to be of use to the defense, but he had just learned that France-Observateur had already publicized his misgivings and conditions, and to his disadvantage. Yet it was not so much political differences as methodology which separated Camus from Ben Saddok's attorney, and now he had been discouraged once and for all. (*Albert Camus,* pp. 611–12)

33. Camus, *The First Man,* p. 29.

34. Fanon, "On National Culture," p. 217.

35. Ibid., p. 218.

36. Bill Readings, *The University in Ruins* (Cambridge: Harvard University Press, 1994), p. 48.

Chapter Four

1. Homi K. Bhabha, "Remembering Fanon: Self, Psyche, and the Colonial Condition," in *Remaking History,* ed. Barbara Kruger and Phil Mariani (Seattle: Bay Press, 1989), p. 137.

2. Henry Louis Gates, "Critical Fanonism," *Critical Inquiry* 17 (1991): 457–70.

3. Alan Read, ed., *The Fact of Blackness: Frantz Fanon and Visual Representation* (Seattle: Bay Press, 1996).

4. Frantz Fanon, *Black Skin, White Masks,* trans. Charles Lam Markmann (New York: Grove Weidenfeld, 1967), p. 219.

5. Dependency, or "underdevelopment" theory, derived from Marxist formulations of political economy under conditions of neocolonialism. Colin Leys, one of the most influential dependency theorists of the late sixties, summarized its central premise as follows: "[T]he predicament of the underdeveloped countries was due to the application to them of western capital know-how and political power, often over several centuries, in ways which had structured (and continue to structure) their economies and societies so as to continually reproduce poverty, inequality and, above all, political and economic subordination to the interests of western capital" (*Underdevelopment in Kenya: The Political Economy of Neo-Colonialism, 1964–1971*

[Berkeley and Los Angeles: University of California Press, 1974], p. xiv).

The "classic" literature of dependency theory also includes Andre Gunder Frank, "The Development of Underdevelopment," in *Latin America: Underdevelopment or Revolution* (New York: Monthly Review Press, 1969); Fernando Henrique Cardoso, "Dependency and Development in Latin America," *New Left Review* 74 (July–August 1972): 83–95; Gavin Kitching, *Class and Economic Change in Kenya: The Making of an African Petite-Bourgeoisie* (New Haven: Yale University Press, 1980); Samir Amin, *Neo-colonialism in West Africa,* trans. Francis McDonagh (New York: Monthly Review Press, 1973). (My thanks to David Apter for bibliographical sources and discussions of dependency theory).

6. Octave Mannoni, *Prospero and Caliban: The Psychology of Colonization,* trans. Pamela Powesland (Ann Arbor: University of Michigan Press, 1990), pp. 85–86.

7. Jock McCulloch, *Black Soul, White Artifact: Fanon's Clinical Psychology and Social Theory* (Cambridge: Cambridge University Press, 1983), p. 214.

8. Fanon, *Black Skin, White Masks,* p. 93.

9. Ibid., p. 94.

10. In the *Carnets* Mannoni marks the beginning of his analysis with Lacan as follows:

> November 13, 1945
> I start here a journal of psychoanalysis that I asked of Dr. Lacan (5, rue de Lille). He asks why I came.
> Reasons I gave: desire to initiate myself (what he calls didactic analysis), and some mild problems: tendency to fail, laziness, money problems.

Lacan checks him over and suggests that they deal with the money problems with regular payments of three hundred francs a session. Bothered by this, Mannoni thinks about how this material would make a good comedy. "Personally," he acknowledges, "I would have liked a more authoritarian attitude. But of course that says more about me than about him" (Octave Mannoni, *Nous nous quittons. C'est là ma route. Carnets* [Paris: Denoël, 1991], pp. 301–2).

11. Ibid., p. 314.

12. On Bataille's pineal eye, see Denis Hollier's essay, "About Some Books Which Bataille Did Not Write," *Parallax* 4 (February 1997): 71–78.

13. Michel Leiris's documentation of the ethnographer's delirium and depression in black Africa in *L'Afrique fantôme,* taken together with his self-deflationary, autoethnography in *L'Age d'homme,* form interesting counterparts to Mannoni's *Prospero and Caliban* and *Carnets.*

14. McCulloch, *Black Soul, White Artifact,* p. 218. McCulloch maintains that Fanon was unjustified "in leaving the reader with the impression that *Prospero* was written in direct support of French colonialism." He insists that "Mannoni was not an apologist for colonialism," because he argued that "the French policy of assimilation could only work at the level of crude charity and blind pedantry." He claims, moreover, that "Mannoni's anguish at the cultural oppression in the older colonies such as the Antilles is very much akin to Fanon's. Furthermore, Mannoni is just as keenly aware as Fanon of the psychological and identity changes involved in Europeanising a small native elite" (p. 219).

15. Lyotard's remarks on French paternalism:

Anyone active in the organizations "of the left" in Algeria before 1954 cannot be ignorant of the fact that paternalism, the very same relationship of dependence they
sought in principle to destroy, persisted in barely veiled form between European militants and Algerian militants. Our course, posing the problem for the Algerians in this
way made it insoluble, because the essential content of the problem was nothing other
than the universal form of social relations in Algeria, namely, dependence itself.

Armed struggle broke the spell. The Algerians, in fighting, no longer call for reforms, no longer demand to be given schools, hospitals, factories; they force imperialism to relinquish its ascendancy, they go on the offensive, and therein lies the literally
revolutionary content of their action. Algerian society ceased to be a society of dependence from the moment when the "subhumans" it oppressed demonstrated con-
cretely that they were not debtors, and that they were prepared to die for this. One
cannot understand the anguish of the Europeans in the face of the resistance unless
one situates it within the framework of the reassuring paternalism that they sought to
practice. The radical critique of the myth according to which the Algerians were created in order to obey, execute orders, and eventually be executed already blasted from
the barrels of the shotguns of the first underground forces. Imagine the stupor of the
true-blooded French! It was no longer their world put to the test; it was, precisely, their
world turned upside down.

Jean-François Lyotard, "The Social Content of the Algerian Struggle," in *Political
Writings*, trans. Bill Readings and Kevin Paul Geiman (Minneapolis: University of
Minnesota Press, 1993), pp. 229–30. See also Françoise Vergès's recent piece in *Critical Inquiry*, "Creole Skin, Black Mask: Fanon and Disavowal" (23 [1997]: 578–95) as
well as her essay "To Cure and to Free: The Fanonian Project of 'Decolonized Psychiatry,'" in *Fanon: A Critical Reader*, ed. Lewis R. Gordon et al. (Oxford: Blackwell,
1996), 85–99, for a more complete consideration of these ideas.

16. Mannoni, *Prospero and Caliban*, p. 89.

17. Fanon, *Black Skin, White Masks*, p. 106. Mannoni records a dream about a
Lebel rifle in which he is in the place of the gun-toting native insurgent, while Lacan
occupies the paternal position of the colonizer/analyst. In the dream, he is standing
in a street that resembles "rue de la Libération" in Tananarive. A young men menaces
him with a revolver. "I explain to him that as a colonial, I have a right to a rifle. . . . I
then dream of spying (rifle by my side) on Lacan as he leaves with his wife and
daughter. L. sits down next to me and proposes leaving the session in order to go to
the theater" (p. 388).

18. If, in the context of Fanon's attack on Mannoni, the Senegalese soldier functions as a reality-check against the European fallacy of projecting Freudian paradigms of the bourgeois family onto non-Western cultures, he also seems to have
been part of Fanon's own racial nightmare, indeed a highly symbolic component of
the Antillean subject's "superiority complex" vis-à-vis black Africans and a reason
why "the Negro is comparison," in Fanon's famous formulation (*Black Skin, White
Masks*, p. 211). In the opening chapter of *Black Skin*, Fanon evokes the unfortunate
case of "Antilles Negroes who are annoyed when they are suspected of being Senegalese. This is because the Antilles Negro is more 'civilized' than the African, that is,
he is closer to the white man" (p. 26). Later in the book, when he audits the free associations of his white patients around the words *rape* or *Negro*, he discovers that
"Senegalese soldier" "evoked dreadful, bloody, tough, strong" (p. 166). And in a famous footnote in the chapter of *Black Skin* devoted to "The Negro and Psychopathology," Fanon inserts an autobiographical anecdote that is not without
relevance to his own Caliban complex:

It is apparent that one would hardly be mistaken in saying that the Antillean does not altogether apprehend the fact of his being a Negro. I was perhaps thirteen when for the first time I saw Senegalese soldiers. All I knew about them was what I had heard from veterans of the First World War: "They attack with the bayonet, and, when that doesn't work, they just punch their way through the machine-gun fire with their fists . . . They cut off heads and collect human ears." These Senegalese were in transit in Martinique, on their way from Guiana. I scoured the streets eagerly for a sight of their uniforms, which had been described to me: red scarves and belts. My father went to the trouble of collecting two of them, whom [sic] he brought home and who had the family in raptures. (Pp. 162–63)

The signs of military savagery—red scarves and belts—infecting the school-child with rapturous horror seem to have become festering mementos or catalysts of a buried Negrophobia. Although it is certain that Fanon attacked Mannoni legitimately for his bungled interpretations of "black bulls" and for ejaculating rifles, it is less clear whether or not his contestation of a Senegalese symbolic in Mannoni's work was a case of "protesting too much."

The Senegalese obsession resurfaced in *Wretched of the Earth* when Fanon records the harrowing case-history of a French police inspector unable to control a brutal penchant for domestic abuse. In the course of linking this penchant to the dehumanizing effect of performing torture, he refers to the blood-chilling role of the Senegalese:

Our problem is as follows: are you able to make this fellow talk? It's a question of personal success. You see, you're competing with the others. In the end your fists are ruined. So you call in the Senegalese. But either they hit too hard and destroy the creature or else they don't hit hard enough and it's no good. (P. 269)

The Senegalese soldier remains unreleased from slavery; thoroughly instrumentalized as a strong arm supplementing a weak European fist, he occupies a place of arrested psychic abjection in this Algerian scenario of "a black man is beating a whiter man of color." In his earlier work, *Black Skin, White Masks* Fanon had exposed the nefarious system of pitting Africans against North Africans, a "procedure" that he called "the racial distribution of guilt" (p. 103).

19. Mannoni, *Prospero and Caliban*, pp. 42–43.

20. G. W. F. Hegel, *Phenomenology of Spirit*, trans. A. V. Miller (Oxford: Oxford University Press, 1977), p. 404. In this section I am indebted to Susan Buck-Morss for her discussion of Hegel.

21. Ibid., p. 522.

22. For more on Frédéric Paulhan and on Jean Paulhan's early associations and intellectual influences, see *La Vie est pleine de choses redoutables*, ed. Claire Paulhan (Paris: Seghers, 1989).

23. See "La Thèse de Jean Paulhan," in *Jean Paulhan et le Madagascar* (1908–10), *Cahiers Jean Paulhan*, no. 2 (Paris: Gallimard, 1982).

24. Mannoni, *Prospero and Caliban*, p. 17.

25. Ibid., p. 5.

26. Mannoni, *Carnets*, p. 313.

27. If a principal motivation of this inquiry is to explore the psychic outer reaches of political and economic dependency theory, I am also concerned, somewhat tangentially, with drawing attention to the *lack* of work on Madagascar in postcolonial studies. Of all the former French colonies and protectorates (from West

Africa and the Caribbean to Indochina), Madagascar, which was subject to French rule from 1890 to 1960, has received scant consideration. Even in the 1940s, when Leopold Senghor's landmark *Anthologie de la nouvelle poésie nègre et malgache de langue française* (1948) appeared, the Malagasy poems by Jean-Joseph Rabéarivelo (whose sense of anomalousness as a Malagasy author writing in French led him to suicide in 1937 at the age of thirty-six), Jacques Rabémananjava (known for his use of royal sources), and Flavien Ranaivo (whose extraordinary poem "Epithalme" draws on the elliptical form of the *hain-teny* described by James Clifford as "gnomic, often amorous poem-proverbs customarily recited in formal disputations"), seem tacked on.

28. For a detailed account of the way in which the murder seems to have indelibly impressed itself on *Aytré,* as well as lesser-known fictions by Paulhan, see John Culbert's "Slow Progress: Jean Paulhan and Madagascar," *October* 83 (winter 1998): 71–95.

29. See *Jean Paulhan et Madagascar.*

30. Jean Paulhan, *Aytré qui perd l'habitude* (Brussels: Editions de la Nouvelle Revue Belgique, 1948).

31. Maurice Blanchot, "Aytré's Paradox," in *The Work of Fire,* trans. Charlotte Mandell (Stanford: Stanford University Press, 1995), pp. 68–69.

32. The dream reads as follows:

> I am in the streets of Tananarive, it is rainy and the earth—a kind of sand—is wet. My feet sink in the mud, I fall on my knees and feel very weak. I ask for aid and stretch out my hand. I think I can manage by myself and that I am perhaps making too much fuss, but I am not so sure, and I must admit to myself that I cannot rise—that is a dream of impotency—Malagasy women, small and young, pass by in the rain, blurred. I stretch out my hand to them, they look at me and pass. I then remember what I know about the Malagasy character; crossing the other way, a man (he has even got mustachio) helps me quickly. He looks like Woulkoff; in my dream Woulkoff too grows a mustachio. I look at him in the face and we part; I am weak no more. Walking along, I see an excavation and the barrier (which must be a color bar!) So it is: so you treated till now the "indigens" (for "natives"). The inscription is in English. I am so astonished that I walk back some steps to look at it. Yes, it is in English! It is propaganda for the strangers, with the hope that the natives and Frenchmen won't know. I almost feel indignation . . . Ends the dream. (Mannoni, *Carnets,* p. 373)

33. Octave Mannoni, *Lettres personelles: Fiction lacanienne d'une analyse* (Paris: Denoël, 1990), p. 9.

34. Ibid., p. 10.

35. Ibid., p. 11.

36. See Octave Mannoni, "The Decolonization of Myself," *Race,* April 1966, pp. 327–35. The essay was reprised in French (preserving the original English title), in *Clefs pour l'imaginaire ou l'autre scène* (Paris: Seuil, 1969), pp. 290–300.

37. Mannoni, *Lettres personelles,* p. 58.

38. Ibid., p. 60.

39. Octave Mannoni, "Je sais bien, mais quand même," in *Clefs pour l'imaginaire,* p. 30.

40. Ibid., p. 21.

41. For a brief discussion of Mannoni's surmise that the dead are to the Malagasy what adults are to European children, see O. Nigel Bolland, "Mannoni and Fanon: The Psychology of Colonization and the Decolonization of Personality," *New Scholar* 4, no. 1 (1993): 29–50.

42. Proof of Mannoni's imperviousness to reality may be found in his *Carnets*. Virtually his only allusion to the insurrection of April 4, 1947, is accompanied by his admission that external events count for little in his memoir: "In this notebook, I hardly note 'impressions' that originate from outside. It is certainly the notebook of an introvert . . . however, I cannot refrain from noting the current period of 'troubles' that began on the morning of March 30—at night—at Moramanga and Manakara. The Antandroy surprised the military camp of Moranmanga and occupied Manakara. Several deaths among the officers and colons" (p. 362).

43. Ibid., p. 387.

44. Ibid., p. 326.

Chapter Five

1. Simone de Beauvoir, *The Second Sex,* trans. H. M. Parshley (New York: Vintage Books, 1989), p. 163; Catherine Clément and Hélène Cixous, *The Newly Born Woman,* trans. Betsy Wing (Minneapolis: University of Minnesota Press, 1975), pp. 68–70, 93; Gayle Rubin, "The Traffic in Women: Notes on the 'Political Economy' of Sex,*"* in *Toward an Anthropology of Women,* ed. Rayna Raiter (New York: Monthly Review Press, 1975), pp. 157–210; Judith Williamson, "The Colonization of Women's Bodies," in *Studies in Entertainment,* ed. Tania Modleski (Bloomington: Indiana University Press, 1986), pp. 99–118; Sandra Lee Bartky, *Femininity and Domination: Studies in the Phenomenology of Oppression* (New York: Routledge, 1990), pp. 22–32.

2. Chandra Talpade Mohanty offers a trenchant critique of *colonization* in feminist discourse, retaining the term for her own purposes as a reference to what Western feminism does to "third world difference" ("Under Western Eyes: Feminist Scholarship and Colonial Discourses," in *Third World Women and the Politics of Feminism,* ed. Chandra Talpade Mohanty, Ann Russo, and Lourdes Torres [Bloomington: Indiana University Press, 1991], pp. 52–54). See also Valerie Amos and Pratibha Parmar, "Challenging Imperial Feminism," *Feminist Review* 17 (1984): 3–19.

3. Gayatri Chakravorty Spivak, "French Feminism in an International Frame" (1981), in *Marxism and The Interpretation of Culture,* ed. Lawrence Grossberg (Urbana: University of Illinois Press, 1988), pp. 134–53.

4. V. Y. Mudimbe, *The Invention of Africa: Gnosis, Philosophy, and the Order of Knowledge* (Bloomington: Indiana University Press, 1988), p. 2.

5. Alain Grosrichard, *Structure du sérail: La fiction du despotisme asiatique dans l'Occident classique* (Paris: Seuil, 1977), p. 177.

6. Victor Segalen, *Essai sur l'exotisme* (Paris: Fata Morgana, 1986), p. 33.

7. The obvious British counterparts would include Rudyard Kipling's *Kim,* T. E. Lawrence's *Lawrence of Arabia,* or E. M. Forster's *A Passage to India.*

8. See *Picasso,* Centre d'Art Contemporain Château de Tanlay, Yonne, June 9–September 30, 1990, particularly the section on gravures 1970–72, "Degas dans la Maison Tellier." A useful essay by Gaëton Picon entitled "Picasso et l'érotisme" (1974) is republished in this catalog. For more on Picasso's play on Degas's brothel monotypes see Carol Armstrong's monograph on Degas, *Odd Man Out* (Chicago: University of Press, 1990).

9. Malek Chebel, *L'Esprit de sérail* (Paris: Lieu Commun, 1988), pp. 118–19.

10. Pierre Loti, *Les Trois dames de la Kasbah,* in *Fleurs d'ennui* (Paris: Calmann Lévy, 1924), p. 100.

11. Jacques Lacan, "The Signification of the Phallus," in *Ecrits: A Selection,* trans. Alan Sheridan (London: Tavistock, 1977).

12. Ellie Ragland-Sullivan attempts to clarify this Lacanian proposition:

> Because her very body serves as a lure to desire, Woman is essentialized by males as containing secret truths, the answers to enigmas, answers from, or to, the Otherness that the masculine denies and rejects and projects onto others. In this sense she is the phallus. Although gender identity evolves as an unconscious position taken toward the phallus, seen as an elemental effect emanating from an uninterpretable fundamental fantasy, such positions can only be deciphered through transference relations and in terms of symptoms whose cause(s) reappear, if at all, as transformed, distorted memories.

"The Sexual Masquerade," in *Lacan and the Subject of Language,* ed. Ellie Ragland-Sullivan and Mark Bracher (New York: Routledge, 1991), p. 60.

13. Guy de Maupassant, *A la Feuille de Rose, maison turque* (Paris: Nouvelle Société des Editions Encre, 1984), p. 58.

14. Ibid., p. 59.

15. Lucie Delarue-Mardrus, *El-Arab: L'Orient tel que je l'ai connu* (Lyon: Les Editions Lugelunum, 1944), pp. 29 and 31.

16. Marc Hélys, *Le Jardin fermé* (Paris: Plon, 1908), p. 4. Marc Hélys was putatively the woman who acted as the model for Loti's Turkish heroine Djénane in *Les Désenchantées.* There was some scandal when it became known that the woman on whose "authentic" report of harem life the novel was based was a "Française" posing as Turkish with two women friends (they in fact were genuine members of the Istanbul bourgeoisie stifled by the social strictures of the harem). When Hélys's book was published shortly after Loti's death, it was assumed by some that Loti had seen through the hoax but had played along for fun. Others justified the adventure, as did Hélys herself, with the argument that her enactment of an *Azyiadé* "part 2" had furnished Loti with wonderful material for a novel. A detailed appraisal of the affair may be found in Pierre Briquet's monumental *thèse d'état, Pierre Loti et l'Orient* (Paris: La Presse Française et Etrangère, 1945).

17. Hélys, *Le Jardin fermé,* p. 14.

18. Maupassant, *Feuille de Rose,* pp. 77–78.

19. Ibid., pp. 78–79.

20. Jacques Lacan, "Anamorphosis," in *The Four Fundamental Concepts of Psycho-analysis,* trans. Alan Sheridan, ed. Jacques-Alain Miller (New York: Norton, 1978), p. 81.

21. Maurice Barrès, *Le Jardin sur l'Oronte* (Paris: Librairie Plon, 1922), pp. 23, 32.

22. Loti, *Les Trois dames,* p. 62.

23. Guy de Téramond, *Schmâm'ha: Roman algérien* (Paris: Simonis Empis, 1901), p. 70.

24. Ibid., p. 84.

25. Ibid., pp. 83–84.

26. Charles Géniaux, *Les Musulmanes* (Paris: Edition du "Monde Illustré," 1909), p. 4.

27. Jérôme and Jean Tharaud, *Fez ou les bourgeois de l'Islam* (Paris: Plon, 1930), p. 193.

28. Isabelle Eberhardt, "L'âge du néant, " in *Oeuvres complètes,* vol. 2: *Ecrits sur le sable* (Paris: Bernard Grasset, 1990), p. 529.

29. Ibid., pp. 530–31.

30. Eberhardt's writing affords a poor model for feminist postcolonialism, containing as it does moments of racism, anti-Semitism, and antifeminism. And yet, she exerts fascination on contemporary women artists (witness the feminist filmmaker Leslie Thornton's 1987 film about Eberhardt, *There Was an Unseen Cloud Moving*). This is how the film is described in the catalog (taken from John Powers's review in the *LA Weekly*):

> Isabelle Eberhardt was a late-Victorian shocker, a writer and poet who left Geneva for Algeria, converted to Islam, traveled around as a man, pushed herself to the borders of annihilation ("drinking and smoking and fucking") and died at 27 in a flash-flood of distinct metaphorical aptness. Leslie Thornton's dazzling video gives us Eberhardt and her world in arresting form—it's an exploded biography and an anti-travelogue. Using written words, still photos, re-created scenes, clips from *Pepe le Moko*, and newsreel footage of the Sahara and the moonwalk, Thornton takes her story in two directions, hoping to suggest the immediate intensities of Eberhardt's experience and to trace this experience's connections to questions of sexual identity, colonialism and representation.

Drift Distribution catalog (New York), p. 23.

31. Isabelle Eberhardt, "La Zaouïa," in *Yasmina et autres nouvelles algériennes* (Paris: Liana Levi, 1986), p. 262.

32. Catherine Millot, *Nobodaddy: L'hystérie dans le siècle* (Cahors: Point Hors Ligne, 1988), p. 37.

33. Isabelle Eberhardt, "Yasmina," in *Yasmina et autres nouvelles, p.* 55.

34. Myriam Harry, *Les Derniers Harems* (Paris: Ernest Flammarion, 1933), p. 23.

35. L.-M. Enfrey, *Le Livre des harems* (Paris: Editions Ernest Leroux, 1920), p. 22.

36. Ibid., p. 132.

37. Ibid., pp. 94–95.

Chapter Six

1. On the relationship between the real and reality see Slavoj Žižek, *Looking Awry: An Introduction to Jacques Lacan through Popular Culture* (Cambridge: MIT Press, 1991), chaps. 1 and 2. See also Elizabeth Grosz, *Jacques Lacan: A Feminist Introduction* (New York: Routledge, 1990). In evoking the category of the "colonial real" I am aware of the multiple slippages and ambiguities surrounding the notion of the real in Lacanian theory. Definable as a term that marks the haunting of the subject by a dream of subjective plenitude or nonseparation with the maternal body (the "lack of the lack," in Lacan's words), immersed in the traumatic moment of the splitting of the subject, identified in its retroactive function in fantasy as the "object-cause of desire" (Lacan) or the "psychic reality of desire" (cf. Žižek), the real in psychoanalytic terms presents itself linguistically and visually on the sly. Intruding itself on the subject at a moment least expected, the real is that sudden and terrifying flash when the subject perceives the gaping hole in subjectivity tenuously papered over by denial.

2. Timothy Mitchell, *Colonizing Egypt* (Berkeley and Los Angeles: University of California Press, 1991), pp. 8–11.

3. Antonia Lant, "The Curse of the Pharaoh; or, How the Cinema Contracted Egyptomania," *October* 59 (winter 1992): 86–112. Lant writes: "The configuring of Egypt and the cinema expressed cinema's twin realist and fantastic character. By

mining the pharaonic archive, the disturbing potential of the cinema to produce pornography through extremely realistic representations of the human body could be diffused, safely channeled, into a distant yet compelling culture, claimed through the imperialism of Egyptology. Roman Egypt, contemporary Arabian Egypt, and the ideas about the harem, the sheik, Arabian nights, and the vamp could then ride into the cinema on the back of pharaonic Egypt, as it were" (p. 109).

4. John Tagg, *The Burden of Representation: Essays on Photographies and Histories* (Amherst: University of Massachusetts Press, 1988), p. 101.

5. Ibid., p. 165.

6. Edward Said, *Orientalism* (London: Routledge and Kegan Paul, 1978), p. 72; and Homi K. Bhabha, "The Other Question—the Stereotype and Colonial Discourse," *Screen* 24, no. 6 (1983): 23.

7. Judith Butler, "Phantasmatic Identification and the Question of Sex," lecture delivered at University of California, Berkeley, February 13, 1992.

8. Naomi Schor, *"Cartes Postales:* Representing Paris 1900," *Critical Inquiry* 18 (1992): 188–244.

9. I take this phrase from Margaret Whitford's account of Irigaray (*The Ethics of Sexual Difference)* in her excellent book, *Luce Irigaray: Philosophy in the Feminine* (London: Routledge, 1991), p. 125. Whitford writes that

> one could put her position like this. In imaginary and symbolic terms, theory, like language, constitutes a house or a home for men: "men continually seek, construct, create for themselves houses everywhere: grottoes, huts, women, towns, language, concepts, theory, etc." . . . We could say, then, that the theory of the male philosophers is equivalent to the maternal body, the body-matter of woman which forms the imaginary infrastructure of metaphysics. But this still leaves women "homeless" in the symbolic order, and it is this homelessness and dereliction with which Irigaray is concerned.

10. By a coincidence of fate, Blidah was also the place where André Gide "came out" in 1894. Espying the names of Oscar Wilde and Lord Alfred Douglas on the hotel register, he felt compelled to erase his own name. Afterward he felt ashamed of his timidity, changed his itinerary, and returned to the hotel where he awaited them in the lobby.

11. Paul Tabet, *Elissa Rhaïs* (Paris: Bernard Grasset, 1982). This book is the somewhat problematic source of much of my information about Elissa Rhaïs's life and reception. Part "talking cure," part factual biography, the author, by his own account, is Raoul Dahan's son. In the book's opening pages he recounts how he came to hear Rhaïs's story on his father's deathbed. When I interviewed Tabet in Paris, he confirmed the factual basis of his autobiographical narrative but did not offer access to family papers or archives. It is therefore advisable that the historically minded reader treat the account of Rhaïs's life offered here with a certain measure of wariness. Natalie Davis has pointed out that a great deal more might be found out about the "real" Rhaïs and her family if one were to investigate records in Algeria on the Jewish community of Blidah. Given the preponderance of portrayals of Jewish life and customs in Rhaïs's fiction, the question of her Jewish origins and her cultural identification with Jewish North African society would certainly constitute a relevant and interesting dimension of her biography to follow up. Davis has also suggested that we might read Rhaïs's novel *Le Mariage de Hanifa* semiautobiographically insofar as it treats the theme of female literacy (at the heart of the enigma surround-

ing Rhaïs's legitimacy as a writer). Hanifa's sad fate can be construed as a kind of so-cial retribution for her Western education.

12. For more on the role of women in French colonial literature and cinema see Yvonne Kniebiehler and Régine Gontalier's *La Femme au temps des colonies* (Paris: Stock, 1985).

13. Jean Déjeux, "Elissa Rhaïs, conteuse algérienne (1876–1940)," *Revue de l'Occident Musulman et de la Méditerranée* 37 (1984): 47–79.

14. I examine a number of harem texts by these women authors in terms of their projection of an "other" eroticism in chapter 5.

15. Gustave Flaubert, *Salammbo*, trans. E. Powys Mathers (New York: Hart, 1976), p. 55.

16. Elissa Rhaïs, *Kerkeb, danseuse berbère*, in *Le Café-chantant* (Paris: Plon, 1923), pp. 71–72.

17. Roland Lebel, *Histoire de la littérature coloniale en France* (Paris: Librairie Larose, 1931). pp. 211–13 and 86.

18. See Graeme Tytler, *Physiognomy in the European Novel: Faces and Fortunes* (Princeton: Princeton University Press, 1982).

19. Rhaïs, *Kerkeb*, p. 72.

20. Roland Barthes, *The Pleasure of the Text,* trans. Richard Miller (New York: Farrar, Straus and Giroux, 1975), pp. 42–43.

21. Rhaïs, *Kerkeb*, p. 73.

22. Malek Alloula, *The Colonial Harem,* trans. Myrna Godzich and Wlad Godzich (Minneapolis: University of Minnesota Press, 1986), p. 18.

23. Rhaïs, *Le Café-chantant*, pp. 35–36.

24. Sarah Graham-Brown, *Images of Women: The Portrayal of Women in Photography of the Middle East, 1860–1950* (London: Quartet Books, 1988), pp. 180 and 185.

25. Théophile Gautier's *Winter in Russia*, trans. M. M. Ripley (New York: Henry Holt and Company, 1877), pp. 117–18.

26. Elissa Rhaïs, *Noblesse arabe*, in *Le Café-chantant*, p. 206.

27. As cited by Tagg, *The Burden of Representation*, p. 178.

28. Elissa Rhaïs, *Saâda la Marocaine* (Paris: Plon, 1919), p. 1.

29. Hubertine Auclert, *Les Femmes arabes en Algérie* (Paris: Société d'Editions Littéraires, 1900), pp. 1–2.

30. David Prochaska situates this problem of flattening in relation to post-cardization in *Making Algeria French* (Cambridge: Cambridge University Press, 1990), p. 215. He refers to the photographic genre of *scènes et types*, generic representations of certain kinds of people (Arabs, Berbers, Jews, Mozabites), practicing certain kinds of occupations (barbers, musicians, shoeshine boys), participating in certain kinds of activities (*fantasias*, making couscous), and depicted in certain kinds of environments (in front of *gourbis*, "under the tent"). The processes whereby individuals are transformed into collectivities, abstracted from three-dimensional flesh-and-blood people living down the street into two-dimensional consumer goods suitable for mailing to friends in the metropole, is a subject full of fascinating possibilities for future research.

31. Chandra Talpade Mohanty, "Under Western Eyes: Feminist Scholarship and Colonial Discourses," in *Third World Women and the Politics of Feminism,* ed. Chandra Talpade Mohanty, Ann Russo, and Lourdes Torres (Bloomington: Indiana University Press, 1991), pp. 52 and 53.

32. Rhaïs, *Saâda la Marocaine*, p. 139.

33. Steven Hause with Anne R. Kenney, *Women's Suffrage and Social Politics in the French Third Republic* (Princeton: Princeton University Press, 1984), pp. 253–54.

34. For a critically nuanced, informed discussion of how the representation of Maghrebian feminism has fared in the postcolonial period (particularly as articulated by contemporary North African women writers such as Fatima Mernissi, Homa Hoodfar, Rachid Boudjedra, Nabile Farès, Assia Djebar, and Leïla Sebbar), see Winifred Woodhull's *Transfigurations of the Maghreb: Feminism, Decolonization, and Literatures* (Minneapolis: University of Minnesota Press, 1993). Her chapter "Wild Femininity and Historical Countermemory" is both urgent and relevant on the issue of North African feminism's task of negotiating between a bigoted anti-Islam in the West and the hard-line fundamentalist restriction of women's rights in the name of a return to traditional Islam.

35. For a vivid picture of Arab feminist concerns as they evolved from country to country from the 1880s to the present, see the excellent anthology of selected writings edited by Margot Badran and Miriam Cooke, *Opening the Gates: A Century of Arab Feminist Writing* (Bloomington: Indiana University Press, 1990).

36. Lisa Tickner, *The Spectacle of Women: Imagery of the Suffrage Campaign, 1907–14* (London: Chatto and Windus, 1987), pp. 126–27.

37. Pétrus Durel, *La Femme dans les colonies françaises* (Paris: J. Dulon, 1898), p. 154.

38. Rhaïs, *Saâda la Marocaine*, p. 193.

Chapter Seven

1. Judith Butler, "The Lesbian Phallus and the Morphological Imaginary," in *Bodies That Matter: On the Discursive Limits of "Sex"* (New York: Routledge, 1993), pp. 57–92.

2. Ibid., p. 234.

3. Ibid., p. 233.

4. Eve Kosovsky Sedgwick, "Queer Performativity: Henry James's *The Art of the Novel,*" *Gay and Lesbian Quarterly* 1, no. 1 (1993): 15.

5. Sigmund Freud, "Character and Anal Eroticism" (1908), in *Character and Culture*, ed. Philip Rieff (New York: Macmillan, 1963), p. 27.

6. Oscar Wilde, *De Profundis*, in *The Soul of Man and Prison Writings*, ed. Isobel Murray (Oxford: Oxford University Press, 1990), pp. 46–47.

7. Craig Owens, "The Medusa Effect; or, The Specular Ruse," in *Beyond Recognition: Representation, Power, and Culture*, ed. Scott Bryson et al. (Berkeley and Los Angeles: University of California Press, 1992), p. 195.

8. Sue-Ellen Case, in *Feminism and Theatre* (New York: Routledge, 1988), p. 57, informs us that Hrotsvit did enjoy a certain popularity in London during the years of the suffragette movement (see above, chap. 6, n. 45). The first major production of *Paphnutius* was directed by Edith Craig (daughter of Ellen Terry and sister of Gordon) in London in 1914. The play was staged by Edith Craig's own ensemble, the Pioneer Players, with Ellen Terry as Thaïs.

9. Nineteenth-century Cleopatras were legion: there were particularly celebrated versions by Delphine de Girardin, Arsène Houssaye, Pushkin, Swinburne and Théophile Gautier, Rider Haggard, and countless others.

10. Peter Wollen, "Fashion/Orientalism/the Body," *New Formations* 6 (spring 1987): 18–19.

11. Mario Praz, *The Romantic Agony*, trans. Angus Davidson (London: Oxford University Press, 1970), p. 397.

12. Lucy Hughes-Hallet, *Cleopatra: Histories, Dreams, and Distortions* (New York: Harper and Row, 1990), p. 280.

13. Alan Sinfield, *Faultlines: Cultural Materialism and the Politics of Dissident Reading* (Berkeley and Los Angeles: University of California Press, 1992), p. 78.

14. Pierre Loti, *Aziyadé* (Paris: Calmann-Lévy, 1987), p. 102.

15. Edward Said, *Orientalism* (New York: Vintage, 1979), p. 103.

16. A Lacanian version of the Oriental "woman with a phallus" theme may be found in a gloss on Lacan's "The Signification of the Phallus (1958; in *Ecrits: A Selection*, trans. Alan Sheridan [London: Tavistock, 1977], pp. 289–91) by Mikkel Borch-Jacobsen. In pointing out that Lacan never fully explains why the phallus is expressive of masculine power, Borch-Jacobsen refers to the fact that Cleopatra and Sémiramis have historically wielded the phallic scepter. Citing Lacan, who states in his article, "It is therefore because it is also the scepter that the phallus prevails," Borch-Jacobsen remarks: "This amounts to saying that we will never know why the 'scepter' is phallic: masculine in fact, it is not so by right (the scepter, as the 'signifier of power,' can legitimately be held by a Cleopatra or a Semiramis)" (Mikkel Borch-Jacobson, *Lacan: The Absolute Master*, trans. Douglas Brick (Stanford: Stanford University Press, 1991), pp. 213–14.

17. Joan de Jean cites François-Jean Desthieux's 1937 *Femmes damnées*, where he insists that "Renée Vivien didn't only imitate Sappho: she certainly believed herself to be Sappho reincarnate." See Joan de Jean, *Fictions of Sappho, 1546–1937* (Chicago: University of Chicago Press, 1989), p. 283.

18. On the issue of sapphism's relation to Orientalism, Jean Goujon writes in his postface to Renée Vivien, *Le Jardin turc: Prose inédite suivi de dix lettres à Kérimé* (Paris: A L'Ecart, 1982), p. 34: "Kérimé rapidly became the romantic 'love from afar' that Vivien had dreamed of for so long, while at the same time symbolizing this Orient that had already fascinated the entire 19th century, from Chateaubriand to Nerval, and from Flaubert to Loti. To object to Mytilène, would be to lose sight of the fact that, beyond the necessary references and pilgrimages, Sappho's island, far from being for Vivien a bastion of Hellenism, took the form of a door opening onto an Orient of love and pleasure."

19. Karla Jay, *The Amazon and the Page: Natalie Clifford Barney and Renée Vivien* (Bloomington: Indiana University Press, 1988), p. 100.

20. Terry Castle's resonant notion of the "apparitional lesbian" is broadly applied to the preponderance of lesbian novels whose plots involve "fantastical" settings or female phantoms. See *The Apparitional Lesbian* (New York: Columbia University Press, 1993).

21. Natalie Barney, *The One Who Is Legion, or A.D.'s After-Life* (Orono, Maine: University of Maine Printing Office, 1987), p. 97.

22. Cléo de Mérode, *Le Ballet de ma vie* (Paris: Editions Pierre Horay, 1955), pp. 46–47.

23. Case, *Feminism and Theatre*, p. 53.

24. Homi Bhabha, "The Other Question: Colonial Discourse and the Stereo-

type," in *The Politics of Theory*, ed. Francis Barker (Colchester: University of Essex Press, 1983), p. 18.

25. Lacan ventriloquizes Cleopatra's nose in "La Chose freudienne," to emphasize contingency. If Cleopatra's nose had been slightly shorter, according to the Pascalian lesson, the course of human history would have been different. Antony would not have fallen in love with her, and the Roman Empire would have maintained its control over Egypt. Lacan writes: "In any case, it is not enough to judge of your defeat to see me escape first from the dungeon of the fortress in which you are so sure you have me secured by situating me not in you yourselves, but in being itself? I wander about in what you regard as being the least true essence: in the dream, in the way the most far-fetched conceit, the most grotesque nonsense of the joke defies sense, in chance, not in its law, but in its contingence *and I never do more to change the face of the world than when I give it the profile of Cleopatra's nose*" ("The Freudian Thing," in *Ecrits*, p. 122; emphasis added).

26. In an interesting article entitled "Isabelle Eberhardt: Portrait of the Artist as a Young Nomad," Hedi Abdel-Jaoud discusses Eberhardt's enactment of the Islamic doctrine of the *hejra*, defined as "a radical departure from beliefs of the past." In *Yale French Studies* 83 (1993): 93–117.

27. Eberhardt, "The Rival," in *The Oblivion Seekers and Other Writings*, trans. Paul Bowles (San Francisco: City Lights Books, 1975), p. 60.

28. Eberhardt, "Pencilled Notes," in *Oblivion Seekers*, p. 68.

29. Wayne Koestenbaum, *The Queen's Throat: Opera, Homosexuality, and the Mystery of Desire* (New York: Poseidon Press, 1993), pp. 84–85.

30. Myriam Harry, *Mon amie Lucie Delarue-Mardrus* (Paris: Ariane, 1946), pp. 8–9.

31. On Orientalist cross-dressing see Marjorie Garber's chapter "The Chic of Araby: Transvestism and the Erotics of Appropriation," in *Vested Interests: Cross-dressing and Cultural Anxiety* (New York: Routledge, 1992), pp. 304–52.

32. Henriette Celarié, *Nos soeurs musulmanes: Scènes de la vie du désert* (Paris: Hachette, 1925), p. 207.

33. Meaghan Morris, "Panorama: The Live, the Dead, and the Living," in *Island in the Stream: Myths of Place in Australian Culture*, ed. Paul Foss (Sydney: Pluto Press, 1988), p. 173.

34. Leslie Thornton has recently completed a feature-length film of Eberhardt's biography entitled *The Great Invisible* that I have unfortunately not yet had the opportunity to view.

35. See Mary Ann Doane's chapter "The Retreat of Signs and the Failure of Words: Leslie Thornton's Adynata," in *Femmes Fatales: Feminism, Film Theory, Psychoanalysis* (New York, Routledge, 1991), p. 178.

36. I am paraphrasing Owens here. The exact quote and its context are from the essay on Barbara Kruger entitled "The Medusa Effect," p. 199. The passage reads as follows:

> Kruger's work, then, engages in neither social commentary nor ideological critique (the traditional activities of politically motivated artists: consciousness-raising). Her art has no moralistic or didactic ambition. Rather, she stages for the viewer the techniques whereby the stereotype produces subjection, interpellates him/her as subject. With one crucial difference: in Kruger's double inversion, the viewer is led ultimately

to reject the work's address, this double postulation, this contradictory construction. There is a risk, of course, that this rejection will take the form of yet another gesture— a gesture of refusal. It can, however, be an active renunciation. Against the immobility of the pose, Kruger proposes the mobilization of the spectator.

37. Sinfield, *Faultlines*, p. 78.

38. Judith Butler, "Performative Acts and Gender Constitution: An Essay in Phenomenology and Feminist Theory," in *Performing Feminisms: Feminist Critical Theory and Theater* (Baltimore: Johns Hopkins University Press, 1990), pp. 270–82.

Chapter Eight

1. Emile Zola, *Nana*, trans. unknown (New York: Random House, n.d.), pp. 179–80.

2. Marcel Proust, *Swann's Way*, in *Remembrance of Things Past*, trans. C. K. Scott Moncrieff and Terence Kilmartin, vol. 1 (New York: Vintage Books, 1982), p. 213.

3. Ibid., p. 83.

4. Ibid., p. 415.

5. See "Le Parc Swann I," in Marcel Proust, *A la recherche du temps perdu* (Paris: Gallimard, 1987), 1:845.

6. *Beauty* is also the word interspersed throughout the notorious scene of homosexual coupling in *Sodom et Gomorrah I*. Though Proust has been criticized for this "monstrous" depiction of sodomitical lovemaking, most famously by André Gide and most recently by Eve Kosovsky Sedgwick, one could argue that these critics had an insufficient grasp of the Proustian sense of beauty.

7. Proust, *Swann's Way*, p. 80. See Richard Dyer's *Stars* (1979; London: British Film Institute, 1998) for a discussion of the burgeoning star system at the turn of the century. His discussion "Stars and 'Character'" is particularly relevant to this chapter.

8. Jean Lorrain, *Une Femme par jour* (Saint-Cyr-sur-Loire: Christian Pirot, 1983), pp. 136–37.

9. Elizabeth de Gramont, *Pomp and Circumstance*, trans. Brian W. Downs (New York: Jonathan Cape and Harrison Smith, 1929), p. 266.

10. Peter Wollen, "Out of the Past: Fashion/Orientalism/the Body," in *Raiding the Icebox: Reflections on Twentieth-Century Culture* (Bloomington: Indiana University Press, 1993), pp. 1–34; Michael Moon, "Flaming Closets," *October* 51 (winter 1989): 19–54.

11. Elizabeth Wood has coined the term "sapphonics" for the equivalent effect in theater of Sarah Bernhardt's acting, that is, for a voice that resonates "in sonic space as lesbian difference and desire" ("Sapphonics," in *Queering the Pitch: The New Gay and Lesbian Musicology*, ed. Philip Brett, Elizabeth Wood, and Gary C. Thomas [New York: Routledge, 1993], p. 28). She writes further on (pp. 40–41),

> What does it mean that [Olive] Fremstad and [Emma] Calvé "may have belonged, like [Mary] Garden, to those who live in the parts they play"? What can we learn of the Sapphonic landscape from roles these singers "lived" in public?
>   In both standard and new repertory, Calvé, Fremstad and Garden built careers as actor-singers on powerful, seductive interpretations of transgressive heroines and travesty "breeches" roles. Each defied stage convention in her uses of dramatic realism, revealing costume, and often scandalous publicity.

12. Natalie Barney, *Quelques portraits-souvenir de femmes* (Paris: Librairie Paul Ollendorf, 1900).

13. Liane de Pougy, *Idylle saphique* (Paris: J. C. Lattès, 1979). It is probable that Natalie Barney ghostwrote the Sarah Bernhardt chapter of this novel.

14. Judith Butler, "Gender Melancholia," draft of paper presented at the Division 39 Meetings of the American Psychological Association, New York, April 1993. A revised version of these arguments was published as "Melancholy Gender/Refused Identification," chapter 5 of *The Psychic Life of Power* (Stanford: Stanford University Press, 1997), pp. 132–50.

15. Sigmund Freud, *The Ego and the Id,* trans. Joan Riviere, ed. James Strachey (New York: Norton, 1960), p. 19.

16. Judith Butler, *Bodies That Matter: On the Discursive Limits of "Sex"* (New York: Routledge, 1993), p. 235.

17. Freud, *Ego and Id,* p. 20.

18. Colette, *Mes apprentissages,* in *Romans, récits, souvenirs (1920–1940)* (Paris: Robert Laffont, 1989), p. 1269. Quoted here: Colette, *My Apprenticeships and Music-Hall Sidelights,* trans. Helen Beauclerk (London: Secker and Warburg, 1957), pp. 129–30.

19. Karla Jay, *The Amazon and the Page: Natalie Clifford Barney and Renée Vivien* (Bloomington: Indiana University Press, 1988), p. 39.

20. Barney, *Quelques portraits-souvenirs,* p. 14.

21. Ibid., p. 39.

22. Jean Chalon, *Portrait of a Seductress: The World of Natalie Barney,* trans. Carol Barko (New York: Crown, 1976), p. 37.

23. Ibid. p. 33.

24. Natalie Clifford Barney, *Traits et portraits* (Paris: Mercure de France, 1963), pp. 209, 36.

25. Richard Wollheim, *Sigmund Freud* (New York: Viking Press, 1971), p. 231.

26. *The Seminar of Jacques Lacan,* book 1: *Freud's Papers on Technique, 1953–1954,* ed. Jacques-Alain Miller, trans. John Forrester (New York: Norton, 1988), pp. 204–5.

27. *The Seminar of Jacques Lacan,* book 7: *The Ethics of Psychoanalysis, 1959–1960,* ed. Jacques-Alain Miller, trans. Dennis Porter (New York: Norton, 1992), p. 10.

28. Walter Benjamin, "Fate and Character," in *One Way Street and Other Writings,* trans. Edmund Jephcott and Kingsley Shorter (London: Verso, 1985), p. 131. Benjamin wrote:

> Physiognomic signs, like other mantic symbols, serve for the ancients primarily the exploration of fate, in accordance with the dominance of the pagan belief in guilt. The study of physiognomy, like comedy, was a manifestation of the new age of genius. Modern physiognomics reveals its connection with the old art of divination in the unfruitful, morally evaluative accent of its concepts, as also in the striving for analytical complexity. In precisely this respect the ancient and medieval physiognomists saw things more clearly, in recognizing that character can only be grasped through a small number of morally indifferent concepts, like those, for example, that the doctrine of temperaments tried to identify.

Chapter Nine

1. Gustave Flaubert, *Salammbô,* trans. A. J. Krailsheimer (1977; New York: Penguin, 1983), p. 166.

2. In 1925 Myriam Harry would echo this idea of a the belly dance as serpentinated national fetish when she described women dancers in Tunis:

> At each movement, the long ribbons of her silver belt unfolded like serpents; her arms twisted, voluptuous swans' necks, and her long hair was either trailing on the ground or apparently coiling itself around an invisible, beloved body. . . . After the Circassian woman, the others took their turn, shaking their flanks, dancing and redancing the eternal dance of the Arabs, the dance of the sex and the belly, which is perhaps a national symbol.

Tunis la blanche (Paris: Arthème Fayard, 1925), pp. 63–64.

3. For a pointed characterization of the Lacanian "gaze" (distinguished from Freudian scopophilia or the Sartrean look), see Elizabeth Grosz's entry "Voyeurism/Exhibitionism/the Gaze," in *Feminism and Psychoanalysis: A Critical Dictionary,* ed. Elizabeth Wright (Oxford: Basil Blackwell, 1992), pp. 447–50.

4. On the "colonial real," see chapter 6, note 1. See also Elizabeth Grosz, *Jacques Lacan: A Feminist Introduction* (New York: Routledge, 1990).

5. On the *stéréorama mouvant* of the World's Fair 1900, whose highlighted attraction was a simulated package tour to Algeria (replete with belly dancing and shopping excursions to the Casbah), see Rhonda Garelick, "Bayadères, Stéréorama, and Vahat-Loukoum," in *Spectacles of Realism: Gender, Body, Genre,* ed. Margaret Cohen and Christopher Prendergast (Minneapolis: University of Minnesota Press, 1995), pp. 294–319, and in particular the section "'A Thousand Marvelous Journeys without Moving a Step': Attractions at the Fair" (pp. 307–13).

6. In sculpture I am thinking specifically of Rupert Carabin's art nouveau rendering of Loïe Fuller performing "La danse du serpent."

7. Ernest Gellner, the section "Ethnomethodology: The Re-enchantment Industry, or the Californian Way of Subjectivity," in *Spectacles and Predicaments: Essays in Social Theory* (1979; Cambridge: Cambridge University Press, 1991), pp. 41–64.

> The pre-packaged ready-cooked and so very contingent subjectivity is similarly convenient; is, so to speak, an industrial, supermarket, ready-to-eat subjectivity. You just warm it up. When Max Weber spoke scathingly of the intellectuals who furnished their private chapels with spiritual exotica and indulged in intellectual antiquarianism, he clearly had in mind an élite hobby, which presupposed privileged access to leisure and resources. It was hand-made Re-enchantment for the Few. But one of the advantages of the affluent society, of the further advance in the equalisation of conditions, is that re-enchantment itself is now mass-produced, standardised, and rationalized. Subjectivity, like the Mexican peasant's meal, is no longer produced in the mud hut of the pueblo; specialists will prepare and package for mass-consumption a variant of it which, when all is said and done is almost as palatable and perhaps much more hygienic. So let us welcome the day when we can be reassured of the existence of our own subjectivity, and be supplied with tools for locating or erecting it, in a way which is no longer restricted to a privileged elite, nursing its nostalgia for enchantment like a badge of rank; but, on the contrary, which is supplied so as to make both the nostalgia and its solace available to *all.* (P. 64)

8. T. J. Clark has pointed out to me that the dates of Picasso's Algiers paintings coincide, perhaps not accidentally, with the beginning of the Algerian Revolution. It would be interesting to explore in another context an interpretation of the paintings that would take the specific historical backdrop of the Revolution into account.

9. Leo Steinberg, "The Algerian Women and Picasso at Large," in *Other Criteria:*

Confrontations with Twentieth-Century Art (New York: Oxford University Press, 1979), p. 177.

10. Ibid., p. 183.

11. Flaubert, *Salammbô*, p. 174.

12. E. H. Gombrich, *The Sense of Order: A Study in the Psychology of Decorative Art* (New York: Columbia University Press, 1979), p. 137.

13. Lacan, "Sexuality in the Defiles of the Signifier," in *The Four Fundamental Concepts of Psycho-analysis,* trans. Alan Sheridan, ed. Jacques-Alain Miller (New York: Norton, 1978), pp. 155–56.

14. Steinberg, "Algerian Women and Picasso," p. 185.

15. Ibid., pp. 185–86.

16. Gustave Flaubert, *Flaubert in Egypt: A Sensibility on Tour,* trans. and ed. Francis Steegmuller (Chicago: Academy Chicago Limited, 1979), pp. 221–22. Steegmuller excerpts and translates this section of "Hérodias" in a note to the passage in Flaubert's Egyptian journal where he describes the bee dance.

17. Ibid., p. 220.

There are multiple literary, cultural, and psychosexual interpretations of the "bee-dance" in recent literary criticism. See Edward Said, *Orientalism* (New York: Random House, 1978); Dennis Porter, *Haunted Journeys: Desire and Transgression in European Travel Writing* (Princeton: Princeton University Press, 1991); Charles Bernheimer, *Figures of Ill-Repute: Representing Prostitution in Nineteenth-Century France* (Cambridge: Harvard University Press, 1989); Lisa Lowe, *Critical Terrains: French and British Orientalisms* (Ithaca: Cornell University Press, 1991). Most recently, in an essay entitled "Vacation Cruises, or the Homoerotics of Orientalism," Joe Boone reminds us through a critique of Said's discussion of the bee-dance, that the "*first* exotic dancer to catch Flaubert's eye is not the female Kuchuk but a *male* dancer and well-known catamite, Hasan el-Belbeissi, whose sexualized pantomime, female garb, and kohl-painted eyes, as Flaubert writes home to his friend Louis Bouilhet, 'put additional spice into a thing already quite clear in itself.'" Stressing Flaubert's connection between Hasan's bee-dance, the availability of boys, and his own sense of obligation to sample sodomy while on tour in the Orient, Boone avoids concluding, as one might, that Kuchuk's bee-dance is simply a surrogate for the homoerotic template, but points out "how contact with different cultural attitudes opens one's perception of *the possible*—and *this* possibility, as references throughout Flaubert's papers reveal, becomes a newly welcome source of stimulation" (p. 8 of manuscript copy). An abridged version of this text appeared in *PMLA* 110, No. 1 (January 1995): 89–107.

18. Steinberg, "Algerian Women and Picasso," pp. 189–90.

19. Gustave Flaubert, "Hérodias," in *Trois contes* (Paris: Garnier-Flammarion, 1986), p. 109.

20. Steinberg, "Algerian Women and Picasso," pp. 207–8.

21. Flaubert, *Flaubert in Egypt,* p. 121.

22. See, as well, the analysis of this passage of the Goncourt journal in Zeynep Celik and Leila Kinney, "Ethnography and Exhibitionism at the Expositions Universelles," *Assemblage* 13 (1990): 35–59 (p. 46 in particular). The authors situate the fashion for belly dancing in relation to the broader culture of popular Parisian dance forms (the cancan, the quadrille, the *chahut,* etc.) in addition to theorizing the "exhibitionism" of Orientalism in the staging of universal expositions during the nineteenth and early twentieth centuries.

23. Edmond Goncourt and Jules de Goncourt, *Journal: Mémoires de la vie littéraire*, vol. 3 (1887–96) (Aylesbury, Great Britain: Editions Robert Laffont, 1989), p. 290.

24. Ibid., p. 287. See Linda Nochlin, "The Origin without an Original," *October* 37 (summer 1986): 76–86.

25. Steinberg, "Algerian Women and Picasso," p. 208.

26. Goncourt and Goncourt, *Journal,* p. 290.

27. Ibid., p. 753.

28. Théophile Gautier, *Voyage pittoresque en Algérie* (1845) (Geneva: Librairie Droz, 1973), p. 76.

29. Homi Bhabha, "Of Mimicry and Man: The Ambivalence of Colonial Discourse," in *October: The First Decade, 1976–1986,* ed. Annette Michelson et al. (Cambridge: MIT Press, 1987), pp. 317–25.

30. Ibid., p. 76.

31. Elissa Rhaïs, *Saâda la Marocaine* (Paris: Plon, 1919), p. 163.

32. Flaubert, *Flaubert in Egypt,* p. 220.

33. See Guy de Maupassant, *Au soleil* (1884), in *Maupassant au Maghreb* (Paris: Le Sycomore, 1982): "Elles vont ainsi, l'une vers l'autre. Quand elles se rencontrent, leurs mains se touchent; elles semblent frémir; leurs tailles se renversent, laissant traîner un grand voile de dentelle qui va de la coiffure aux pieds. Elles se frôlent, cambrées en arrière, comme pâmées dans un joli mouvement de colombes amoureuses. Le grand voile bat comme une aile. Puis, redressées soudain, redevenues impassibles, elles se séparent; et chacune continue jusqu'à la ligne des spectateurs son glissement lent et boîtillant" (p. 112).

34. Malek Alloula, *The Colonial Harem,* trans. Myrna Godzich and Wlad Godzich (Minneapolis: University of Minnesota Press, 1986), p. 5. Alloula's book can be easily criticized, indeed has been criticized, for its lack of historical precisions and blinkered sexism. The female models are left anonymous and undocumented: no mention is made of their vastly differing facial expressions (mutinous and resentful of the camera's eye in one collective harem picture [p. 33]), and nothing is made of the fact that many of the same models reappear, some in vastly different contexts and guises (i.e. the chaste young girl in a "scènes et types" lovers shot [p. 43] is astonishingly reincarnated later on as the lasciviously smiling, bare-breasted, tattooed model of "la belle Mauresque" [p. 124]). Individual photographers are amalgamated into a composite figure of *the* colonial photographer whose gaze is assumed to be homogenous and whose camera seems to operate according to a common point of view that uniformly embodies colonial ideology (see Alloula's footnote 26). The albums and photographic agencies from which the cards were selected are insufficiently described. The messages on the cards are haphazardly reported (with little attention to the class, gender, or geographical status of addressees). A colonial phantasm is put on the divan as if it were an anonymous, poststructuralist subject, and no explanation is given for the absence of male, homoerotic counterparts to the female models (for which there was a corresponding photographic archive, though perhaps more underground). On the other hand, Alloula's brilliant configuration of psychoanalytic interpretations of scopic eroticism and the politics of decolonization (prefigured in Franz Fanon's chapter "Algeria Unveiled," in *A Dying Colonialism,* trans. Haakon Chevalier [New York: Grove Press, 1967] must be recognized as a kind of landmark in cultural studies, particu-

larly in light of when the book came out in France (1981) under the shadow of Roland Barthes's spellbinding, idiosyncratic *Camera Lucida* (1980), trans. Richard Howard (New York: Hill and Wang, 1982).

Chapter Ten

1. Manthia Diawara, "*Noirs* by *Noirs:* Toward a New Realism in Black Cinema," in *Shades of Noir,* ed. Joan Copjec (London: Verso, 1993), p. 262.

2. Leo Bersani and Ulysse Dutoit, excerpt from *Caravaggio's Secrets* (Cambridge: MIT Press, 1998), in *October* 82 (fall 1997): 17.

3. Edgar Morin, *Le Cinéma ou l'homme imaginaire* (Paris: Edition de Minuit, 1958).

4. Louis Delluc, "Photogénie" (1920), in *Ecrits cinématographiques,* vol. 1, in *Le Cinéma et les cinéastes,* ed. Pierre Lherminier (Paris: Cinématheque française, 1985), pp. 35–39.

5. Richard Dyer's chapter "The Light of the World" takes up the "economy of race" built into the technical procedures for creating "the glow of white women" in photography and film. Distinguishing glow (characteristic of blond hair, or white skin, which tends to absorb light) from shine (which bounces off skin, especially dark skin), Dyer demonstrates that "the promotion of black female beauty" could never be "modelled on glowing white ideals" (Richard Dyer, *White* [London: Routledge, 1997], p. 122).

6. Jacques Lacan, *The Four Fundamental Concepts of Psychoanalysis,* ed. Jacques-Alain Miller, trans. Alan Sheridan (New York: Norton, 1977), p. 96.

7. Roland Barthes, "William von Gloeden" (1978), in *The Responsibility of Forms: Critical Essays on Music, Art, and Representation,* trans. Richard Howard (Berkeley and Los Angeles: University of California Press, 1985), p. 196.

8. Malek Alloula, *The Colonial Harem,* trans. Myrna Godzich and Wlad Godzich (Minneapolis: University of Minnesota Press, 1986), p. 78.

9. Rachid Boudjedra, *Les 1001 années de la nostalgie* (Paris: Gallimard, 1979), pp. 223–41.

10. Marcel Ohms, "L'Imaginaire colonial au cinéma," in *Images et colonies: Iconographie et propagande coloniale sur l'Afrique française de 1880 à 1962* (Nanterre: Bibliothèque de Documentation Internationale, 1993), p. 105.

11. Ibid.

12. Gilles Deleuze and Félix Guattari, *Mille plateaux (*Paris: Editions de Minuit, 1980), pp. 205–9.

13. Ibid., pp. 216, 218.

14. Jean Epstein, "Grossissement" (1921), in *Ecrits sur le cinéma,* vol. 1 (Paris: Editions Seghers, 1974); trans. as "Magnification and Other Writings," by Stuart Liebman, *October* 3 (spring 1977): 11. I quote Liebman's translation here; subsequent translations from Epstein are my own.

15. Epstein, *Ecrits sur le cinéma,* p. 143.

16. Ibid., p. 93.

17. Ibid., p. 131.

18. Georges Bataille, "Le Coupable," in *Oeuvres complètes* (Paris, Gallimard, 1970), 5:500, as cited by Michel Surya, *Georges Bataille. La mort à l'oeuvre* (Paris: Librairie Séguier, 1987), p. 263.

19. Robert Smithson, "Hidden Trails in Art" (1969), in Eugenie Tsai, *Robert Smithson Unearthed* (New York: Columbia University Press, 1991), pp. 83–84.

20. Jean Tharaud and Jérôme Tharaud, *Paris-Saigon dans l'Azur* (Paris: Plon, 1932), p. 17.

21. Ibid., p. 79.

22. Ibid., p. 197.

23. Mary Louise Pratt, *Imperial Eyes: Travel Writing and Transculturation* (New York: Routledge, 1992), pp. 202–4.

24. Epstein, *Ecrits sur le cinéma*, pp. 94–95.

25. Jean Tharaud and Jérôme Tharaud, *Marrakech ou les seigneurs de l'Atlas* (Paris: Plon-Nourrit, 1920), pp. 274–75.

26. Lacan, *Four Fundamental Concepts*, p. 96.

27. André Malraux, *La Reine de Saba: Une "aventure géologique"* (Paris: Gallimard, 1993), p. 45.

28. Ibid., p. 73.

29. Le Corbusier, *La Ville radieuse* (Paris: Editions Vincent Fréal, 1964), p. 231. *La Ville radieuse* was prefaced by a heroic portrait of the French pilot Coste celebrating his Atlantic crossing of 1931. Le Corbusier also paid homage to the airplane in *Aircraft,* published in 1934.

30. Glissant is evoked by Jean Bernabé, Patrick Chamoiseau, and Raphaël Confiant in *Eloge de la créolité* (Paris: Gallimard, 1989), p. 103.

Chapter Eleven

1. Edith Wharton, *In Morocco* (New York: Scribner, 1920), pp. viii–ix.

2. Louis Bertrand, *Le Mirage oriental* (Paris: Perrin, 1934), pp. 3–8. This book is rather remarkable as an early example of antitourist literature. Bertrand was a follower of Emile Zola, and his text bears the mark of Zola's stylistic influence in its use of a naturalist Orientalism luxuriating in the enumeration and documentation of scrofulous detail.

3. Jean Tharaud and Jérôme Tharaud, *Rabat ou les heures marocaines* (Paris: Emile-Paul Frères, 1918), pp. 61–62.

4. Jean and Jérôme Tharaud, *Fez ou les bourgeois d'Islam* (Paris: Plon, 1933), pp. 19–20. This nontransformative view of Moroccan culture is reiterated in another variation on the above theme: "In Fez, there is certainly a culture, but this culture, purely exterior and formal, hardly transforms the intelligent spirit" (p. 23).

5. Abdelkebir Khatibi, *Figures de l'étranger* (Paris: Denoël, 1987), p. 19. In French: "[L]a France classique est une unité imaginaire entre la langue courtisane, le pouvoir charismatique et le nationalisme théologique."

6. The expression "virtual tourism" is coined by Anne Friedberg as a way of talking about the "mobilized gaze" that purchased experience by visual proxy common to early cinema, tourism, and the commercial arcade. See her *Window Shopping: Cinema and the Postmodern* (Berkeley and Los Angeles: University of California Press, 1993).

7. Paul Bowles, *The Sheltering Sky* (1949; New York: Vintage, 1977), pp. 3–5.

8. Paul Rabinow, *French Modern: Norms and Forms of the Social Environment* (Cambridge: MIT Press, 1989).

9. Mary Louise Pratt, *Imperial Eyes: Travel Writing and Transculturation* (New York: Routledge, 1992), p. 2.

10. Georges Van Den Abbeele, *Travel as Metaphor* (Minneapolis: University of Minnesota Press, 1992), p. xiv.

11. Dean MacCannell, *The Tourist: A New Theory of the Leisure Class* (1976; New York: Schocken, 1986), p. 183.

12. Meaghan Morris, "Banality in Cultural Studies," in *Logics of Television,* ed. Patricia Mellencamp (Bloomington: Indiana University Press, 1990), p. 14.

13. Jean Bonnerot, *Jérôme et Jean Tharaud: Leur oeuvre* (Paris: La Nouvelle Revue Critique, 1927), p. 27.

14. Jean Bonnerot writes of the reception of *La Fête arabe* that "P. Lasserre leur a reproché de faire du Fromentin, déclarant que 'là où Chateaubriand, Flaubert, Théophile Gautier et autres avaient passé, pour longtemps on ne passerait plus parce que l'azur et le vermillon de la palette littéraire étaient fatigués'" (ibid., p. 26).

15. Michel Foucault, "La Peinture photogénique" (1975), in *Dits et écrits, 1954–1988* (Paris: Gallimard, 1994), 2:710.

16. Quoted in ibid. p. 708.

17. Ibid. p. 256.

18. Walter Benjamin, "A Short History of Photography," in *One Way Street and Other Writings,* trans. Edmund Jephcott and Kingsley Shorter (London: Verso, 1985), pp. 243–44.

19. Tharaud and Tharaud, *Fez,* pp. 72–73; emphasis added.

20. Tharaud and Tharaud, *Dingley. L'illustre écrivain* (Paris: Plon, 1906), p. 104.

21. Ibid., p. 105.

22. George Orwell, "Rudyard Kipling" (1942), in *The Penguin Essays of George Orwell* (London: Penguin, 1984), p. 209.

23. André Chevrillon, *Three Studies in English Literature: Kipling, Galsworthy, Shakespeare,* trans. Florence Simmonds (London: William Heinemann, 1923), p. 39.

24. Sara Suleri, *The Rhetoric of English India* (Chicago: University of Chicago Press), p. 112.

25. Tharaud and Tharaud, *Rabat,* p. 68.

26. Tharaud and Tharaud, *Dingley,* p. 229.

27. Ibid., p. 104.

28. The work of Paul Rabinow, Gwendolyn Wright, Pat Morton, and most recently Jean-Louis Cohen and Monique Eleb-Vidal has recently illuminated the history of Lyautey's colonial urbanism in Morocco.

29. Tharaud and Tharaud, *La Fête arabe* (Paris: Emile-Paul, 1912), p. 253.

30. Ibid., p. 287.

31. See Janet L. Abu-Lughod's case study *Rabat: Urban Apartheid in Morocco* (Princeton: Princeton University Press, 1980). Abu-Lughod shows that although French Moroccan planners may have been more sensitive to preserving local architectural traditions than they had been in Algeria, they did little to prevent what the author characterizes as the "concretization of the caste city" (p. 3).

32. Rabinow, *French Modern,* p. 311. On a more concrete level, Rabinow gives an incisive rundown of Lyautey's protectorate urban policies, which he usefully distinguishes from the doctrine of assimilative colonization:

> The society Lyautey sought to create, the society he hoped would spring to life in his new cities, was doubly hierarchical. Moroccan society exhibited a viable hierarchy: the requisite social forms existed, as did the range of virtues necessary to activate

them. During the course of Moroccan history, an order had gradually defined social and spatial forms. Lyautey's adherence to the protectorate form (rather than to a doctrine of assimilative colonization) derived from this evaluation; the task consisted in identifying and strengthening these existing social forms and practices. He laid down the following imperatives: "Vex not tradition, leave custom be. Never forget that in every society there is a class to be governed, and a natural-born ruling class upon whom all depends. Link their interests to ours." It was time to introduce a technical modernity, with its advantages of hygiene and science, so as to reawaken Morocco's dormant energies without destroying its social forms. (Ibid., p. 285)

33. Tharaud and Tharaud, *Marrakech ou les seigneurs de l'Atlas* (Paris: Plon, 1920), pp. 98, 103, 114.

34. Rabinow, *French Modern*, p. 300.

Chapter Twelve

1. Postcoloniality, as I would define it, refers to a condition of being-in-identity linked to specific historical, social, material, racial, and class situations. Postcolonialism, by contrast, can be said to apply to a body of theoretical and historical work that, in the last decade, has branched out from "subaltern studies" (as practiced by Gayatri Chakravorty Spivak, Gyan Prakash, Dipesh Chakravorty, or Homi Bhabha) to include the critique of Orientalism, new minority discourses, and Fanonism as a reminted *tiermondiste* idiom (particularly in former French colonies and protectorates).

2. Homi K. Bhabha, *The Location of Culture* (London: Routledge, 1994), pp. 248–49.

3. Ibid., p. 254.

4. Raphaël Confiant, "Confiant sur son volcan," *Magazine Littéraire*, November 1994, p. 77.

5. Philip K. Dick, *Do Androids Dream of Electric Sheep* (New York: Ballantine Books, 1982), p. 12.

6. Cynthia Kadohata, *In the Heart of the Valley of Love* (New York: Penguin, 1992), p. 209.

7. Scott Bukatman, *Terminal Identity: The Virtual Subject in Postmodern Science Fiction* (Durham: Duke University Press, 1993), p. 156: "So cyberspace is a financial space, a space of capital; it is a social space; it is responsive; it can be modified; it is a place of testing and the arena for new technological rites of passage (Tomas). . . . The passage of the subject into the pixels and bytes of 'invisible' terminal space addresses the massive redeployment of power within telematic culture."

8. Donna Haraway, "A Manifesto for Cyborgs," in *Coming to Terms: Feminism, Theory, Politics,* ed. Elizabeth Weed (New York: Routledge, 1989), pp. 175 and 174 respectively.

9. As Janet Bergstrom comments,

> *Blade Runner* has the look, sound and ambience of the totally designed perceptual experience. It is built up out of unnaturally colored beams of light and glowing neon shapes that activate parts of the screen space, filtered through haze, shadows, smoke, steam and rain. People use degraded, hybrid languages, and costumes, to move in a disorderly, decaying urban-industrial environment. Characters emerge out of this delirium, sometimes competing with their environment for the spectator's attention. Anachronistic elements from the past are able to invade and disrupt, if not ultimately

control, this "future" city. The iconography of *Blade Runner,* and also of *Alien* and *The Road Warrior,* is striking in its use of composite figures that condense the obsolete and the technologically advanced, the biomorphic and the mechanical. For example, a flying machine drifts through the night skies in *Blade Runner* resembling both a heavily armored, metallic blimp and an archaic, deep-sea puff fish, with spiked feelers protruding from its sides. Flashing lights are strung over its surface, emphasizing the "ribs" of its skeleton. An irregular patch of light is located where a fish's eye would be. This "creature" carries an electronic billboard advertising the off-world colonies, while a reassuring male voice repeats a slogan that reinforces the image verbally.

. . . The status of characters within this complex scheme is not obvious; they seem to rise and fall in importance, like an irregular pulse. Part of the rhythm of the differentiating characters decor is tied to strong generic expectations: there will be characters, but they might not be human. Androids, replicants and aliens are not human, but more or less, depending on the film, they can approximate human physical, mental and emotional characteristics.

. . . Where the basic fact of identity as a human is suspect and subject to transformation into its opposite, the representation of sexual identity carries a potentially heightened significance, because it can be used as the primary marker of difference in a world otherwise beyond our norms.

"Androids and Androgyny," in *Close Encounters: Film, Feminism, and Science Fiction,* ed. Constance Penley et al. (Minneapolis: University of Minnesota Press, 1991), pp. 34–35.

10. William Gibson, *Neuromancer* (New York: Ace Books, 1984), p. 3.

11. Ibid., pp. 10–11.

12. The Japanese cult film *Tetsuo: The Iron Man* (1989) would qualify, according to Mark Dery's analysis, as the epitome of this genre: "steeped in the style and subject matter of *manga*—the ultraviolent, often scatological comic novels devoured by millions of Japanese, Shinya Tsukamoto's film is a descent into a maelstrom of body loathing, cyborg fantasies, mechano-eroticism, information anxiety, agoraphobia, castration complexes, and fear of phallic mothers. Biological metaphors for machinery fuse with mechanical metaphors for biology in animated sequences of swarming wires and pulsating metal excrescences" (Mark Dery, *Escape Velocity: Cyberculture at the End of the Century* [New York: Grove Press, 1996], p. 271).

13. F. T. Marinetti et al., "Futurist Manifesto of Women's Fashion" (1933), trans. Emily Braun, in "Futurist Fashion: Three Manifestoes," *Art Journal* 54, no. 1 (1995): 40.

14. Mark Dery, "I Have Seen the Future and It Is Morphed," in *Escape Velocity,* pp. 230–31.

15. Robert J. C. Young, *Colonial Desire: Hybridity in Theory, Culture, and Race* (London: Routledge, 1995), p. 181.

16. Lance Olsen, *Tonguing the Zeitgeist* (San Francisco: Permeable Press, 1994), p. 35.

17. William Gibson, *Virtual Light* (New York: Bantam Books, 1993), p. 215.

18. Octavia Butler, *Parable of the Sower* (New York: Warner Books, 1993).

19. Kadohata, *Heart of the Valley,* p. 12.

20. Ibid., p. 194.

21. Frantz Fanon, *Black Skin, White Masks,* trans. Charles Lam Markmann (New York: Grove Weidenfeld, 1967), p. 161.

22. See, in particular, Homi K. Bhabha's chapter "Interrogating Identity: Frantz Fanon and the Postcolonial Prerogative," in *The Location of Culture,* pp. 40–65; Henry

Louis Gates, "Critical Fanonism," *Critical Inquiry* 17 (1991): 457–70; Kobena Mercer, "Black Hair/Style Politics," *New Formations* 3 (winter 1987): 33–54; and Diana Fuss, "Interior Colonies: Frantz Fanon and the Politics of Identification," *Diacritics* 24, nos. 2–3 (1994): 20–42.

23. Fanon, *Black Skin, White Masks,* p. 162.

24. This future anterior may respond in small measure to Paul Gilroy's call for a new periodization whose coordinates reckon with the history of slavery: "Defenders and critics of modernity seem to be equally unconcerned that the history and expressive culture of the African diaspora, the practice of racial slavery, or the narratives of imperial European conquest may require all simple periodizations of the modern and the postmodern to be drastically rethought" (*The Black Atlantic Modernity and Double Consciousness* [Cambridge: Harvard University Press, 1993]), p. 42 Gilroy's point seems incontrovertibly well taken: clearly we must reconceptualize historical periodization—from battleship history to *posthistoire* or history *longue durée*. That said, it will no doubt be a monumental labor to modify "white" paradigms of pre- and postmodern, no matter how subject to revision and critique; these periodizations (supposedly racially neutral) are resilient.

25. As a symptom of the changing times, I note that Homi Bhabha, opened a polemical piece on the "victim art" controversy, globally and temporally relativizing it with an account of an E-mail intervention from Bombay: "[T]he kind of 'connectivity' that comes with the entanglements of E-mail turns us all into vernacular cosmopolitans," he writes, "and it is unwise, anymore, to presume we know where the center lies and where the periphery falls" (Homi K. Bhabha, "On Victim Art," *Artforum,* April 1995, p. 19).

Chapter Thirteen

1. Peter Høeg, *The Woman and the Ape,* trans. Barbara Haveland (New York: Penguin, 1996), p. 174.

2. Ibid. p. 175.

3. Will Self, *Great Apes* (New York: Grove Press, 1997), p. 94.

4. Arjun Appadurai, "Off-White," *Architecture New York* 16 (1996): 58.

5. Gilles Deleuze and Félix Guattari, *What Is Philosophy?* trans. Hugh Tomlinson and Graham Burchell (New York: Columbia University Press, 1994), pp. 102 and 112 respectively.

6. Gilles Deleuze and Félix Guattari, *Anti-Oedipus: Capitalism and Schizophrenia,* trans. Robert Hurley, Mark Seem, and Helen R. Lane (Minneapolis: University of Minnesota Press, 1983), pp. 329–30.

7. Jean-François Lyotard, *The Inhuman,* trans. Geoffrey Bennington and Rachel Bowlby (Stanford: Stanford University Press, 1991), pp. 182–83.

8. Deleuze and Guattari, *What Is Philosophy?* p. 86.

9. Gilles Deleuze and Félix Guattari, *Nomadology: The War Machine,* trans. Brian Massumi (New York: Semiotext(e), 1993).

10. Fredric Jameson, "'Art Naïf' and the Admixture of Worlds," in *The Geopolitical Aesthetic: Cinema and Space in the World System* (Bloomington: Indiana University Press, 1992), p. 206.

11. Jean Bernabé, Patrick Chamoiseau, and Raphaël Confiant, *In Praise of Creoleness,* trans. M. B. Taleb-Khyar (Paris: Gallimard, 1990), p. 90.

12. Tahar Djaout, *L'Invention du désert* (Paris: Seuil, 1987), p. 79.

13. Amitav Ghosh, *The Calcutta Chromosome: A Novel of Fevers, Delirium, and Discovery* (New York: Avon Books, 1995), p. 3.

14. Ibid. p. 9.

15. In using the expression "race aliens" I am inspired directly by the Black Audio Collective's video *Last Angel of History,* in which George Clinton pronounces that "we're descended from stars, switched genetically." This outerworldliness of African-Americans is alluded to again when Eddy George speaks of "sounds unheard before," in discussing the electronic music of George Duke, Stanley Clark, and Jimi Hendrix.

16. Nathaniel Mackey, *Bedouin Hornbook* (1986; Los Angeles: Sun and Moon Press, 1997), p. 47.

17. Mark Dery, "Black to the Future: Interviews with Samuel R. Delaney, Greg Tate, and Tricia Rose," in *Flame Wars* (Durham: Duke University Press, 1994), p. 211.

18. See Renée Green, "Affection Afflictions: My Alien, My Self/More 'Reading at Work,'" in *Loving the Alien: Diaspora, Science Fiction, and Multikultur,* ed. Diedrich Diedrichson (Berlin: ID Archive, 1998).

19. In posing the question "Why do so few African Americans write science fiction, a genre whose close encounters with the Other—the stranger in a strange land—would seem uniquely suited to the concerns of African-American novelists?" (especially in light of the fact that "African-Americans, in a very real sense, are the descendents of alien abductees"), Mark Dery coined the term *Afrofuturism* to denote "speculative fiction that treats African-American themes and addresses African-American concerns in the context of twentieth-century technoculture—and, more generally, African-American signification that appropriates images of technology and a prosthetically enhanced future" ("Black to the Future," pp. 180–81).

20. Scott Bukatman, *Terminal Identity: The Virtual Subject in Postmodern Science Fiction* (Durham: Duke University Press, 1993), p. 169.

21. Samuel Delany, *Dhalgren* (1975; Hanover, N.H.: Wesleyan University Press, 1996), pp. 382–83.

22. Ibid., p. 373.

23. Ibid., p. 225.

24. Ibid., p. 228.

25. Ibid., p. 532.

26. Ibid., pp. 578–79. The Scorpion idiolect draws heavily on ebonics, or Black English. But Delaney seems to be parodying, *avant la lettre* (that is, before the term ebonics was coined), Afrocentric notions of linguistic "genetic inheritance." This idea, most clearly articulated in the 1996 Oakland School Board resolution declaring Black English to be a separate language, implies the existence of an Africanist language gene that carries over from slave languages to "mess with" Standard English. While the linguistic essentialism of much of the ebonics literature seems problematic, I think the phobic reactions to the Black English controversy obscure the most controversial aspect of the debate, which devolves around whether or not the memory of slavery should be kept alive within active patterns of speech and communal exchange.

27. Ibid., pp. 668, 373.

28. Ibid., pp. 418, 412.

29. Black technobodies are often part and parcel of "technologies of the sacred." "It's worth pointing out," Mark Dery writes, "in the context of what I've chosen to call 'Afrofuturism,' that the mojos and goofer dust of Delta blues, together with the lucky charms, fetishes, effigies, and other devices employed in syncretic belief systems, such as voodoo, hoodoo, santeria, mambo and macumba, function very much like the joysticks, Datagloves, Waldos and Spacegloves used to control virtual realities. Jerome Rothenberg would call them technologies of the sacred" ("Black to the Future," 210).

30. Ibid., p. 192.

31. Ibid. p. 193.

32. Delany, *Dahlgren,* p. 753.

33. Ibid., p. 754.

34. Compare Delany's remarks elsewhere: "But somehow black critics . . . just don't seem to be all that interested in how black a writer's work is; or, when they are, they express that interest in—how shall I say?—a different tone of voice. The white, worried about some black's 'blackness,' always seems to be expressing the troubling anxiety that, indeed, you may not really *be* black, and that, therefore, somehow they've personally been fooled, taken in, or duped, either by your manipulative intentions or by some social accident" (Samuel R. Delany, "The Semiology of Silence," in *Silent Interviews: On Language, Race, Sex, Science Fiction, and Some Comics* [Hanover, N.H.: University Press of New England, 1994], p. 50).

35. Samuel R. Delany, *Trouble on Triton: An Ambiguous Heterotopia* (1976; Hanover, N.H.: University Press of New England, 1996), p. 144.

36. Dery, "Black to the Future," p. 180.

37. Delany, *Trouble on Triton,* p. 184.

38. Deleuze and Guattari, *Nomadology,* p. 48.

INDEX

Abbeele, Georges Van Den, xiii, 200, 271n
Abdel-Jaoud, Hedi, 263n
Abu-Lughod, Janet L., 209, 271n
Afrofuturism, xi, 225–27, 229–30, 232, 235, 275–76nn
Agéron, Charles-Robert, ix, 239n
Akomfrah, John, 225
Albes, Wolf-Dietrich, 249–50nn
Algren, Nelson, 217
Allegret, Marc, 183
Alloula, Malek, 107, 122, 176, 182, 260n, 268–69nn
Althusser, Louis, 26, 41–43, 47, 55–56, 114, 243n, 246n, 248n
Amin, Samir, ix, 79, 252n
Amrouche, Jean, 62, 116, 249n
Anderson, Benedict, 10, 213, 240–41nn
Apollinaire, Guillaume, 102, 181
Appadurai, Arjun, ix, xiv, 4, 227, 241n, 274n
Armstrong, Carol, 256n
Auclert, Hubertine, 124–25, 260n
Augé, Marc, 32, 244n
Austin, J. L., 132, 248n

Bachelard, Gaston, 8, 36, 245n
Badis, Ben, 127
Bahr, Hermann, 162
Bailly, Jean-Christophe, 4, 239n
Bakst, Léon, 136
Baladier, Charles, 83
Balibar, Etienne, ix, 15, 42, 241–43nn, 245n
Balibar, Renée, 15, 241n
Balint, Michael, 163
Ballard, J. G., 228–29

Balzac, Honoré de, 27, 92, 108, 113, 120, 167
Banks, Russell, xiii
Barnes, Djuna, 161
Barney, Natalie Clifford, 136, 139–42, 155, 158–61, 262n, 265n
Barrès, Maurice, viii, 12–13, 25–26, 28–29, 31, 35–36, 54, 69, 106, 188, 195, 198, 201, 243–44nn, 248n, 257n
Barrucand, Victor, 143
Barthes, Roland, 121, 134, 182–83, 185, 260n, 269n
Bartky, Sandra Lee, 99, 256n
Bashkirtseff, Marie, 26–27
Bataille, Georges, 47–48, 50–51, 82, 185, 187, 246n, 252n, 269n
Baudelaire, Charles, 151, 203
Baudrillard, Jean, 13, 134
Bazin, André, 187
Beauvoir, Simone de, 98–99, 256n
Belboeuf, marquise de, 135
Benitez-Rojo, Antonio, 219
Benjamin, Walter, 4, 20, 163, 176, 194–95, 203–4, 265n, 271n
Bennington, Geoffrey, 9, 240n, 274n
Benoist, Alain de, 13
Ben Jelloun, Tahar, 30
Ben Saddok, 72–73, 251n
Bensmaïa, Réda, 4, 60, 66, 250n
Bergman, Ingrid, 40
Bergstrom, Janet, xiv, 216, 272n
Berkley, James, 7, 239n
Bernabé, Jean, 31–32, 244n, 270n, 275n
Bernhardt, Sarah, x, 116, 137, 139, 142, 145, 153–56, 159, 265n
Bernheimer, Charles, 267n

Bersani, Leo, 180, 269n
Bertolucci, Bernardo, 182, 199
Bertrand, Louis, 118, 195, 197, 270n
Bhabha, Homi, ix, xiv, 4–5, 10, 32, 67,
    77–79, 114, 143, 175, 213, 222,
    239n, 241n, 250–51nn, 259n,
    262n, 268n, 272–74nn
Bigne, Valtesse de la, 159
Blache, Vidal de la, 188
Black Audio Collective, 225, 236
Blanch, Leslie, 144
Blanchot, Maurice, 90–91, 255n
Boleyn, Ann, 158
Bolland, O. Nigel, 255n
Bonnerot, Jean, 201, 271n
Bonnet, Jean-Claude, 247n
Boone, Joe, 267n
Borch-Jacobsen, Mikkel, 262n
Borland, Christine, 226
Bouceb, Mahfoud, 3
Boudjedra, Rachid, 62, 183, 192,
    261n, 269n
Boumedienne, Houari, ix, 66
Boumendil, Rosine (alias Elissa Rhaïs),
    117
Bourdieu, Pierre, ix, 35
Bourget, Paul, 151
Bouveresse, Jacques, 11
Bowles, Jane, 146
Bowles, Paul, 144, 146, 182, 199,
    263n, 270n
Brahimi, Denise, 144
Braudel, Fernand, ix, 67, 70, 198
Brée, Germaine, 69
Breker, Arno, 13
Brennan, Timothy, 70, 251n
Breton, André, 20, 246n
Brooks, Romaine, 161n
Bukatman, Scott, 214–15, 232, 272n,
    275n
Buck-Morss, Susan, 242n
Buñuel, Luis, 185
Burke, Edmund, 68, 187
Butler, Judith, x, xiv, 43, 115, 131–33,
    143, 147, 236, 246n, 259n, 261n,
    264–65nn
Butler, Octavia, 220–21nn, 236n,
    273n

Cabanès, Dr. Augustin, 48, 50, 246n
Caillois, Roger, 20, 243n
Calvé, Emma, 153, 157, 161, 264n
Camus, Albert, viii, ix, 60, 65, 67–74,
    249–51nn
Carabin, Rupert, 266n
Card, Orson Scott, 236
Cardoso, Frenando Enrique, 252n
Caron, Rose, 142, 153
Carroll, David, 244n
Case, Sue-Ellen, 142, 261n
Castle, Terry, 140, 149
Celan, Paul, 29, 244n
Celarié, Henriette, 145, 195, 263n
Çelik, Zeynep, 267n
Césaire, Aimé, ix, 64, 79
Cha, Theresa Hak Kyung, 41–43,
    245n
Chakravorky, Dipesh, 272n
Chalon, Jean, 160, 265n
Chamoiseau, Patrick, 31–32, 192,
    244n, 270n, 275n
Chanel, Coco, 159
Charles-Roux, Edmonde, 144
Chateaubriand, François René, 195,
    202, 262n, 271n
Chatterjee, Partha, 241n
Chebel, Malek, 103, 256n
Chevrillon, André, 195, 205, 271n
Chirac, Jacques, vii
Chivas-Baron, Clotilde, 118
Chomsky, Noam, 235
Chow, Rey, 222
Cixous, Hélène, 3, 62, 98–100, 256n
Clair, Jean, 13
Clark, Timothy J., xiii, 266n
Clemenceau, President Georges, 44
Clément, Catherine, 256n
Clérambault, Gatian de Gaeton,
    20, 44
Clifford, James, 5, 239, 255n
Clinton, George, 225, 231, 275n
Cocteau, Jean, 160, 246n
Cohen, Margaret, xiv, 266n
Colet, Louise, 171, 176
Colette (Sidonie Gabrielle), 116, 135–
    36, 139, 157–58, 161, 196, 265n
Colley, Linda, 16, 242n

Confiant, Raphaël, 31, 32, 214, 229, 244n, 270n, 272n, 275n
Conley, Tom, xiv, 60–61
Conrad, Joseph, 82
Constable, Elizabeth, 243n
Constant, Benjamin, 4
Copjec, Joan, 42, 269n
Corneille, Pierre, 92
Courbet, Gustave, 173, 174
Crébillon, Claude Prosper Jolyot de, 135
Crevel, René, 20
Culbert, John, 255n
Curtiz, Michael, 182
Cuvillier, Charles, 141

Dagen, Philippe, 241n
Dalí, Salvador, 20, 185
Darwin, Charles, 27
Daudet, Alphonse, 101
Daudet, Léon, 54, 195, 248n
Davis, Natalie Zemon, xiv, 259n
Debord, Guy, 51
Debray, Régis, 13
Degas, Edgar, 102, 256n
de Jean, Joan, 262n
Déjeux, Jean, 117, 117, 118, 260n
Delacroix, Eugene, 102, 103
Delany, Samuel R., 232–37, 275n, 276n
Delarue-Mardrus, Lucie, 105, 118, 139, 144, 145, 161, 257n, 263n
Deleuze, Gilles, 31–33, 184–85, 225, 227, 229, 232, 235, 237, 244n, 269n, 274n, 276n
Delluc, Louis, 181, 183, 185, 269n
de Man, Paul, 7
Déroulède, Paul, 28
Derrida, Jacques, 8–10, 16, 62, 240n, 242n
Dery, Mark, 218, 273n, 275–76nn
d'Esmé, Jean, 183
Deutsch, Michel, 4, 239n
Diawara, Manthia, 178, 179, 269n
Dick, Philip K., 215, 272n
Diderot, Denis, 87, 100
Dieulafoy, Jane, 118, 195
Djaout, Tahar, 3, 59, 62, 229, 249n, 275n

Djebar, Assia, 62, 261n
D. J. Spooky, 232
Doane, Mary Ann, 146
Douglas, Alfred Lord, 134, 259n
Doyen, René-Louis, 144
Dreyer, Carl, 39–41
Dreyfus, Albert, ix, 25–26, 29, 53, 58, 201
Drinka, George Frederick, 247n
Droit, Roger-Pol, 244n
du Camp, Maxime, 180
Duchamp, Marcel, 102
Durel, Pétrus, 128, 261n
Durkheim, Emile, 25
Dutoit, Ulysse, 180, 269n
Duvivier, Julien, 182
Dyer, Richard, 264n, 269n

Eberhardt, Isabelle, x, 108–10, 128, 131, 143, 195, 209, 257–58nn, 263n
Einhorn, Richard 39–40
Eisenstein, Sergei, 185
Ellis, Havelock, 48–49, 247n
Eloui-Bey, Nimet, 161
Elys, Marc, 118
Enfrey, L. M., 110–11, 118, 258n
Engels, Frederick, 124
Epstein, Jean, 180, 185–87, 189–90, 269–70n

Falconetti, Renée, 40–41
Fanon, Frantz, ix, xiv, 4, 6, 64, 66–67, 74, 77–81, 83–85, 87–88, 92, 94, 107, 198, 222, 250n, 252–55nn, 268n, 273–74nn
Farès, Nabile, 261n
Favre, Lucienne, 118
Feraoun, Mouloud, 62
Ferry, Luc, 11
Feyder, Jacques, 182
Fichte, Johann Gottlieb, 18, 242n
Finkelkraut, Alain, 11–12, 240n
Flaubert, Gustave, xvi, 104–5, 113, 118–19, 159, 167, 171–73, 176, 195, 202, 260n, 262n, 265n, 267n, 268n, 271n
Flers, Robert de, 195

Flici, Laadi, 3
Foch, Marshall, 44
Fokine, Mikhail, 136
Foster, Hal, x, 239n
Fottorino, Eric, 244n
Foucault, Michel, 26, 47, 56, 134,
    202–3, 243n, 246n, 248n, 271n
France, Anatole, 53–54, 135
France, Hector, 118
Frank, Andre Gunder, 252n
Franklin, Sarah, 19
Frazer, James, 247n
Fremstad, Olive, 153, 264n
Freud, Sigmund, 19–20, 81, 88, 92–
    93, 102, 109, 133, 143, 150, 156–
    57, 161–63, 247n, 261n, 263n,
    265n, 266n
Friedberg, Anne, 199
Fromentin, Eugène, 202, 271n
Fuller, Loïe, 142, 266n
Fumaroli, Marc, 12–14, 241n
Fuss, Diana, 222, 255n, 274n

Gandersheim, Hrotsvit von, 135
Garbo, Greta, 185
Garden, Mary, 153, 264n
Garelick, Rhonda, 266n
Gary, Romain, 40, 264n
Gates, Henry Louis, 4, 8–9, 78–79,
    222, 240n, 251n, 274n
Gaulle, Charles de, vii, 82
Gautier, Théophile, 118, 123, 135,
    175, 195, 202, 260–61nn, 268n,
    271n
Gellner, Ernest, 17, 168, 242n, 266n
Genet, Jean, 47, 51
Géniaux, Charles, 107, 118, 257n
Gérôme, Jean-Léon, 103, 175
Ghosh, Amitav, 229–30, 275n
Gibson, William, 216, 220, 222, 232,
    228, 273n
Gide, André, 25, 33–34, 60, 69, 92,
    102, 184, 201, 244n, 259n, 264n
Gilroy, Paul, 33, 241n, 244n, 274n
Girardin, Delphine de, 261n
Glissant, Edouard, 4, 31–32, 79, 192,
    219, 244n, 270n
Gloeden, Baron von, 181–182

Gobineau, Joseph Arthur, comte de, ix
Godard, Jean-Luc, 40, 187
Goethe, Johann Wolfgang von, 26,
    160
Gombrich, Ernst, 169, 267n
Goncourt, Edmond and Jules, 48, 104,
    118, 173–74, 190, 200–201, 267–
    68nn
Gordon, Louis, 253n
Gorra, Michael, 16, 242n
Goujon, Jean, 139, 140, 262n
Gourevitch, Philip, 57–58, 248n
Gourmont, Remy de, 136, 160
Graham-Brown, Sarah, 122, 260n
Gramont-Tonnerre, Elizabeth de,
    154–55, 161, 264n
Grave, Jean, 201
Green, André, 243n
Green, Renée, 231–32, 236
Grégoire, abbé Henri, 15, 241n
Grenier, Roger, 69
Grosrichard, Alain, 100–101, 256n
Grossberg, Lawrence, 19, 20, 243n,
    256n
Grosz, Elizabeth, 258n, 266n
Guattari, Félix, 31–33, 184–85, 227–
    28, 233, 244n, 269n, 274n, 276n
Guéhenno, Jean, 79
Guin, Ursula le, 236

Hachette, Jean, 128
Haggard, Rider, 261n
Hall, Radclyffe, 161
Hall, Stuart, 79, 243n
Halperin, David, 47, 246n
Haraway, Donna, 19, 216, 243n, 272n
Hardy, Thomas, 16
Hardy, André P., 191
Hari, Mata, 139, 157, 158, 161
Harry, Myriam, 109, 110, 118, 144,
    145, 195, 258n, 263n, 266n
Harvey, Andrew, 206
Hartland, Sidney, 247n
Hassoun, Jacques, 32, 244n
Hause, Steven, 126, 261n
Hegel, G. W. F., ix, 8, 17, 78–79, 84,
    86, 242n, 254n
Heidegger, Martin, 36, 47

Heine, Maurice, 48, 246n
Hélys, Marc, 105, 257n
Herder, Johann Gottfried, ix, 4
Herr, Lucien, 200
Hersant, Yves, 247n
Hill, Ernestine, 145–46, 269n
Hirschfeld, Magnus, 48
Hitchcock, Alfred, 182
Hitler, Adolf, 13
Høeg, Peter, 226, 274n
Hobsbawm, Eric, 127
Hogarth, William, 169–70, 246n
Hollier, Denis, 250n
Houssaye, Arsène, 261n
Hughes-Hallet, Lucy, 262n
Hugo, Victor, 48, 101, 203
Hume, David, ix, 14, 15, 241n
Humboldt, Wilhelm von, 242n
Hurt, Mary Beth, 40
Husserl, Edmund, 8
Huysmans, Joris-Karl, 47, 50, 51, 247n

Ingres, Jean-Auguste-Dominique,
    102–3
Irele, Abiola, 239n
Irigaray, Luce, 115, 141, 259n

Jacob, Max, 160n
Jacob, P. L., 48
Jacobs, Gabriel, 54, 248n
Jacoby, Jean, 54
James, Henry, 132
Jameson, Fredric, 18, 215, 242n, 274n
Jaurès, Jean, 200
Jay, Karla, 140, 158, 262n, 265n
Joan of Arc, viii, 18, 39–44, 47, 51–54,
    56–59, 127, 128, 141, 245–46nn,
    248n
Jospin, Lionel, 58, 248n
Jouve, Pierre, 248n
Julien, Charles André, ix, 239n
Julien, Isaac, 78

Kabbani, Rana, 144
Kadohata, Cynthia, 215, 221–23,
    272–73nn
Kafka, Franz, 92
Kahina, 59

Kamuf, Peggy, 240n
Kant, Immanuel, ix, 13, 26, 27, 47,
    248n
Kassewitz, Mathieu, 64
Kedourie, Elie, 17
Kenney, Anne, 126, 261n
Khair-Eddine, Mohammed, 30, 244n
Khatibi, Abdelkebir, ix, 4, 62, 198,
    270n
Khomeini, Ayatolah Ruhollah, 3
Kinney, Leila, 267n
Kipling, Rudyard, 201, 204, 205, 271n
Kitching, Gavin, 79, 252n
Klein, Melanie 19, 94
Klossowski, Pierre, 47, 48, 50, 51,
    247n
Kniebiehler, Yvonne, 260n
Kobak, Annette, 144
Koestenbaum, Wayne, 144, 263n
Kojève, Alexandre, 8
Krafft-Ebing, Richard von, 48–49
Kruger, Barbara, 134, 239, 251n, 263n,
    264n

Lacan, Jacques, 20, 41–42, 44–46, 78–
    77, 81, 82, 92, 95, 100, 104, 106,
    143, 150, 161, 163, 168, 170, 173,
    183, 185, 190, 222, 246n, 252n,
    253n, 257n, 258n, 262–63nn,
    266n, 267n, 269n, 270n
Lamarr, Hedy, 40
Lang, Jack, 13
Lanson, Gustave, 14, 30–31, 118,
    244n
Lant, Antonia, 114, 258n
Laporte, Dominique, 15, 241n
Larkin, Philip, 16
Lawrence, T. E., xiv, 19, 243n
Lebel, Roland, 119, 260n
Le Corbusier, 102, 191–92, 270n
Le Guin, Ursula, 236
Leiris, Michel, 102
Lemon, Ralph, 232
Le Pen, Jean Marie, vii–viii, 13, 48,
    56–58, 248n
Le Somptier, René, 181
Levinas, Emmanuel, 8
Lévi-Strauss, Claude, 13, 235n

Levy-Bruhl, Lucien, 88
Lévy-Valensi, J., 44
Lewis, Wyndham, 182, 196
Leys, Colin, 79, 251n
Littré, Emile, 103
Lloyd, David, 242n
Lorrain, Jean, 118, 151, 154, 195, 264n
Loti, Pierre (Julien Viaud), 103–6, 118–19, 128, 136, 138–39, 143 195, 256–57nn
Lottman, Herbert R., 70, 71, 249n, 251n
Louÿs, Pierre, 136
Lowe, Lisa, 4, 243n, 245n, 267n
Lyabès, Djilali, 3
Lyautey, Louis-Hubert-Gonzalve, 108, 188, 198, 202, 208, 271n
Lyotard, Jean-François, ix, 84, 227, 253n, 274n

MacCannell, Dean, 200, 271n
Mackey, Nathanael, 230–31, 236, 275n
Magoudi, Ali, 248n
Maigret, Julien, 108
Maistre, Xavier de, 4
Mallet-Stevens, Robert, 191
Malraux, André, 5, 6, 190–91, 239n, 270n
Manoni, Maud, 81
Mannoni, Octave, ix, 77, 79, 80–89, 91, 93–95, 107, 252n, 254–55n
Mapplethorpe, Robert, 184
Marat, Jean Paul, 50, 247n
Marcilly, Jean, 57
Marinetti, Filippo Tommaso, 273n
Marx, Karl, 100
Mary Queen of Scots, 128
Massenet, Jules, 135
Matisse, Henri, 102
Maupassant, Guy de, 104, 106, 118, 176, 195, 268n
Maurras, Charles, vii, ix, 33, 34, 54, 248n
Mbembe, Achille, ix, 4
McClintock, Anne, 9, 10, 240–42nn
McCulloch, Jock, 83, 252n

McMichael, Philip, 11, 240n
Mehlman, Jeffrey, 246n
Meilhac, Henri, 159
Memmi, Albert, ix, 32, 64, 107
Mercer, Kobena, 79, 222, 274n
Merles, Robert, 62
Mernissi, Fatima, 261n
Mérode, Cléo de, 141, 142, 159, 262n
Messaoudi, Khalida, 62, 249n
Michelet, Jules, 2, 36, 48, 50–53, 55, 248n
Migault, Pierre, 44
Mille, Pierre, 26, 243–44nn, 269n
Miller, Christopher, 4, 239n
Miller, D. A., 138
Miller, Jacques-Alain, 257n, 265n, 267n, 269n
Millot, Catherine, 109, 258n
Mitchell, Timothy, 4, 114, 258n
Miyoshi, Masao, 4
Modleski, Tania, 256n
Mohanty, Chandra Talpede, 125, 256n, 260n
Mohanty, Satya, 4
Monselet, Charles, 48
Montagnon, Pierre, 249n
Montesquieu, Charles Louis de Secon-dat, baron de, 4, 100
Montherlant, Henri Marie Joseph Mil-lon de, 69
Moon, Michael, 155, 264n, 275n
Morand, Paul, 116, 151
Morin, Edgar, 180–181, 269n
Morny, Mathilde de, 161
Morris, Meaghan, 145, 200, 263n, 271n
Mudimbe, V. Y., 4, 100, 239n, 256n
Mussolini, Benedetto, 184
Mulvey, Laura, 122

Nadar, 141
Nairn, Tom, 242n
Nalpas, Louis, 181
Nancy, Jean-Luc, ix
Nandy, Ashis, 4
Nietzsche, Friedrich, 47, 121, 246n
Nixon, Robert, 9, 240n
Nochlin, Linda, 173, 268n

Noiriel, Gérard, 243n
Nora, Pierre, ix, 2, 239n, 241n
Noury-Bey, Nouryé and Zennour, 136, 140

O'Barr, Jean, 239n
O'Brien, Conor Cruise, 60–61, 68–70, 249–50n
Offenbach, Jacques, 159
Ohms, Marcel, 269n
Ollier, Claude, 35–36, 245n
Olsen, Lance, 219, 220, 273n
Orwell, George, 16, 196, 205, 242n, 271n
Owens, Craig, 134, 146, 261n, 263n

Palmer, Eva, 159
Panizza, Oskar, 48
Parker, Andrew, 241n
Paulhan, Jean, 31–32, 48, 50, 77, 88–91, 244n, 246–47n, 254–55n
Paulhan, Frédéric, 88, 254n
Péguy, Charles, 43, 53, 188, 200–201, 246–48n
Peignot, Colette, 187
Péladan, Joseph, 135
Penley, Constance, 273n
Perec, Georges, 35, 245n
Perrault, Charles, 49
Pétain, Marshal, 54, 58
Petrey, Sandy, 30
Picasso, Pablo, 5, 13, 102, 168–69, 171, 174, 181, 256n, 266–68nn
Pierrefeu, Jean de, 120
Pike-Barney, Alice, 159
Pizan, Christine de, 39
Polke, Sigmar, 193
Poiret, Paul, 141
Pontalis, J.-B., 94
Porete, Marguerite, 40
Porter, Denis, 265n, 267n
Pougy, Liane de, 141, 153, 155, 159–61, 265n
Poulantzas, Nicos, 79
Prakash, Gyan, 272n
Pratt, Mary Louise, 189, 199
Praz, Mario, 135–36, 262n
Prochaska, David, 260n

Proust, Marcel, 152–54, 264n
Pushkin, Alexander, 261n

Rabéarivolo, Jean-Joseph, 255n
Rabémananjava, Jacques, 255n
Rabinow, Paul, 199, 209, 210, 270–72n
Racine, Jean, 100, 154
Ragland-Sullivan, Ellie, 257n
Ranaivo, Flavien, 255n
Rais, Gilles de, 46, 49–53, 55–56, 58, 246n, 247n
Randau, Robert, 118, 143
Rappaport, Mark, 40
Read, Alan, 251n
Readings, Bill, 74, 251n, 253n
Reed, Ishmael, 236
Reich, Wilhelm, 162
Reinach, Salomon, 53, 160, 248n
Renan, Ernest, ix, 4, 17, 18, 242n
Retamar, Roberto Fernandez, 79
Rétif de la Bretonne, 48
Rhaïs, Elissa, x, 113, 115–24, 126–29, 175, 196, 259–61nn, 268n
Rhaïs, Jacob-Raymond, 117
Riefenstahl, Leni, 184
Riviere, Joan, 94, 157, 162
Robespierre, Maximilien, 50
Roblès, Emmanuel, 62, 249n
Rolland, Romain, 200, 280n
Ronnell, Avital, 55, 248n
Rose, Jaqueline, xi, 16, 242n, 275n
Ross, Kristin, 14, 241n
Roudinesco, Elisabeth, 246
Rousseau, Jean-Jacques, 48, 69, 100
Rousseau, Samuel, 116
Roy, Jules, 62
Rubenstein, Diane, 26, 243n, 248n
Rubenstein, Ida, x, 136, 139, 141, 153
Rubin, Gayle, 99, 256n
Rushdie, Salomon, 3, 242n

Sade, Donatien Alphonse François, Marquis de, 47, 50, 51, 246–47nn
Said, Edward, ix, 4, 60–65, 69, 120, 138, 197, 250n, 259n, 262n, 267n
Saint-Juste, Louis de, 50

Samary, Jeanne, 154
Sanderson, Sibyl, 141–42
Sardou, Victor, 137
Sartre, Jean-Paul, 6, 36, 51, 78, 80, 239n
Sayad, Abdelmalek, ix, 35, 239n
Schneiderman, Stuart, 50
Schor, Naomi, 115, 259n
Scott, Paul, 206
Sebbar, Leïla, 62, 261n
Seberg, Jean, 40, 245n
Sedgwick, Eve Kosovsky, 106, 132–33, 261n, 264n
Segalen, Victor, 4, 101, 136
Segond-Weber, Mme, 153
Self, Will, 226–27, 274n
Senhadri, Hafid, 3
Senocak, Zafer, 29
Serres, Michel, 13, 29
Sharpe, Jenny, xiv, 10, 240n
Shaw, George Bernard, 40
Shohat, Ella, 4, 240n, 241n
Shreber, Daniel Paul, 43, 46, 246n
Sinfield, Alan, 137–38, 146, 262n, 264n
Smithson, Robert, 187, 270
Somptier, René le, 181
Soon, Yu Guan, 41
Soury, Jules, 26
Spivak, Gayatri Chakravorty, 4, 9, 99, 239n, 256n, 272n
Stam, Robert, 240n, 241n
St Denis, Ruth., 141
Steinberg, Leo, 168–74, 266–68nn
Sternberg, Max von, 182
Suleri, Sara, 4, 206, 271n
Sun Ra, 225
Swinburne, Algernon Charles, 261n

Tabet, Paul, 115, 117–18, 126, 259n
Tagg, John, 114, 259n, 260n
Tahimik, Kidlat, 229
Taine, Hippolyte Adolphe, ix, 14, 26–28, 48, 205
Tansi, Sony Labou, 29
Tate, Greg, 231, 275n
Téramond, Guy de, 106–7, 118, 257n
Terry, Ellen, 140, 149, 261n, 262n

Tharaud, Jean and Jérôme, 107, 118, 188–89, 192, 196–200, 202, 204–11, 257n, 270–72nn
Thornton, Leslie, 146, 258n, 263n
Tickner, Lisa, 127, 261n
Toqueville, Alexis de, 4
Todorov, Tveztan, 4
Toumi, Alawa, 62
Touraine, Alain, 11
Tournier, Michel, 47, 50, 52, 248n
Trautmann, Catherine, 57
Trophimowsky, Alexander, 144
Troubridge, Una, 161
Turkhan-Pacha, Kérimé, 139–40
Tytler, Graeme, 260n

Valéry, Paul, 36
Vergès, Françoise, 79, 253n
Vernant, Jean-Pierre, 13
Vertov, Dziga, 185
Viaud, Julien (Pierre Loti), 137
Vieuchange, Michel, 118, 195
Virilio, Paul, 188
Viswanathan, Gauri, 242n
Vivien, Renée (Pauline Tarne), 139, 140, 155, 158, 161, 262n, 265n
Volney, comte de, 210
Voltaire, François-Marie Androuet, 135, 187

Wallerstein, Immanuel, ix, 70, 241n, 250n
Walter, Eric, 50, 247n
Ward, Nari, 232
Warner, Marina, 245n, 248n, 273n
Warner, Sylvia Townsend, 149
Weber, Sam, iv, 20
Weil, Simone, 35, 245n
Weill, Nicolas, 29, 244n
Weiss, Peter, 50
Wells, Laurette, 161
Wharton, Edith, 196, 270n
Whitford, Margaret, 259n
Wilde, Dolly, 161
Wilde, Oscar, 133–34, 136, 144, 161, 259n, 261n
Williamson, Judith, 99, 256n
Wittgenstein, Ludwig, 11, 235n

Wollen, Peter, xiv, 136, 155, 262n,
264n
Wollheim, Richard, 162, 265n
Wong, Nadine, 161
Wood, Elizabeth, 264
Woolf, Virginia, 149
Wright, Elizabeth, 266n
Wright, Patrick, 243n

Yacco, Sada, 142
Yacine, Kateb, 62, 117
Young, Robert J. C., 219, 273n

Zéghidour, Sliman, 107
Žižek, Slavoj, 56, 248n, 258n
Zola, Emile, 25, 104, 120, 151, 153,
264n, 270n